THE MEMOIR OF WING COMMANDER B
ONE OF **THE MOST PROLIFIC PILOTS**
OVER 3,160 LOGGED FLIGHT HOURS IN 42 DIFFERENT AIRCRAFT

BRIAN ANTHONY ASHLEY

TWO HAWKS
AND A PELICAN

I_AM SELF-PUBLISHING

🐦 @iamselfpub
www.iamselfpublishing.com

TABLE OF CONTENTS

Sketch by Pat Rooney 1952

DEDICATION

This book is for Jenni,
who was not born, was too young to remember
or was away at school.

WG CDR BRIAN ASHLEY AFC

A few years ago I was seeking contact with Meteor pilots for a book I was writing about the type. I had not been searching for very long when I received an email from Brian Ashley, telling me that he had flown Meteors operationally in both RAF Germany and Singapore. I was immediately struck by his huge enthusiasm for my book project, his love of the aeroplane and his pride in what, I would soon discover, had been a long and distinguished Royal Air Force career.

Brian had a quite extraordinary time from joining the Royal Air Force in 1949, making his first flight in Rhodesia in April 1950, to his final retirement in 1977. During these long years he experienced and flew an enormously varied range of aircraft types, from the biplane de Havilland Tiger Moth on which he started to learn his trade, to the mighty Panavia Tornado strike aircraft of today, a project in which he was deeply involved. As aircraft service lives seem to get stretched ever longer (the Tornado itself is now over 40 years old), today's pilots do not perhaps, have the same opportunities for type variety as those of Brian's era. He certainly maximised his chances when he attended the Empire Test Pilot's School, flying an extraordinary range of aircraft types and obviously enjoying every one of them. Throughout this excellent book, his love of flying shines through in so many stories, some exciting, some scary and a few sad.

During his time in Singapore he found himself as one of a pair of Meteors PR.10 photo reconnaissance aircraft, airborne on their very last operational sortie anywhere in the RAF before being retired. He recounts the fun he and his wingman had going round and round in the circuit at the end of the flight, vying with each other to claim the bragging rights as being the last one to land – Brian won! The role of the single-seat, high-flying reconnaissance aeroplane had been a key element in air force strategy during the Second World War and Brian was immensely proud of not only continuing that tradition, but being the very last practitioner of the art. He even managed to salvage a souvenir from the cockpit of his faithful Meteor before it was scrapped.

By the 1970s Brian found himself at the forefront of the RAF staff allocated to the Multi-Role Combat Aircraft (MRCA) project, which ultimately entered service as the Tornado. At one time he was being lined-up to command the multi-national training station at Cottesmore in Rutland. Although he subsequently decided to take early retirement instead, his legacy lives on in the superb Tornado and for many years, in the tremendous Tri-national Tornado Training Establishment (TTTE) at Cottesmore, on which I had the pleasure to serve during the late 1980s and into the early '90s.

Brian was one of a very special generation of servicemen, who were part of the transformation of the service from one that was only just beginning to change from the shape it was in at the end of the Second World War, to a true late 20th century, high-tech, professional organisation. Proud though he was of his part in all that change, the love of his family, from his marriage to Marlies in 1954 and then the joy of his daughter Jenni, comes across very strongly throughout these pages as the dominant factor in his life. There can be little doubt that all who knew him must feel privileged, I certainly do.

Dr Steve Bond PhD CEng FRAeS
Shropshire
April 2017

INTRODUCTION

WHEN Jenni heard The Old and Bold reminiscing, with the hangar doors wide open, and recalling The Good Old Days she often said that she had never heard that before and over the years she has cajoled me to write it all down before it is too late. I was either too busy or too idle so I put it off. However my conscience nagged me and when I stirred myself I found that I already had in my computer several articles I had written for squadron, unit and society histories that I might be able to top and tail and pad out. Several years ago or more I began to stab at my laptop computer with my two typing fingers and slowly the book has grown. My memory seems to me to have served me well but, over the eighty years the book spans, unperceived errors may have crept in. If so they are all mine and I apologise to anyone who has been offended by them. My only aide memoire has been my Pilots Flying Logbook so at least most of the dates are accurate. I have scraped together photos all my life and I have brought together all that I thought suitable for the book. Most of them are mine or ones which have been given to me by my fellow travellers. Others I have no idea where I found them and if anyone would like to lay claim to them I will readily make an acknowledgement.

The book will never be finished because every time I revise the chapters more memories come flooding back. One advantage of typing slowly with two fingers is that it gives one more time to think and remember. As long as I live the book will grow but Jenni's copy will always be kept up to date. I am also most grateful for Mickie Moss's daughter, Susan, who has given me unstinted support and encouragement

My eternal thanks go to Marlies who has been part of this book since 1954 and who had to put up with long absences while I chased around the RAF or more recently stabbed at my notebook. She has neither complained about reams of papers strewn around or in the waste paper basket and upturned boxes of photos nor protested at my incessant pecking at my laptop like a geriatric woodpecker.

CHAPTER 1
In the Beginning

THREE little lads were hurrying over the fields at their best cruising speed. For those who do not know this method of yomping over the southern Lincolnshire Wolds it involves running for 100 yards and walking for another 100 yards and continuing ad infinitum, or so it seemed. One disadvantage of the system was that the paces were set by the big boy at the front and the little lad at the back had to run 150 paces or so. I was the one at the back continually calling, "Wait for me". It was 1935 and the leader was my brother Jack who was 11 years old. Then came Ray who did about 120 running paces because he was 10. I, who always trailed along behind, was only 7 and the world was just not fair. The day was very special because we were heading across country to a large grass field to see Alan Cobham's Flying Circus and fate had blessed us with a lovely summer's day. Lincolnshire was well used to the Royal Air Force squadrons who seemed to look upon the county as their own. We were well acquainted with aircraft going about their business but on that day we were going to see aircraft close up for the first time and my world was about to change.

Lincolnshire Wolds farmer in the 1930s

The crowd was already gathering when we arrived and although the show had not started my eyes must have been like saucers as I tried to take in everything at once. A Westland Wessex three engined transport was parked near the crowd picking up passengers and sundry smaller aircraft were landing or already draped around the field. The smell of exhaust fumes and oil together with the noise of engines running or being run up to high revolutions on test all boosted a young boy's vivid imagination.

The day was far too exciting to remember everything in detail but a small fleet of Moth aircraft plied their trade carrying passengers. A wing walker draped himself around wing struts of an aircraft cavorting in front of the crowd, an inebriated stranger tricked his way into a cockpit and put on a drunken crazy flying display which frightened me nearly to death and Clemm Sohn demonstrated what a Bird Man could do. He was a free fall parachutist and he wore a flying suit with canvas webs sewn between his legs and between his arms and his sides. He was carried aloft in a Moth and then launched himself overboard and gave what seemed to be long swoops, glides and turns before opening his parachute and landing in front of the crowd. Seventy five years later this may be old hat but parachuting in 1935 was a black art and very unreliable and his display was magic. We had a close up view of an Autogyro demonstrating its short take off and landing capabilities just in front of us. I wish I could have seen more because I was certain I was missing something behind me while my attention was distracted.

We stayed until very little was still moving and then set course to trudge home at what must have been our maximum endurance speed. The only things operating at high speed were our tongues as we tried to outdo each other in recounting the things we had seen. By the time we arrived home I knew I wanted to be a pilot. I slept like a log but next day I still wanted to be a pilot and it never went away.

School Days

Prime Minister Chamberlain declared war on Germany the week before I was due to start my secondary education at Queen Elizabeth's Grammar School in Horncastle but much to my surprise nothing much happened. When the Air Training Corps was introduced the School formed a Squadron but I was too young to be enrolled. Because of my obvious enthusiasm I was allowed to attend the lectures and I learned much about the RAF.

I was a proficient carpenter and helped to build an elementary trainer which was suspended from the ceiling by ropes which passed through pulleys. By moving a control column the attitude of the contraption could be moved to simulate the movements of an aeroplane in flight. I don't know if it eventually helped my flying but it certainly did no harm.

The Royal Observer Corp built a new observation post about 3 miles from home and I soon became a regular visitor to the Observers. In time they began to welcome my visits because they could leave me to maintain a very alert look out while they performed the essential duties such as making tea, playing cards or listening to the radio. While in the post one day we heard reports that a German Junkers Ju 88 bomber was heading east towards us from inland and was low flying to avoid the unwelcome attention of 2 Spitfires. Very soon we saw the Spitfires diving to try to get at the evading bomber. As we watched the battle approaching a Beaufighter appeared from the north. This was the first time I had seen one as it was new but I knew it was armed with 4 cannons and 6 machine guns. It came in steadily from the left of the Ju 88, turned in on a nicely judged curve of pursuit and when in range fired one mighty burst and the Ju 88 seemed to fall apart. The wreckage was spread over 2 fields. I didn't stop talking about it for days.

One bright Saturday morning the Army were exercising in a valley just over the hill from home and 2 Hurricane fighters appeared to be making simulated attacks on them. I leapt onto my bicycle and headed up the hill to get a grandstand view of the fun and games. As I approached the brow of the hill one of the Hurricanes came over the hill top in a slow roll. When it came over the hill it was inverted and then the pilot allowed the nose to drop and it followed the curvature of the hill until it hit the field still inverted about 400 yards away on my left. I can still remember the dull thump as it hit the ground, scrunched together and gave a little hop before it subsided. The crash was catastrophic and the aircraft disintegrated. There was nothing I could do and when ammunition began exploding I decided it was time I went to get help. This did not deter my ambition to fly but it taught me not to let the aircraft nose drop while flying inverted.

I followed the progress of the Battle of Britain and the rest of the air war with great interest and gobbled up every piece of information I could find but all the time I fretted that I was about 5 or 6 years too young and could not join the fray. I began to realise that the war might end before I could join in.

The BBC

The British Broadcasting Corporation had lost many of it younger engineers to fill gaps in the Armed Services' requirements and they canvassed around many Grammar Schools to ask Headmasters if they could recommend suitable school leavers who could be trained to make up the shortages. I had just finished my School Certificate, or Matriculation, a year early and my headmaster put my name forward. I had an interview with a senior engineer and was offered training to qualify me for the Engineering Division. I had no hope of joining the RAF for perhaps 3 years and the offer was an attractive alternative for me and I accepted. My training course was arranged at the BBC's most senior transmitter site at Daventry and after slogging through electrical and radio theory and some practical radio engineering I was declared to be safe enough to go and earn my living. I was posted to a transmitter station at Woofferton Junction, just south of Ludlow in Shropshire.

Personnel Branches to look after the welfare of the employees were not invented in 1943 therefore I, a fifteen year old who was away from home for the first time, was faced with the problem of finding somewhere to live in a strange town. I arrived in Ludlow on a dark evening and I decided to seek help at the police station. Fortunately the sergeant on duty was an excellent example of an old fashioned local Bobby. I think he was Dixon of Dock Green. He scratched his head, deliberated for a few minutes and then decided to phone a large transport café. He then announced I had a bed for the night. The Mitre transport café was run by Mrs Teague, a large, imposing Welsh lady. The house was down at the bottom of the north end of the town and was surrounded by a large open area for parking a collection of huge lorries. I felt somewhat intimidated as I presented myself and my case in the noisy, smoky café but Mrs Teague's bark soon turned out to be worse than her bite. She listened to my tale of woe and then declared she would help me for the night and I could find somewhere more suitable next day. The café only had small dormitories for the transport drivers but she would move out of the front bedroom and I could use that. This was an extremely generous offer and the room was a quite large comfortable nest. I then sought for a meal in the café and I found the drivers to be very friendly and welcoming. I joined them for my meal and was astonished to find that it was the best meal I had tackled for a long time. Food throughout the UK was strictly rationed but the café had special supplies to produce meals at all hours of the day and night for drivers whose work was essential for the British economy. I always loved fish and that was one food Mrs Teague could obtain readily. Breakfast was a typical wholesome meal with a huge mug of tea and I felt I could tackle the day with renewed energy. After breakfast Mrs Teague surprised me by asking if I would like to make the café my long term base and after very little hesitation I agreed.

Many of the drivers operated well established routes and paid regular visits to the café. I soon discovered they were strands in a country wide web which exchanged information and co-operated with each other. When they discovered that I lived in Lincolnshire they suggested I should travel with Jim who left Ludlow every morning at 5 o'clock to deliver milk to Birmingham. He would hand me over to a friend who would be returning to Derby and a further lift to Lincoln would follow. It was a great family which many people never knew existed and I enjoyed my stay at The Mitre.

When I reported for duty at Wooferton Junction I found a huge building and a few smaller huts surrounded by a large marshy site with many aerial arrays suspended from a semi-circle of 300 foot high masts. The transmitter hall housed 10 transmitters, each of 100 kilowatts, and I was to be in charge of one of them as they transmitted what is now the BBC World Service 24 hours a day. Each transmitter was about 20 yards long and 5 yards deep. Doors in the front panels allowed access to the inside to make frequency changes or repairs. Every component could be identified and repaired or replaced if necessary. The small low power circuits could be handled easily but the large output circuits had to be moved on their carriages which were mounted on miniature railway lines in the rear half of the transmitter.

After transmitting for 5 or 6 hours for example to the Far East on the 35 metre band the transmitter would have to be closed down exactly on cue and the safety interlock door key returned to the chief control engineer. We then had a hectic few minutes during which the components were changed and adjusted to prepare it for transmitting on perhaps the 25 metre band to the Middle East. When the change was complete the interlock key would be collected from the controller and then the transmitter switched on at low power and fine tuned to bring it up to optimum performance. Then it would be closed down until the exact time for resuming transmission. In the mean time, while the interlock key was with the control engineer, a new aerial would be connected to the transmitter and a new programme network and frequency had been fed in by the control room. As the time signal to resume transmitting came up the transmitter would be switched on at full power and fine tuned to take over the transmission from the transmitter somewhere else in UK which was just giving it up. The whole process had to be completed within 15 minutes and I never knew of a late hand over.

The transmitter duties were interspersed with spells in the control room where the programmes were received from London and distributed to the transmitters. A bank of oscillators was used to provide the frequencies which had to be set by hand before being connected to the transmitters. All transmissions were checked for frequency accuracy by a monitoring unit in Kent and a mighty fuss would be raised if the error was more than 1 in a million cycles per second. The competition to have the best record was very keen and I managed to compete well and escaped the indignity of being out of the limits.

To ensure that we were never bored we also had to take our share of aerial duties. This mainly involved tramping around the huge transmitter site which was part moor and part marsh to adjust the aerials before connecting to the transmitters for their next transmission. This involved moving the aerial feeder wires from one set of hooks to another perhaps 20 yards away. The wires were about 12 feet above ground and we used a long pole with twin hooks on the end to manoeuvre them. This was not a great problem in good weather but not relished on a black night with freezing rain when the only source of light was a plain torch held alongside the pole. This had to be completed quickly and a mad dash made to a nearby phone to the control room so that the transmitter safety key could be released. Maintenance work on the masts and aerials such as changing cracked insulators or dud warning light bulbs had be done whenever possible and I soon realised that aerials usually had to be climbed in freezing, wet, windy winter weather and rarely on a lovely summer's day.

The transmitter station had to have a guaranteed electrical supply and we had an emergency power house built on to the end of the transmitter hall. It was equipped with 3 large ship's diesel engines which turned alternators to provide the required power. The engines were about 10 feet high and the fly wheels for the alternators were about 8 feet in diameter. All engineers were trained to start the engines and if there was a mains power failure the nearest engineers would race for the diesels and the first three to arrive would begin starting them. After much hissing, clanking and chuffing they slowly came up to operating speed by which time a senior engineer would have arrived to synchronise the alternators and bring them on line. I loved this exercise and I was very fast to the power house. When the diesels were eventually closed down they had to be reset ready for instant restarting. This included cranking the fly wheel round with a long iron bar until it was in the correct position for a quick start.

What a toy for a young boy!

All this was exciting stuff for a teenager but I was also given much more theoretical and practical training on what was new technology in the 1940s. We had a very good engineer in charge of the engineering workshop and I also managed to improve my basic engineering skills to add to those I had already acquired on the farm. Later I was moved to other tasks which further expanded my electrical and radio experience.

Ludlow 1944

My time in the BBC filled the gap until I was old enough to be conscripted into the armed forces. Eventually, immediately after the war ended, I was invited to report to the Recruiting Centre for enrolment and I trotted along with a light heart as my time had at last come and I was no longer too young. Alas the fickle finger of fate had not yet finished with me and when I eagerly told the Recruiting Officer of my ambitions to be a pilot he asked me if I had not heard that RAF pilot training had been suspended and only a small number were being trained at Cranwell. The RAF had too many trained pilots and they all had to be paid. Just after the war the official attitude was to prepare for everlasting peace and money was being diverted away from the armed services. My bubble had been burst and I was at a loss for ideas. When the recruiters noticed that I had been trained by the BBC they had plenty of ideas to fill my dazed mind. They decided to enrol me in the Royal Navy as a Radio Mechanic. I had never considered any alternative to joining the RAF and here I was heading for a spell in the Royal Navy for an unknown number of years. Such are the quirks of life.

The Royal Navy

I duly arrived at HMS Royal Arthur to begin the attempt to turn myself into some semblance of a sailor. My attitude was that the next few years were inevitably committed to the Navy so I might as well try to enjoy it. I was still in my teens and still had much to learn. We were issued with sailors' suits and instructed how to climb into them and generally introduced to the unique ways of the Navy and then sent to HMS Gosling in Lancashire for our seamanship training. Most of the training seemed to centre round the parade ground but much of the rest was useful for the rest of my life. Although on shore establishments we usually slept on beds most ships including HMS Gosling were still run as in Nelson's time. Hammocks were used for sleeping and life centred around the mess deck where groups of 8 or 10 sailors based their daily existence. We took turns to be bubbly bosuns whose onerous duties were to collect the daily rum ration and distribute it absolutely evenly or we were mess orderlies who collected and shared out the food which was eaten at the mess table. Every sailor became self contained when it came to looking after oneself and washing, ironing, mending became routine chores and we never seemed to go anywhere without our laundry buckets. Training in knots, bends and hitches was good value and rowing and handling of sea boats on Leigh Flash was fun but very competitive. During this time I sustained a broken jaw while boxing and finished in Rainhill Hospital for an operation in the area of my left temple. While sorting out the broken bone the surgeon managed to sever some nerves. This resulted in a paralysis of the left side of my face which gave me a very cynical grin. I still have the residual paralysis over 70 years later. The fact that Rainhill was the main mental hospital for Lancashire provided plenty of opportunity for slanderous remarks but there may have been some justification for them because I found it difficult to differentiate between some of the Naval patients and the regular inmates.

The dominant feature for me was the availability of all types of sport. My boxing days were now over but I could fill up all my spare time with hockey, cricket, squash, badminton, rowing and rugby. Life was good.

All this rich living was managed with a princely income of 4 shillings (20 pence) a day. It was the custom to allocate 1 shilling a day to a Post Office savings account which was safeguarded by one's mother and riotous living was thus avoided.

The fun and games eventually came to an end and the Lords Commissioners of the Admiralty decided that, because of my BBC training, I would be excused basic radio training and be sent to join a more advanced course devoted to RN operational radio and radar equipment. I was sent to HMS Collinwood near Fareham in Hampshire, which as the centre of radio training, became my regular base while serving ashore.

No 136 Radio Course HMS Collingwood
Me front row, 3rd from left Beetle first left

My previous education was expanded to include radar which was still in a very rudimentary state and ships' systems. Much more engineering workshop practice was given and when I finished my course I was equipped with a wooden tool box which contained the latest sophisticated tools such as hammers, chisels, pliers, spanners, screw drivers, hacksaws, etc. As I moved from ship to ship I was issued with an Avo test meter and a Mega insulation tester. With this comprehensive range of tools I was required to tackle any problem which might be remotely classified as radio. Electronics was yet to be invented.

When I joined the new course for the second half of my training they had already been together for 14 weeks and when I told them my name was Brian I was told that they had two already and I would be Bill. When I left Collingwood I was accompanied by some of my old comrades and I continued to be Bill for the rest of my time in the Navy. The new course had a preponderance of Geordies from Teesside and although I had not encountered any before I soon realised what a great bunch of people they were. They were always singing and I was soon up to speed with the Blaydon Races, Cushy Butterfield and Keep your feet still Geordie Hinnie. The ballad of the Lampton Worm was often recited. I have retained my admiration for Geordies to this day.

The time passed quickly and I was delighted to find that almost every kind of sport was available when ashore. Boxing was now finished after my operation but squash, rugby, hockey and badminton soon filled the gap. Rugby was much more competitive and eventually I was invited to play for United Services Portsmouth. On one occasion I thought I was about to reach the high point of my rugby career while playing for USP. I had nearly reached the touchdown line to score a try but I was slowly being dragged down by evil people trying to prevent me. I was just short of the line but nearly on the point of going down when I saw my old friend Beetle Beeston, from my radio course, roaring up on my left side and I was able with my last gasp to smuggle the ball to him and over the line he went. Just after the war we still had many international players in the services and playing with some of them lifted one's own game. Fuel was still rationed in civilian life and lines were painted in baths at a depth of 4 inches to indicate the maximum amount of hot water but we had plenty of hot water and one of my luxuries was soaking in a steaming bath after a hard and muddy game. Several times I was woken by the cold water from the cooling bath.

I resumed my acquaintance with radio and radar masts again. Nearly all ship's aerials were located at the maximum possible height and as in the BBC most aerial troubles occurred during freezing wet weather. A rolling ship also adds charm to the aerial work. Towards the end of my time I was posted as an instructor to HMS Mercury, the RN Signals School at Leydene House high in the hills near Petersfield, and I had my first taste of the noble art of teaching. Time whizzed by and eventually Demobilisation Group 78 loomed over the horizon and my time was up. I collected my utility civilian suit and I was a free man again.

Soon afterwards I was in Lincoln and I met an old RAF friend who I had not seen for a long time. We took the opportunity to have coffee in Stokes Café on the High Street bridge and I learned that he was running the RAF recruiting office in Northgate. When we were leaving he asked me if I had heard that RAF pilot training had started again. Although his office was on top of the hill I was able to surprise him when he returned by sitting outside his door waiting.

CHAPTER 2
At Last – Into the RAF and off to Rhodesia.

AFTER 14 years of frustration I was about to take my first step towards fulfilling my abiding ambition to be a RAF pilot. I was invited to attend the RAF Aircrew Selection Centre at RAF Hornchurch. This was doubly welcome to me because I had never been on an RAF flying station and Hornchurch had played a major part in the Battle of Britain. I waltzed into the station and was accommodated in a barrack block with a host of other applicants. During the next few days of fun and games I paired up with Brian Kail who was also aiming for pilot training.

A new question now entered my mind for the first time. Would I be able to fly? I knew the failure rate for student pilots was high but in my enthusiasm I had never imagined the possibility of failure and the approach of my first testing time suddenly brought it into focus. What an alarming possibility! All the applicants must have been feeling similar apprehensions but when the testing procedures began the doubts were eased. I had no worries on medical and educational grounds but the special aptitude tests which had been the downfall of many young hopefuls proved to be logical and very enjoyable. At school I had a liking for geometry and it had no mysteries for me. I sailed though the aptitude tests and began to feel more confident. After a few days of enjoying the companionship of the other applicants I was eventually called to hear the all important verdict. The Judge and Jury gazed upon me and I was prepared for the death sentence but they had decided that I was very highly suitable to be a navigator and my heart descended into my shoes. They then added I was also well suited for pilot training and as outstanding pilot candidates were rarer than navigators they had given their vote to pilot training. Hurray!

Probably because I was only a farmer's boy I was offered an engagement for 7 years in the RAF as a sergeant pilot with a further 5 years in the Reserve. I had no hesitation in accepting the offer. I later discovered that very few candidates were pre-selected for commissioning. The first hurdle had been overcome but the question of my ability to survive pilot training still remained. Brian Kail had the opposite verdict and he was offered navigator training. I kept in contact with him for several years and he was soon very happily navigating Sunderland flying boats from Singapore.

The next step along the way was to report to the RAF Reception Unit which was located at RAF Cardington with the RAF Barrage Balloon Depot. While hauling my suit case through the main gates I was confronted by the 2 enormous airship sheds which were erected in 1930 to accommodate the R100 and ill fated R101. I had read much about this episode of British aviation history and I felt I was becoming part of the aviation community. I joined a large number of young men milling around while the RAF tried to sort them out. I was issued with uniforms, equipment and webbing and took my oath of allegiance to King George VI. The next few weeks were a jumble of mundane tasks such as polishing floors, cleaning brass buttons and buckles, queuing for injections, hours of drill on the parade ground and lectures in the classrooms. We were dragged around Air Crew Transit Units at RAF Kirton in Lindsey, RAF Digby and the Personnel Despatch Centre at RAF Hednesford as we were slowly beaten into shape. We were vaccinated against small pox and inoculated against typhoid, tetanus and TABT. About half the group became ill and the fitter members polished floors and scrubbed bath houses while the invalids polished our buttons and webbing buckles. When queuing for inoculation we were always put into alphabetical order and I went into bat first. I soon discovered that Bob Barnden was always the next victim. Before joining our party he had worked at the Traffic Research Centre in the Ministry of Transport before being conscripted to serve in the Army in the Royal Engineers. He was slightly younger than I but we had much in common and as we plodded our way through the morass we formed a strong friendship which lasted until Bob died at the age of 80. I don't remember when we realised that 60 of us were to form a flying course or when we discovered we were to be trained in the Rhodesian Air Training Group and that could only mean Southern Rhodesia. We were to be known as No 13 Course but we were not superstitious. Soon came news that we would travel out to Rhodesia by ship to Cape Town and then by train to Bulawayo.

We took the boat train from Waterloo to Southampton Docks and you can imagine the joy of 60 young lads when we were confronted with the flagship of the Union Castle line, the Pretoria Castle. For 12 glorious days we were to be not only the lowest rank in the RAF but also passengers on a luxury liner. Life has its ups and downs but this was definitely up. We were allocated three to quite small cabins but who cared? The ship was full of affluent South African families going home after summer in England. They accepted us very well and the living was easy. We held a small discrete parade every morning to attend to the usual administrative chores but were then free to savour our luck. We proposed to give a concert to the passengers and we soon discovered that the course had a wide range of talent. Bob Barnden had brought his violin with him and as he had been the leader of the National Youth Orchestra he was our star turn. The show was well received by the passengers and we had sung for our suppers. England was in a long period of austerity since the war and we were delighted to see the gorgeous array of food which was offered to us every day. Few youngsters from a wide range of backgrounds have the marvellous introduction to such a wide range of gourmet food and the experience served us well for the rest of our lives.

We had a much appreciated break when the ship called in at Funchal on Madeira Island and we immediately found the boat surrounded by all manner of small bumboats offering an assortment of bric a brac and fruit on which the tourist trade thrives. We were impressed by very small boys with their boats who urged us to toss coins into the water way below us so that they could dive for them. I don't think they missed a penny and they had a lucrative morning. Bob and I went ashore together and after a stroll through the town we took a taxi up the hill to Reid's Hotel which had an excellent reputation. The view from the veranda was marvellous and after delicious morning coffee we bummelled our way back down the hill though the streets of Funchal to the ship. I discovered that when bananas are ripening on the tree they point upwards. I always imagined they would obey the laws of nature and hang down.

With memories of Madeira fading behind us the uninitiated met Father Neptune and suffered the usual indignities as we crossed the Equator before we cruised down to Cape Town. As we sailed into Cape Town Bay we found that the view of Table Mountain with its table cloth of cloud hanging over the side was just like the well known post cards. We said goodbye to all our South African friends and reluctantly disembarked. There would be a three day delay before we could set course again by train for Bulawayo in Rhodesia but the South African Air Force provided us with accommodation. We were billeted in the old Cape Town Castle in an enormous room equipped with 60 beds, single wardrobes and bedside lockers. We used communal bathrooms and ate in a canteen and we lamented the contrast with the Pretoria Castle. During our stay we were able to explore the city and we were all dismayed to note the strictness of the apartheid laws. After the freedom of English we were appalled by the situation.

After three days we lugged our luggage on board the Rhodesian Railways Matabeleland train which would haul us back up north. We were allocated three to a cabin but if that is what we had to pay for going to fly; so be it. As the enormous steam engine chuffed its way out of Cape Town we soon left the city behind us. Most of the first day was spent travelling through pleasant green country side with many vineyards in the southern part of Cape Province but by the end of the day we were introduced to the Karoo desert. The countryside was flat, brown and sparsely covered with scrub and occasional thorn bushes. The temperature slowly increased and without any form of cooling we had to rely on airflow from the open windows. As the train chugged along the novelty soon palled and we began to be bored and as night fell the heat was oppressive. I had a top bunk and found some relief by sliding down the bunk and sticking my bare feet out of the window. At every railway station along the route, which appeared regularly after a few hours the train stopped and was immediately surrounded by all manner of traders plying their wares. Buxom women with large baskets of fruit carried on their heads, food trolleys and locally produced drinks. We had been warned by our doctors to avoid any native produced drinks and foodstuffs but lively trade was done with the African passengers.

The desolation of the Karoo was replaced by the even bigger Kalahari Desert and the sight of a single ostrich produced great excitement. The stops were leisurely and we all disembarked, stretched our stiff legs and then took our places in the dining car for whatever meal was appropriate for the time of day. When all the strays had been rounded up the train lurched into motion and we were on our way again. We had a slightly longer stop to allow us to have a brief walk around Pretoria and we also revised our history of the Boer War as we stopped at places with familiar names such as Kimberly or Beaufort West. Eventually, on the third day we passed from South Africa into Bechuanaland and Francistown was our last stop. We knew that Southern Rhodesia would soon be looming over the horizon. Our patience was eventually rewarded and we were home and dry in Bulawayo.

Leaving the train was a leisurely process and we were pleased to see that Bulawayo was a good looking town of two story buildings with broad streets lined with all manner of flowering trees such as Jacarandas, Magnolias, Flamboyants, etc. Soon our transports appeared and we then discovered strip roads for the first time. Instead of having a few metres of asphalt making up the road two strips were laid which were spaced a distance apart equal to the width of the track of a large selection of vehicles. Two vehicles heading in opposite directions charged towards each other and at the last possible moment moved over to their left side so that their offside wheels were still on the nearest strip and the nearside wheel was running on the bundu. The local drivers found this procedure absolutely routine and I never heard of collisions caused by the strip roads. Our buses set course to the east on the Salisbury road and after about twelve miles turned off to the right into the bundu. After another three miles we arrived at the main gates of RAF Heany which was to be our home for the next eighteen months. The train journey from Cape Town to Bulawayo did not seem to be too high a price to pay for a flying training course.

CHAPTER 3
No 4 Flying Training School.
RAF Heany, Southern Rhodesia

AT last No 13 Course had reached a home of its own but it did not look inviting. For many miles the landscape was a dull light brown picture of flat dry hard packed earth with a liberal scattering of thorn bushes which we would come to know as the bundu. Although we were at about 4,500 feet above sea level we could see in the hazy distance ranges of hills reaching up a few more thousand feet. We were in the middle of nowhere and a long way from green England. I was pleased to discover that RAF Heany was the base for one of the RAF's oldest flying training schools, No 4 FTS, that served for many years before the war in RAF Heliopolis in Egypt and where my mother's youngest brother, Uncle Terry, served as a sergeant instructor in the 1930s and had been one of my heroes. I was happy to follow in his footsteps.

It could well have been the inspiration for the opening lines of the immortal RAF ballad, The Shaibah Blues.

> A little bit of muti fell from out the sky one day
> And it landed in the bundu so very far away
> But when the Air Force saw it there,
> it looked so bleak and bare,
> They said "That's what we're looking for
> We'll send our Air Force there"
>
> So they sent out fighting squadrons,
> armoured cars and AHQ
> and sent out 4 F T S
> to show them what to do.
> But peachi I'll be going to the land that's so remote
> the only words you'll hear me say is
> "Roll on that mucknoon boat".

I've got the Shaibah blues, Shaibah Blues.
I'm fed up and fed up and I'm blue.

The main part of the RAF Station, including most of the domestic and administrative buildings, was contained within a circular road and the hangers, workshops and the Air Traffic Control buildings and fire services were outside this perimeter next to the airfield. All the accommodation was in single story prefabricated buildings and we soon found out that we were to live in 2 long huts near to the aircrew cadets dining hall.

We were divided into 2 batches of 30 cadets and shepherded into our barrack huts. 15 beds were placed on either side of the room and each one had a bedside locker on one side and a single wardrobe on the other. Blankets and sheets were neatly folded on the beds together with a knife, fork and spoon and an enamel all purpose mug. By hook or by crook we sorted ourselves and claimed our bed spaces and I was pleased to find that Bob Barnden had settled just over the aisle from me. In a corner of the room was a small cabin which was provided for the senior student to demonstrate his importance. We were A Flight and we had no problem with finding a senior student. Bill Wing was a Flt Sgt signaller who was attempting to remuster to a pilot and he automatically took possession of the single room. Behind our hut was another single building which contained the wash basins, toilets and showers and that completed the Heany Hilton. We soon discovered that one of our flight was an amateur hairdresser who had brought his tools of trade with him. He had a captive clientele, his waiting list was continuously full and he made much pocket money during the next 18 months.

It was springtime in Rhodesia so our working dress was KD shirt, shorts and stockings but with full KD suit and tie for formal parades. We were briefed on the daily routine and discovered that our first 5 months would be devoted solely to ground school which included a liberal dose of parade ground arms drill and marching. Our day revolved around breakfast, lunch and supper when we returned to our barrack hut for a wash and to collect our spanners and mug and hurried to join the cafeteria queue in the cadets' mess for plain but satisfactory food. After the austerity and rationing in UK we had no complaints. The dining hall was furnished with wooden tables with 10 places and the ubiquitous wooden forms. Some hungry lads occasionally attempted to rejoin the queue for a second helping but the kitchen staff was very smart at spotting those trying to swing round the buoy.

RAF Heany

In our leisure hours Bob could often be persuaded to play his violin and his expertise was enjoyed by all of us. One of his favourite pieces of music was Danse Macabre by Saint Saens which he normally introduced by announcing, "It is midnight in the grave yard. Enter Death playing a violin".

In UK potential pilots were given about 10 hours flying to assess their ability to learn to fly and then sent to an Initial Training Wing to complete the ground school phase before going to an FTS. We were surprised that we should be sent all the way to Rhodesia without these stages and thus risk the expense having to return to UK those who failed to solo. The failure rate at this stage was quite high.

For me the next 5 months were full of interest when we were introduced to principles of flight, navigation, meteorology, flight instruments, administration, customs of the service and RAF law. I particularly looked forward to pilot navigation lectures which seemed to be so logical to me.

The classroom lectures were interspersed with parade ground drill and I was amused by our drill instructor who was an RAF Regiment corporal of the old school. We had to endure very elementary instruction and when introducing the rifle he would begin with, "The Short Magazine Lee Enfield MK 111 rifle is 44½ inches long and weighs 8lbs and 10 ounces. It has a bore of ·303 inches, etc". If he was queried on any detail he would begin again at the beginning and repeat the whole sermon word for word. We were particularly amused by his demonstration of how to throw a hand grenade over a high wall. He ran at the wall, put one foot high up the wall surface, leapt up and hurled the grenade over the wall. Unfortunately there was no wall and after his spirited demonstration he collapsed in a heap on the ground. We admired his enthusiasm.

Local security was entrusted to a regiment of native soldiers who were incredibly proud to be members of the Rhodesian Army Rifles. Their turnout was impeccable with stiffly starched uniforms and highly polished boots. They loved marching and it was difficult for their drill instructors to restrict the height to which they swung their arms. Their parade ground drill was crisply precise with much enthusiastic banging of boots. We discovered later that they dreaded punishment which included being deprived of their boots and reduced to walking behind their marching comrades.

We took it in turn to pass by the Mail Office to collect our letters on our way back to our hut for lunch and then distribute the mail to our flight. We normally gathered by the front door of our barrack hut while the mail bearer called out the names and handed over the precious envelopes. Mail travelled slowly to Rhodesia and was often more than 3 weeks in transit. We soon realised that some people got more mail than others and I was saddened to note that some members invariably stood on the fringe of the group obviously waiting with little hope before turning away disappointed. I was heartened to observe the happy days when their names were called out and the world became a better place. Bob received regular letters from Daphne, his regular girl friend, and we used to share selected parts of our letters to increase the flow of news from UK.

I quickly discovered that our sports pitch had a hard gravelly surface. When playing rugby I was prone to spending much time surfing along the ground and I soon had a mass of raw scrapes on my knees and arms which were slow to heal. As there were lots of other sports such as hockey, squash, tennis and swimming I gave up rugby in Rhodesia. Much of our off duty time was spent around and in the swimming pool and soon came our first experience of a tropical Christmas. Of course the prime location for the celebrations was the pool. We also had a sailing club which had a fleet of 12 foot dinghies based at a dam in the Matopos Hills adjacent to Rhodes' grave. The dam was surrounded by small steep hills and as we usually had fresh winds the hills formed eddies which gave constantly changing winds across the water. Sailing was very competitive and soon became one of my main sports and, as usual in sailing clubs, it also involved continuous maintenance work. Although it was frustrating not to be allowed near the Tiger Moths and Harvards which were daily in evidence in the air the five months passed by quite quickly. I was lapping it up and enjoying all the information I could get and in the periodic exams Bob and I competed for first place. During this period we began to see several students failing to make the grade and returning back to UK. We had 2 senior courses ahead of us and several of the cadets failed to go solo on the Tiger or Harvard and they also began the lonely trek back to England, home and beauty. It was obvious that I was making good progress but in my reflective moments I was still haunted by the old question of whether I could learn to fly. I was now to find out.

We had a short holiday during which I spent most of my time sailing on the Matopos dam and returned keen to tackle the flying phase. Before we began flying we moved from our barrack room to a block of 2 bed cabins with a communal bathhouse adjacent to our new building. This was welcomed but our time in the barrack block had built up a bond of camaraderie which has survived among the survivors until today.

Bob and I reported to A Flight of No 1 Squadron with our flying kit and were welcomed by our Flt Cdr and instructors and saw on the blackboard that Ashley and Barnden were allocated to an ex-wartime fighter pilot, Flt Sgt Ken Wilson, although at that period in the RAF he was known as a Pilot 1. He was a stockily built man of less than average height and we immediately took a liking to him. During our training he was always called Sir but later he became a close friend for the rest of his life and I will refer to him as Ken. We quickly settled in and Ken took us out to meet the Tiger Moth. I felt very lucky that we were to receive our initial instruction on what was generally accepted as the best trainer in the world. It was the last of the wood and canvas biplanes of the RAF. It was small and its empty weight was only 1,100 pounds and looked very frail. Its faithful Gipsy Major engine with its wooden propeller only produced 130 hp at sea level and much less at our height of 4,500 feet. Many small cars these days are heavier and more powerful. I had known the Tiger Moth since I first became interested in aeroplanes and I loved it.

Tiger Moth on the flight line

Our only flying kit was light cotton flying overalls and a leather helmet with earphones and we were soon fitted with our personal parachutes. The engine was started by hand swinging the propeller and we had to have a session of training in the art before we were issued with the first certificate to find a place in my flying logbook. Not many pilots have them today. After several general briefings on 12th April 1950 Ken and I lugged our parachutes out to Tiger Moth 6975 for my first flight. My adrenalin was flowing and I was excited and raring to go. We then made the first of several thousand pre-flight inspections as we walked around the aircraft, including removing small stones from under the propeller, to make a thorough check and then struggle into our parachutes. If I could stand up straight my harness was not tight enough. Ken flew in the front cockpit under the top wing and as we stepped up on to plywood walkway by the left wing root the aircraft leaned over to the left. I lowered myself into the snug little rear cockpit, strapped into the safety harness and plugged my helmet into the intercom, closed the entry door and was ready to go.

Ken shepherded me through the engine starting procedure. I checked that the ignition switches were off and the throttle closed before an airman turned the propeller to draw fuel into the engine. The throttle was then opened and the airman turned the propeller backwards one turn to blow out excess fuel. All was the ready for the cry of "Contact" and the throttle set partly open before the switches were turned on and the airman began to swing the propeller a few times until the engine fired, coughed and then settled down to a steady beat. The aircraft rocked gently on its soft undercarriage and for the first time I felt the airflow past my face. We waited a while until the engine warmed up as we checked the instruments. Ken signalled for the chocks to be pulled away from in front of the wheels and we were free to taxi. The Tiger had no wheel brakes and no tail wheel. We had to increase power to give enough airflow over the rudder to turn and our tail skid acted as a weak brake. Usually an airman tugged on a wing tip to help the turn out of the flight line but then great care was needed to taxi along the edge of the airfield. As we could not see straight ahead because of the engine we had to swing the aircraft from side to side to ensure the way ahead was clear. Taxying was quite straight forward in calm conditions but as soon as the wind strength increased the aircraft showed a will of its own as it continuously tried to turn into wind and a very strong wind could blow the aircraft over. Trying to taxy downwind was another test of wills.

Tightening the parachute

Now close the door

The airfield was an almost circular patch of bundu with a 900 yard runway cutting across the middle. The runway was used by the Harvards and the Tigers normally used the open area on the camp side in front of the control tower and to the left of the runway. We zigzagged our way along the edge of the airfield towards the runway controller's caravan at the downwind end of the landing area and Ken guided me through my first efforts at mastering this new art. Before takeoff we had to perform the pre-takeoff checks which I was to repeat for every flight I made during my flying career and as we had no radio we waited for the runway controller to give us a green light from his Aldis lamp. This first flight was intended to be a demonstration and I settled down to watch carefully as Ken began the takeoff. All tail dragger propeller driven aircraft try to swing off line during takeoff and the Tiger tried to swing to the right. The Harvards on our right tended to swing to the left so a little extra care was called for. The acceleration was slow but soon the tail came up and the wheels bumped less and less. A little later we were airborne. At last I was flying.

We set our altimeters to zero when we on the airfield so that while we were flying we always knew how high we were above the ground but we had to remember that we were in fact 4,500 feet higher above sea level. The Tiger was under powered and in UK it rejoiced in a rate of climb of about 650 feet per minute but at our height and temperature it was considerably less and we were continuously struggling to gain or retain height. Eventually we arrived at 3,000 feet and Ken made a clearing turn to ensure we were on our own in the area and then showed me how the controls worked. All the reading I had done now paid off and I was usually ahead of him as he patiently explained everything and he let me try my hand at the everyday manoeuvres. I was enjoying the whole situation and to be sitting in a Tiger with the wings above and below me, the airflow streaming past my ears, the back of Ken's head in front of me, the marvellous view of the Rhodesian landscape and my first attempt to keep check on our position confirmed that this was what I wanted to do. At last we came to the bits I had been waiting for; the stall and the spin. Ken closed the throttle and held the Tiger level. The speed quickly reduced and I began to feel the trembling as the airflow over the wings began to break up. The trembling became a judder and with the control column, or stick, held firmly back the Tiger began to sink. Ken used the rudder to keep the aircraft heading straight until he eased the nose down and re-applied power to regain flying speed. This was as I had expected but it was a great kick to experience it for the first time. We clambered back to a safe height and checked around for other aircraft. What I was really waiting for was my first spin and it was about to be demonstrated. Ken advised me to try to watch what was going on as some students closed their eyes and hung on tightly. He then repeated the approach to the stall but just before it happened he pushed on a boot full of left rudder and moved the stick back into his stomach. The nose reared up and the left wing began to roll down. The nose dropped down below the horizon and the rolling continued. The right wing was still providing lift but the left wing had gone on strike. We were falling down like a sycamore seed and a view from the back seat was spectacular. I could see the wings rolling around with the nose mainly pointing down but varying from nearing vertical to nearly horizontal. The Tiger was out of control but as it was my first spin Ken did not prolong it and as soon as he eased the stick forward and pushed on full right rudder the Tiger obediently stopped spinning and entered a steep dive. Ken gently eased out of the dive and applied climbing power. I was elated and my adrenalin was flowing freely. This was the heart of flying.

Tigers can bite

We had at last to return to the airfield and Ken showed me the procedure for joining the circuit and fitting in safely with the other traffic. We flew along the downwind leg of the circuit at 1,000 ft, turned on to the base leg and Ken closed the throttle. The standard approach was made in the glide and any adjustments required to bring the aircraft to the correct touchdown point were made by judging the turn in point to line up on the landing direction and side slipping to lose any excess height. After crossing over the airfield threshold the trickiest part of the whole exercise began and I watched carefully as Ken continued the descent to within a few feet of the ground and then eased the nose up to fly almost level. The speed reduced quickly and Ken kept the aircraft off the ground until it began to stall with the nose quite high in the correct landing attitude. As the wings began to lose lift the Tiger sank gently down until the wheels touched the surface simultaneously with the tailskid. This was the well known 3 point landing which was demanded by the air force as the only acceptable method of landing a Tiger in normal conditions. This was the major stumbling block for many students and thousands never mastered it and were "scrubbed".

The Tiger, like all tail dragger aircraft, was directionally unstable on the ground and if it was allowed to begin to yaw during the landing roll the tail would try to go to the front and the aircraft finish up running backwards. This was the infamous ground loop. I was in a group on the flight line when a landing Tiger began a ground loop. As the turn to the right reached 90 degrees the left wing dipped and touched the ground, the nose was pitched down and the propeller hit the ground. The nose dug into the earth and the tail began to rise until it reached the vertical. It paused in this position and then slowly continued on its way until the Tiger was lying on the top wing and the tip of the fin. The pilot was still safely sitting in his seat with his head about 2 feet off the ground and as we ran towards him we were calling, "Don't release your harness" but before we reached him he did just that and we watched him fall on to his head. Fortunately he did not break his neck but he had a sore head for some time.

Bob turning me from flight line

Now for a coffee

Now began the most important fortnight of my flying career. We made 4 flights during which we covered all the upper air exercises such as straight and level, climbing, descending, turning, steep turns, climbing and descending turns, etc. I had no problems with this phase and I knew that with practice it would improve. We then moved on to flying the circuit and trying to master the art of landing. The airfield surface was hard earth with a few tufts of rough grass and I, like many of my friends, found great difficulty in judging the correct height to round out before touch down. Occasionally the wheels would hit the ground before I intended. The shock absorbers would compress and then expand again and push the nose of the aircraft back up into the air and we were all set for a series of embarrassing bounces. At other times I would round out and then discover that I was too high and had to face either putting on some power or risking a heavy landing. The only answer was practise and more practise. Initially Ken gave very useful snippets of advice but slowly the flow dried up and his head sank deeper and deeper into his cockpit until I could only see the tip of his helmet. Occasionally an apple core would be propelled out of his cockpit. After one landing I was trying to take off again but the Tiger just was not accelerating properly and I was only bouncing along on the wheels when I heard Ken chuckling from the front seat. When I checked around to find what was tickling him I discovered that I had only put on half throttle. When I pushed the throttle fully open the Tiger flew much better.

Ken Wilson

Me, Bob and Ken

During this period I managed to get an extra flight as passenger during an air test but then I was back to circuit bashing. Slowing I was getting it all together and then after my 4th session I had a flight with my flight commander and on 28th April 1950 after 7 hours of flying he sent me solo. Several members of our course were falling by the wayside at this stage but my sense of relief was enormous. Bob also flew solo at this time and our joy was unbounded. We had a great party with our successful friends and we could see the way ahead. If I had failed my world would have collapsed.

More bundu

After a full day's flying we helped to return the Tigers to our hangar. One person would pick up the tail to protect the tailskid from the tarmac and several others pushed from behind the lower wings and we trundled across the hard standing into the shade of the hangar. Putting them to bed was one of the most satisfying parts of the day.

Often when Ken and Bob were flying I would walk out with them to start the engine and help them out of the flight line. Sometimes the engine was reluctant to start even after many swings of the prop. I learned that the recognised RAF procedure for such an occasion was to open the engine cowling on the right side, find an apple sized stone and then look at the magneto to find several prominent scratches. This was where one clouted the magneto with the stone. The treatment never failed.

Putting a Tiger to bed

May and June were full of absolute joy. We still flew many circuits and landings but the upper air work was consolidated and expanded to include aerobatics, formation and instrument flying and our first navigation flights. I knew I could master the exercises and was always waiting for anything new. Unfortunately we now began to have the first of our fatal accidents. One student spun into the bundu in his Tiger and soon afterwards an instructor and his student followed suit. We had already attended funerals for members of the senior courses but to lose someone so close to us had a heavy impact.

During this time the rumour was spread that "The Trappers are coming". Soon our instructors introduced us to something like The Inquisition, namely the periodic visits of the Examining Wing of the Central Flying School whose task it was to regularly visit all flying instructional units of the RAF worldwide to fly with a large proportion of instructors and students to ensure that good standards were being maintained. A spring cleaning of flying orders and publications was made and flight line procedures were tightened up. At last the team of experienced and highly qualified QFIs appeared and we did not find any two headed monsters among them. They quickly settled into normal routine among the flights and some carefully briefed students were offered up to fly with them as sacrificial lambs. They were surprised to find that they were asked to fly perfectly normal general handling sorties and they felt no pain. The first Trapper I saw was the leader, Sqn Ldr John Barraclough, and little did I realise I would meet him often in the future during our careers until he became Air Chief Marshal Sir John; a great stalwart of CFS.

The wind was normally fairly light and generally along the runway but one morning it was suddenly quite strong and blowing across the runway. The decision was made to fly into the wind and across the runway and this was really no great problem. I was detailed to fly a solo exercise which finished with circuits and landings and all went well until I was taking off again for my second circuit. Although the Tiger had performed well so far it was very reluctant to accelerate and I checked to ensure that I had put on full throttle. The engine instruments showed that it was behaving well but the Tiger staggered into the air and I soon realised that I must not throttle back. Even at full power the aircraft was not going to accelerate to normal circuit speed or climb to 1,000 ft for a normal circuit. We staggered round the circuit at about 400 ft still at full throttle and when I arrived on the approach to land I only had to reduce the throttle a little before it began descending to the touch down area. As I landed I pulled the power off and the Tiger immediately sat down firmly on the ground. Even to taxy to the flight line needed much more throttle than usual and I was glad when I could close the engine down and ease my weary body out of the cockpit. Several people from the flight line had noticed the unusual behaviour and quickly gathered around to find the cause. The reason was immediately obvious because I had about 30 yards of electric cable trailing behind the tail skid. As I had crossed the runway after my first landing the tailskid had hooked into a cable which had been laid alongside the runway, torn it out of position and taken it for a ride round the airfield. The Tiger flew much better again when the cable was removed.

Tigers over Heany

In the middle of June I flew a progress check with my flight commander and towards the end of the month I also flew my final handling test with him. Bob and I had been lucky to have all our instructional flights with Ken Wilson and his teaching had set us both on the way to very rewarding flying careers. My last flight for this first part of our course was with Ken and we had a great session of aerobatics with a practice forced landing followed by low flying thrown in for good measure.

We now had the vast total of 40 hours flying on the Tiger Moth and we had to move on to our next challenge, the Harvard. We had seen from the 2 courses ahead of us that even after the Tiger Moth flying several students failed to master the Harvard and were sent home. Back came the doubts in my mind.

Wood and canvas burn easily

We were made welcome by E Flight when we dragged our flying kit to their offices. I was pleased to note that I would begin my Harvard flying with our new flight commander. This was another stroke of luck because Flt Lt Ted Colehan was another exceptional instructor. He was a big, heavy, flat footed, quiet, thoughtful man who I immediately liked. In later years I followed his career as he became AOC Malta, Commandant at Cranwell and an Air Vice Marshal. All were well deserved. The Harvard was a monoplane with a big 600 hp engine, retractable undercarriage and wing flaps and a radio. It was 4 times heavier and had at least twice the performance of the Tiger Moth and the student sat in the front cockpit.

The Flt Cdr took me out to the flight line on the hard standing and showed me around my new chariot. I clambered up onto the wing trailing edge, went forward to the front cockpit and installed myself into the seat. I immediately noticed that the big, circular engine obscured much of the forward view while the tail was still on the ground. When all was ready 2 airmen stood on the left wing root next to my cockpit, inserted a huge crank handle into a hole just behind the engine and began the heavy task of accelerating a flywheel up to sufficient speed to turn the engine over. When they were ready I engaged the flywheel to the engine and it slowly began to turn over. I had then to use a hand priming pump to judiciously pump fuel into the engine until it fired and commenced to run. If I primed too much the engine became too rich, if I primed too little the mixture was too lean and on both occasions the engine turned slower and slower until eventually it stopped. The resentful looks from the airmen as they began to wind again was to be avoided at all costs.

The Harvard had wheel brakes operated by pressure on the rudder pedals and a tail wheel instead of a tailskid and could therefore be parked on the tarmac. They flew from the runway and reached it by taxying along a tarmac taxiway. The big engine hid the forward view and we had to zig zag our way along the taxiway to ensure all was clear. After performing all the pre-take off checks and obtaining take off clearance by radio the Flt Cdr demonstrated a take off to me. The engine rotated clockwise, the opposite direction from the Tiger Moth, and the tail wheel made it easier for the aircraft to swing to the left on takeoff. Extra care was required to keep away from the Tigers. He gave me control and I climbed up to a safe height and after checking around we flew all the air exercises including stalling, spinning and action in case of fire before we returned to the airfield to begin the inevitable circuit bashing. Landing on the runway required a little more precision and I found that the tarmac runway had fewer surface characteristics to help me to judge the round out height. My head was about 10 feet above the ground and I knew that the landing would need plenty of practice. I flew my next flight again with the Flt Cdr and I enjoyed his quiet style. He told me what to do and then let me get on with it and afterwards told me how to improve it next time. Again the landings were a varied mixture but he seemed satisfied with my progress.

Strapping in to the Harvard

He had then to concentrate on his other duties and he handed me over to my own instructor which proved to be my first set-back. He was a small, dark, taciturn Canadian and from the beginning he never stopped talking and nagging me. While climbing he would be chanting "95, 95, 95 etc" in his nasal Canadian accent and I would switch off my microphone and mutter "Shut up, shut up". I found it hard to concentrate and felt that I was making no progress. After 4 frustrating flights I was programmed to fly again with my Flt Cdr and I feared that it was a scrub check. My heart was in my boots but the big comfortable man climbed into the back, told me to take off, climb to 3,000ft over Mielbo, make a stall and a spin and then return to the circuit. He then settled back and let me get on with it. I told him what I was doing and when we returned to the circuit I tried to produce my best landings. After 2 reasonable attempts he told me to taxy to the control tower. When we were parked he said, "Off you go and do a couple of circuits. Good luck" and climbed out. I could not believe the change in my fortunes and I don't remember anything about my first Harvard solo flight.

After he had de-briefed me he told me that he knew my instructor was not easy to live with but he assured me that if I stuck with him I would benefit from it. I formed the impression that my instructor was newly qualified and was still under supervision. I flew the remainder of the basic phase uncomfortably with him. My friends and I were continuously talking about our flying and anything I had missed I picked up from them.

After my first Harvard solo flight

On my second solo flight a little excitement entered my life. I was making an approach and concentrating hard when lined up on the runway at a few hundred feet I saw a bright red flash right in front of me and the cockpit suddenly began to fill with acrid smoke. I did not know what was going on but I thought the best action was to continue my approach and land as quickly as possible. I managed to make a reasonable arrival then applied the brakes as hard as possible and when the aircraft stopped I applied the parking brake, undid my harness, opened the canopy and leapt out amid a whole cloud of red smoke and ran to a safe distance before looking back while waiting for an explosion. What I saw was a Harvard parked in the middle of the runway with smoke streaming from the cockpit but with the engine still ticking over. In my haste to escape it had not occurred to me to switch off the engine. Subsequently I discovered that as I was concentrating on my approach a student in a Tiger Moth had misjudged his approach and was flying into the runway centre line but below me where I could not see him. The runway controller in his caravan saw this quite late, grabbed his Verey pistol and fired off a red cartridge to warn me to overshoot and go round again. Unfortunately in his haste he fired directly at my aircraft and the ball of burning phosphorus entered my radial engine, passed between the cylinders and lodged in the cockpit air intake and threw a cloud of smoke into my cockpit. I have since maintained my claim that on my second Harvard solo I was shot down by Air Traffic Control.

Out of the blue came the news that Tony Partington had crashed. He was flying with his instructor and the aircraft spun into the bundu and both were killed. This hit us very hard and again we had to go through the routine of a military funeral. We were becoming well rehearsed in the procedure. The price of learning to fly was high but we had to carry on.

My Flt Cdr flew with me for a 20 hour progress check and he also gave me my first night flying exercises. Again I was able to relax and I began to love night flying. The navigation exercises in the Harvard were much longer than in the Tiger and as the Rhodesian countryside was so barren they were more demanding. My fascination with pilot navigation slowly increased. We had practically no cloud in Rhodesia but we had to practise instrument flying and the students flew from the back seat with a canvas hood over the cockpit. This was an essential part of pilot training but it was a new art which required careful thought and much practise. We ploughed steadily through the course and eventually the Flt Cdr flew with me on my final handling test which thankfully went well. The basic phase came to and end and I was always grateful that Ted Colehan had been my perceptive flight commander. We had a short break before moving to F Flight for our Applied Harvard phase during which several of us travelled down to Durban and spent a week mainly in the highest and strongest surf I had ever seen. When we returned I had the opportunity to fly again with Ken Wilson in a Tiger in a formation practice. I had now flown a grand total of 100 hours.

Dennis Coop, Bill Sleigh, Doug Holmes
Geof Bradford, Bob Barnden

While we were having fun in the air RAF Heany had been preparing to introduce a bundu survival course and was ready to try out their plans. Volunteers were required and 6 of our course stepped forward and were selected as guinea pigs. Bob Barnden, Doug Holmes, Geof Bradford, Dennis Coop and I together with Bill Sleigh, who was a few years older than us and had been a flight test engineer with Rolls Royce aero engines, were given bush hats, one rifle, one pistol, machetes, water bottles and a one day ration pack for each of us. We used our flying maps. Kitted out with such advanced equipment we were loaded on to a lorry and driven out well into the bundu. We were instructed to make our way across the bundu to a bridge over a dried up river bed about 10 miles away and as they left us we were told we would be picked up there in 5 days times. We could see nothing except flat bundu well peppered with 50 foot high round topped kopjes and over head was a 100% blue sky. The marching would not be difficult so we had plenty of time to make our target. We could enjoy our stroll through the bundu and our biggest tasks would be acquiring food and water, protecting ourselves from the sun and avoiding injury. We had no problem with finding food although we did not have gourmet menus. Water we found in bamboo stems and by digging deep holes on the outside of bends in the dried up river beds. When we found damp soil in the hole we left it and after a while water would slowly filter into the hole. It needed further filtering through any cloth we had and it was adequate to keep us alive. We were a happy team and we spent much time tracking springboks or climbing kopjes for fun. In the evening we chose our camps site, improvised beds and then lit our camp fire. We prepared whatever food we had gleaned and then sat around the fire and chatted the cooler evenings away. Inevitably the subject of food came round and we selected the meal we would have if we were in a top class restaurant. As the days passed and we became hungrier my choice of fictitious food became more basic with items such as my mother's bramble and apple pie. Hunger is a great leveller. I have nothing but pleasant memories of these days and it provided a splendid break from the course. Needless to say we were waiting when the lorry turned up to rescue the survivors.

Before we began the applied phase we were upgraded to Officer Cadets and we moved into twin berth cabins next to the Officers Mess and were made mess members. During the remainder of the course we were also introduced to the customs and procedures of mess life. We were very fortunate that our Station Commander was Gp Capt Don Geddes who was a pre-war officer who had flown with distinction and reached the rank of Air Cdre during the war. He set a very high standard of behaviour in the Mess and I was always glad for it.

As usual we assembled in the offices of F Flight but my designated instructor was not there. I soon discovered that he had little interest in flying and attempted to minimise the amount he had to do. Before the first flight of the day the students went out to the aircraft and inspected them. They started the engines and before the engines were warmed up their instructors had arrived and off they went. Day after day I would be the last one sitting in my aircraft and then I would see my instructor scurrying around the end of the hangar and into the crew room to pick up his flying kit. We were starting a very important part of our course and I was missing out on good instruction and I tried to fill the gaps by discussions with my fellow students.

We were introduced to steep dive and low level bombing and air to air gunnery which I loved but I had very little help from the back of the aircraft. We had our own bombing range at Mielbo, about 30 miles to the east of Heany. We carried 4 x 25 lb smoke bombs and for low level bombing we dropped them from 250 ft. We tried to aim the bomb rack at the target but the release sighting point was below the top of the engine cowl so we had to release by guess work. We flew on a northerly heading over the target and then turned left to make another approach towards the east. Then left again on to a southerly heading and finally to the west. Of course after each bomb we had to take a quick look back to see where the puff of smoke showed our error. Two airmen on the range with theodolites calculated the error and passed the news to us. Initially we threw bombs all over the bundu but slowly I realised that the smallest amount of side slip would throw a bomb off track and getting the Harvard flying straight was absolutely essential. My instructor in the back could not see the target on the bombing run so he was less use than normally. During this phase Blondey Derbyshire flew into the ground while watching over his shoulder to see the smoke puff from his bomb. He was a popular lad and we missed him greatly but life had to go on.

I liked low level bombing but steep dive bombing was much more exciting. We started at 4,000 ft and dived at 60°. We tried to position the target close by the side of the cockpit and flew straight until it had disappeared under the leading edge of the wing. When we judged the time to be ripe the aircraft was rolled 120° to the left and the nose pulled down and the wings rolled level again in the dive when the target was seen. The speed built up very quickly so we entered the dive at about 60 mph, the lowest safe speed, and we tried to find the sighting point before we reached the maximum permitted speed but usually we exceeded it before we pulled hard on the controls to recover from the dive and clamber back to 4,000 ft for the next run. During the dive the speed was changing very quickly and we had to continuously move the rudder pedals to try to keep the aircraft flying straight. We again threw bombs all over Rhodesia but as we learned to control the side slip our bombs crept nearer to the target until eventually one heard the welcome call, "Delta Hotel" (direct hit). The scores were published in the flight offices and we became very competitive. We also knew that the last series of scores would be used to find the winner of the Bombing Trophy.

Harvard rolling into dive

At the same time as bombing we began air to air gunnery. The Harvard had a camera gun and we used other Harvards as targets. We practised all manner of attacks leading up to the final exercises when we flew head on attacks. The target approached very quickly and we were relieved when we passed the target and were still flying. After the flights the films were processed and we then learned whether we would ever make fighter pilots.

We were introduced to formation flying and practiced it regularly. The adrenalin flowed quite freely and fierce concentration was required for long periods of time. Instrument flying was also continuously practiced and our navigation flights became longer. While I was slogging my way through this phase with very little help from the back seat I had a stroke of good fortune. Within 6 weeks of the end of the course I was suddenly transferred to a new instructor. Flt Lt Bill Tait must have been our oldest instructor, well into his thirties. He had a well lived in face and a rather fatherly image. He was burly and well tanned with thinning hair. He lived with his wife in a native village where his wife was the school teacher. Immediately I met him I liked him and sensed that he would be a great help to me. He was a quiet man but full of good common sense, only said what was necessary and pushed me hard to improve. Bill Tait saved my course and I was eternally grateful to him. The changeover came just in time to make dramatic improvements in my low level and dive bombing and he immediately began to work on my aerobatics. He not only improved the precision of my aerobatics but also insisted on a smooth transition between manoeuvres to give a continuous flow and build up a reasonable display. My love of aerobatics increased and I never forgot the teaching of Bill Tait. Life became very pleasant again and I hoped I could make up any lost ground.

Soon we began the phase when all our results were being assessed for the aerobatics, bombing and navigation trophies. The aerobatic trophy would be decided between the 4 leading contenders during a public display and Bill worked very hard to lick me into shape and when the great day came I flew in front of the control tower with judges on the ground and with an impartial judge in the back seat. My display went well and I was well pleased with it. Bill in his quiet way also seemed well satisfied but we would have to wait until the end of the course for the results.

I flew my final night navigation exercise with our Chief Instructor and my Flt Cdr gave me my Final Handling Test and suddenly the end of the course was looming into sight. We had lost half of the course through fatal accidents or failures but those of us still flying were confident we would pass the course. I managed to get flights to and from RAF Thornhill near to Gwelo for an inter station squash match and then it was time to smarten up our marching and rifle drill for our passing out parade. The date was set for 21st March 1951 and Air Commodore Allinson, the AOC of the Rhodesian Air Training Group, would be the reviewing officer. Bob, who was very impressive on the parade ground, was nominated to command our course. We then imagined we were on Horse Guards Parade. The parade went well and then we formed up in front of the parade for the presentations. We were all presented with our wings and my long

53

term ambition was achieved. The presentation of the trophies followed and Don Roland had won the Navigation Trophy and I was second. Geof Bradford won the Bombing Trophy and I was second. Phil Crawshaw won the Aerobatics Trophy and again I was second. I was musing about always being the bridesmaid when I heard the announcement that I had won the Cup of Honour.

No 4 FTS had a proud place in RAF history and I was delighted that my name would be added to the list of winners. My uncle had been on the staff of the unit at Heliopolis in Egypt in the 1930s and he would have been proud of me. I was given a small replica of the Cup and it is still one of my proudest possessions. All my doubts were over. I had learned to fly. Our flying log books were made up to date and sent to the Chief Instructor for his signature and I received the first of many Summaries of Flying and Assessments of Ability. When I received it back again I found that I had been assessed as Above the Average as a pilot under training, as a pilot navigator, in bombing and in air gunnery. In instrument flying because of our lack of cloud and, like all other students, I was assessed as Average. I now had 205 flying hours and Uncle Terry would have been proud of me.

No 4FTS Cup of Honour

Only 33 of the original course members had passed out and 10 of us were commissioned as Pilot Officers. The remaining 23 were promoted to Sgt Pilots and we devoted our new found wealth to the mother and father of all parties.

The survivors

We then had to wait while preparation were made to return us to UK and I began my new trade of aircraft stealer and in no time at all I had secured the part time job of flying the daily Mielbo bombing range delivery service for personnel and mail. Usually I flew a Tiger Moth but some days a Harvard was provided. One passenger to Mielbo was Cpl Aikenhead of the Rhodesian Army Rifles. He stood about 6 ft 6inches tall and must have weighed nearly 18 stones. After I had briefed him and fitted him with a parachute I invited him to enter the front cockpit. He stood on the small walk way on the left wing and the Tiger leaned more to the left than usual and I thought I heard it groan. When level with the cockpit he turned smartly to the right and then took a step back. His right boot went straight through the top and bottom canvas of the wing and he sank down above his knee into the wing. Hauling him out of the hole without doing more damage proved to be a major task but he was uninjured while the poor little Tiger was very sick. He behaved himself when we attempted a re-run in another aircraft and he was safely delivered to Mielbo.

Eventually a Hastings transport aircraft was on its way to collect us from Livingstone airport, immediately over the Zambesi River from Victoria Falls. Our happy group of new pilots enjoyed a very relaxed train journey from Bulawayo to Victoria Falls and spent a carefree night in the superior Victoria Falls Hotel. Next day we embarked on our personal Hastings, took off and discovered that the undercarriage would not retract. We landed back at Livingston and as soon as it was ascertained that spare parts were required from UK we rejoined the train and returned to Bulawayo to wait for another aircraft to be sent out for us. Instead of returning to RAF Heany we were accommodated at RAF Kumalo which was the HQ of the Rhodesian Air Training Group and situated just outside Bulawayo. It had an airfield and I reverted to my new job of aircraft stealing. I managed to get 2 flights in an Anson and then I had the opportunity to fly a Sergeant in a Harvard up to Livingstone. It was a quite long flight but much of the journey was over thick jungle. The first 50 miles or so I could see the railway line on my left but then it wandered off to the west and all I could see was dense trees. With only a single engine to rely on I hoped it would prove to be reliable. I paid more interest than usual to the engine instruments and all seemed well. Every time I moved my head the note of the engine changed and I had to check again. As usual the Harvard did not let me down and soon I could see ahead of me the huge plume of water spray over the Victoria Falls. The remainder of the journey was all downhill. An airman was waiting for me and after I had re-fuelled we set course back over the jungle and I was greatly relieved when the railway line to Bulawayo came out of the jungle from the west to meet me and lead me home. I enjoyed the 2 flights and felt that I was earning my keep at last.

Another Hastings arrived at Livingstone and we repeated our journey to join it. On 3rd May the undercarriage decided to retract and we set course for Nairobi where we spent the night in The New Stanley Hotel. Next day we chugged along to Aden where we sampled the charms of the RAF Khormaksar officers mess. On 5th May we were given an aerial tour of the Red Sea and landed at RAF Fayid alongside the Great Bitter Lake in the Canal Zone of Egypt. We sampled the austerity of tented transit accommodation at RAF El Hamra and were glad to resume our travels next day and fly past the Mediterranean islands and land at RAF Luqa in Malta. We stayed in the Officers Mess and felt as if we were getting nearer to Europe again. We wandered around Valetta City during the evening and it was inevitable that we found ourselves in the notorious Gut. We were becoming rather short of cash by this time and we found a novel solution to our problem. One of the establishments had a small band which included a violinist and in very short time he had been persuaded to lend his fiddle to Bob. While Bob gave one of his virtuoso performances some of our group took a hat around a collected a goodly sum of money. We never let Bob, even when he was a Gp Capt, forget the time when he played the violin for monetary gain in a house of ill repute. It was time for us to return to UK and next day our faithful chariot delivered us to RAF Lyneham. We were home.

A Hastings (foreground) during the Berlin Air Lift

CHAPTER 4
Rhodesia Refresher Course

BEFORE our 33 newly qualified pilots could be any use to the rapidly expanding RAF they still had much to do. The most immediate requirements were to gain experience of flying in England and to find plenty of cloud for us to increase our instrument flying capability. The other need was for us to gain some experience of living in a real Officers Mess. The RAF's solution to the problem was to give us the most enjoyable 3 months flying holiday I can remember. No 13 Course re–assembled on 20th June 1951 at No 2 FTS to partake in a Rhodesia Refresher Course.

RAF South Cerney was a pre–war permanent station with a small grass airfield. The Officers Mess was a large 1936 pattern brick building with all the normal facilities; it looked good with a large flight of steps before the main entrance and it was comfortable. The flying field was a circular area of grass of about 1,000 yards diameter. The airfield was about 3 miles south of the delightful old town of Cirencester. What more could we want?

Percival Prentice

Of course we needed aeroplanes and a generous Air Force gave us the mighty Percival Prentice. We Rhodesian trained pilots were proud to be aces of the Tiger Moth and Harvard which had rules which must be obeyed and if you disobeyed they would, and did, kill you. The Prentice was the main elementary trainer in UK at the time and we were amazed to discover that it was a great big pussy cat. If you were very determined, and with a bit of luck, it might be persuaded to kill you but I don't know of any successful attempts. Student and instructor sat side by side and to give an extra bit of mutual support a second student could be seated in the middle behind them. It had a 50 foot wingspan which was large for an elementary trainer and was hauled around by a faithful DH Gypsy Queen engine. This lovely engine was suitable for a pussy cat.

Our course in Rhodesia had been set very high standards and the failure rate had been 50%. Ten of the successful students had been commissioned and the remaining 23 were made Sergeants for a seven year engagement. When we arrived at South Cerney the pass rate for UK students was 95% and all survivors were commissioned. I believe that our Sergeants were better pilots than nearly all of their UK counterparts but as far as I know only two were subsequently commissioned. The Cold War was getting colder and that was one of the prices we were paying.

After settling into the Mess and finding our way around half of us assembled in J Flight and met our instructors. They were mainly ex–wartime pilots and experienced instructors but we soon discovered that the Flight was closely supervised but run on a relaxed and friendly basis. The jewel of the Flight was the Flight Commander, Flt Lt Grzybowski, alias Grib, one of the many Polish pilots who gave such splendid service during the war. He was short but what he lacked in height he made up for by fire in his belly. He was imbued with an indomitable press–on spirit and on bad weather mornings he would be the one to fly the weather test. He would purr off into the cloud and within a short time the message would be received, "Fit for flying". Then individual instructors would decide if they shared his judgement. The Flight was operated like a well run flying club and very soon we were introduced to the Prentice which seemed to be quite capable of flying itself. After a few flights to check our general competence, some instrument flying and a cross country flight to check our navigational capability we were considered to be fully paid up members of the club. Then the fun started.

Nearly every day requests came into South Cerney from other RAF bases to either deliver passengers or move spare parts. Among general training exercises such as formation, aerobatics and night flying the day's tasks were allocated at morning briefings and we eagerly waited to receive our share of the fun. One day I flew two airmen to Shawbury in the west of England, dropped off one of them and flew the other on to Manby, in the east of England, and then returned to base. Four days later I retraced the route to bring them home again. This was typical and I visited airfields all over England. The summer weather was generally good and I became very familiar with the beauty of England.

During all the trundling around England I came to like pilot navigation more and more. With good map reading and a deft use of simple maths it was possible to achieve very satisfying results and soon I was trying to improve my navigation. This liking for pilot navigation continued to increase and I never lost it. If the weather was bad, so much the better, it allowed us to build up our cloud flying time. Every morning during the weather briefing we watched for airfields around the country which were badly affected by low cloud or fog. If the airfield had Ground Controlled Approach radar (GCA) somebody was bound to head there so that he could fly approaches in the claggy weather until forced to return by low fuel. South Cerney had only a manually operated radio direction finder which was sited not on the airfield but a little distance north. After descending to the homer the pilot had to fly south to the airfield which was guarded by the line of huge pre–war hangers. After scraping over these obstacles all that was required was to close the throttle and collapse on the grass: home and dry.

The only way to fly a Prentice

During this wonderful summer Bob and I took every opportunity to fly together and we were soon trying to outdo each other with manoeuvres which the Prentice never expected. We discovered that when making practice forced landings it could be side slipped very aggressively to lose height rapidly on the approach. This had been used extensively in past years but it seemed to have gone out of fashion. We brought it back into use. The manoeuvre at which the Prentice really excelled was inverted flying and we thought it might have been made with the plans upside down. On one occasion we even joined the airfield circuit upside down until we thought it prudent to return to normal. The view from the cockpit was excellent and invited pilots to try low flying much lower than usual. We exercised this feature regularly and on one occasion we crossed a sunken lane at only a few feet when we discovered in front of us a man bending down with his back towards us while pumping up his bicycle tyre. The aircraft passing about 6 feet above his head must have been terrifying

Part way through our summer flying holiday we discovered that a group of pilots met on Friday afternoons in the Chedworth area to take part in a free for all dog fight. As many as ten or more Prentices were vigorously attempting to get on the tail of anyone in sight. Aircraft were all over the place, going in all directions and in a small chunk of sky. It was exciting and I developed a manoeuvre which I christened an Upward Osseltwissle to stop an attacker getting on my tail. I would haul the nose up to the vertical and then force it into an inverted spin and hold it in the spin. As the aircraft gyrated around the sky the spin somehow or other fell into a normal upright spin by which time my startled pursuer had disappeared into the distance wondering what had happened.

One morning the airfield was covered by a thick layer of cloud with a base of about 800 feet. As this was just in our limits I was despatched to get as much cloud flying as possible. I climbed up to about 10,000 feet into a beautiful sunny sky. I began a descent to base and all was nice and smooth until I reached a height of about 2,000 feet when my radio began to fade and soon gave up the ghost. I climbed away in a safe direction and as I neared the top of the cloud the radio was resurrected. I called base and explained my problem and as I had plenty of fuel I tried another let down but again the radio packed up before I reached the homer. Up I went again and made my total of failed approaches up to 4. The cloud covered nearly all of southern England and I was not prepared to make a blind let down into the Cotswolds Hills area without precise knowledge of my location. I decided to keep trying to complete a let down until my fuel was too low to continue. Then I would set the aircraft flying in a safe direction and step out and take to my parachute. After a careful check that my parachute was in good order I began another descent. Again it failed and I reckoned I had fuel for one last attempt. At least I was getting lots of cloud flying into my logbook. The descent was like all the previous ones but as I passed through 2,000 feet I was still in contact with the tower. Perhaps holding my breath helped but eventually I reached the homer and turned to confront the hangars. I never thought I would be so happy to see these huge buildings in my path but it was no problem to slide over their roofs and settle down on the lovely grass.

We came to realise that soon a major decision would have be made about our future. New pilots were divided into streams and we could be sent to light piston engined aircraft such as Mosquitos, Hornets, Beaufighters, etc or to large multi engined aircraft such as Lancasters, Sunderlands, Hastings, etc. The lucky lads were selected for jet training and from what we had learned Bob and I were certain that we wanted to be in that group. The most exciting future of the RAF would be the jet fighter squadrons and we wanted to be there. We did our best to ensure we were in the top group and we also indulged in gentle lobbying at every opportunity. Shortly before the end of our course news of our postings filtered through and about ten of us were destined for jet conversion courses. Bob and I were in the group and from now onwards it was all down hill.

Sqn Ldr Charlie Holdway was the Senior Air Traffic Controller and when I could get away during night flying and he was on duty in the Control Tower I would have a mug of coffee with him. He was nearing retirement after a long flying career and it wasn't difficult for a keen youngster to get him reminiscing about pre–war RAF days. For me it was fascinating to chat with a pilot who had lived through days I had dreamed about. He recalled the period before the war when he was flying in one of the RAF's three Bristol Bulldog squadrons and the Squadron had been on summer camp at Leuchars, in southern Scotland. The squadrons, as ever, were very competitive and were always looking to achieve new records. His squadron decided they would make the first ever squadron long distance formation navigation flight by flying back to base at Tangmere on the south coast of England en masse. After much, hectic preparation they set course on a sunny day full of high hopes. Alas, as they crossed the border into England they could see, towering before them, the huge cloud formations of a cold weather front. Flight instruments were still rudimentary and instrument flying was regarded as a black art but who wanted or dared to quit? Of course the formation plunged on into the black mass and the squadron formation return to base ended there. Charlie recalled with great gusto the adventures of various members of the formation who were scattered all over the north of England but he concluded with the good news that no one was injured or aircraft wrecked and three aircraft eventually arrived at Tangmere in formation. Perhaps a very small record was claimed.

Nearly all of Charlie's controllers were ex–wartime aircrew but one distinguished Australian became a good friend of 13 Course. He was Flt Lt Toby Foxley also known as Digger, who is recorded in the annals of RAF history as the rear gunner in Micky Martin's Lancaster crew on 617 Sqn and a survivor of the Möhne and Eder Dams raid. He had an irrepressible sense of humour and was prone to request Prentice pilots on the final approach to land "Check undercarriage down and welded." Most controllers had printed forms on which they would log continuous details of aircraft making a controlled descent through cloud but Digger scribbled down the details all over various bits of paper. It looked to be a shambles but the aircraft always arrived safely. When we were flying night cross country details we would gang up on Digger; the first pilot would delay his request for a let down and the last would call in early in an attempt to overload Digger. We never succeeded.

Almost at the end of our course South Cerney was involved in producing an Empire Air Day flying display. Preparations went ahead for all the usual elements of the display including the old favourite from Heston flying displays, 3 aircraft flying formation aerobatics while tied together from the wing tips by string.

Practising for the display
You can't see the string

Grib heard that RAF Hullavington had 3 Tiger Moths on charge and by devious means he persuaded them to lend one to South Cerney to use in the display. The Tiger Moth was rather limited for power and it was not possible to fly continuous aerobatics and hold altitude. A pilot would normally begin his display at a higher than usual height so that he could complete his show before running out of height. This technique was not in keeping with Grib's version of a display and as expected his performance was spirited and quite unbecoming for a staid old lady. On his second practice he concluded his show with a masterpiece as he slow rolled at low level and continued the roll into the ground. The sound of tearing canvas and splintering wood as the aircraft was converted into a heap of fire wood will rarely be heard again. Fire engines and ATC vehicles homed in to the wreckage and hauled a battered but undefeated Grib from the pile of wood. Grib's remarks in his native Polish were not translated.

Grib was carted off to Wroughton hospital and a couple of days later I came down from a flight and heard that Max Walker and Maurice Wells had scrounged a Prentice to fly down to Wroughton to visit our revered Flt Cdr. I was just in time to pile into the rear seat to join the party. We set course to the south and soon discovered that neither Max nor Maurice had a map but as Wroughton was quite nearby they soon found a likely airfield. They called he tower for landing instructions but could get no answer. After several attempts they tried to read the signals square but then realised they did not know the identification letters. They decided to land on what seemed to be the disused airfield but after taxying up to a likely looking hangar they decided to leave the engine running until they found out where they were. Soon a civilian appeared from the hanger dragging a pair of chocks which were as high as the Prentice's wheels and more suitable for a heavy bomber but they would serve their purpose. We were relieved to learn that this wilderness was indeed Wroughton and we soon found transport to the ATC tower. A single controller was on duty and was within arm's reach of a mug of coffee and several empty plates. As we greeted him one of the three loudspeakers in front of him gave a call from another aircraft wishing to join the circuit. He grabbed a microphone positioned in front of the speaker but after trying a couple of times to talk to the visiting aircraft he put down the microphone and seized the one next to it. This did not work either so he then tried the third one. Much to his surprise he made contact and sanity was restored. After answering the call he grabbed the jumble of wires of the three microphones and tried to sort them out muttering as he did so, "I always have this problem".

We made our way to the hospital and soon found Grib securely tethered in his bed with one leg in an enormous plaster and one arm also in a plaster but held up above his head by a Heath Robinson pulley. He was soon complaining to us that the hospital staff would not let him out. The Ward Sister came in and told us, "I don't know what I can do with him. I came in this morning and found him in the armchair". Such was our well liked Flt Cdr.

Suddenly the end of the course loomed over the horizon and the world became a more ordinary place. I was to go to RAF Middleton St George with three others and Bob was posted to RAF Driffield for his next course. The RAF had given us a marvellous summer holiday but the big news was that we were going to try to fly the mighty jets.

CHAPTER 5
Higher and Faster

RAF Middleton St George, the home of No 205 Advanced Flying School, was built on the north bank of a particularly pretty part of the River Tees between Darlington and Middlesborough and I was surprised to find that it was much more attractive than I had imagined. The 1930s style Officers Mess was very similar to the one I had just left at South Cerney and was equally comfortable. When I had settled in to my room I paused to take stock of my place in the great scheme of things.

I had always wanted to be a pilot and now I had my wings but I was only on the first step of the ladder. My world was limited to below 5,000 feet and below 250 knots. The RAF was trying to expand as fast as possible and the front line fighter squadrons were nearly all equipped with jet aircraft and I knew from the 2 years I had been flying that this is where I wanted to be. I had come to Middleton St George to face my next challenge. Could I master the exciting new fighter? The outcome was becoming very important to me and I was itching to get at the new aluminium pursuit ships.

The course members were a motley mixture of ab initio students like Dave Parry, Derek Mortar, Maurice Wells and me all from 13 Course, experienced piston engine pilots converting to jets and sundry flight engineers, air gunners and signallers seeking to remuster to pilots. The Meteor was much more complicated than our previous chariots and we were dragged through about 8 days of technical lectures on hydraulics, pneumatics, fuel and electrical systems before we were allowed to touch the mighty machine. A session of training in the station swimming pool in full flying kit with our single seat dinghy packs included the usual horror of leaping off the high diving board into the pool where we worked our way through the various routines until we were on board our dinghy with protection covers in place. We were subsequently pushed in from the edge of the pool blindfolded to repeat the process in darkness. As part of our training for high altitude flying we had a session in the decompression chamber. Six of us at a time, in full flying kit, were herded into the chamber which was then depressurised until we were at the equivalent height of 38,000 feet. Three of us were told to switch off our oxygen and begin writing down a series of numbers decreasing by seven. Eventually as each victim lost consciousness the remaining three switched the oxygen back on. The exercise was then repeated with the other three. After being wound down to earth again we reviewed what had been written by the guinea pigs. All samples began in a neat and orderly fashion but soon deteriorated into various versions of pudding. Some denied that they had ever lost consciousness. Anoxia affects people in many different ways.

I was in my element and readily lapped up all the detail I could garner and in no time at all we presented ourselves at our flights ready to go. It seemed to be quite an anomaly that our flying kit for this new adventure was exactly the same as we had been using for the puddle jumpers; ie, a simple cotton flying suit, a leather helmet with flying goggles, oxygen mask and tube. Underwear and shoes were optional extras

After the usual opening ceremony of having mugs of coffee pushed into our hands we met our instructors and we were glad to note the very friendly yet business like atmosphere. I was allocated to the most junior instructor I had encountered so far. He was Fg Off Hugh Williams who came from a family of tea merchants in the Channel Isles. He had completed one tour of duty on a squadron and was newly arrived from the Central Flying School instructor's course. He was a delightful man and I was well pleased with my master.

Meteor T Mk 7

22nd August 1951 was a lovely summer's day with a little high cloud and it was to be one of the greatest days of my life. I wandered into the Operations Room and there on the Operations Board was:

Meteor 7 WA720   Fg Off Williams, Plt Off Ashley   Exercise 1.

I was about to find out what jet flying was all about. Hugh had already given me a careful briefing and shown me the pre-flight external checks of the aircraft so we were ready to go. Out on the tarmac our fleet of Meteor Mk 7 trainers and Meteor Mk 4 single seat fighters were lined up ready for another day's flying. We inspected WA720 and I clambered up to the cockpit which was way above my head with the help of the step and kick in toe hold, over the edge of the cockpit and down on to the seat. A friendly airman helped me find and fit the parachute harness and then the seat harness. On with my helmet and then plug in my microphone lead and oxygen lead while Hugh disappeared into the back seat. I was deep down in the cockpit with the side rails level by my shoulders but the view ahead was marvellous with no big engine and propeller to spoil it. The cockpit was almost exactly the same as the single seat fighter.

Hugh followed me through the cockpit checks and start up procedures and the big heavy cockpit hood was brought down and locked. This was my first flight with a nose wheel undercarriage and as Hugh taxied out with the nose dodging up and down when he used the brakes I admired the view and appreciated the relatively little noise from the engines. He was given clearance to take off so he taxied on to the beginning of the runway and opened up the engines against the brakes and the nose nudged down as we reached take off thrust. The engine instruments and brakes were checked and we were clear to go. This was it.

The nose bounced back up again as Hugh released the brakes and a big fist pushed me in the back as 7 tons of metal began to accelerate smoothly down the runway. Slowly at first but quicker and quicker as the speed built up and very soon at about 80 knots Hugh lifted the nose slightly and the nose wheel came off the runway. Almost immediately afterwards we were airborne and really getting into our stride. The undercarriage and then flaps were raised before we reached their limiting speeds. The aircraft was now getting the bit between its teeth and by the time I had had a look around we reached the climbing speed of 300 Kts.

Hugh raised the nose and we began rocketing upwards like an archangel going home. By the time I had taken a few breaths we had reached the region around 15,000 to 20,000ft and Hugh reined our monster in. After a look around to check our position and a clearing turn to ensure no one else was in our area Hugh quietly said the instructor's magic words, "You have control."

First I took another breath and then gave a thought about where to begin. A few progressively tighter turns, rolls and wing overs showed that the controls at medium speeds were firm and pleasant and as the manoeuvres became more adventurous I began to realise I had all the room in the world to play with my new toy and soon we were up and over in my first jet age loop. All too soon Hugh brought me back to reality and it was time to find our way home. I dived smoothly for base and then tried the airbrakes but as we returned to Teesside Hugh took control and showed me the airfield rejoining routine followed by a standard circuit and landing. I had my first view of a lovely flat 2,000 yard runway. The approach and landing was better than I had ever seen and the undercarriage was so soft and forgiving that every landing was a masterpiece. The flight had lasted for 35 minutes and all the time fuel had been swilling down the pipes and we were approaching our minimum fuel state of 40 gallons per engine before landing. While returning to dispersal Hugh guided me through taxying which in comparison with piston engined aircraft was a pleasure. Hugh parked the aircraft and I closed the engine and bits and pieces down. After clambering back down the side of the cockpit with the aid of a prominent black line to guide my foot into the toe hold I was glad to see Hugh again after about 40 minutes. What a day? I had joined the jet age.

Such delights have to be paid for and now we had to buckle down to the serious business of learning to master the aircraft with all its emergency systems and the new operating procedures. The fatal accident rate at the Meteor training schools and squadrons had been quite high with too many pilots being killed, particularly when attempting to land with only one engine. Jet engines were not as reliable as today and turbine blade failure on take-off was fairly common. One had to constantly remember that the Meteor, although a delight to fly, could kill you more effectively than any other machine I had encountered. With Hugh to guide me we quickly completed the general handling phase and began to tackle circuit work. The most critical part of the course was single engined flying which must be well understood if one hoped to survive. For the asymmetric flying phase I was eternally grateful to be allocated to Flt Sgt Ray Davis as my mentor. This was a very significant decision for me for he became my prime example of an exceptional flying instructor. The RAF had many NCO pilots at that time who gave excellent value to the service. Ray used his vast knowledge of Meteor flying for problem solving but he limited the information he gave to students when in the air to the essentials. He was thorough but patient. He said only what was necessary in flight and then sat back quietly and observed the results. Later I used Ray as my guide during my instructing years. His teaching kept me safe and I never forgot it while flying many hundreds of single engine landings throughout my career. After my session with Ray I returned to Hugh for consolidation. A key part of any flying training was always circuits for no matter what one does in the air the aircraft must always be returned safely to earth in all weather conditions and all states of serviceability. While knocking the circuit procedures into my head I adopted a system which I continued to use until the end of my flying days. When preparing to fly a new aircraft before going to sleep I would sit on the edge of my bed, close my eyes and fly circuits and landings with all the correct checks and procedures. This worked so well that 60 years later I can still fly a simulated circuit in copybook style. For those who love nitty gritty detail the annex for this chapter should make your day.

Flying the circuit lasts only about 5 minutes so all the procedures have to be smartly performed and a strong cross wind may add a few complications. It is therefore imperative that the routine is thoroughly mastered and I did my utmost to ensure the drills came automatically. I think I could land a Meteor in my sleep.

Meteor F Mk 4

With circuits and single engine flying well established we began to cover the remainder of the syllabus with aerobatics, formation and instrument flying and navigation exercises. Soon the time came to make my first solo flight and we were lucky to have the Meteor F Mk 4 for our solo flying. Until recently it had been the RAF's front line fighter and had been the first aircraft to push the world's high speed record above 600 mph. I had no problem with this major event because the cockpit was identical with the Mk 7 and Hugh was never in sight while we were airborne. The weather must have been specially selected for student pilots and the three months sped by in a state of rapture but we did have few blips. One day when I was rejoining the circuit I heard a rather excited voice call, "405, I have just had a brake failure." A calm voice came back with, "Roger 405. What is your position?" The excited voice concluded the conversation with, "I'm just going through the fence – Now." I looked over the side of my cockpit and, sure enough, there was Dave Parry's Meteor 4 charging across the grass field off the end of the runway with parts of the half sawn fence dangling around its nose like a mad bull in full charge. Dave was back in the crew room with a mug of coffee when I eventually arrived. The episode must have prepared him to cope with his next escapade which followed soon afterwards. He was practising high level handling when he suffered a double engine failure. In spite of his best efforts he could not get them started again and was committed to gliding back to base and making an engine out landing. The weather was on his side and by following all he had been taught and exercising considerable skill he made a safe landing on the airfield and No 13 Course had upheld the highest traditions of the RAF. A few beers were drunk.

In the early 1950s middle England had only one airway running up the middle from London to Prestwick and it only went up to 25,000 feet. There was no surveillance radar and all pilots were responsible for maintaining a sharp look out for other aircraft. This meant that all of northeast England was available for enthusiastic pilots to use as their playground and we took every opportunity to make use of it. I was having the time of my life.

Bliss!

When I discovered that Joe Crawshaw, one of our QFIs, had managed to get the job of Chief Flying Instructor at West Hartlepool Flying Club I leapt at the chance to go with him at every opportunity. One of the fairly new civilian pilots had bought a Miles Magister monoplane elementary trainer with open cockpits and was learning to use it. It was a mid 1930s contemporary of the Tiger Moth and I was very attracted to it. He had never flown aerobatics and was keen to learn. With my vast knowledge from 40 hours flying in Tiger Moths within the last year I offered to teach him all I knew and he gladly accepted the offer. What could be better than flying Meteors during working hours and a Magister during my spare time and it was all free? The gods were being kind to me.

Miles Magister

On a grey morning with the top of the clouds at over 20,000 feet I was sent off to practise some high level handling followed by a few let downs through cloud. Hugh went off with Peter Poppe, from a later course, to introduce him to high level aerobatics and instrument flying. While flopping over the top of a wobbly loop the aircraft dropped into an inverted spin. Recovery was very reluctant and as the aircraft entered the cloud Hugh ordered Peter to bail out in accordance with the standing orders. Peter released the hood which jettisoned cleanly. He released himself from his safety harness and shot out from the aircraft like a champagne cork from the bottle. As soon as he was clear from the aircraft he pulled his rip cord and was relieved to find that his parachute opened like a charm and he was left suspended in cloud with apparently no motion.

Hugh had a tougher problem evacuating from the rear seat. He pushed himself out along the top of the wing and was quickly whipped away. Unfortunately the inverted aircraft was spinning around rapidly and as Hugh was passing it the tail plane came round and dealt him a mighty blow across his body and damaged his right arm. He thought he saw a white flash and imagined his parachute was damaged. He was unable to pull his rip cord with his damaged right hand but eventually he managed to grip his right wrist with his left hand and after a struggle he forced the rip cord out of the parachute pack and to his immense relief the parachute opened. Meanwhile Peter was gently floating down in the cloud wondering how high he was when suddenly a great swishing sound disturbed him as Hugh shoot past him while still struggling with his parachute. Soon afterwards Peter came out of the clouds at about 5,000 feet just in time to spot Hugh as his parachute opened and he descended on to a remote area of the Yorkshire Moors near Richmond. With all the space available in this vast area Hugh contrived to end the saga by landing dead centre on the back of a bull which was quietly lying down and contemplating the infinite. Peter soon arrived on the scene to join him. Next morning the incident was reported on the front page of a national tabloid newspaper and apparently the reporter who interviewed Hugh in hospital asked him if he was frightened when he landed on the bull. Hugh reply was, "I wasn't but you should have seen the bull!" It was last seen high tailing it over the horizon.

And so this idyllic summer sped by and I was the happiest man alive. Amidst all the fun I was introduced to high level navigation and I developed a great fascination for it. We had no navigation aids except for a compass, a watch and maps. Our aircraft had only enough fuel for flights of several hundred miles but that was sufficient to show the challenge of navigating on one's own at over 30,000 feet to find small targets. I had always been fascinated by the wartime exploits of the single seat photographic reconnaissance squadrons flying unarmed Spitfires at the highest possible altitude deep into Europe and the feeling never went away. The only problems were the extreme cold and, in the Meteor 7 which did not have a pressurised cabin, the effects of sitting at 30,000 feet or more for long periods of time. We began to encounter Diver's Bends for the first time which could lead to severe pain in the limbs and even loss of consciousness.

As winter drew closer we began to have periods of bad weather and one morning the weather briefing showed that there was no hope of flying until fog cleared away, maybe after lunch. We were up to date on all ground lectures so we retired to the mess. John T, a student from a senior course, settled into an armchair before a roaring fire and was immediately fast asleep. Soon our concentration on our crossword puzzles etc was disturbed by his loud snoring as his head dropped back and his mouth gaped open. One of our likely lads quickly produced a tube of toothpaste and promptly dropped a long worm of toothpaste into John's awaiting mouth. Unfortunately it touched a tooth and curled around into ball and produced no immediate effect. A second likely lad then produced a box of matches and after carefully inserting several match heads into the gap between the upper and the sole of his shoe he lit the matches and waited for the reaction. As the match heads flared up the sight was spectacular but the result was disappointing. John's foot was obviously not in contact with that part of the shoe. The thwarted audience then ran out of patience and seized pages of readily available news papers, lit them and when well alight held them near his head and called "Fire, Fire" until the message filtered through to his addled brain. The result was quite spectacular as he leapt up, partly swallowed the toothpaste, put his foot down into his hot shoe and prepared to escape from the fire.

We were very fortunate to have Flt Lt Roger Emmet as one of our instructors at Middleton. He was the RAF's No 1 solo aerobatic display pilot and we could regularly watch his practices. Roger was the best Meteor display pilot I have seen and in later years I attempted to model my displays on his examples. Some display pilots use a strong right arm to hammer their aircrafts into submission but Roger used firm persuasion which seemed to me to be the way ahead.

Alas, all good things must come to an end and soon we were thinking of moving on to the fighter Operational Conversion Unit and out first fighter squadrons. I was rather surprised when I was given my final handling test slightly before the other students and was even more concerned when I was told to report to the Station Commander for an interview. I reviewed the recent few weeks and could think of nothing which could have dropped me into the mire but a new haircut and extra polishing of my shoes were obviously required. I was relieved to see that the Group Captain was not wearing his cap and I was invited to sit down and have a coffee. He explained to me that because of the rapid expansion the RAF was becoming short on flying instructors. The senior pilots who would normally be going to the Central Flying School for instructor training were needed in the new squadrons as flight commanders and senior pilots. The RAF was about to make a new experiment whereby specially selected students from the AFSs would be sent to CFS to discover if they could be made into qualified flying instructors (QFIs). I had been selected to be one of the first creamed off QFIs as we became known but the scheme would be voluntary. He knew I was hoping to go to an operational squadron but he offered a taste of honey to make it more palatable. He had been authorised to say that my first posting would be limited to 2 years and then, if possible, I would be given a choice of my next posting. This was a mighty relief because I had already noted that when a pilot was dragged into the instructing net he usually stayed there until old age rescued him.

I had come to regard CFS with great respect. It was the oldest military flying unit in the world and had pioneered what had become the best system of flying instruction in use in all the major air forces. I could see great advantages in having an instructor's rating so early in my career and I readily agreed to give it a go. Soon afterwards the usual doubts began to enter my mind. Could I cope with the challenge?

I still had to complete my flying exercises but eventually all my old friends packed their bags and departed for their Operational Conversion Units and I prepared to head into an unknown future at CFS. At last I was leaving No 13 Course but would still be a student.

A little while after I left the station I was told that as I was leaving a student was attempting a single engine overshoot from the short runway but he could not gain any height and flew directly into the first floor of the Officers Mess and was killed. It was the first fatal accident during my stay.

I also heard that a few weeks after I departed Hugh was flying a practice instrument rating flight from the back seat when the aircraft dived out of cloud into the ground and both pilots were killed.

The Meteor Circuit

A FTER getting safely airborne retract the undercarriage and climb at 170 kts up to 500 feet. Throttle back to 13,500 rpm and enter a 180 degree climbing left turn while maintaining 170 kts. Aim to arrive at 1,000 ft on the downwind heading then throttle back to 10,500 rpm. Check that the port wing tip is running along the runway and call, "Downwind". Perform the pre-landing checks:

1. Airbrakes in.
2. Undercarriage down and don't forget to put on right rudder until the left wheel is down.
3. Check undercarriage locked down with 3 green lights.
4. Wheel brake pressure sufficient and brakes off.
5. Flaps selected to ¼.
6. Fuel not less than 40 gallons per engine. Balance cock closed.
7. Harness tight and locked.

Check that the wing tip is still tracking along the runway and the airspeed is reducing to 150 kts. When the leading edge of the port wing reaches the runway caravan at the beginning of the runway begin a left turn and lower the nose aiming to bring the aircraft lined up on the runway centre line at 140 kts and 400 feet. When half way round the turn check undercarriage locked down and call. "Finals, 3 greens". When certain that it is possible to land select full flap and with judicious use of the throttle taper off the speed until the touchdown point is reached at 100 kts. Let the aircraft sink on to the soft undercarriage, close the throttles and then hold the nose high off the runway until it is ready to go down. Use wheel brakes as necessary until you can safely turn off the runway. Resume breathing.

Time – about 5 minutes.

CHAPTER 6
No 136 Course - Central Flying School

BEFORE I set out on my pilgrimage to the Pilot's Mecca I was told that although the HQ and main base of the Central Flying School was perched on a hill in the Cotswolds at RAF Little Rissington my course would begin at RAF South Cerney. Of course I was delighted to be returning to the lovely little airfield which I had only left in August. No 2 FTS, at which I had recently flown my Rhodesia Refresher Course, was still based there but it was also the base of CFS A which was still equipped with the mighty Percival Prentice aircraft. Settling in to the familiar Mess was no problem and I was glad to discover that my old sparring partner, Bob Barndon, would be joining me as a creamed off student instructor.

During our previous visit to Cerney we had been flying for fun to improve our flying experience but now we had to settle down to serious work. We were about to start playing with the big boys. We had a total of 4 creamed off students and the remainder of No 136 Course were all ex-wartime pilots varying in rank from our senior student, Wg Cdr Don Pevelar, who was destined to become the Chief Flying Instructor at the RAF College at Cranwell, to quite a few NCO pilots. Pilots who had not previously encountered the Prentice were given a few hours to tame the ferocious monster while Bob and I did a little more inverted flying and aerobatics. Then the serious business had to begin but I was pleased that Bob and I were in the same flight.

Since the method of teaching flying had been pioneered by Lt Col Robert Smith Barry at the School of Special Flying at Gosport in 1917 it had been continuously refined until it was almost universally used by all major air forces. The particular syllabus was divided into separate sequences such as effect of controls, straight and level, turning, climbing, descending, stalling, spinning, etc. Each sequence was presented in detail in a lecture room by a CFS instructor and discussed. This would be followed by individual QFIs briefing their students on how the exercise would be demonstrated. The exercise would then be flown with the CFS QFI in the instructor's seat and the QFI student acting as Plt Off

Bloggs in the student's seat. The exercise would then be repeated with the instructor's second student QFI. Student A would then go into the instructor's seat and repeat the exercise to Student B. They would then swap seats and Student B would do the honours. By this time the penny was beginning to drop but to be completely sure each student QFI would then make the CFS instructor's day by again going through the sequence. The method seems to be tedious but it has been proven to produce good instructors all singing the same song.

Bob and I made our first working flights with our Flt Cdr, Kit Urwin, who I believe was the mother hen checking the chicks. We were apparently given the seal of approval because from then onwards we were not treated any differently from the rest of the students. Work began in earnest to slog our way through all the sequences. I usually flew what were known as the mutual exercises with Bob but I also flew 8 times with other students. Bob and I had had 3 big advantages over the big boys.

1. We had recently been given very similar exercises only 8 months previously on our FTS course.
2. We had been continuously under training for the last 18 months and were completely familiar with absorbing instruction. Most of our companions had been flying on squadrons and were out of touch with the learning process.
3. We were very familiar with the innocuous Prentice and could devote most of our time to learning the sequences.

The work rate was high and we rapidly worked our way through the course but eventually the autumn weather began to close in. One evening we attended a weather briefing before night flying but the forecast ruled out any possibility of flying and we all retired to the Mess bar. One of our instructors who shall be known as Len was a tall, thin, lugubrious character who was only happy when he was miserable. During the jollifications and when he was carrying a good load of alcohol he suddenly realised his wife was waiting for him to return home. He searched the bar shelves for an appeasement offering and chose a hip flask shaped bottle of brandy, pushed it into his hip pocket and weaved his way out of the mess. Almost immediately noises off invited us to come and witness a major event. In front of the mess was a large flight of steps and Len had fallen neck and crop down them. Friends were very carefully mopping him down as the bottle had broken and he had brandy flavoured trousers with blood and glass splinters in his nether region. At last he set course very gingerly for his married quarter and peace was restored. Next morning the weather was still miserable and we were draped around our crew room when Len appeared looking utterly miserable. When we inquired about the state of his health he told us that his wife had given him a hard time and accused him of drinking. He tried to deny it but realised it was useless when his ball and chain told him she had just been into the bathroom and found sticking plaster all over the mirror!

Progress continued steadily and all too quickly the end of our period at South Cerney loomed into view. All members of the course were still with us when we bade farewell to our instructors and their lovely little airfield and prepared to resume the battle at RAF Little Rissington.

Little Rissington had always been planned as a Flying Training School and a Maintenance Unit and was therefore a large station. It was perched on top of the Cotswolds at 730 feet above sea level and had 3 tarmac runways but the longest was only 1600 yards long. Most modern RAF airfields usually had a 2,000 yard runway which would happily accept the new jet aircraft. We arrived in January and when the surrounding area had low cloud we were in fog. If they were in fog we would be the only airfield open in the area. This would be Bob's and my first winter flying in England. We did not have many flying hours and not a lot of experience of bad weather flying. The course would be hard pressed to stay on schedule or the whole station program would suffer.

The Officers Mess was another big mess built during the expansion period in the mid 1930s and we were becoming quite familiar with the lay out. We soon settled in and reported to our flights and with hardly any pause for breath we were launched into the second part of the course. We would be flying that renowned noise generator, the North American Harvard, and as Bob and I were in recent practice from our Rhodesian days we needed only one familiarisation flight with our new CFS instructor, Plt Off Alfie Camp, to bring us up to speed. Unlike the Prentice the Harvard was no pussy cat. It had all the vices of its contempories such as swing on take off, dropping a wing on landing and a ready ability to stall and drop into a spin. During its long career it had killed many pilots. A major change from our previous flying was that we were expected to fly all instruction from the back seat and the forward view was almost nil.

The mighty Harvard

We lost no time in pressing on with the course. On our first day I had a quick dual check with Alfie Camp and was then sent solo to try and remember everything I knew about the beast. Next morning I was invited to become acquainted with the delights of back seat flying and I had a session of circuits and landings with Alfie in the front seat to maintain a sense of order. From then onwards the flying continued without pause with either Alfie or Bob. After 14 flights in 14 days I had our Flight Commander, Flt Lt Crawford, as my instructor as he took the opportunity to check our progress. Soon afterwards I was detailed to fly a solo exercise while Alfie and Bob went off with Bob in the front seat and Alfie in the back to "give" Bob a low flying training sequence. As part of my flight I needed to make a practice forced landing and was setting myself up and looking for a suitable field in the Chedworth area, south west of Rissington, for my practice approach when my attention was attracted by the flash of rather bleak sunshine on an aircraft low flying across my intended forced landing area. It was flying very low and entering a left turn. As I watched the left wing tip touched the ground. This upset the balance of forces on an aircraft that we had been taught in Ground School and the next few seconds were quite spectacular. The engine hit the ground and the aircraft cart wheeled. The starboard wing separated from the fuselage closely followed by the port wing. The tail section broke off just aft of the cockpit. The engine broke away and continued bounding along and it left a very sorry looking cockpit section lying on its side.

I abandoned any idea of a practice forced landing and called Little Rissington and described what I had seen. The scene looked like a scrap merchant's yard and I could not imagine there would be any survivors. I went down low to make a better assessment and I soon saw the identification letters on the fuselage side which told me that it was Bob and Alfie's aircraft. I was passing this devastating information to Rissington when I noticed movement in the front cockpit and very slowly Bob dragged himself out of the aircraft. He took a few wobbly steps to orientate himself and then set about the task of rescuing Alfie. In a few minutes he had Alfie out of the cockpit and I was happy to tell Rissington that they were both on their feet again.

Later, back at the base, I was discussing this with a bruised but otherwise intact Bob and he told me that Alfie had given him the copybook low flying exercise and then said, "That's for the students. Now I'll show you the real thing". The real world is always full of interest!

The weather was beginning to close in. It was early January and we began to encounter fog in the evenings just as we were due to begin the night flying phase and then it snowed. The temperature stayed below freezing level and the snow on the ground became hard. The end of the course was approaching and the decision was made to fly from the hard snow. To complicate the issue further a fresh wind settled in from the north and we had no option but to fly from the short north westerly 32 runway. I think it was about a 1,000 yards long but it had no permanent approach or runway lighting. All RAF airfields had a ready supply of kerosene fuelled goose neck flares to line the runway so the only remaining problem was that the lack of approach lights meant that the approach and undershoot areas were just solid blackness.

A pilot in the front seat of a Harvard could not see a lot at night because of the broad engine cowling but from the back seat all that could be seen was the back of the head of the lucky lad in the front seat. Before take off the most important check was to ensure that the aircraft was accurately lined up on the centre line of the runway. A little help from the front seat was always welcome. On what was virtually an instrument take off it was essential to curb the ever present tendency of the aircraft to swing to the left and then check both sides of the cockpit to ensure that the flares were passing by at the same distance. With any luck the aircraft became airborne before it ran off the runway. The whole exercise was complicated further by the requirement to give a running commentary, also known as patter, to the pseudo student usually known as Bloggs in the front seat.

Having got the beast into the night sky the next trick was to get it back on the ground again. On our first night flying session Alfie Camp, our instructor, gave both Bob and I the night flying sequence from the back seat. Then we climbed in again with Bob in the back seat to give the exercise to me. In the next 40 minutes we discovered a lot about landing a Harvard at night but fortunately the wind was not straight down the runway and the drift allowed glimpses of the runway to be seen down the side of the nose. The next night I went into the back seat to give the sequence to Bob and, to make life more exciting, the wind was straight down the runway. The most essential requirement was to fly the downwind leg and base leg as accurately as possible to ensure that the straight in final approach was commenced from the correct place. From then onwards everything ahead was black. The absence of approach lights meant that we had nothing to help us line up on the extended centre line of the runway. If a runway light was seen it indicated that you were not lined up and a correction was urgently needed. The use of the correct throttle setting ensured that the aircraft usually reached the runway and not the undershoot area but it was a great relief to see the flare path appear with lights on both sides of the aircraft. At this stage I had a conflict of interests between either keeping the patter going as if I was completely in charge of the situation or holding my breath. The short length of the runway did not allow us the luxury of landing well down the runway and one was often grateful for a suggestion from the front seat that a little more power would be appropriate. This was a good safety factor while on the CFS course but a working QFI was not likely to get much assistance from Bloggs.

The easy solution to landing from the back seat on snow at night would be to make a landing on the main wheels with the tail still off the ground but this was an anathema at CFS and we were required to make three point landings. Any lack of concentration after the landing would invite a ground loop and an embarrassing interview with the Squadron Commander. We completed all our night flying on the short snow packed runway without incident but the bar profits showed a significant improvement over this period.

On the morning after my final night handling test we heard the sad news of the death of HM King George VI and we then followed the journey from Kenya of our new Queen back to UK. We had all been commissioned by our very popular King who had performed so well in difficult circumstances but we looked forward to serving our beautiful young Queen. For the remainder of the course we wore black crepe armbands on the left sleeves of our uniforms.

The high intensity of the course made a relaxed life in the Mess absolutely essential and I was fortunate to have an excellent batman. He was a retired policeman and he felt that as I was only a Plt Off he needed to keep a special watch over me. Every morning he would arrive in my room and if I was awake I would hear a click of his tongue as he survived the wreckage. All his generation of batmen must have been given special training because they could all produce exactly the same cup of tea. I was usually tired and suffering from stress and overwork in the morning but when I sleepily took a mouthful or two of his magic potion I was instantly launched into the new day. The Devil's Brew was very strong and well stewed with a generous helping of sweet condensed milk. Who knows what a vital part this played in CFS's success?

After one very convivial evening in the bar I readily fell into a deep sleep but was startled when I woke up to discover that while I slept my bed had been moved out of the mess on to the top of the steps by the front door. Officers who were collecting their mail before going to work were as surprised as I. On yet another morning I was slowly surfacing from a deep sleep when I began to hear a very faint voice calling, "Sir, Sir" and it slowly became stronger. As I finally surfaced all I could see was a strip of light about 6 inches wide above me and a puzzled batman's face peering down at me. My alleged friends had raided my room and taken the edge of my bed and tipped it over against the wall. I was so well anaesthetised that I merely moved my pillow to the lower side of my head and continued sleeping.

We steadily worked our way to the end of the course and I survived my final night test with our Sqn Cdr, who was a USAF major, and my day final handling with a visiting member of Examining Wing. I had made it.

RAF Little Rissington had qualified for the final of the RAF Station Rugby Championship. The match was to be played at RAF Halton and our Station Commander, Gp Capt Bill Coles, decided that to show support for our team he would lead a mass formation of Harvards to Halton. As many

Harvards and pilots as possible were mustered for the occasion and as Ron Bradley and I had just finished our last flight on No 136 Course we were fitted into the quickly improvised formation. I drew the short straw and was authorised to fly the outbound flight.

By hook or by crook we all got airborne and set course in a formation of about 30 Harvards for the sleepy Chilterns. The sound of 30 odd Harvards formating is guaranteed to put paid to any sleepiness. The arrival at RAF Halton called for some clever juggling but we all finished up approaching en mass down the hillside side by side into the small grass airfield. It was quite a sight to behold. The greatest problem was trying to taxy back without been sat on by another landing Harvard. Due to the superb piloting skills of CFS pilots we all arrived intact and the rugby match began.

Formation flying was over for the day so we set course independently for our return to Rissington. I settled down in the back seat with my rudder pedals pushed fully forwards to enjoy my return to base and savour the view of the English countryside. Our arrival in the circuit at Rissington was right out of the manual and the approach was as steady as a rock. The three-point landing was on the runway markers and all was well with the world until the nose of the aircraft began to swing left. The swing continued and at 90 degrees to the runway the starboard wing tip hit the tarmac. The rate of turn was reduced but we still finished slowly rolling backwards along the runway. It was a beautiful evening for one's first and last ground loop and it was beautifully executed. I learned many years later that the beginning of that particular runway 23 had a slope across the runway of 6½ degrees from right to left and as that was the way the Harvard loved to swing it may have helped Ron to complete his education. I never managed to make a ground loop during my FTS course but the training at CFS was very thorough and comprehensive.

Instead of the usual B2 category which was awarded to probationary QFIs Bob and I were both graduated with B1 categories. This boded well for the creamed off QFI scheme. Having been given an excellent QFI training on Prentices and Harvards Bob was posted to instruct on Vampires at RAF Merryfield and I was sent to Meteor instructing at RAF Full Sutton

Postscript to Chapter 6

So Bob and I, who were like brothers by then, at last went our separate ways. He went into Fighter Command and did all the things which a promising young pilot was expected to do. He married Daphne and his postings were similar to mine. We kept in contact but did not meet. While he was a Group Captain and Station Commander at RAF Little Rissington I heard that his chronic asthma had flared up and he was in RAF Wroughton hospital. Soon afterwards I was told that he had died. Very sadly I removed his details from my address book.

Long after I had left the RAF in 1998 I receive from CFS an updated list of members and among all my old friends was "Group Captain R J Barnden". Within ten minutes I was on the phone and we were in contact again. He was living in Arundel. The reason for his greatly exaggerated death was because he had been in hospital with a Group Captain with a similar name and he was the one that died. The false rumour quickly spread and even Daphne was cruelly told the terrible news. It was quickly corrected but the scars remained with her. In 1999 Doug Holmes located several members of No 13 Course and arranged a re-union on the 50th anniversary of our first meeting at RAF Cardington. 14 survivors with their wives met at Northampton while Marlies and I were in England and it was as if we had only met the day before. Waists were thicker and hair much thinner but the voices and body language were the same. We met Daphne for the first time and she was exactly what I had always imagined. During the night at the hotel we had a false fire alarm and we had to evacuate our rooms and I found myself in the garden with her in her night clothes. Another re-union was arranged in 2001 at the RAF Club in Piccadilly to celebrate the 50th Anniversary of our Wings Parade. It was a lovely weekend and during the period the four of us managed to sneak away for a visit to the Savoy Theatre to see a performance of Gilbert and Sullivan's Pirates of Penzance. Bob, Daphne and I were great enthusiasts but Marlies had never seen one of the operas and the chance to see a performance in their old home was not to be missed. It was a lovely evening for all four of us.

Bob left the RAF at about the same time as I and had a very successful career in civilian life but he had no contact with the RAF. In 2002 No 84 Squadron was planning a great occasion to mark the last flight in the RAF of the Westland Wessex helicopter. When I reminded them that Bob had been CO of No 84 Squadron in Aden when they flew Beverley transport aircraft they included him in their VIP guest list. Bob and Daphne came to stay with us and we had a most comfortable week living like brothers and sisters. Bob's chest troubles were increasing and needed careful attention. On the great day I escorted Bob to the final flight ceremony and introduced him to modern day 84 Squadron. In the evening we went to a splendid guest night in RAF Akrotiri officers' mess. It was the first one that Bob had attended for nearly 20 years and the station had pulled out all the stops. The evening was presided over by AOC in C Strike Command who was an ex-Wessex pilot. The dining room was impressive with mess and No 84 Squadron silver, flowers and mess dress of many nations. Bob was fascinated and early next morning I escorted a very tired Bob home. He had been shown a reminder of his best RAF days and he and Daphne returned very happily to England.

Soon after they reached home we were told that Bob was very ill and had been admitted to hospital. He never returned home but we believed he died as a very happy man. Daphne by this time had become a very accomplished violinist and consoled herself by playing regularly with the Chichester Orchestra. Within two years she also died.

It is more than 65 years since No 13 Course first assembled at RAF Cardington but I am still in regular contact with Douglas Holmes in Bristol, Bill Sleigh in Hereford, Jim Vigar in Kent, Dave Parry in Farnham and Eddy Coates in Atlanta, USA.

CHAPTER 7
The Creamy Years — No 207 AFS

MARCH 1952 was not a good time to go searching for RAF Full Sutton. I arrived at York railway station in the early evening and as my taxi headed east out of York darkness was falling. The weather was cold and drizzly and the headlights of the car showed absolutely nothing of interest. After about 10 miles we arrived at a large black Nissen hut and I discovered it was the Officers Mess. I was not expected but I was in time for an evening meal but very few people were around. A young steward found that a room had been allocated to me so he collected a small trolley on which he loaded my case and headed out into the fields. We followed a path past 3 fields and arrived at a smaller Nissen hut which was to be my home. The hut had been divided into two and I was to occupy one half with six other Pilot Officers who had arrived recently to join No1 Course at the AFS. The room was heated by one of the old type of circular coke stoves which, thank goodness, was already in use. The bath house was in another building about 50 yards away. My last five messes had all been brick built 1936 pattern buildings which had been warm and comfortable and I could not believe I had fallen so far down the social order. I had been in the training machine for 2 years and this was to be my first productive job. I was to be one of the new creamed off flying instructors who had been taken from Meteor training direct to the Central Flying School for instructor training. Now I was going to instruct on Meteor fighters for a couple of years but I never dreamed it would be like this.

Full Sutton had been one of the many bomber airfields hastily built in Yorkshire during the war and later a triangle of tarmac runways had been added. Most airfields in the area had a main runway running from east to west to make use of the prevailing westerly wind. The fact that we had an 800 foot hill just to the east made it prudent to orientate our 2,000 yard runway from north to south. At the end of the war the airfield had been allowed to deteriorate but when the Cold War began getting much colder the RAF had to expand as quickly as possible to meet the threat from over the Iron Curtain. Several airfields similar to Full Sutton were quickly resurrected and brought back into use to allow a big build up in training for the new air force. I soon realised that the RAF got extremely good value for money out of these relics. The resilience of the ground crews and the enthusiasm of the instructors and students continuously produced many hours of valuable productive flying. It was a politically dangerous time but the ring was held.

Since October 1949 I had been given what I now realise was the best possible flying training. I had been taught on Tiger Moths, Harvards and Meteors, all of them excellent trainers, which would not only teach you all the tricks of the trade but also kill you if you ignored vital rules. I had been fortunate to have been taught by six excellent instructors and some not so good. In future I modeled my own teaching on all of them. Now, 2½ years on, it was my turn to put something back into the pot. The circumstances could not have been better. I had been sent to a new unit and the students were still undergoing their ground school training. With any luck I could be in at the beginning of No 207 Advanced Flying School but first I had to get myself up to speed.

Next morning I started my joining procedures and was told that as the Station was just opening up again and had not yet begun flying instruction everything was in chaos. New living accommodation was being finished and my present room was only temporary. I was told I had been posted to No 2 Squadron of the AFS but it was located across the other side of the airfield. After lunch I joined other members of the Squadron on a shuttle bus which drove round the edge of the airfield to my new work place. We had a large corrugated iron hangar and a few small Nissan huts for offices. Half of one hut was the Sqn Cdr's office while the other half was used by A Flight flying instructors (QFIs) and I had to fit in by hook or by crook. Other huts were similarly divided for B Flight instructors and all our ground crew.

As a start to this new life I pushed open the door of the instructors' crew room with some trepidation but I was not prepared for the chaos going on inside. Flt Sgt Bill Farrer was sitting on the hot coke stove shouting, "Lift me off." Flt Lt Josef (Steve) Stivar was chasing his Boxer dog, Nimrod, around the room trying to retrieve his cap and a tall lugubrious Flt Lt noticed my entrance and came ambling over to me saying, "Hello Boy, my names Enoch. Bloody hard luck, ain't it?" A Pilot Officer QFI was a novelty but after having the inevitable mug of coffee pushed into my hand I soon discovered that although they might be unconventional they were very friendly. It looked like being an interesting tour.

I was dragged round to see my new Boss, Sqn Ldr Keith Rogers, a New Zealander, and my Flt Cdr, Flt Lt Dean Jones, an American, and I explained that although I was a B1 QFI my CFS instructors' course had not been on Meteors but Prentices and Harvards. The only advantage I had over my future students was that I had already survived the Meteor course which they were about to begin. This was no great problem. I had been well taught at Middleton St George and could remember the instructional sequences quite well but I had never flown the Meteor 7 from the back seat. Although the view from the front seat was far better than any previous piston engined fighters the view from the back seat was restricted by the heavy framework of the canopy. The view out of the side was adequate but ahead was a detailed view of the canopy frame and the back of the student's head. All my fellow QFIs rallied around and in the next four days I flew thirteen sorties including checks by my Boss and finally with the Chief Instructor and I was ready to start instructing on No 1 Course. The next day I flew my first sortie with a real live student in the front seat. The partially sighted was leading the blind.

Outside on the flight line were about 6 Meteor 7 trainers and about 6 Meteor 4 fighters. The Meteor 7 was becoming a well-established advanced trainer which would continue giving excellent service for the next 20 years. The Meteor 4 was a very good choice for the students in which to fly their solo exercises. Together with the Vampire it had been the back bone of Fighter Command since the end of the war and had only been replaced by the Meteor 8 in the last few years. A few years ago it had twice established a new world air speed record and had pushed it over 600 mph for the first time. If the speed was pushed up to about 550 mph during a low level fly past as part of a display it would produce a howling noise known as the Blue Note and on a humid day the wings would flash with clouds of condensation around the wings. It was always impressive. Now our students would have this well tried warrior to play with. It was the last front line fighter without an ejector seat and I would still have to climb the side of the fuselage to enter the cockpit with a parachute hanging from my backside. Just for good measure we did not have any hard helmets with sound protection. Instead we still wore the old wartime leather helmets with inset head phones. The small cockpit canopy was manually operated and I would still have to crank it backwards and forwards with a winding handle mounted on the cockpit wall. It had an idiosyncrasy which reminded me of Tiger Moth biplanes. If an engine did not light up when starting the normal drill included taking a good sized stone and disappearing into the port wheel well. A round cylinder with many scratches on it showed one where to administer a standard RAF thump to encourage the relay to do better next time. With a Tiger Moth the blow was delivered under the starboard engine cowling on to the scratch marks on the magneto.

Thus began one of the best flying periods of my career. We flew hard, drank and sang happily and chased a few girls in what spare time we had. My first student was given a check by the Boss before he flew his first solo but I still had to cycle out to the runway controller's caravan to bite my nails while he tried to demonstrate that my instruction made any sense. After that I was cleared to send my students solo.

Although the flying was very interesting it was also demanding. We normally flew 40 minute duration sorties and they were often above cloud cover. The old pattern of gyro instruments were air driven and as soon as the aircraft was inverted the artificial horizon would topple and just when it was needed to recover through cloud it would wander around aimlessly and be more confusing than if it had remained still. The directional gyro would also go walkabout and had to be re-set by reference to the large magnetic compass behind the control column. While maneuvering during the lesson the pilot had to keep in his head a good estimate of his position, particularly in a strong wind. A jet fighter could travel over a 100 miles in a few minutes and at the end of the instructional sequence you had to be near to base to begin a letdown otherwise all the fuel would quickly disappear. The only navigation aid we had was a primitive manual homer whereby an airman sat in the receiver cabin near to the runway and when you transmitted for a course to steer for base he read a bearing off his display for you to steer. Our homer was not very accurate and on one occasion Fg Off Paddy Cardwell was flying with Plt Off Lew Levitt and when they broke cloud after a letdown they found themselves not near Full Sutton but over the North Sea in the Scarborough area. Fuel was short so Paddy closed down one engine to conserve what little he had and headed towards base wondering if he could reach it. At last he passed Garrowby Hill and Full Sutton was ahead but with very little fuel sloshing around the bottom of the tanks. He was well placed for an approach on to our shortest runway and he opted to do that. It involved crossing over a railway line just short of the touch down point. He flew a beautifully judged approach but just before he reached the runway a railway train passed in front of him. He had no extra height or speed in hand and the aircraft nose passed between two trucks of fish. Several trucks were knocked off the track but the aircraft finished on the grass in the undershoot area. The crash was near to our hangar and we charged across to the wreckage. The canopy had burst open and we were able to drag Lew Levitt out of the front seat where he was almost submerged in small smelly fish. He had a broken arm but was savouring a close up view of a train crash. Paddy Cardwell was almost unharmed in the back seat but was in danger of suffocating in the stinking fish. He was soon extricated from the wreckage and was on his feet almost immediately. He had shown great skill to recover from a desperate situation. In very short time a small tractor drawn convoy of rescue equipment came chugging around the perimeter track accompanied by our Engineering Officer on his bicycle. As he approached the sick aircraft Wilkie Wilkinson took one look and a deep smell and declared, "I'm not having that bloody thing in my hangar."

At this time little was known about the effects of compressibility as the aircraft approached the speed of sound. The Sound Barrier was a popular topic of discussion. The Meteor course was a good opportunity for students to discover what happened to the Meteor if a pilot attempted to break the sound barrier. We began the exercise above 30,000 feet by accelerating at full throttle until the speed stabilised at about Mach .82 or so depending on the condition of the aircraft. Then the nose was lowered and speed increased until something untoward happened. Usually the controls twitched and snatched and the whole aircraft juddered and banged around but recovery was soon affected by closing the throttles and putting out the air brakes. A much more convincing demonstration was made by accelerating straight and level and then rolling upside down, pulling the nose down about 45 degrees, rolling upright again and continuing the acceleration in a steep dive. Things happened much more quickly as the aircraft ran into compressibility. Along with the usual banging and twitching the aircraft might flick on to its back or any other attitude and the controls could be completely ineffective. Recovery action was to throttle back, put out the airbrakes and wait until the aircraft came to its senses again at about 20,000 feet. Behaviour was quite unpredictable and older aircraft gave the most exciting rides. Present day service pilots are not now allowed to fly their aircraft into situations where all control is lost but that was life in the early 1950s.

Meteor F Mark 4

The Meteor had the most powerful engines which the students had encountered and they had to be very thoroughly taught to control the aircraft on one engine, particularly at low speed and high power. I had been taught asymmetric flying by an excellent instructor, Flt Sgt Ray Davies, and I remembered it well. The instruction was being continuously improved and most students were given a very sound understanding of the problems. In the early days of Meteor 7 instructing this had been the greatest cause of fatal accidents but the rate was steadily improving. Our first fatal accident occurred to an aircraft of my flight while Flt Lt Bill Enoch and his student were flying a single engined circuit with one dead engine. Towards the end of the downwind leg at 1,000 feet the aircraft yawed to the left and entered a steep spiral dive into the ground. Bill and his student were both killed. This was an example of the infamous Phantom Dive.

Asymmetric training was a major part of the course and soon after the flying instruction began we were told to enter all landings with a dead engine into our logbooks. We found we were averaging between 15 and

17 per month. Before I finished my tour the High Priced Help at Group HQ decided that practice landings with an engine flamed out were too dangerous and all practice landings were to be flown with one engine throttled back. It was certainly safer but it took away the incentive to get it right.

Much emphasis was placed on training to control an engine failure immediately after take-off and it had to be regularly practiced. Unfortunately students soon became very watchful and an attempt to pull back one throttle immediately warned the student. On one occasion I pulled off the main fuel cock to the port engine at low speed just after take-off and the student was caught unawares. I was prepared to give a hefty push on the right rudder if he was too slow but I was taken by surprise when he pushed hard on the wrong rudder pedal. The aircraft began a quick yaw and roll to the left and as my right leg had been forced back by his action I could not generate enough push to overcome his straight right leg. While calling, "I have control", I decided the only way to avoid a fatal accident would be to continue the roll to the left and complete a full roll. By much stirring of the controls we made an ugly looking roll during which the student gave up his efforts to land us upside down in a Yorkshire field and we lived to fly another day but we had been given a close up view of the trees off the end of the runway. My pride was hurt when after landing I received a phone call from the Chief Instructor with a rollicking for doing unauthorised low level aerobatics. I thought he would have realised that if I had done it deliberately it would have been better than the ugly thing he had seen.

In among the flying we managed to fit in plenty of other activities. Squash could be arranged at short notice but on Wednesdays we usually slogged around the rugby field. We played away matches with local clubs which included the RAF bases at Linton on Ouse and Church Fenton. Both stations had Meteor fighter squadrons and we fought out needle matches. On the way back home we usually called in at favourite hostelries in York where the local ale was evaluated. One evening one of our more enterprising members phoned the local theatre from the pub and booked seats in the middle of the two front rows. The Empire Theatre was staging one of many leg and belly shows which did the rounds in those days. Normally they played to meagre audiences of caps and mackintoshes but the chorus girls had a surprise to find some red blood in the two front rows and the show soon developed into a dialogue between us. During the interval a bus was hired and after the show the whole cast was taken back to our Mess. Rarely had such a party been seen there and it soon spread through the dining room into the billiard room and even into the telephone kiosks. Perhaps it was well that the Station Commander, whose house was nearby, came home at about two o'clock and one short telephone emptied the Mess in record time. Next morning did not figure prominently in our memoirs.

The lasting impression I have is that the flying was fun. Instructors and students showed lots of enthusiasm and it produced excellent results. We flew hard all day and often had four flights with associated briefings and debriefings per day. I flew up to nearly fifty flights per month but it only added up to about thirty to thirty five hours. One day I led a formation of students on an advanced formation exercise and after carrying out the usual formation drills I led them into a tail chase which began gently and worked up to a spirited chase around the sky. After a few minutes I came up behind the last member of the formation who had obviously lost us. I called, "Red four, can you see us?" After a slight pause the reply came, "Er. Red Leader, No." I told him I was right behind him and he came back with, "Red Leader, in that case you had better follow me!" and he led off into another exciting tumbling around the sky. Spike Jones became a good fighter pilot.

No 2 Squadron with Nimrod in front of Sqn Ldr Keith Rogers

About this time we were joined by a RCAF Exchange Officer and the Canadian Air Force had made a very good choice. He was an extremely likable man with a lovely wife and a baby girl. He fitted into our flight easily and we soon discovered that his family sent him every week a packet of local newspapers. One of the magazines was Pogo the Possum which was far too advanced for his daughter but highly suitable for RAF flying instructors who could appreciate the antics of Pogo and his friend Rackety Coon, the raccoon.

We flew and worked hard but much of our spare time was devoted to raising the noise level in the bar. Behaviour was never riotous but we had an extensive hymn sheet and many were the lusty renditions of Pretty Redwing and The saga of Lady Jane.

Lady Jane
To the hymn tune of "For those in peril on the sea"

It fairly broke the family's heart
when Lady Jane became a tart.
But blood is blood and race is race
And so to save the family face
Her father bought an expensive beat
On the shady side of Jermyn Street

In six months' time she was doing well
With a most exclusive clientele
And it was rumoured without malice
she had a client at the palace
And long before her sun had set
she worked her way right through Debrett

Further verses about young Sir Percy's fall from grace are restricted to consenting adults only but the Ballad of Eskimo Nell and sundry other sacred works of English literature were regularly recited.

Meteor Mk 4 EE521 when part of the High Speed Flight

Soon after the flying part of the course began we were told by Group HQ that spinning was to be introduced into the syllabus. Before the students could spin the Meteor 4s the aircraft had to be air tested to ensure they did not have any evil habits. Suddenly all the old and bold instructors on the flight seemed to have essential duties which required immediate attention and as the only Pilot Officer I was popularly elected to get on with the air tests. I had not spun a Meteor during my training so I approached the first test with more than average interest. At 25,000 feet I throttled back, came to the point of the stall and booted on full left rudder. The aircraft yawed and rolled into a steep left dive and I thought it was going to be a nice smooth classical spin when suddenly all hell broke loose. The nose rose up above the horizon and then pitched down steeply and the rate of roll increased. The extreme pitching continued. My head was banged on the side of the cockpit and the control column was snatched out of my hand. When I tried to grab it again it lashed around and hit the back of my hand painfully. I then reached down below the joint and brought my hands up the column holding fast as I did so. From then onwards the recovery was quite straight forward. After that I always held on to the control column tightly with both hands when entering the spin

Spinning continued in the syllabus for about 6 months but then it had to be stopped. The control rods to the ailerons had to pass through a fairing inside the engine intake and when a cover was removed we discovered that the rods were buckled under the high forces produced during the spin. The rods had been flattened on the underside to pass over rollers and this had made a weak spot. I heard that after I finished my tour spinning used to go in and out of the syllabus like a fiddler's elbow.

The Meteor Mk 8s in Fighter Command had ejectors seats and although we did not have such luxuries our students still had to be trained in their use. As the number of ejections increased it became apparent that a significant number of back injuries were being sustained because of incorrect ejection procedures. It was decided that all of our student courses would be taken by bus over the hill to Driffield where an ejector seat trainer was located. Each course had to be accompanied by an instructor who would conduct the training before making the return journey. This chore was not popular with most instructors but it was obvious that it was an excellent task for a Pilot Officer QFI. We only had one so I was elected by majority vote.

The trainer was a 30 foot ramp which was erected with at an angle of about 70 degrees from the vertical. An ejector seat was mounted on the forward face of the ramp and when the seat was fired the seat and occupant were propelled up to near the top of the ramp where it was held by a ratchet device. It was then wound down by hand. After giving the briefing on the use of the seat I then demonstrated my mastery of the art. Each student had his turn and then, to make the return bus journey more palliative, I had another go. During my time at Full Sutton I repeated this procedure until I had made about 30 practice ejections. After I had moved on the High Priced Help at Command HQ discovered that more spinal injuries were caused by the trainer than in actual ejections so the practice was discontinued. No wonder I have a bad back.

During this period I read for the first time the wonderfully evocative poem High Flight. The Comet jet airliner was just entering service and the few airways only extended up to 25,000 feet. With a sprinkling of cumulus cloud to set the stage we had a marvelous aerial playground. The poem captures well the freedom of the skies which we enjoyed for a few more years. The author was a young fighter pilot during the war but unfortunately he was killed soon after writing it. I have kept a copy ever since.

In May 1952 we received 2 new Meteor 7s and I had a chance to fly acceptance air tests on them. I remember WH205 and WH226 particularly because they were the best handling Meteors I ever knew. They had no quirky characteristics and were very accurately rigged. They flew beautifully and even when pushed hard into compressibility they juddered but still flew straight. It is rare for aircraft to leave such an impression but I flew WH226 very often and it became my first choice for aerobatic displays. Little did I realise I would use it again nine years later while on No 81 PR Squadron at Tengah in Singapore to give aerobatic displays for the opening of the new Payar Lebar International Airport. It became a good friend and never let me down.

In the middle of this great flying period I was selected to be a solo aerobatic display pilot and after checks by the Station Commander and the 25 Group AOC I was added to the list available to the RAF Participation Committee which allocated pilots to fly in their extensive list of displays. My first display was a Battle of Britain display at West Freugh near Stranraer and I took WH226. It was an MOD bombing trials airfield and did not have any jet aircraft. The longest runway was only 1,400 yards long but when I arrived the wind was blowing along a 900 yard secondary runway. Meteors were normally flown from 2,000 yard runways and 900 yards would be a bit of a challenge. The approach to land had to be very accurately flown with the touch down speed as low as possible. With a Meteor this was not the end of the problem because it had drum wheel brakes which overheated when heavily used and then faded. I well remember the brakes becoming less effective as the end of the runway rapidly approached. The brakes lasted just long enough to slow the aircraft sufficiently to turn off on to the taxi way and avoid running on to the grass. Next morning I flew a practice display which proved to be a good advertisement and alerted the local people to the presence of a jet fighter. Next day people came from all over the Mull of Galloway, some of them walking across the fields, and a big crowd filled the airfield. The display went well and in the evening almost everyone seemed to have been invited to the Battle of Britain cocktail party. Rarely have I met such a delightful collection of people. They were fascinated by the Meteor which made such a change from their usual Mosquito and Lincoln bombers.

I was fortunate to return in 1953 and was pleased to meet my old friends again. However this time the weather turned sour and during the display the cloud base was less than 1,500 feet. The people had made so much effort to get to the display that I felt I had to put on a show for them. We normally rehearsed an alternative display for such conditions and I flew a routine of rolls, Derry turns, inverted flying and steep turns to keep them amused. I pulled hard round for an inverted run along the runway and I lined up, rolled over and pushed the control column forward to keep the nose up and suddenly blacked out. When I regained my vision I was in cloud but my immediate check on the instruments showed that I was climbing. As I was gratefully absorbing this information the aircraft appeared out of the top of the shallow layer of cloud and right way up. I don't know how this happened but I immediately turned about and descended back through the cloud. By great good fortune I appeared with the runway straight ahead. After a few more manoeuvres I landed and climbed out absolutely exhausted and rather shaken by the experience. During the party in the evening some people thought it was a very good part of the display and asked how I did it. I did not divulge my secret.

Round about this time I began to realise what an interesting character Flt Lt Josef (Steve) Stivar was. He was one of many Czechs who had escaped from Czechoslovakia after it was overrun by the Germans and had managed to find their way to England. He joined the RAF and flew, mainly on fighter aircraft, until the end of the war. He then left the RAF but rejoined when the Cold War began to look dangerous. He was retreaded, sent to CFS for instructor training and converted on to Meteors. He arrived at Full Sutton just before me and was therefore in time to begin instructing on the first course. Although he was new to instructing he was a very experienced pilot on piston engined fighters and like many of his fellow Czechs he possessed great dash and fighting spirit. We were flying a training exercise together when he decided to show me his aerobatics and I was greatly impressed by the enthusiasm with which he threw the aircraft around. Towards the end of his show he dived down quite low to pick up high speed and then pulled up to the vertical and began rolling until the speed had almost disappeared and then made a stall turn to the left. When we were heading vertically downwards he began to roll continuously. He left the throttles fully on and the airbrakes in and although the manoeuvre looked very impressive the speed was increasing rapidly and the height was disappearing almost as fast. I began to worry and was faced with an awkward decision. Steve was much more experienced than I but my limited experience told me we were heading fast to a monumental hole in the ground. At last my fear overcame my reluctance and I called, "I have control," closed the throttles, put out the airbrakes and hauled back on the control column. We both almost disappeared into the bottom of the cockpit with the high G force but at last we reached the bottom of the dive at below 2,000 feet. We resumed breathing but at a faster rate than usual.

A little later Steve was giving his student a lesson on single engined landings at our relief landing ground at Breighton. To conclude the exercise he closed down the port engine and told the student to make a full stop landing. The student flew a faster than usual approach but Steve was hoping he would realise it in time and correct it but unfortunately the student delayed selecting full flap and they crossed the threshold at about 130 Kts. Steve thought they would not be able to stop on the runway and decided to try to make a roller landing and go round again. It was a forbidden manoeuvre but it was possible if very good judgment was used to feed on the throttle only as fast as the speed allowed. Steve overcooked the increase of throttle just as the aircraft was becoming airborne again. He could not hold the increased power and the aircraft yawed to the left and drifted off the runway. The yaw developed into a roll and normally it would have resulted in a fatal accident, probably upside down on the grass. Fortunately the aircraft was so low that as it rolled about 60 degrees the left wing tip hit the ground and bounced the aircraft back to the right. By this time Steve had decided to abandon the overshoot and closed the throttle and landed on the grass. An inspection of the port wing tip showed no obvious damage so Steve relit the stopped engine and then flew the aircraft back to base.

Meteor T Mark 7

Steve became very irritated when he was teaching his student to make maximum rate turns at about 10,000 feet. This was a basic manoeuvre used when a pilot was attacked without warning and it had to be mastered. Steve could not persuade his student to give it the required urgency and decided to demonstrate again what was needed. He took control and increased speed and then threw the aircraft into a hard left turn and applied full power. It must have been very effective because suddenly both Steve and his student blacked out. Steve regained his vision again while the aircraft was still turning left but at 3,000 feet. On the way back to base they flew some aerobatics and then some circuits and landings before calling it a day. Soon afterwards our Flt Sgt came into our crew room and suggested we take a look at the aircraft. From the side it was obvious that all was not right. The fuselage had a slight bend in the centre section where the fuel tanks were fitted. The covers over the tanks made the fuselage weaker in that area and the tail unit was tilted upwards by a noticeable amount. The Meteor was strong but Steve was stronger. The aircraft had to be rebuilt at a Maintenance Unit.

Low level navigation exercises were a part of the course which I enjoyed but one particular sortie on 17th July was more interesting than usual. A student and I were flying at 450 knots and 200 feet off the coast by Scarborough when we heard and felt a hefty thump. As we looked around for the source we saw that a large bird such as a seagull had struck the leading edge of the starboard wing about a foot in from the wing tip and punched a hole bigger than a small plate in the leading edge. As we watched the force of the airflow began to tear the metal skin off the wing and as it lifted it was torn backwards so that eventually we lost almost a foot of skin from the wingtip back as far as the aileron. We had throttled back and climbed to reduce speed and we had good control of the aircraft. We made a distress call and then began heading back for base. This was a good opportunity for the student to obtain some useful experience so I asked him what he was going to do next. He made all the correct checks and found that he could control the aircraft safely down to 120 knots and decided we could land at base using the higher approach speed. I allowed him to fly the landing but my hands were never far from the controls. After we landed he was about eight feet tall and I would have loved to have heard the story as told in the students' crew room.

Towards the end of 1952 I began to have trouble with my left knee. Normally it gave no problems but occasionally it would lock and require some fiddling around to get it loose again. This obviously was dangerous in a Meteor and at last I was sent to Halton hospital for an inspection. The Orthopaedic Specialist pulled me around quite severely but could not find the cause so he sent me to the RAF Medical Rehabilitation Centre at Headley Court for further tests. Although rehabilitation was their main trade in my case they were tasked with trying to break me down and make the knee lock so that the cause could be diagnosed. I spent most days playing all the rough sports they could devise. I would suddenly be attacked and wrestled to the ground or have medicine balls thrown at my leg but my contrary knee resisted all efforts to put an end to the fun. This was too good to last and after a week I was sent back to Halton hospital for an examination under anaesthetic. On 18th December I was trundled into the operating theatre and when I came out it was with my left leg strapped to a back board from my thigh to my ankle and a five inch hole on the inside of my knee through which they had removed almost all of the medial cartilage. Apparently when they opened up the knee and tried to remove the cartilage the front three quarters fell out. The operation to remove the remaining part would have required a further incision from the rear of the knee so they decided to leave it in place.

From then onward I was supposed to have ten days in bed with my left leg rigid. The ward was a very lively place and seemed to be more like a kindergarten than an officers' ward. Wg Cdr Tony Smyth, the OC Flying Wing at Leconfield, was the major terrorist and one evening towards the end of my strict bed period he sneaked me out into a taxi and we spent the evening at The Bell Hotel in Aston Clinton for the best meal I had had for a long time.

The nurses were magnificent and could be very unobservant when they chose to. Walking patients would invariably bring back to the ward bottles of beer tucked into their coat pockets and our bed side lockers were as well stocked as a minor bar. When the lockers were pushed forward every morning for the floor cleaning they rattled like brewers' drays but the nurses never noticed.

All good things must come to an end and I was soon bundled out of Halton and returned to Headley Court for my rehabilitation. The MRU was a world leader in returning injured aircrew to their cockpits in the minimum of time and life was hectic but fun. Our days would begin by loosening up our joints in a heated hydrotherapy pool and then the exercises would be increased in difficulty as fast as we could absorb them. In the afternoons we were encouraged to get out into the countryside and Ascot Races were very popular when we walked, cycled or were taken by bus to exercise our limbs between bookies' stands. The MRU was widely known and we had sufficient complimentary tickets for such events as rugby international matches and Inter Services Championships at Twickenham and theatre tickets in the West End. Inmates who were too exhausted on return to the Mess to climb the stairs would be bundled into the dumb waiter and hauled up to their bedroom floor by fellow inmates. The morale of the patients was very high and progress was very rapid. At first the staff could not understand why patients' progress always slowed down towards the end of their treatment but they then realised that the patients were waking up to the fact that their rate of progress would soon result of them being returned to their units. All incentive to improve disappeared and the MRU had to throw them out to complete the task at base.

I enjoyed myself immensely and was helped by Bill Bedford, who became the renowned Chief Test Pilot of the Hawker aircraft company. Bill was a fellow inmate after having a kidney removed. The beginning of our day's work was a breakfast time competition to complete the Daily Telegraph crossword puzzle in the shortest time. Bill could usually beat me but I still remember the Tuesday morning when I completed it in six minutes. Tuesday was the easiest day for me. Part of our treatment was Occupational Therapy and Bill decided to take up weaving and he made a large piece of tweed. When it returned from being finished he found that he had more than enough to make a jacket and trousers so he had two pairs of trousers made, just in case of accidents. However Murphy's Law of Tailoring says that if you have two pairs of trousers you will burn a hole in your jacket. This is exactly what Bill did! I stayed in contact with him for the rest of his life.

I was joined in my Early Legs group by Jim Campbell who became a very enthusiastic inmate and a good friend. He had been an RAF Physical Training Instructor for several years but had seized the opportunity to take a pilot's course and was nearing the end of his training when he damaged his leg. Fortunately he was able to resume his training when released from Headley Court and go on to become a very sound pilot. He would re-appear in my life later.

The exercises were normally very vigorously performed but one morning Gp Capt Hockey was exercising with Flt Lt Hugh Peebles. They were sitting on the floor facing each other and gripping each other's hands. They then see sawed their alternate hands backwards and forwards. Gp Capt Hockey was much larger than Hugh and the outcome was a broken neck for Hugh, fortunately only a minor break. Hugh immediately regrouped from Late Legs to Early Necks.

In early 1953 the RAF decided to make a film of the work of the MRUs and they searched around to find suitable cases to be included. Obviously the case had to be successful so they had to delay a choice until they were sure the recovery would be completed. A representative had to be found for each class of operation and my case fitted very nicely into the schedule for the film and I became Mr Menesectomy of 1953. The early stages and the operation had to be simulated but soon the filming caught up with real time and then we had a very entertaining period. We visited the other MRUs at Chessington and Collerton Cross, near Exeter. We played golf at Bigbury Bay and Leatherhead Golf Clubs, climbed into and out of Meteor fighters at RAF Biggin Hill and played tennis and croquet at Headley Court. In spite of my efforts the film was a success and if anyone can find the 1953 Rehabilitation Film they will see all the gory details. I tried my utmost to resist the inevitable but in February 1953 they threw me out and I had to return to working for a living. In retrospect my operation was badly handled and I have had serious limitations in my knee movements ever since that time. My rugby days were soon over and I played squash for another couple of years before having to admit defeat.

When I arrived back on my squadron a new Boss had taken over. Sqn Ldr Mike Birt was an amiable, tall, gangling character who turned out to be an excellent Boss. It was immediately noticeable that that he only had 3 fingers on his left hand. During the war he had been flying a Beaufighter in Burma when he had been hit by a cannon shell from a Japanese fighter. The impact destroyed his left thumb and forefinger but the surgeons had made an amazing modification for him. His middle finger was turned around until it could be used as a thumb. About a year later he had to attend a medical board to check his progress. All was as well as could be expected and at the end of examination the President of the Board asked what he was doing at that time. Mike told him he was still flying and when the President objected that he should not be flying with his wrecked hand

Mike replied, "No one told me to stop and I've managed for a year now so I'm going to continue."

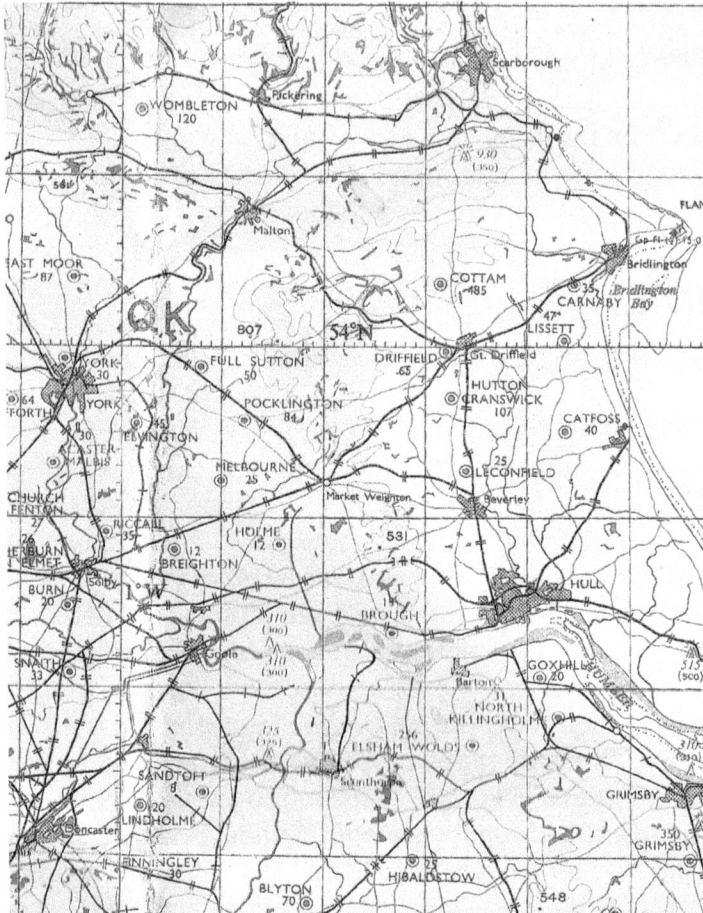

Part of 1951 edition of widely used general purpose map

As part of his rehabilitation he had learned to knit and had become an expert. When he was not flying he would happily make a very professional piece of knitted ware for any of us or teach any of our wives to knit. He was also expert at cake making and was very busy before Christmas and weddings.

Soon after he arrived he asked me to go to his room to collect his greatcoat and I was intrigued to find in his wardrobe items of uniform with Flt Lt, Sqn Ldr and Wg Cdr badges of rank on them. When I mentioned it to him he explained that he had been involved in 7 courts martial. He had been under instruction, defending officer, junior member, senior member and accused twice. No doubt his extensive experience made him such a good Boss. During one of our festive evenings in The Sun at Colton the assembled multitude rendered a spontaneous performance of the popular song Oh My Papa for him and the effect was remarkable. He was quite overcome with emotion. On the way to Colton we had run into thick fog which was not unknown in Yorkshire. Tony Goorney was driving and I was his passenger and we were groping our way along the York to Tadcaster road in very hazardous conditions when we were picked up by a very friendly motor cycle policeman. He then led us and our mini convoy to the door of The Sun and he was not waiting with a breathalyzer when we came out. It was splendid service but it was over 50 years ago.

Soon after my return to Full Sutton I received a phone call from Tony Smyth at Leconfield. He told me he was bringing a Lincoln bomber over to Full Sutton for me to fly and I should be waiting by the control tower in an hour's time. Nothing would have stopped me from being there and on time the Lincoln appeared and taxied around to pick me up as arranged. As I climbed the steep hill up the fuselage to the cockpit Tony began taxying again. As I reached the cockpit he turned to greet me and almost immediately came cries from the crew to stop. The taxiway passed through A Squadron's dispersal and the port outer engine was nicely lined up with the tails of about six Meteors and the propeller was prepared to slice them into ribbons. The airmen had to turn out to push the Meteors forward until the Lincoln could taxi past. After we were airborne Tony flew to our relief landing ground at Breighton and showed me a landing. He took off again and then climbed off the throne and invited me to have a go. Before taking off in a tail down aircraft I normally take care to note where the horizon crosses the cockpit canopy so that I know what the landing attitude should look like. In this case I had not seen this so some guess work would be involved. The Lincoln was by far the biggest aircraft I had flown and I was very conscious of the fact that if I bounced it or dropped it on landing there would be a lot of metal lurching around the sky. On the approach to land I found that everything was going quite slowly but as I looked out I was surprised to see the wings gently waving up and down. The Meteor was much stiffer. The aircraft was nice to fly but the only problem would be judging the height at which to round out for the landing. If I went too low it would hit the runway and bounce. If I rounded out too high it would eventually drop on to the runway. I made a guess and slowly brought the nose up until I thought it would be in the correct landing attitude. So far so good but I still had not found the runway. Before I could worry about putting on more power I felt the beast slowly mushing down and it settled on to the runway as if it belonged there. Having seen the correct attitude further landings were no problem but they were not as good as the first one which I rated as beginners luck. Having had my day out Tony took me back to Full Sutton but this time all of A Squadron's aircraft were pushed well forward

Avro Lincoln

The social life in the Mess was still flourishing. Most of our girl friends were far away and could not travel to all the parties but someone in the early days of the AFS had discovered that York had both a teachers' training college and a large nurses' hostel. It had become a routine to offer a block invitation to the girls and we always had a good representation. It was an admirable arrangement and usually the parties were very enjoyable. Before one dance some clown suggested we should have a Grimmy Party with a competition to see who could find the plainest partner. The party was in full swing when one of the nurses told Brian Clayton that they believed we were having a Grimmy Party but she had news for him. They were also having one and at that time he was in the lead.

Percival Proctor

While I was regaining full fitness to resume instructing I took the opportunity to fly our Percival Proctor and Airspeed Oxford as much as possible. They were both descended from well-known pre-war civil aircraft and they made a great contrast to Meteor flying. We used them for general communications flying and I spent many a happy hour touring around England carrying passengers or fetching spare parts. Both aircraft had a similar characteristic. When a pilot was attempting to make a text book three point landing the aircraft would sink on to the runway just before the tail wheel was near the runway. All that was required to produce the real thing was to give a little tug on the control column just before the aircraft was ready to touch down. If it was timed well the tail wheel would be flicked down and arrive on the runway at the same time as the main wheels. QED. The Proctor was available for training flights over the weekend but not many of the pilots took advantage of the offer and it was quite easy to stake a claim for the next weekend. Several times we flew to Turnhouse, the airfield for Edinburgh, on Friday afternoon and returned on Monday morning. Sqn Ldr Tony Goorney, our Station Medical Officer, had completed his medical training at Edinburgh University and still had fond memories of the place. After checking into a hotel we would make all speed to the Students' Union to check the program of events so that we could arrange our activities around it. A good weekend was guaranteed.

Tony was one of the group of flying doctors from the Institute of Aviation Medicine (IAM) at Farnborough which was investigating the new problems resulting from flight at high speeds and extreme altitude. While making tests on low temperature or great height I have seen them push themselves until they lost consciousness. I thought they were mad but the contribution they made to the future of high performance flying should never be under estimated.

While at Farnborough before he came to Full Sutton he had been cajoled by Wg Cdr Conrad Basanik to fly in the back seat of a Meteor 7 to operate some equipment while Conrad flew a high speed low level test. While cantering along at 450 knots the cockpit canopy decided to play a part in the test and swung open and went down the starboard side of the aircraft and hit the leading edge of the wing. Tony had no windscreen to protect him and he took the full force of the airflow which gave him quite a battering. Conrad managed to retain control of the aircraft and reduce speed but the hydraulic system had been put out of action. He managed to make a very hazardous wheels up landing at Farnborough. The ventral tank was punctured and the remaining fuel burst into flames. Tony claimed the fastest part of the high speed test was the rate at which both he and Conrad left the aircraft. Tony sustained flash burns to his head and hands and lost part of his ear and had to be patched up at the burns unit at Halton Hospital. It was typical of the flying doctors that he was very soon back at his bench again.

The RAF in the early 1950s were constantly looking for economies and some bright spark in the postings branch decided that Tony ought to have a Meteor conversion course but to get full value for their money they hit upon the novel idea of also making him the Station Medical Officer. If he gave us any trouble we could always decide that he needed more training in spinning. In return we did not give him a lot of trouble: we were a pretty fit outfit but he became very proficient at cuts, spots and sneezes

Airspeed Oxford

He achieved instant fame when Steve's idiot Boxer dog, Nimrod, during a station defence exercise, picked up in his mouth a Thunderflash explosive with the fuse burning. Everyone expected to collect bits of a daft dog but he was only knocked out. He soon came round and looked about with a severely blackened face. The ambulance was called and the exercise was abandoned. All then rested on Tony's surgical skills but he proved up to the challenge and much to our surprise Nimrod survived to create further havoc long after he and Steve left Full Sutton. We thought Tony should have had an OBE but the RAF was not responsive.

Chris Bush, Gp Capt John Hill, Steve Stivar, BA in The Sun at Colton

He played another very important part in our lives because he owned a car. Cars were scarce on squadrons in those days and we could not arrange a party off base unless all car owners were included in the list. Tony had a Triumph Dolomite which could carry a good number of mess members to parties but the gear box was temperamental. To cater for all emergencies Tony had acquired a spare gear box and when we asked him if he would join us for a party he usually replied, "I would love to but I'll have to change the gear box first". He became an adept engine mechanic but I was told that on one occasion when the gear box was being particularly uncooperative he used the ambulance to tow the wretched thing out of its mounting. He claimed that he could change the gear box or the cylinder head gasket within 1½ hours. It was amazing that with so few cars we could arrange to transport so many of our group 20 miles or more for a very convivial party at the Sun at Colton or the Punchbowl at Martin cum Grafton. It was another indication of the high morale of the Station. When he returned to Farnborough after his flying tour he continued work on oxygen masks and followed up the P type with the Q type. He then moved on to developing the first pressure helmets for the RAF.

In mid-April 1953 my life entered a new phase when Flt Lt Noel (Micky) Moss poked his head around the crew room door and asked if he could join us. He was in his late 20s and appeared to be a smart, dedicated RAF officer. The only defect in his impeccable appearance was his habit of wearing his hat at an angle like a drunken sailor but he could be stubborn and we could not reform his evil ways. The first impression proved to be correct but little did we guess that he also had a quirky sense of humour and was a great party man. He had been trained to fly in the USA towards the end of the war and just after it came to an end he found himself flying Mosquito bombers in Malaya and Burma. During his tour he was suddenly posted to No 205 Squadron to convert on to Sunderland flying boats without a formal conversion course. I had not heard of such a posting before but Micky just got on with it and in due course became a Sunderland captain. On return to UK his flying boat experience was put to good use in the usual Air Force manner when he completed the CFS course and became a Chipmunk instructor at Cranwell. I think the RAF was trying to discover how versatile he was because after his tour they sent him back to CFS to convert him to a Meteor QFI. Possibly to improve the tone at Full Sutton they sent him to join us.

Very soon we became almost inseparable. We had so many things in common. We loved our flying; we sang the same songs and drank the same beer. We played rugby and squash and we had a similar bizarre sense of humour. We were also founder members of the Society for the Preservation of the English Language. I think we were the only two members. The big difference was that Micky was older and more experienced than I but that worked in our favour. It was certainly a big help to me to keep me heading in the right direction when I needed it most. The final major advantage was that Micky owned an Austin 7 coupe two seat car known as Hortense. Hortense soon became well known around the Yorkshire hostelries, very often parked next to Tony Goorney's Triumph Dolomite.

At about this time our domestic arrangements markedly improved. We had new offices built along the front of our hanger and we also moved into new living accommodation. The SECO buildings had separate rooms with anthracite stoves which we could keep slowly burning all night. We still had to walk past two fields to reach the mess but the bath house was only 20 yards away. We were only a couple of hundred yards from the squash court. This increased the occasions on which we played but Micky could normally beat me. He played No 3 in the station team whereas I could just scrape into No 5.

In May I was flying an air test on a Meteor 4 and to check the handling I performed some aerobatics. I made a roll to the left but when I tried to stop the roll I could not move the control column to the right. I had to keep on rolling while I thought about my next trick. I tried moving the stick in all directions without removing the obstruction. I put on some negative G and then gave a hefty yank to the right and at last the stick broke free. After a careful check I returned gently to base to resume business as usual. When the aircraft was inspected a four inch spanner was found in the bottom of the cockpit and it had become jammed in the joints at the base of the control column.

In mid-1953 we had a fancy dress ball in the Officers Mess and Micky and I decided to go as an elephant. Micky used his seniority to claim the front end and I knew my place. We fabricated a presentable but rather small elephant and converted Brian Clayton into a Mahout for the evening. When the time came for our grand entry we were led on to the dance floor. After a very dignified parade around the floor our Mahout extolled the many virtues of his excellent animal and to demonstrate its docility he asked Gp Capt John Hill, our Station Commander and therefore only ranked just below God, to lie on the floor so that the elephant could walk over him. John Hill was an experienced officer and was very wary about the whole thing but he agreed to do so. The elephant slowly advanced and made great play of being very careful. After the front feet had successfully passed over to the other side my moment came. In the back half I had a loaded soda siphon. One quick splash and it was time for us to exit stage left at a brisk canter. That was the intention but the fickle finger of fate intervened and as I put my hard board shod right foot on to the floor it landed in a pool of soda water and slipped. I toppled backwards and dragged Micky down onto both myself and John Hill. The task of two people trying to stand up when enclosed in an elephant suit is almost impossible and our act ended in chaos. It was perhaps a better end to the event than originally planned..

Gp Capt Hill was the best Station Commander I served under during my RAF career. He was a very smart, smallish man with impeccable manners. He ran his station strictly but absolutely fairly. His management of all the station personnel was superb. In my case he realised that I had a hard road to tread and he took a personal interest in my development. He frequently had me in his office to read my palm and keep me out of trouble. Occasionally he took me with him on official visits as an unofficial ADC to give me more experience of RAF life. He had fought in the Battle of Britain and when the memorial to the Battle of Britain pilots was erected on the Embankment I sponsored the carving of his name on the memorial. In acknowledgement I received a summary of his career during the Battle of Britain and it included the time in 1940 when he commanded No 504 Hurricane Sqn in France. He was shot down by a Me109 and bailed out. As he was about to land he was fired on by French peasants with shotguns. He convinced them he was not German but then a British Army patrol appeared and assumed he was a fifth columnist. When he reached for his identity card they began firing. He dived into a ditch and then managed to convince them he was British. The French peasants again became very suspicious and attacked him, knocking him out. He came to being attended to by a French Air Force Commandant who he had known in Rouen. He was evacuated by ambulance train from Lille but the train was dive bombed by a Ju 87 and the driver and fireman abandoned ship. John Hill and another pilot found out how to control the train and drove it to Boulogne. No wonder he was a good Station Commander.

Note the King's Wings

During early 1953 we had heard many rumours about a Queen's Review of the RAF and at last details were released. A major review would take place at RAF Odiham where all units of the RAF and all aircraft in service would be displayed for Her Majesty's inspection and a fly past of about 650 aircraft would take place after lunch. This would be the biggest RAF event ever produced and would almost certainly never occur again.

We then heard that No 25 Group, which controlled all the jet AFSs, would be represented in the fly past by a formation of 12 Vampires aircraft and another of 12 Meteors. As more information seeped through we discovered Full Sutton would provide a 4 Meteor formation and I was delighted when I was nominated as one of the four pilots. We had Alan Hoult and Eric Pike from 1 Sqn and Don Geddes and me from 2 Sqn. Alan would be the leader and I was his deputy

On 20th June we departed with our aircraft and a team of airmen for RAF Oakington where we were to be based for our work up and rehearsals. Oakington made available a good sized building for our offices and a separate dispersal pan for our aircraft and we were made very welcome. Most of the 25 Group QFIs knew each other and it was similar to a great big reunion party. It is interesting to note that five of the twenty four pilots were creamed off QFIs. Then began a feast of flying. We flew a mixed bag of three or four sorties per day usually including a solo training flight, a four aircraft formation, a 24 ship formation and, later on, a flight along the route which would be used for the Review Flypast.

The task of putting 641 aircraft before the Queen in 27 minutes with faster aircraft passing the slower ones demanded careful planning, precise navigation and strict discipline. The plan was for all formations to pass over a "gate" at Leavesdon airfield, near Hatfield, at an exact time and then fly at a fixed speed over the saluting base at RAF Odiham and continue until over another "gate" at RAF Lasham. From that point each formation had its own escape route to return to base. Many of the formations had been deployed to airfields within reasonable distance of the Leavesdon gate and as most of the fighter aircraft had no navigators much of the early practice was devoted to devising methods of positioning the formation over the gate within the one minute tolerance we were given. If the formation was not within its time slot it was not allowed to continue along the route. In the early practices it was only the large slow aircraft such as Lincolns which had to abort the exercise because if they were approaching the gate late they could not accelerate to make up time.

The first aircraft in the flypast was a Sycamore helicopter towing a Royal Ensign at 75 knots. The slower aircraft came next and when my formation, the 26th, passed through exactly on time at 1600 feet the speed was 300 knots. After us came the Meteors of Fighter Command, the Canberras of Bomber Command and the Sabres of RAF Germany and the RCAF all at 300 knots. The prototype Swift and the first 5 production aircraft swept through at 400 knots but soon after over flying Odiham one of them had an engine failure but managed to make an emergency landing at Chilbolton. The prototypes of the Victor, Valiant and Vulcan bombers trundled past at 250 kts, 300 kts and 400 kts respectively and finally the first Javelin at 500 kts and the Hunter and Swift Mk 4 whipped in the tail of the procession with a flourish at 580 kts. Each formation had a set altitude to adhere to and all was neat and orderly until RAF Odiham was passed. Then the fun began as the formations began to catch up with the previous ones. My formation was planned to turn right at Lasham and then continue over the Chilton Hills on our way back to Oakington. A formation of 24 Chipmunks also followed this route back to their base at RAF Halton and we normally passed close to them but they were five hundred feet below us. One hazy day we passed over them just as they were breaking formation to land at Halton and we suddenly found a stream of Chipmunks passing from right to left very close below us. Our lowest member was Eric Pike in the box and Allan Hoult called "Yellow four, are you still there?" and we were all relieved when Eric replied, "Yes, but why do you ask?" He had seen nothing.

On another occasion in the same area our formation had been put into open formation when a small civilian light aircraft appeared from ahead and passed almost through us but did not waver in his flight. We debated afterwards whether he had seen us at all.

During one of the first runs along the route two Meteors collided and the crews were killed but fortunately that was the only flying accident. When we returned to Oakington we approached the airfield in formation, broke away to the left separately and followed in line astern downwind to land. As a matter of pride we stayed close behind the aircraft before us and tried to get all 24 aircraft on to the runway before the leader turned off at the upwind end. We normally managed to do this but it had its hazardous moments. I was number twenty two in this stream landing and the approach path was very turbulent from all the jet wakes. One day we had a small cross wind from left to right and Allan Hoult had to apply some extra power to manoeuvre to the left side of the runway. My aircraft ran right into the centre of his jet wake at about 300 feet and began to roll hard right. In spite of full control to restrain it my left wing rolled ninety degrees and I could not reach the runway. I put on full power to climb away but in this extreme position I noted that in front of me, on the railway line which crossed the runway threshold, two railway workers were travelling along the line on a small truck which was propelled by a large lever with handles which they pumped up and down. This picture filled my windscreen and as I watched they saw me coming and bailed out in unison but they left the truck still trundling along the line with the lever still pumping away. By the time I had savoured this cameo my aircraft had been thrown out of Allan's jet wash and I was able to recover and climb away for a solitary landing.

No 25 Group pilots and aircraft (Photo - Charles Brown)

The time passed very quickly and the fly past became more accurate. We approached Leavesdon gate from straight along the route but the formation before us came in from the left and the one behind us from the right. As we approached the gate all we could see was the bellies of the formations as they turned to slip into position. It seemed as if a collision was imminent but in the last few seconds the jigsaw fitted together. I led our formation down the route a couple of times which added more interest to life and one day I had the opportunity to swap my Meteor with Peter Cornish's Vampire. We were paid a visit by Charles Brown, the renowned aerial photographer, and he produced some excellent photos both in the air and also group photos on the ground.

Any pilot who has flown in multi-aircraft formations knows that tension builds up before the flight and the pilots become quieter. Last minute cigarettes are smoked and the edge of the dispersal pan is frequented by several pilots having a final nervous pee before climbing into the cockpit. On return after the flight there is a huge release of tension, voices are louder and there are many recriminatory cries of, "Why the hell did you do this or that?" After one run down the route a gaggle of us were unwinding outside our building when Joe Lestrange picked up a pebble and aimlessly hurled it towards the grass next to the pan. In flight it was intercepted by a small bird which was instantly killed. As one man all the pilots turned on Joe and condemned him for his cruelty to harmless birds and animals. It was an effective means of releasing the tension.

As we worked up for the real thing we all tried to improve our performance but sometimes it could be overdone and on one occasion Alan moved in too close and led me into the jet wake of Mike Norman's aircraft. In spite of all my efforts my aircraft was being forced down into the box where Eric Pike was flying. Fortunately Eric was expecting me and very politely moved away until I had finished with his place.

No 25 Group Meteors practicing for the Queen's Coronation Fly Past
(Photo - Charles Brown)

On 15th July the Great Day arrived and the weather was good. Everyone performed well and the whole fly past was quite exceptional. The average error in timing as the formations passed the saluting base was 5 seconds. It was a unique occasion which I am sure will never be attempted again. We were privileged to be part of the Review; we were proud of our young Queen and I hope she was proud of us. Next morning we were on our way back to Full Sutton and back to the coal face. After the Review a Coronation Medal was distributed. RAF Full Sutton was allocated four and the Station Commander decided to award them to members of the station ground staff who had served with distinction. The aircrew had always been given enthusiastic support by our ground staff and the four of us from the formation had been extremely lucky to have taken part in such a historic event and we supported the Station Commander's decision

Soon after our return Micky received an invitation to visit an uncle and aunt who lived in the north eastern part of Leeds and he arranged for me to go along too. We bowled along in Hortense and found the family, which included two daughters of almost our age, waiting for us. We were made extremely welcome and the weekend just slipped away. On Sunday, after fond farewells we steamed back to Full Sutton and on the way exhausted our repertoire of songs which was quite considerable by this time. The weekend made a welcome change for us because Full Sutton was the kind of place where one could spend all one's time without a break. With the cobwebs cleared away we could get back to work again.

When the next free weekend came up we decided to go and have a look at Nottingham which was rumoured to have lots of pretty girls. We stayed overnight and during our investigations we found the Trip to Jerusalem which was claimed to be the smallest pub in England. That may be true but there was enough room for Micky and I to raise our elbows.

Evaluating the trip to Jerusalem

I had been instructing for eighteen months and was surprised when I was told that it was time I thought about taking the exam to qualify as an A2 flying instructor which carried an above average assessment. I flew with the Chief Instructor and he recommended me for the test and arranged a date on 1st October for me to take an aircraft to CFS Little Rissington to visit Examining Wing for the test. I buried my head in books at every available opportunity because the test included 5 ground subjects in addition to the flying tests and eventually set course for the Cotswolds with some trepidation. Little Rissington sat on top of a hill and its main runway was only 1,600 yards long instead of the usual 2,000 yards and I had not flown a jet aircraft from it.

My examiner was Flt Lt Jock Agnew who was known as a strict but fair Trapper and we soon got down to business. When it came to the flying phase scattered cloud had developed at around 1,000 feet and so our circuit work consisted of either low level circuits at 500 feet or high level at 1,500 feet. Because I had not flown a jet aircraft at Little Rissingtgon before I was not prepared for a complication caused by the fact that the runway had a hill about halfway along it. On the approach as the aircraft passed below about 200 feet the far end of the runway disappeared and only reappeared when you were halfway along it. By then it was considerably closer than expected. Both Jock and I lost a lot of sweat but at the end of the day he gave me the nod and I became one of the first creamed off A2 QFIs. Of course this meant much more profit for the bar at Full Sutton but no more pay for me.

Normally our flying log books were signed each month by the Squadron Commander but periodically they were sent to Flying Wing HQ for checking and signing by the Chief Instructor and occasionally by the Station Commander. Soon after my A2 recategorisation my logbook came back having been signed by our Chief Flying Instructor, Sqn Ldr Stan Wandzilak. He was one of many Polish Air Force officers who had fought the Luftwaffe in Poland and then escaped and reached England. He then had a distinguished wartime career in the RAF and was still continuing to give excellent value. He was a charming character and I was glad to come across him again in later years. When I received my logbook I found tucked into the page that he had signed a postcard showing the well-known painting by Pieter Brueghel of The Fall of Icarus. Daedelus and Icarus decided to escape from their island by attaching feathers to their arms with wax. Icarus was warned not to fly too near the sun but he ignored the advice and the wax melted and he fell into the sea. It was probably the first recorded incident of over confidence. This was Stan's gentle way of reminding me not to fly too near the sun. It was typical of him because he knew that I was at a stage when many young pilots become over confident, often with fatal results. I still have the card in my logbook and many years later when he was OC Flying Wing at RAF Oakington and I was leading a team of Trappers I showed it to him. It had served its purpose.

I would have been happy to continue at Full Sutton but suddenly the end of my tour loomed over the horizon and I had to move on. When I was first told that I was being sent to CFS for QFI training I was promised that I would do only a 2 year tour and then, if possible, given a choice of posting. For many years I had wanted to be a single seat photographic reconnaissance (PR) pilot and emulate the work of the war time pilots flying special unarmed Spitfires from Benson. Now was my chance to fulfill my ambition and as the end of my tour approached I asked for a posting to single seat PR and was very relieved when the RAF kept their promise and I got my choice.

In January 1954 I paid my mess bill and packed my bag. It was inevitable that Micky should drive me to York station in Hortense. When I was seated the only place for my case was for it to be wedged on to my lap. Mickie bowled up to the main entrance of the station in a grand style, as befitted the occasion, but then I had a problem to open my door. With my case on my lap I could not reach the door handle but Micky solved the problem by leaning on me and squeezing his hand through a gap to release the handle. As the door burst open our combined weights propelled me out of Hortense on to the tarmac with my case on top. As I picked myself up and dusted myself down the last I heard was Micky roaring with laughter. It was not the way I had imagined leaving Full Sutton.

High Flight

Oh, I have slipped the surly bonds of earth

and danced the skies on laughter-silvered wings;

sunward I've climbed,

and joined the tumbling mirth

of sun-split clouds – and done a hundred things

you have not dreamed of – wheeled and soared and swung

high in the sunlit silence. Hovering there,

I've chased the shouting wind along and flung

my eager craft through footless halls of air

Up, up the long delirious, burning blue

I've topped the windswept heights with easy grace

where never lark, nor even eagle flew.

and, while with silent, lifting mind I've trod

the high untrespassed sanctity of space,

put out my hand and touched the face of God

John Gillespie Magee, Jr, USAF
Flying with RCAF Sqn in UK.
Killed in Action. 11th December 1942

CHAPTER 8
The Meteor PR OCU – RAF Bassingbourn

I had decided when I was about 7 years old in 1935 that I wanted to be an RAF pilot and as a teenager during the war I scavenged every piece of information I could find about the war in the air. Like many other youngsters I was daft enough to worry that the war might end before I could get into it. The Battle of Britain attracted most of my attention and then the fighter sweeps over France but slowly I became aware of the work being done by the newly developed photographic reconnaissance units (PRUs). Information was hard to come by but slowly news filtered out about the efforts of Sidney Cotton to form a unit with unarmed Spitfires fitted with cameras which was intended to take high level photographs over occupied Europe. I admired the skill and determination of the PR pioneers such as Shorty Longbottom, Bob Niven, Bill Wise and Alistair Taylor who proved the concept to be feasible. Initially I had wanted to be a fighter pilot but slowly I came to realise that the demanding but lonely, cold and dangerous role might be the challenge for me.

At last, in January 1954, I was on my way to join No 237 PR OCU at RAF Bassingbourn to begin my training as a single seat PR pilot. Bassingbourn was very busy training aircrews for the Canberra bomber force and No 231 OCU was the main occupant of the station. In 1954 the Cold War was becoming much colder and the build-up of the Canberra squadrons was a high priority. Tucked away in half of the second hangar from the A14 road was No 237 PR OCU. A smaller number of crews were being trained for the Canberra PR3 which was just being introduced into the UK. The only high level PR cover for the RAF overseas was provided by 3 squadrons of Meteor PR Mk 10s which were holding the fort until the Canberra PR version could take over. Because of the low number of Meteor pilots involved the turnover of pilots was quite small. I discovered that I was the only Meteor pilot on the course.

After 2 years living in prefabricated accommodation at the old wartime airfield at Full Sutton I was delighted to return to a well-appointed permanent 1936 type RAF station with a comfortable Officers' Mess. I soon noticed that the way of life changed from the rough and tumble of a hard flying AFS to the more sedate style associated with pilots who operate on their own.

When I reported to the PR squadron I met my new CO, Sqn Ldr Dougie Lowe, who I soon discovered was a very intelligent and capable officer who ran the squadron firmly but with a light touch. No one was surprised when he eventually became ACM Sir Douglas Lowe and a member of the Air Force Board. The Meteor instructors were Flt Lts Harry Clerbould and Vic Cramer and I had almost individual training rather like a flying club. As an A2 QFI on the Meteor I did not have to fly a general Meteor conversion but I had to meet my new war horse, the Meteor PR Mk 10.

The PR10 had been developed from earlier Meteor fighters. It was basically an F Mk 8 but the long extended wingtips had been stolen from earlier Mk 3s to give more wing area. The Mk 7 tail unit was fitted together with a FR Mk 9 camera nose complete with a forward or side facing F24 camera. The armament and ballast weights had been removed and two F52 vertical cameras were fitted in the rear fuselage. The aileron spring tabs which were fitted to other Meteors were removed to make the PR less sensitive in the rolling plane. Two 100 gallon under wing fuel tanks were a standard fitting. Only 57 were built and they equipped 541 Squadron in Germany, 13 Squadron in the Suez Canal zone at Kabrit and 81 Squadron at Tengah in Singapore. Such was the RAF's overseas photographic force. The most surprising fact was that there were no navigation aids other than maps, a compass and our wrist watches. It had two VHF radio sets but as the pilots usually operated with minimum use of radio these were utilities rather than navigation aids.

Meteor PR Mk 10 of No 81 PR Squadron

I had a conducted sector recce around the Bassingbourn area in the Meteor 7 and then I was ready to get acquainted with the Meteor 10. I was pleased to note that at last I would be able to fly with an ejector seat. No longer would I have to strap my parachute on before climbing up the side of the fuselage and down into the cockpit. The seat was an early model and could only be used above a height of 200 feet and a speed of 250 knots. After ejection the pilot still had to separate himself from the seat before pulling the rip cord to deploy the parachute but it was better than no ejector seat

My first flight in the PR 10 produced no surprises but I enjoyed the bigger single piece canopy and the better view ahead through the gap where the gun sight normally sat. It had been removed and replaced by the smaller controller for the F52 cameras. I thought that the idea of using the water bottle in the survival pack as a cushion for the ejector seat was a clever way of providing a soft incompressible seat. It was not long before I discovered that on long high level flights it became a block of ice and froze your backside. The aircraft was very steady on the approach to land and it could be flown over the runway threshold as low as 95 knots, however at such a low speed the bottom of the tail fin was very close to the runway and any twitching of the controls could result in the tail banging the runway.

Almost immediately I had to start learning the art of taking photos. I did not find much difficulty with taking forward or side facing low level photos but the high level tasks were another kettle of fish. Most peace time high level survey tasks were standardised and taken from 30,000 feet which produced photos with a scale of 1:10.000. The photographic interpreters were well used to this scale and it made their difficult task a little easier. We had three main types of task. The first was a pinpoint target where only 3 overlapping photos were required to give a stereo image. The second task was a feature line which could extend for 20 miles or more. This required careful planning to be able to track along the required line without being able to see the ground underneath and without being blown off by strong winds. The third task was a Small Area Cover which required 2 or more feature lines side by side. The basic requirement for all 3 tasks was for the pilot, who could not see underneath the aircraft, to be able to position it over a spot on the ground, heading in the correct direction at the correct speed and with his wings level, all at precisely 30,000 feet. That was the theory.

Before the sleight of hand could begin the exact point on the ground had to be identified and kept in sight while manoeuvring for the photo run. For feature lines the switch on point could be a field, a part of a wood or a point near a bend in a river. We normally used 1 inch to the mile Ordnance Survey maps to give us the required detail but one had to learn a special discipline for handling the maps to avoid being submerged by paper in the small cockpit. To produce good results the switch on should be within 100 yards of the selected point and the only way to hope to achieve this accuracy was practice, practice and practice. Just north of Bassingbourn was a very easily visible crossroads known as Caxton Gibbet which was an excellent target for beginners. The recommended approach to the target was to approach at 90 degrees to the photo run and bring the target close down the side of the fuselage. When you were almost alongside it you turned hard left so that you had a good last look at the target and then tried to roll out on the required heading with the wings exactly level and then switch on the cameras. Worrying about maintaining exact height and speed could come later. After my early efforts when my film had been developed I often wondered where Caxton Gibbet had gone. It was important to try to remember the method you had used last time and make improvements but it was a tedious process. Slowly I managed to keep my photos within Cambridgeshire and I could move on to trying feature lines. We used the same procedure to begin the run but then the heading had to be held precisely and the wings rock steady. I used the long straight Bedford Levels Canals as my practice targets and if the heading varied lots of photos of unidentified fen land were brought home and if the wings wobbled the successive prints looked like the footprints of a drunken man on his way home. If the nose of the aircraft was allowed to rise or fall the overlap between prints varied from a lot to almost nil.

The efforts to improve my photography went on all through the course but we also had to brush up our pilot navigation. This was one of the attractions of the job for me and I enjoyed all the navigation exercises I could get. Low level navigation was fun. I had always delighted in map reading and to be able to practise it from a fast moving aircraft added spice to the task. It was also a pleasant way to become more familiar with the lovely English countryside. High level navigation in the Meteor 10 was equally pleasing but in a completely different way. The dual checks were flown in the Meteor 7 which had no cockpit pressurisation. Under wing tanks were fitted which made it heavier and less nimble than my old friends. In everyday use the Meteor 7 would only spend less than half an hour above 30,000 feet but flights of more than an hour were cold and tiring. It also produced the risk of decompression sickness or Divers Bends which were usually very painful. Fortunately I never had an attack.

The solo navigation exercises in the Meteor 10 were new to me. At last I could reach out to a range of about 1,000 nautical miles without any navigational aids other than my maps, my compass and my eyes. Planning had to be precise and flying had to be accurate. Corrections to the flight path were only to be made when sure of your new information and the mental calculations to reach the target had to be quick and reliable. The flights would have been splendid if only it had not been so cold. The engines could not push much warm air into the cabin at altitude and the temperature soon dropped well below freezing point. We had no special clothing and we could use pullovers etc. but the biggest problem was cold hands and feet. I had my old fur lined sheepskin flying boots from Tiger Moth days but I could not decide what to wear inside them. I tried thick socks, up to 3 pairs of thin socks, silk socks and on one occasion no socks. All were equally cold.

Amidst all this work I received an invitation to return to RAF Full Sutton for a Dining Out Night which had not been possible to arrange before my posting. I welcomed this and immediately began pestering the Boss to allow me to take a Meteor over for the weekend. He would have been happy to grant my request but we ran into a period of shortage of aircraft. The day before I was due to go he asked me if I could fly the Avro Anson, a twin piston engined aircraft, which we had on the Squadron for general communications flights. I told him I could because I was sure I was capable of handling it. I did not tell him that I had not flown one before. He agreed that I could fly up on Friday and return on Monday morning. With that settled I then went to find the Pilots Notes for the Anson but was rather perturbed when none could be found. Overnight I tried to remember all I could about piston engines and decided that if I could get the engines started there should be no major problems. Next morning the Anson had been pushed out on to the tarmac and as I signed the authorisation book I had a shock when I discovered that 4 airmen were waiting for a ride to Full Sutton en route to a weekend in York. While I walked around doing the external checks I was learning as much as I could about the aircraft. When I was settled into the cockpit I was pleased to note that I could recognise all the important knobs and switches. Using a combination of the techniques I had used on Oxfords, Harvards, etc., the engines started without problems. Everything fell into place and I was soon ready for take-off. The weather was good and the airmen were well settled in so off we went.

Avro Anson

I was glad that it was a more modern Anson and I did not have to wind the undercarriage up with about 20 turns of a big wheel. Even the Anson had acquired a button which did the trick. Soon I settled down on course for Full Sutton and then I had a chance for a good check around to review the situation. All seemed to fine except that I could not find a control for the landing flaps. I checked around the cockpit very carefully and tried to put a name on all the knobs and levers. Only a knob on the cockpit floor just outside my right knee seemed to be spare. I had the choice of trying the knob or making a flapless landing at Full Sutton. I considered the option for a while and decided that as there were no yellow and black stripes around the knob nothing was likely to fall off if I pulled it. With some trepidation I pulled up the knob and guess what happened? The flaps came down. When I joined the circuit at Full Sutton the controller asked me if I could fly that thing and I had to admit I did not know but would let him know after landing. The airmen were very grateful for their lift and the return flight was downhill all the way.

At last the end of the course loomed in sight and the Boss decided that for my final check he would fly with me on a long high level navigation sortie. He chose a route up to the north west of UK and then down to the Cornwall peninsula and back to Bassingbourn. I certainly did not want to foul up this trip and I put a lot of effort into the careful planning. Apart from a strong gusty surface wind it was a lovely clear day and the Boss was an ideal passenger. Apart from responding to my oxygen checks he was very quiet and every time I checked behind my tail I could see him looking over the side. Whether he was checking the navigation or enjoying the marvellous view I never knew. I was relieved that all went well but when we returned to Bassingbourn the strong gusty wind had swung across the main runway and the short northwest runway was in use. I had flown earlier in the morning on the same runway and had found that where the last few hundred yards of the approach crossed over the main A14 road and quite near to the Coach and Horses public house there was quite severe turbulence. As the aircraft flew through what was known as a wind gradient up to 20 knots of airspeed could be lost with the danger of landing short of the runway. On a long runway this could be prevented by adding another 20 knots on to the approach speed but in our case we had a short runway for a Meteor 7 with wing tanks fitted and with not very good brakes. It was imperative that we arrived at the end of the runway at the lowest safe speed. This was a good situation for testing students on their final tests but I had rather it had not happened to me. I set up a good approach and was using more power than usual to carry me through the wind gradient as we approached the Coach and Horses. The Boss must have been aware of the problems but he did not offer a word of advice and of course he had not flown through it earlier in the day. As we passed the pub he told me to take off the power and with much trepidation I eased it off as slowly as I dared and then the aircraft began to sink and we just made the first few yards of the runway for a firmer landing than usual. A good point of the Meteor was that it had an excellent undercarriage and it took the strain. I was once told that any landing you could walk away from was a good landing. The Boss never mentioned it in his debrief.

We had to keep our proficiency in night flying and a few night sorties were included in the syllabus. We waited until the sun had gone down and a respectable darkness had settled on the countryside before I took off but very soon I had two new experiences. As I climbed away from Bassingbourn I realised I could climb high enough to bring the sun back over the horizon and by 25,000 feet there it was again. Harry Potter has not done this yet and I was fascinated by being in bright sunlight and looking down through a clear sky on England in darkness. At that time in 1954 the airways network only reached up to 25,000 feet and to the south I could see from a distance of 50 miles or so the lights of London. I decided not to forego a great opportunity and swung south to cruise over the top of Central London at 30,000 feet. By great good fortune the night was unusually clear and not even the prevalent smog was lurking over the City to spoil the view. The black snake of the Thames was a convenient marker and it was quickly possible to pick out all the major features of London in marvellous colour. The range of colours was almost limitless. Every stretch of street lights seemed to have different hues and the advertisements filled in every colour of the spectrum. It was an extraordinary sight and I had time to savour it. Alas it is not possible any more.

I had a few more exercises to complete before the end of the course but my mind was now focussing on my next posting and Air Ministry teased me by not giving any clues. I knew I had the three possibilities of Singapore, Egypt or Germany but I was well pleased when at last I discovered that I was bound for Germany. This meant I was posted to No 541 PR Squadron and I was delighted because it meant I was going to follow in the footstep of Sidney Cotton's pioneers. The original PRU had become No 1 PRU and as the force expanded it became No 541 Sqn and eventually changed its Spitfires for Meteor PR 10s. Everything was going my way and I was a very happy man.

CHAPTER 9
Alone Above All.
No 541 (PR) Squadron

LIVERPOOL Street Station was cold, damp and full of smoke, steam and coal dust when I arrived there on the evening of 20th March 1954. It was a miserable picture but I didn't care. I had a travel warrant to travel on the troop train to Gütersloh, somewhere in the middle of Germany to join No 541 PR Squadron which was the direct descendant of the first high level Spitfire PR squadrons which were developed during WW2 mainly at RAF Benson. The pilots of 541 Sqn at Benson noticed a tiny pretty deep purplish blue flower which grew in profusion around their hangar and when they discovered that its common name was Birds Eye Speedwell they decided to adopt it as their squadron crest. As a motto they chose "Alone Above All" for, as they were unarmed, they certainly hoped they would be and remain just that.

Squadron Crest

The first problem was to survive the journey by troop train to Gütersloh. When all passengers and luggage were aboard the train huffed and puffed its way to Harwich where it disgorged its contents on to the dark and wet platform. After humping my case over several railway lines and platforms I found myself on the Harwich to Hook of Holland ferry boat where I quickly decided a visit to the bar might provide the necessary anaesthetic to guarantee a good night's sleep. It could only get better.

Next morning my case was lugged around again until I was settled in to another steam train which regularly made the journey through Holland and the Ruhr industrial complex and then through most of the British Sector of Germany to Berlin. Most of the journey to Gütersloh was through flat uninteresting countryside which gave a completely false impression of Germany but I was intrigued to make acquaintance with many names which had been so familiar during the war. Who hadn't heard of the marshalling yards at Hamm? I was sharing a compartment with a family which included a lively little boy of about five. As the train arrived in Duisburg station with clouds of smoke swirling under the canopy and much chuffing from other engines he stood at the window with eyes as big as saucers. As he watched from the slowly moving train a German porter came into sight dressed in a splendid uniform and a Rommel type hat. He was calling a long list of German names and after listening intently for a while the boy turned and said "Mummy, he's talking Scribble!"

Gütersloh railway station was just as dull and uninteresting as that of any other small industrial town but life began to improve when I recognised an RAF officer obviously waiting for me. Gerry Mayer was my first contact with 541 Squadron and as we drove through the middle of the town I realised that it was more attractive and interesting than I had expected. Another few miles to the north and I arrived at my first German air force base and my favourable impressions continued to increase. When we approached the Officers Mess my cup of happiness overflowed. In front of a large area of grass was an attractive building quite unlike the standard pattern of RAF Messes. It was partly covered by creeping ivy and a small tower graced the right side. In front of the Mess on either side of the grassy area were three accommodation blocks which were in good condition and seemed to be inviting.

The next hour or so is rather blurred in my memory but at some time I was taken over to my room to off load my kit and to meet Frau Kuhnemann, my batwoman. She was a plump little lady who was old enough to be my mother and she looked after three officers. She spoke no English and I spoke no German but it did not seem to be a problem. I spoke careful English and she spoke Wesphalian German and we got along fine.

"Good morning, Frau Kuhnemann."

"Guten morgen, Herr Ashley". Frau K opens the curtains.

"How's the weather today?"

"Ach! Es gibt ein bischen Regen. "

"Do you have a blue shirt for me? "

"Ja, ja. Kommt sofort."

Later I discovered she had a son who had been killed during the war when he was about our age and she seemed to look upon us as her boys. I became very fond of her.

After dinner in the very pleasant dining room, complete with minstrel's gallery, a group of the squadron pilots decided to complete my first day in Germany with a visit to a local hostelry. Everything was still being given high marks in my assessment when I was instructed to go over to a buxom wench and say, "Fünf Bier, bitte". To my surprise she soon reappeared with five large glasses about three quarters full of beer and a quarter full of foam. My first day's education was complete.

After breakfast next morning I was led the short distance through some trees to the Operations Block where the day began with the Met briefing. It was the custom for a duty pilot to visit the Met Office earlier, be briefed on the weather situation and then bring the synoptic chart to brief the assembled pilots. Sometime later on a miserable day we were given a briefing which forecast a bright sunny day. When the assembled multitude protested we discovered that the duty pilot had been late and he had grabbed the chart and raced for the briefing. He then briefed us from the wrong side of the chart! Economy was the order of the day in the early 1950s but using both sides of a met chart was a false economy.

Another short walk across the road from the Ops Block to a concrete built hangar and at last I was really on 541 Squadron.

Meteor PR Mk 10 over Nijmegen My old Charlie

Our Squadron Commander was Sqn Ldr Peter Thompson and my Flight Commander was Flt Lt Peter Bridger who had been with me on the same Meteor course at Middleton St George in 1951. After meeting all available squadron members over the usual mug of coffee I departed on my round of joining procedures which to my disappointment were just as lengthy and boring as in UK. This kept me away from the flight line for a day but then I was ready to go. The first two days were a sample of the future: a sector recce with Peter Bridger in the Meteor T7, a solo sortie in a PR Mk10, an instrument flying sortie with Gerry Mayer in the back seat and then a high level photo sortie over Hamburg. The third day I gave dual instruction to our OC Eng Wing, which is always a good investment, and then a low level photo sortie on the east coast of Schleswig Holstein. After a weekend break came my first high level sortie down over the American sector. Unfortunately my targets were covered in cloud but I was back home in time for a night flying test on a PR10 with an instrument let down and some Ground Controlled Approaches (GCA) at Jever. In the late evening I flew a night check with Peter Bridger and then I was off on a night sortie which included a let-down and GCAs at Wunsdorf. The next two weeks were a similar mixed bag of sorties.

During this time I was told I had been selected to go on the next squadron exchange to No 13 PR Squadron at Kabrit in the Canal Zone of Egypt. This was one of the squadron's most sought after tasks and I

135

could hardly believe I had been selected after only three weeks on the squadron. After a return journey to Sylt and two more dual sorties with our Wg Cdr Eng I started to prepare for our detachment.

I was allocated Meteor PR 10 WB156 for the journey and it required air testing after a thorough servicing. I had heard many tall stories about the maximum height reached in a PR10 but as I was quite new on the type I decided to find out for myself. I left the height climb part of the test until the end of the sortie when I had little fuel remaining. The climb was normal until I reached 45,000 feet but then the flying became very sensitive while seeking the best climbing speed. A variation of a few knots would result in reduced rate of climb or even descent. By milking every bit of climb the aircraft eventually reached 49,700 feet but it was difficult to maintain and I let it sink to a sustainable height of 49,500 feet. After such a struggle I had to tell someone about it so I called Gütersloh tower for a controlled let down. The controller on duty was Flt Lt Toby or Digger Foxley who had been Micky Martin's rear gunner on the Möhne Dam raid. As expected he asked for my height and I proudly but breathlessly told him "49.5" whereupon he immediately came back with "Roger Blue, make it 50.5. I already have one there!" I could think of no appropriate answer.

I was paired with Flt Sgt Ron Waugh for the detachment and on 14th April we set off for the sunshine. We were two bachelors with all our worldly possessions packed in zipped travel bags tied into the rear fuselage and ready for anything. Ron led me on the first leg of our journey to Istres, the French test centre just north of Marseilles. We flew in loose formation and I could admire the scenery as I kept a check on the navigation. Istres was one of our frequently visited air fields and I always enjoyed the food in the Mess. Carafes of both white and red wines were kept well topped up. Fortunately we were staying overnight and we had no restraints.

After an excellent breakfast we continued on our way towards RAF Luqa on the island of Malta. I was leading and was taking good care to keep a close check on possible diversion airfields because the weather chart had shown the possibility of heavy thunder storms in the Central Mediterranean. All went well until we were about 200 miles from Malta and then my radio died. I was able to attract Ron's attention and by hand signals ask him to take over the lead. Fortunately he had been monitoring our navigation and he pressed on towards Malta. Soon afterwards we began to see evidence of cumulonimbus clouds building up along our track. As we approached Malta the cloud rose above us and we were soon in thick cloud and I had to stay close to Ron as he was my only hope of a safe arrival at Luqa. My fate was in his hands. We entered rain and severe turbulence which increased until we were having a very uncomfortable ride and keeping close formation required vigorous handling. By this time we had insufficient fuel remaining to enable us to divert to an alternative airfield and all I could do was hang on to Ron like glue even though at times I could barely see him from a few yards. I was immensely relieved when I began to see glimpses of the ground as we descended through about 800 feet and when Ron eased on to the runway I was right there alongside him. It had been the longest 2 hours and 10 minutes of my life. Even then our problems were not over. As we taxied into the dispersal the rain was heaving it down in bucketfuls. If we opened our cockpit canopies not only ourselves but also the aircraft cockpits would be soaked in water and while our skins were waterproof the cockpit was much more sensitive. Fortunately the servicing crew had the good sense to leave us in our cockpits until the storm abated. Ron enjoyed his free beer all evening and I slept well all night.

My radio was patched up overnight and next morning we had to do the old PR pilot's trick of changing the radio crystals. Different frequencies were used around the Mediterranean and most of us on long journeys carried a pocket full of crystals to meet all eventualities. We disappeared into the rear hatch underneath the fuselage and took the cover off our radios. The redundant crystals were removed and the new ones inserted. We had spare aerial connecting plugs with small bulbs wired in and with the bulbs in position we tuned the radios to give the brightest light. This technique was not the preferred solution in Engineering Wing but it enabled us to operate independently.

The next day I led Ron to RAF El Adem near to Tobruk on the North African coast and then Ron led me over the El Alamein and other renowned WW2 battlefields on the way to RAF Fayid, the main transport airfield in the Canal Zone where we cleared customs. A ten minute flight across the Great Bitter Lake and we had reached our new temporary home at RAF Kabrit.

RAF Kabrit was situated at the southern end of the Great Bitter Lake and the Suez Canal passed along the east side of the airfield. The accommodation was in prefabricated buildings or Nissen huts and from my room I could walk 100 yards to the Officers Mess or 120 yards to bath in the lake.

In the early summer the daytime temperature was already very hot and to avoid flying in strong turbulence flying would normally begin at 6 o'clock in the morning and cease about noon. If I was on the first sortie I would surface about half past four and call my bearer to bring hot water and then a quick trot to the Mess for breakfast in the dawn light before heading for 13 Squadron offices. One day I awoke to find it was already quite light and my bearer was summoned to produce hot water quickly. In very short time I was scuttling over to the Mess when I encountered some officers working on their sailing boats! In the confusion after an afternoon siesta I had thought it was morning instead of evening.

We were kept busy during the next two weeks by 13 Sqn. Several PR tasks were flown in the Canal Zone and visits made to No 208 FR Squadron at Abu Sueir and to RAF Nicosia in Cyprus. A long low level flight took me across barren desert to St Margaret's Monastery at the base of Mount Sinai. On the return flight I came across an Arab with his camel plodding steadily in a westerly direction. My curiosity was aroused so I turned and set course in the direction he was following. Within about 20 miles I flew over a small oasis and I am still amazed that he could navigate so accurately. I frequently complained about having no navigation aids but he did not even have a map and compass

On April 22nd we took part in a night exercise during which minimum airfield lighting was used. I was not very familiar with Kabrit airfield but with only small glim lamps to mark the taxiway I had to proceed with great care. While groping my way to the end of the runway I realised that I was passing through a line of Meteor night fighters which were parked on both sides of the taxiway. This could have been a very expensive operation! When I was airborne I was amused to note that all the Canal Zone airfields were easy to locate because they were the only dark patches in a large brightly lit area. Getting back to the airfield again was no problem.

When we left Kabrit on 28th April on our return journey to Germany we gave them the customary low flypast. As I passed the control tower I was pleasantly surprised to see that I was way below the wind sock. We retraced our way to RAF El Adem and continued on to RAF Benina in Cyrenaica. This area had been fought over several times during the war and it was a military junk yard. The airfield was strewn with many German aircraft in various states of wreckage and an equal number of abandoned vehicles. We were soon on our way and after an easy flight reached our night stop at RAF Idris, just south of Tripoli. It was the old Italian Castel Benito airfield and obviously part of an ex-Italian colony and the whole atmosphere reminded us of the fact. It was attractively laid out and the staff still maintained their old customs and produced excellent food. The Mess buildings were all stone built and the gardens were full of bright flowers and the streets were lined with palm trees. We had a very enjoyable overnight stay.

Next day was another relaxed flight to the Tunisian base at El Aouina in the outskirts of the city of Tunis. We had left behind a small piece of old Italy to find ourselves in an equally enjoyable piece of the old French colony. The base was not as attractive as Idris but the welcome by the French speaking Tunisians was very warm. We took the opportunity to visit the attractive city and very much enjoyed sitting on the terrace of the old French Air Force club next to the main boulevard in the centre of the city. Life on a PR Squadron had few perks but this was one of them. After our taste of North Africa we had to get back to Europe again so we set course next morning for Istres. During the flight I flew in close formation behind Ron's aircraft and positioned myself just behind and above his tail plane and took a series of photos with the forward facing camera. When we were back at base they won me the Photo of the Month. We did not stop to enjoy another night at Istres but continued on our way to Gütersloh. On 30th April we were home and dry and my laundry was in the safe hands of Frau Kuhnemann

It was good to be back with the Squadron again in our lovely Officers' Mess. It was smaller than the normal 1936 pattern Messes in UK and a unique layout. We shared it with our sister Squadron, No 79 Fighter Reconnaissance Sqn, and we fitted in very comfortably. 79 Sqn claimed a small ante room on the left of the entrance and we occupied a similar one on the right plus the library. If someone was rash enough to venture into enemy territory the error was soon pointed out. We shared a cellar bar and a small bar at the top of the tower which was known as Goering's bar. A much used wartime expression was, "If I tell a lie may the beam (on the ceiling) bend". If a metal ring which was fitted into the floor was pulled sure enough the centre of the ceiling beam descended about six inches.

While we operated singly and quietly at long distances from base 79 Sqn normally flew in small formations at low level on tactical photo sorties for the Army near the battlefield forward area. The character of the two squadrons could not have been more dissimilar. They were brash and noisy and had the highest flying accident record in RAF Germany while we went about our tasks quietly and we hardly had an accident record. We fought tooth and nail in the Mess but if strangers tried to intervene we would unite to see them off; rather like brothers.

In the years after the war discipline had become rather too relaxed and we heard that our Station Commander, Gp Capt Dudley Moore, had been tasked with getting RAF life back to a proper peacetime footing. As part of this process all officers were required to dine in the Mess every Friday evening and every Saturday morning was a Station Commander's parade. The Dining In Nights were certainly not looked upon as a punishment and they were usually very spirited occasions. One beautiful evening we took our drinks out on to the patio and were amazed to observe David Moffet sprinting along the flat roof next to the patio waving aloft a large sun umbrella and launching himself in the direction of a large flower bed. David was equally amazed to find that the aerodynamics of the umbrella were terrible and he landed in a crumpled heap with a broken ankle. Much later in the night a group of us decided to go swimming in the pool in our white dress shirts and bow ties. Jim Taylor, the Flying Wing Adjutant, had obviously been impressed by Dave Moffet's experiment and he decided to test the aerodynamics of a bicycle by riding it off the end of the diving board. The result was as bad as the sun umbrella. While we were elegantly wandering back to our rooms we met the two Flight Commanders of 79 Sqn going for an early morning swim in swimming trunks and dressing gowns. We decided they were very casually dressed.

We normally paid a high price for the Dining In Nights next morning, particularly in hot weather. A formal parade was quite long and standing still for a long period with a thumping head ache was a formidable challenge. Any unfortunate officer who should faint on parade was normally rewarded with several extra Orderly Officer duties. It was a great test of character to stand still while watching your perimeter of vision slowly decreasing and knowing that if you allowed the hole to fully close you would have little leisure time in the near future. The incentive to stay vertical was very strong.

Orderly Officer duty came round quite frequently and often produced unexpected tasks. At first we used Land Rovers as our all purpose vehicles but soon after I arrived we began to use the relatively new Volkswagen Combie. I was amazed to find that in spite of their larger size they were surprisingly manoeuvrable and nippy. One night in a Land Rover I had to check on the German security guards on the flight line. While I was signing one of the guard's log book his vicious guard dog was trying to climb over the tail board to get at me. To judge by the noises he was making his intentions were not benign. I must have produced the shakiest signature in my life. In the Combi we were much more comfortable and efficient and I am not surprised that over 50 years later it is still in production and widely used.

Meteor PR Mk 10 over Geneva

The next few weeks were filled with a mixture of high and low level photo tasks with the aim of getting myself declared "Operational" for future NATO tasks. I flew night navigation and instrument flying sorties and a task in the south of France which involved a refuelling stop and lunch at Istres. For light entertainment I used the Station Flight's Percival Prentice, a basic trainer, for liaison flights and for giving instruction to station staff. During this period we had to produce a formation for the Air Officer Commanding's (AOC) flypast. My main memory of this day was watching 79 Squadron landing as we taxied in to our dispersal. As a matter of pride they had to fly a curved approach all the way to the beginning of the runway. As Paul Worthington was approaching the threshold he must have flown into some jet wash from the aircraft in front and he made a beautiful three point landing in the undershoot area, on his nose wheel, left wingtip and the left wing tank. He then bounced on to runway, finished his landing run and returned to dispersal as if it was his normal method of arrival.

After four months on the Squadron I was getting very well acquainted with the Meteor PR10. I was very familiar with other types of Meteor but the PR10 seemed to have a personality of its own. It was very reliable and never let us down. It could fly much further than the others and although heavier on the controls because the aileron spring tabs had been removed it was very manoeuvrable. All that was needed was a strong right arm. Occasionally I had the opportunity to fly an air test without wing tanks or cameras and it was great fun to fly a full range of aerobatics.

Charlie misbehaving

The old boy was very stable on radar approaches and it could be flown very accurately. The radar controllers could recognise the difference between a PR10 sitting steadily on the glide path and a FR9 of No 79 Sqn yo-yoing its way home to roost. I became very fond of the PR10 particularly VW376 A-C, Charlie, which I flew as often as possible. It was a great shame that the RAF expected us to fly such a demanding role without any navigation aids other than the compass, the pilot's own watch and maps. On a long flight when detailed maps were needed in the target area a high degree of cockpit discipline was essential to avoid the cockpit becoming full of used maps. When the same maps were required in the reverse order for the return flight the pilot could easily get involved in the game of Hunt the Map.

In June Fg Off Denzil (Denny) Beard and Fg Off Lew Levitt departed on the next of the Sqn detachments to No 13 Sqn at Kabrit. Just before they were due to return we heard news that Denny's aircraft had last been seen spinning into the Mediterranean Sea without a tail unit. No parachute had been seen. Lew Levitt was reported to have landed safely at Istres. The Squadron members went about their tasks as usual but a great sense of gloom was pervasive. I was given the task of making an inventory of Denny's kit and locking his room. The next day was miserable while the Boss flew down to Istres to check on Lew. The following day news came through that Denny had survived. He had been picked out of the sea after many hours by a French freighter and taken back to Tunis and was staying with the British Air Attaché's family which included two attractive daughters. Immediately the whole atmosphere changed and the bar was opened. When both Denny and Lew returned to base we learned that on the flight from Tunis to Istres Lew's aircraft had hit the tail of Denny's aircraft. The tail unit was knocked off and the aircraft fell into a spin. Denny was taken by surprise and almost immediately ejected and found himself on his parachute just below 30,000 feet. The temperature was extremely cold and the parachute began to swing. Soon he became air sick and continued to be so until he landed in the sea. He managed to inflate his dinghy and clamber on board but then became sea sick. The next few hours must have been an absolute misery for him. Towards the end of the day a passing French freighter, by incredible good fortune, found him and fished him out of the sea. It was bound for Tunis and that is where Denny found himself after a not to be forgotten journey.

After the collision Lew's aircraft pitched up and went into a spin from which he was able to recover just above 20,000 feet. He circled around looking for Denny's aircraft and eventually saw it spinning down into the sea without its tail unit. He saw no sign of a parachute and feared for the worst. Although he did not know it Denny was swinging on his parachute up above him. Lew made the appropriate distress calls and then continued on his way to Istres. He returned to base soon afterwards but it took a little longer for Denny to be flown back. They both received a tremendous greeting and a dinner was arranged at the Quellental Hotel, near Bielefeld, which was reputed to be the best in the area. I can't recall a happier party or a better meal. Eventually Lew had a very one sided interview with the AOC.

A British Forces school was situated in Gütersloh town and the female teachers were accommodated in a large requisitioned house in the park. Our Squadron had a very friendly relationship with them and we normally invited them all to our Mess parties. Frequently we were invited to their house for tea or a party and we all enjoyed the happy arrangement.

We had a Wg Cdr Church of England padre on the station but we very rarely saw him. We also had a Roman Catholic padre, Flt Lt George McCurrogh, who everyone knew. He regularly paid visits to nearly all sections on the station and I was often visited by him either when I had just settled into the cockpit for a sortie or when I had just climbed out. He was an excellent pianist who usually graced the bar in the evening and led the sing songs. If the party became too boisterous George was suddenly missing. When asked why he spent so much time in the bar he would reply "Because that is where my flock is". He was also a connoisseur of single malt Scotch whisky. When I was married to Marlies in the following year he was an honoured guest with his own bottle. When he came to the end of his tour he was diligent in showing his replacement all the most important places to watch over. We had an Officers' Club in the centre of Gütersloh town and George took his replacement to visit the club on a Saturday evening which was, no doubt, a suitable time. They decided to cycle into town for the occasion and a very educational evening was soon approaching midnight and, as was usual, George and the new padre left to cycle back to base. Within minutes an officer came into the club crying," Come and look at this". We all piled outside to view the unforgettable scene. The two padres had set off along the street and at the T junction at the end George, on the right side, had turned left while his companion had turned right. In the middle of the T junction were the two padres on the road with bicycles around their necks. By good fortune no photos appeared in the local press

A mixed bag of very enjoyable flying followed and I was soon declared Operational and thereby qualified for any NATO tasks. The high level sorties were very demanding and because of our lack of navigation aids they required careful planning and accurate flying. We normally climbed en route to about 43,000 feet and then settled down at maximum continuous engine speed and allowed the aircraft to slowly climb as fuel was used. The Meteor was originally designed as an interceptor fighter with a normal flight time of about 40 minutes. We soon discovered that after an hour or so the cockpit heating was completely inadequate. The engines produced very little thrust above 40,000 feet and very little warm air was available for heating. After an hour or so the cockpit temperature was very much below freezing temperature. When sitting on an ejector seat a soft cushion could not be used and some ingenious designer had the bright idea of using the emergency water bottle in our dinghy pack as a soft but incompressible cushion. After a long period at high level the water bottle froze and we were left sitting on a block of ice. At first we had a numb backside and then cramp would set in. I often debated with myself if I should take my broken backside back to base or divert to a lovely looking warm airfield. As far as I know no one fell to the temptation but I often wondered why I had chosen this as my favourite role and why I had volunteered for it. We often reached 47,000 feet towards the end of our sorties but our oxygen system was the same as the old Meteor fighters and was not cleared up to that height but we pressed on regardless. Although PR was a daytime activity we still had to maintain our night flying proficiency and one evening, after checking the weather forecast, the Boss, who was a man of few words, declared, "Everybody to Bristol and back!" As I was approaching the English east coast westbound at about 44,000 ft I saw an aircraft coming directly towards me but about 2,000 above me. It was Derek Webb on his way home. Either the navigation was good or we were both lost.

Even when we returned to base our troubles were not over. After more than 2 hours at a temperature of about minus 55 degrees Celsius the aircraft was cold soaked down to near that temperature. Over the winter period Germany was usually covered in a layer of moist cloud and as the cold aircraft entered it we were immediately cocooned in a thick layer of rime ice all over the aircraft surface including the cockpit canopy. We did not have enough fuel to fly around and let the aircraft warm up and so we found ourselves flying a radar controlled approach with nowhere to go if we missed the approach. Fortunately the radar controllers were in very good practice after the Berlin Airlift which had just finished and they gave us excellent service. The Meteor PR 10 was very stable on the approach and could be flown very accurately. Nothing could be seen out of the cockpit so we flew under radar control down to about 300 feet above the ground and then opened the canopy and shoved our heads over the side. Invariably a friendly looking runway or a forest of runway lights was just in front of us.

Good navigation was essential for our role and we had very few errors but one incident created quite a stir. One of our pilots had been on a long sortie down to the Austrian border and on his return leg of his flight he was over full cloud cover. His let down point for Gütersloh was in the Frankfurt area but he misread his navigation log and instead of setting the correct compass bearing he set the number of miles to run. This took him in a heading just north of east. He broke through the cloud base at about 3,000 feet and was surprised to find he was in a strange area. A quick run around his map and he realised he was near to the River Elbe in East Germany. He immediately pulled up into cloud again and began heading west. A little later he passed through a hole in the clouds and saw below him an airfield well sprinkled with MiG fighters. He disappeared again into cloud with a much increased heart beat rate and continued tip toeing home. Eventually he reached West Germany and scraped into RAF Wunsdorf with remarkably little fuel.

As a pleasant change from undiluted jet flying we had on our Station Flight a Tiger Moth trainer. Just over four years previously this had been the primary trainer for several of us and we were well versed in all the tricks of a tail dragging biplane such as swing on take-off, ground looping, dropping a wing or entering a spin. Now only a few years later none of the nose wheel only pilots would fly the Tiger Moth. We made it a challenge by insisting it was flown exactly as in the earlier flying schools but from an 800 yard grass strip in front of the control tower from where any untoward antics could be savoured.

Operating in the PR role made us very familiar with our operational area and we came to know all the well-known places. In the course of our tasks we collected photos of such house hold names as Belsen and Möhne Dam.

The Squadron had a Photo of the Month competition and the entries were always interesting. It was amazing how many amorous couples erroneously thought that if they drove miles into the depths of Luneberg Heath they could avoid the cameras of 541 Squadron. While returning one day through central Westphalia at low level to Laarbruch I noticed smoke beginning to escape from the roof of a typical farm building which had most of the farm buildings under one large roof with the animals at one end and the domestic accommodation at the other. I altered my course to investigate and found that a major fire was gaining ground. I climbed and called Bad Eilsen Air Traffic Control Centre and gave them the details. They passed it on to the local emergency services and after a while I saw the fire services approaching and was able to guide them, via Bad Eilsen, to the farm. Before I had to leave the area I flew over the house to take a photo and as I approached my switch on point the roof began to collapse and flames and sparks shot upwards. I had to fly through the smoke but it made a good photo.

Mass graves at Belsen Concentration Camp

Burning Wesphalian Farmhouse

Möhne Dam 1954

On another low level cross country flight I was crossing a large shallow lake known as Dümmer See and as I approached the far bank I noticed a group of girls bathing. I immediately circled round with the intention of obtaining another photo of the month. When the girls saw the aircraft returning they climbed out of the water on to the bank. I had an F24 side facing camera fitted but it was designed in 1925 and to obtain a good close up picture we had to fly low and slow. As I approached to take the photo I saw they the girls were all naked and realised this would make a much better picture. I was not satisfied with my first pass so I decided to go round for a better one. This time I was lower and slower and to add value to the picture the girls were waving. As I took the photo the aircraft began to shake and I realised it was on the point of stalling. I hit the throttles and by great good fortune normal flight was regained. During my return to base I pondered on how I would have explained to the Boss how the aircraft came to be resting in water nearly up to the cockpit rails while flying a low level cross country.

No 541 PR Squadron was a mobile unit and we had to be capable of flying our aircraft away and then pack all the Squadron equipment and vacate our base within 2 hours. We had all our transport including fuel bowsers, runway controllers' vans and a Mobile Field Photographic Unit for processing our films. This was a demanding task and we often practised it. Most of our heavy transports were old wartime Thornicroft lorries which had crash gear boxes but no self-starters. All new personnel including pilots had to be trained to handle the beasts but the worst problem was trying to get them started on a cold winter's morning. The starting handle would be inserted under the number plate into the engine and as one man could not swing it a rope was attached and as many as 4 or 5 people would heave on it again and again until the monster reluctantly fired. Soon after I arrived the Squadron Commander ordered a surprise evacuation. We taxied the aircraft to the far side of the airfield and then the packing of the lorries began. Each lorry had a crew of 2 nominated and they each had various items of the equipment allocated to them. When all was on board the convoy departed from the station and we had a practice convoy run along the autobahn to The Windmill YMCA Restaurant near Rheda. After the standard tea and a bun we then returned to base. While we were away the Squadron Commander had inspected every corner of our buildings and discovered a great amount of equipment left behind. After the dust settled orders were given to get rid of everything which was not on our inventory. Some of the lorries had been overloaded so we had to re-allocate loads and then ascertain how many vehicles were required and then demand extra vehicles to enable us to meet our task.

During a similar exercise later on I was sitting on the first floor of the The Windmill drinking coffee with a fellow officer when I heard footsteps coming up the stairs. Suddenly and without any reason I thought, "My God, it's Tony Goorney!" and sure enough within a few seconds the head and shoulders of my old friend who had been our Station Medical Officer and Meteor student at Full Sutton came into view. Tony did not appear surprised to see me either and a warm re-union over YMCA coffee and buns ensued. Tony and his friend were on a staff visit from UK and while travelling along the Autobahn had decided on the spur of the moment to drop in for a break.

It was well that we got our lorry problem sorted out because in July the Squadron was detached to RAF Buckeburg while our runway was repaired and resurfaced. I led the main convoy in a Landrover and was rather disconcerted on the downhill sections of the autobahn to find a high speed 3,000 gallon fuel bowser driven by our Flight Sergeant sitting close behind my rear bumper. The detachment was like a holiday. We left our Administration and Engineering Wings behind at Gütersloh. RAF Buckeburg, which did not have their own squadrons, welcomed us and No 79 with open arms. We flew our usual tasks but during the detachment I also acted as Adjutant to our OC Flying Wing, Wg Cdr John Blount. He had for his own use a Vampire F Mk 5 which was usually parked outside his office and if it was free I was able to use the Kiddie Car.

Two new pilots arrived on No 79 Sqn and as their QFI was away I was asked to give them dual checks before they were released on the unsuspecting German population. The first check was uneventful but the second one aged me a few years. Immediately after take-off while still very low I pulled off the fuel cock to the port engine to give the pilot a practice engine failure after take-off. I was ready to push on the right rudder pedal if he did not react quickly enough but he surprised me by pushing hard on the left pedal. The aircraft began to roll hard to the left and I could not overcome his mistake because my right leg was forced back and I could not generate enough strength to overcome him. While shouting that I had control I decided that the only way to save the day was to complete the roll to the left. By much stirring on the control column I was able to make a lifesaving but very ugly roll and by the time we regained level flight he had stopped pushing on the wrong pedal. A vivid memory was the sight ahead of us of Buckeburg Schloss rotating in the centre of the roll. This had happened to me before while I was instructing at Full Sutton but I certainly wasn't keen to try another one.

The Command Headquarters was based at RAF Bad Eilsen and Buckeburg was the nearest airfield. The AOC in C's Devon aircraft was stationed with us and that gave me the opportunity to fly with his pilot on his training sorties. One day I was Orderly Officer and I had to go to our airman's quarters at Obernkirchen, about 5 miles away on the other side of the Autobahn. I phoned for some transport and was told that the only vehicle available was a Thornycroft lorry which I accepted. The lorry duly arrived driven by a very young airman. Soon after leaving the Squadron I noticed he was still driving in first gear and I asked why. He shamefully admitted that he had not been trained on crash gear boxes and couldn't change gear. We swapped seats and on the journey I taught him the art of double declutching and on the return journey he made a good fist of the task. Life was always interesting.

A fine diversion at Buckeburg was a visit to the Officers' Club which was situated in a wing of Buckeburg Schloss, the home of the Prince of Schaumburg Lippe. The Schloss was a beautiful building and we enjoyed the club immensely. On Sundays we would go to the Club for a curry lunch and if the weather was good we would walk back along the railway line to the Mess.

I had applied to sit my Promotion Examination for Flight Lieutenant but all my relevant books were at Gütersloh and the Exam Centre was to be there too. I spent a lot of time driving along the autobahn in the evening while preparing for and then sitting the exam. About the same time I was ordered to visit Command HQ for an interview with the AOC in C. This would be the final step in my application for a Permanent Commission. While waiting in his outer office I saw several worried looking junior officers leaving. When my turn came I was ushered into the presence of Air Marshal Sir Harry Broadhurst who was often referred to as Black Harry. I waited while he continued looking down at his notes and then he fired a series of questions at me the answers to which were all in the notes before him. Eventually he bid me good day and he had not looked up at me once during the whole interview. I then knew why the previous victims had looked so worried. I was surprised when, sometime later, I was told I had been granted a Permanent Commission.

In September we returned to Gütersloh just in time for a 2nd ATAF exercise Battle Royal in which we worked with a USAF reconnaissance unit. Apart from the usual tasks I had a lot of fun flying John Mclaren of Flight magazine in our Meteor 7 while he took air to air photos of the various aircraft. He was a very experience photographer and guided me into many interesting positions. My next sortie was with a television cameraman who was taking video films and he was quite surprised that I could put him in so many good positions. Thank you, John Mclaren. I also did a good trade in exchanging flights in the front seat of our Meteor Mk 7 for the USAF pilots on condition that I could fly their RB 26 Invaders. We also had an excellent arrangement with the British Army tank regiment at Sennelager and we were able to barter rides in our Meteor Mk 7 for chances to drive their Main Battle Tanks on their practice range.

Meteor T Mk 7

One evening all the pilots were invited to a birthday party in Gütersloh town and while the party was in full session the sister of the birthday girl returned home and joined the party. Who can resist a lovely, tall, blond, elegant girl? I certainly could not and Marlies very quickly removed me from the eligible bachelor's list. Soon afterwards we drove to Lippstadt for a very enjoyable evening at a restaurant with a very good band but on the return journey to Gütersloh my car stopped. The night finished with a lift in a huge lorry with trailer into the centre of town. Marlies was just in time to change and get to work and I returned to the airfield on a bus with a collection of batwomen who found the situation intriguing.

For about a year we had been taking photos of the new airfield which was being built at RAF Laarbruch on the Dutch border near to Wesel and we knew that it would be the new base for the RAF Germany reconnaissance squadrons. Now 541 and 79 Sqns were being joined by No 69 Squadron with Canberra PR Mk 3s and later by the Dutch No 304 Sqn with their RF84 Thunderflashes. On 28th October No 541 Sqn was detailed to be the first unit to move into Laarbruch. Our Sqn Cdr was away and the Sqn was in the hands of OC B Flight. I was OC A Flight at the time with the splendid rank of Flying Officer. During the briefing for the flight to Laarbruch OC B Flt stipulated that his flight of 4 aircraft would take off first and A Flt's first 4 aircraft were not to take off until 10 minutes after they had departed. At the appointed time my flight watched them take off and climb sedately to the west. After waiting exactly 10 minutes we began our take off and kept heading west at full throttle until we reached the maximum speed with wing tanks fitted. We thundered over the Rhein at low level and Laarbruch was soon dead ahead. The flight went into echelon starboard and we roared down the runway at very low level and pulled up to break into the circuit for a tight circuit and a landing in quick succession. B Flt was nowhere in sight. We were directed to our new hangar in the south west corner of the airfield and found the Station Commander, the Burgomaster of Weeze and the station senior officers waiting for us with Champagne. Eventually B Flt arrived and demanded their share of the bubbly while we were bundled into the station's Avro Anson to return to Gütersloh to collect another four aircraft. On 1st November I led another 4 ship formation into Laarbruch and we were all home and dry.

After a series of sector recce flights the PR business was resumed as normal. Apart from as much flying as I could crowd into a day I spent my weekends driving for a couple of hours back to Gütersloh to see Marlies and this is when I discovered how cold a pre-war car could be. Germany had a heavy fall of snow which froze and traffic on the autobahn packed it into a drivable surface and it remained so for several weeks. The main problem, apart from the freezing cold, was recognising the edges of the road. Great care was needed. At the beginning of December I broke my right ankle and was fitted with a plaster cast with a wooden block in the base to prevent rough surfaces wearing the base of the plaster away. I was not allowed to fly but it did not stop my weekend drives to Gütersloh. The only problem was taking the wooden block off the accelerator and trying to hit the brake pedal with it. During this time I also developed an iritis of my left eye. It was an inflammation inside the eyeball which the doctors knew was caused by an allergy. I was packed off for a holiday in the RAF Hospital at Wegberg while a series of tests were made to identify the allergy. Atropine was put in the problem eye to dilate the pupil fully and I had to wear an eye patch over my left eye to protect it from glare. The good right eye was dosed with a soothing lotion to ease the strain. One morning a keen game of cards was taking place in the lounge when a junior nurse came to drag me off for my periodic treatment but I had a promising hand of cards and pleaded for a stay of execution. As soon as I had lost the hand I cavorted down the corridor to the treatment room where the bonny girl awaited me. I sat in a chair, lifted my eye patch and put my head back while the nurse sloshed atropine into one eye and lotion into the other. Within a minute I was on my way back to the dissolute life. Within minutes of resuming play I found that I could no longer identify my cards. The distracted nurse had put the drops into the wrong eyes. As my right eye also dilated I lost all ability to focus and I felt as if I was looking through a heavily frosted window. My ward mates made great play out of the situation and I was immediately equipped with a white stick to tap my way around the ward. Fortunately they could not find a guide dog.

I was soon out of hospital although the type of allergy had not been identified but I was still wearing the eye patch. Next time I arrived at Marlies' home with my leg in plaster and the eye patch Marlies' mother began to wonder if I was a pilot or Long John Silver. All I needed was a parrot.

541 Squadron Pilots 1955

L-r Mike Somervell, Jim Campbell, Geoff Legget, Toby Meyer, Geoff Stafford, Dennie Beard, David Pownell, David McCoy, David Goodsir, BA, Mike Sander, Ron Waugh, Tom Benson, Brian Dove-Dixon and Lou Swailes, squatting

In April a new Squadron Commander was posted in. Sqn Ldr Howard Kelsey was a small, lively officer with a sharp mind and a distinguished war record. He had won his DSO and two DFCs while flying Mosquitos on night intruder patrols over Germany. He probably knew Germany better by night than he did by day. Almost at the same time as his arrival the Squadron received an invitation from the Netherlands government to take part in a flypast over The Hague on 29th April. The fly past was designed to commemorate the dropping of food over Holland by Bomber Command in April 1945 when the people were desperately short of food. A squadron of Lincoln bombers from Upwood was invited to make three passes over the city centre and drop tulip petals. Our Squadron was in great favour in Holland for flying every day in very bad weather during the catastrophic winter of 1951/52 to keep a watch on the dykes that were under great threat during the exceptional high tides and floods. As a show of gratitude we were invited to fly past the Lincolns on the inland side as they were dropping the tulip petals and repeat it for all three runs. As we would have only one rehearsal with the Lincolns as they flew in from Upwood it would be very difficult to co-ordinate. The Boss was new on the Squadron but he wished to lead Operation Tulip Drop so he decided to lead in our Meteor Mk 7 while I tried to maintain reasonable order from the rear seat. I had to phone Upwood to ascertain such details as time over target, the planned route, cruising speed, turning radius and time to turn 180 degrees. They did not even know that we were also taking part in the fly past but I managed to get enough information to plan a rehearsal on the day before the real thing. On the rehearsal day we took off with a nine aircraft formation from Laarbruch and managed to contact the Lincoln formation while it was still over the North Sea. They were hopelessly late but we were committed to our flight. We passed over the Town Hall on the agreed time and then made our turn for the second fly past. We met the Lincolns coming in the opposite direction and did not see them again. Both Squadrons landed at Valkenburg for a wash up before we returned to Laarbruch. Unfortunately our Dutch hosts had arranged a party for us which interfered with our planned debriefing. The Lincoln Sqn Cdr was having a hell of a good time and we could get nothing out of him. Fortunately his navigation leader was taking things a little more seriously and we were able to make the most important plans. The problem of co-ordinating the flights of two squadrons with one flying twice as fast as the other was complicated and did not give us much confidence.

We returned to Laarbruch muttering all kinds of oaths against Lincoln crews and I spent the evening trying to work out a flight plan for us which could be altered as much as possible to fit in with the Lincolns' vague wanderings. Next day we returned along our route and were able to contact the Lincolns as they took off from Valkenburg. They were late again but we were able to adjust our flight path and as we swept over the Town Hall the Lincolns were dropping their tulip petals. During the two 180 degree turns I was able to check with their navigation leader and we managed to pass inland from the Lincolns as they were showering The Hague with tulips. We returned to Laarbruch leaving the Lincoln squadron to enjoy another party. I slept that night like a log. Soon afterwards our pilots received handmade Delft plaques from the Queen of the Netherlands to commemorate our operations during the floods and our participation in the fly past. As I was not flying as a pilot I did not get one!

In between exercises I managed to get married to Marlies. Just to make sure we did a good job of it we had two weddings. The first, in the morning, was a German ceremony at the old Gütersloh Rathaus, a lovely old building which has since been demolished. I thought I was in the unique situation whereby Marlies was married to me but I was not married to her. However Marlies kept a close eye on me until, in the afternoon, we had our second wedding, at the lovely old Apostle Church in the centre of the town. The ceremony was performed by our Padre from Laarbruch and then all was ship shape and Bristol fashion. After a honeymoon at the Winterberg mountain resort we returned to Laarbruch.

Before I left I had been assured that 23 married quarters were standing empty and I could take my pick. When we returned I reported to the Station Adjutant, who controlled quarters, to arrange my take over. He told me there had been a slight complication. In my absence an RAF Regiment Wing with two Squadrons had been posted in and I was now 12th on the waiting list. Public accommodation was very scarce in those days and we were rescued by Squadron members letting us live in their houses while they were on summer leave. This involved moving every few days.

Gütersloh Alte Apostel Kirche

The second wedding

The decision was made that the newly built RAF Goch would not be used as a Group HQ and our Station Commander took over the AOC's house. We moved in to his old house at Laarbruch with three other families and shared it until we were allocated a new Married Quarter at Goch. Marlies began to wonder what kind of mad house she had joined. I didn't have a good answer to that question.

No 304 Sqn of the RNAF had settled in quite well with their RF84 Thunderflash aircraft and one day we heard that the Squadron Commander was going to fly initial tests using 4 small rockets attached to the rear fuselage to reduce the take-off distance. Such events were rare on an operational station and we all turned out to watch the fun. When all was set up the take-off began and after a short while the rockets were fired. We all expected to see the aircraft disappear into the distance at high speed in a shower of flame and smoke but instead the nose of the aircraft rose high off the runway and created so much drag that the aircraft ceases to accelerate. After travelling half the length of the runway at a steady speed the attempt was abandoned and we never heard of the project again.

Marlies at Winterberg

I was getting used to being a Flight Commander by this time and one morning I sent one of our newly arrived pilots to fly a quite straight forward task on the east coast of Schleswig Holstein. I went over the sortie with him and off he went. When he returned he confessed that he could not find the target. This was not a good start for a PR pilot so I checked his flight plan with him and all seemed in order so I sent him back for another go. When he came back and reported another failure I showed a rare arrogance and muttering, "I suppose I will have to do it myself," grabbed my helmet and stomped out of the office. In due course I arrived over the target and, guess what? I couldn't find it. I made a thorough search for it but nothing like a radar station was in the area. As I left the area wondering how I was going to escape paying for my arrogance I had a new idea and flew exactly 60 miles south of the target position we had been given and to my intense relief there was a nice new radar station. The target position was wrong by 1 degree of latitude. I always thought someone was looking after me but he was working hard that day.

A rare photo of 4 PR10s in formation

At last we managed to get rid of our older vehicles and instead of the ancient Thornicrofts NATO provided us with modern Magirus Deutz lorries and a new range of German fuel bowsers, fire engines, cranes, runway control caravans, etc. We were proud of our new fleet and when the local town of Weeze organised a Grand Carnival we were happy to take part and show off our new toys. At the height of the entertainment an old aircraft was set on fire in front of the crowd and with sirens sounding and bell ringing a brand new fire engine passed behind the spectators at high speed and at the end of crowd turned hard left to approach the burning aircraft. Unfortunately the speed had been slightly misjudged and the fire engine heeled to the right and slowly toppled on to its side. We then had the opportunity to demonstrate our new crane.

During the summer we sharpened our skills by taking part in various NATO exercises. In July our flight moved lock, stock and barrel to the south side of RAF Wildenrath's runway for Exercise Carte Blanche and we were not allowed onto the north side. We operated from temporary buildings and sited our tented Mess in the woods about 3 miles away. Our Sgt Chef was in his element. He usually supervised his meals in a red, silk dressing gown and he produced lovely sauces to accompany his delicious meals. Our Photographic unit was in another wood 3 miles away in another direction. This was a time when NATO was prepared for an attack from the East and we planned to avoid being completely wiped out in a pre-emptive strike. I was still Flight Commander as a Fg Off and was king of all I surveyed. In this exercise the northern air forces in Europe faced south and fought against the USAF and Canadian Air forces. This was good for us because the USAF Sabre fighters were slightly better than the Russian MiG 15s which were deployed against us over the Iron Curtain. We were pleased to discover that by flying to our limits we could avoid interception.

I was waiting one morning for one of our pilots to return before I went to lunch. I heard the aircraft taxi into its dispersal but the pilot took a long time to come into the operations room. I decided to walk out to the dispersal and I climbed the blast wall which protected the dispersal pan. Down below the pilot was on his knees hammering part of his aircraft with a stone beating it back into shape. I decided to retreat and wait until the pilot came in to de-brief. I asked if he had completed his task and if the aircraft was serviceable and he assured me that he had got the target and the aircraft was OK. After he left to go to lunch I collected our Flt Sgt and went to survey the scene. The pilot, while turning inside the pan, had scraped his wing tip along the revetment wall. He knew all aircraft were needed to meet our tasks so he unscrewed the wing tip with a coin and then used a round cobble stone to beat it back into shape. Chiefy and I agreed he had done a good job and a coat of paint could wait till later. PR pilots were noted for their resourcefulness.

My only exciting moment was when I was intercepted by 2 USAF Sabres while on a low level task in the hills of the US Sector. I dived into a deep and winding valley and flew as low as I could while hauling my faithful old Charlie round the tight bends of the valley. The Sabres tried diving into the valley behind me but by the time they were getting close I was away round another bend. Fortunately I was getting nearer home and they were flying away from their base and eventually they had to break off their attacks just before I arrived out of the valley into flatter countryside.

In September came Exercise Beware when we acted as attackers against England to test the UK air defences. The Hunter was the newest fighter in the RAF and again we found that we could avoid them. After a few days we were asked to limit our height to 45,000 feet to give them a more realistic target. This gave a boost to our confidence. During the exercise I flew an endurance test and logged a flight of 3 hours and 15 minutes which is the longest I know of in a standard Meteor aircraft.

Immediately after Beware came Exercise Foxpaw and we again operated against the UK. One of my tasks was to find a Russian fleet which was carrying the USSR President to Portsmouth for a Summit Meeting. They were in the north part of the great expanse of the North Sea but the estimated position I was given was very good and I found them in excellent weather conditions and I collected some very rare high level photos of a major Russian fleet.

This period was one of the coldest periods of The Cold War and the political situation was very tense with our V Bombers standing at readiness on their bases, armed with their nuclear weapons, ready for immediate reaction to an attack. This was brought home to me when the Boss came alongside me while I was walking across the hangar and told me I was to go to a briefing in a couple of days' time and I was to talk about it to no-one. The briefing was given by two men in civilian clothes in a secure room and I was given a special target. I was left to prepare the flight myself without restriction. I chose my aeroplane, cameras, maximum fuel and time. Occasionally the Boss would quietly ask if everything was going well and I am sure he did not know my target. Before I departed on the sortie I had to authorise the flight myself and use a typical task number. When I returned to base I was debriefed by one of the men in civilian clothes and a stranger. Normally all our films were processed, printed and plotted by our own photographic unit but this time the films were taken away by the visitors and I never saw or heard of them again. I only realised much later that if anything had gone wrong the RAF could have denied all knowledge of the sortie. The only evidence was my signature in the authorisation book. Because of the secrecy I do not know if any other pilots were involved in these missions but if so it could only have been one of the other three officers who were able to authorise flights.

Even though we were based well inland we still had to perform our periodical dinghy drills and one sunny morning our Sergeant Admin drove a group of our pilots down to the station swimming pool for a practice. I sat in the front with him and as we arrived near the pool he was obviously distracted and when I asked him about his problem he pointed to an attractive girl lying on the grass and reading a book and said "Cor, look at her. She's new". This gave me the chance to tell him, "Yes, Sergeant, she's my wife".

Marlies

In October 1955 Laarbruch was visited by CFS Examining Wing, known as the Trappers. Their task was to fly with as many pilots as possible to assess their performance and ensure that the standard was as high as possible. We went through a phase of reading up our Pilot's Notes and any other relevant books and I did a few back seat landings in the Meteor T Mk7 in case I should be checked as an instructor. The team leader visited the Squadron to arrange the test programme and the Boss told me I would not be on the roster. On the first day of the Squadron programme one of our fairly new Fg Offs was put in to bat but he must have been very nervous and he did not put up his usual sound performance. Later in the day the Boss came round and told me that all had been changed, which was normal RAF practice, and that I would be on the program next day. Flt Lt Tommy Atkins was our Trapper and he told me he flew plenty of general handling flights but he would like to fly a typical low level navigation sortie. I let him choose the turning points and as we had been talking the previous evening about the marvellous party we had at the Quellental Hotel when Denny Beard returned he suggested that I should show him that. I threw a few other suggestions at him and he chose the marshalling yards at Hamm which had figured in news bulletins so often during the war. As they covered a big area

I proposed we should take the signal box as our target. I briefed him carefully and prepared a very detailed map with more information than he could possibly use. As an instructor I put him in the front seat of the T Mk7 and settled into the back. The weather was good and we expected a good flight. I flew as accurately as possible and I had the advantage that we were heading from our present base towards our recent base at Gütersloh and I knew the area very well. I gave him a detailed account of various features as we roared past them and plenty of small heading corrections to keep us near to our required track. Little did Tommy realise that the Quellental Hotel sits on the side of the Teuterberger Wald range of hills and that I would be able to spot it from a good distance. As we approached the target I warned him to look ahead and then put the right wing down so that he could have a good look at the hotel as we passed directly overhead. The next leg to Hamm was over the very flat Westphalian countryside but I kept him plied with information on expected villages, railways lines and roads etc. I pointed out several features out on either side of our track to divert Tommy from looking ahead too much and realising as we approached Hamm that the signal box was the highest building in the area. Needless to say we passed right overhead and set course back to Laarbruch. Any good pilot should know his way home in any weather and on a good day it was a piece of cake. After a back seat single engine landing we were soon back in the coffee bar. He had enjoyed his ride, I got an exceptional rating and the Squadron's reputation was saved.

Before the Trappers left Laarbruch I was asked if I had ever thought of applying for the Empire Test Pilots Course at Farnborough and I confessed I did not think I was ready for it yet. I was having too much fun on the Squadron and was only half way through my tour. After a bit of arm twisting someone phoned Farnborough and my application was submitted. I was not too worried about it because I did not think I stood a chance. Soon afterwards I was notified that I would be on the next ETPS course at Farnborough.

When I joined the Squadron all our aircraft were camouflaged with grey and green upper surfaces and PR blue underneath but a single silver aircraft WH181 was always tucked away at the back of the hangar. I was told it was a night trials aircraft but no one seemed to know anything about it. When we moved to Laarbruch it accompanied us and it resumed its place in the corner. When Howard Kelsey arrived he wanted to know what was supposed to happen to this poor lonely aircraft. Some of the longer serving squadron members believed it had been sent from Boscombe Down for night photographic trials. Apparently the previous CO wanted nothing to do with it and we could find no documentation to go with the aircraft. Howard Kelsey regarded this as a challenge and as he knew I had an electronic engineering background he gave me a clear briefing, "Get it working". I usually spent a lot of my time poking around the inside of our aircraft so I put on my dust coat and disappeared into the rear fuselage of WB181 which became known as Flash Harry. It had been fitted with a prototype night camera which later became the Type F97. One of the under wing fuel tanks had been cut in half horizontally and 66 dischargers for 1½ inch photo flash cartridges had been fitted in the bottom half of the tank. The two halves were fitted together with 36 Dzus fasteners. A scout around the squadron revealed several boxes of 1¼ inch cartridges with sleeves to adapt them to the dischargers and a provisional copy of an Air Publication for the F97 camera which had a typical aircraft wiring diagram. After much crawling around inside Flash Harry I discovered that its wiring did not correspond to the book and the only way to get it working would be to fit a blank plug to one of the camera output sockets and short out two pairs of pins. This seemed to be a good time to visit Boscombe Down to talk to them.

I flew over in the Station Prentice and at last found someone who remembered Flash Harry. When I explained the problem he scratched his head and then recalled that there had been such a shorted out blanking plug delivered with the aircraft. Back at Laarbruch I made and fitted the required plug and, Heigh Ho, the camera banged away quite happily. The next step was to load some cartridges and find out if it would fire them. The technical staff was reluctant to tackle this potentially dangerous task on unfamiliar equipment without specific authorisation so I did the dirty work myself. The circuits were checked, the camera tested and cartridges loaded in the dischargers. The bottom half of the wing tank containing the dischargers was lifted by a team of men with ropes passed under the tank rather like a burial party hauling up a coffin rather than lowering it while I struggled to fix the 36 Dzus fasteners.

On board the Percival Prentice T Mk 1

When all was ready for the great baptism on 23rd August 1955 Fg Off Mike Somervell flew Flash Harry and I formated on him to obtain a grandstand view of the firework display. Over the main runway Mike switched on and two cartridges were discharged before the fickle finger of fate intervened and the camera stopped. The problem could be either the camera or the cartridges so I decided to check the cartridges first. I found a short length of steel scaffold tubing which had an inside diameter of 1¼ inches and thus made an ideal breech for the cartridge. A plug from a disused battery trolley could be made to fit on the end of the tube so I modified the plug to have one central contact instead of the usual two and Fg Off Dicky Dyer cut a thread on the outside of the tube with a triangular file which was a work of art. A cartridge could be loaded into the tube and our home made breech block screwed on the end and we had a test device. We set it up facing into the remains of an old Siegfried Line bunker which was just off the end of the runway and connected a battery trolley to supply the firing current. The Boss fired the first cartridge, the Flight Commander the second and I had a go with the third. We had three bird's eye views of photo flashes exploding in the bunker. Three bulls eyes.

While mulling over possible causes of the misfires I discovered that the 1½ inch cartridges for which the camera was designed were a British product but the 1¼ inch cartridges which we had were American. I flew down to the main USAF reconnaissance base at Spangdahlem to have a chat with their experts. I discovered that their cartridges needed a 10 ampere firing current which was greater than the British one. I did not want to get involved with modifying the aircraft more than necessary but I found that by wiring a landing light bulb in parallel with an existing resistor it would give a suitable increase in firing current. Flash Harry was prepared again on 25th August and off we went. This time all went well and a stream of cartridges were discharged until Murphy struck again and a fuse blew. Obviously the firing current was now too high. This time I found a fuselage interior light bulb which I could wire in series in the circuit and reduce the current slightly. On 8th September we flew another test flight and Flash Harry banged away quite happily but I never did discover if the bulbs lit up every time a cartridge was fired. We tested it at night and found that it was taking good photographs. This ended the first part of the trials. The next phase would be low level night navigation and photography but before I could start on this my posting to ETPS came through and the Boss asked me to write up all the work that had been done in minute detail so that the trials could continue and the aircraft be restored to its original state before being returned to Boscombe Down. My detailed notes in all their gory details were intended to be used only by our own people but soon after I left the Squadron Boscombe Down asked for a report on the trials. To save time and energy my successor topped and tailed my notes to make them into a report and sent them to Boscombe. I would love to know what their reaction was and if I would have been flayed alive. I will never forget Flash Harry.

As we settled in at Laarbruch some of the pilots looked for cheap means of transport to get around the large airfield and they quickly discovered that there were several pre-war small two stroke motor cycles available which the local population would not be seen dead on. They made ideal runabouts but one good thing leads to another and very soon the owners realised that a road and part of the taxi way around our hangar made a very good mini racing circuit. The hangar was tucked away in the south west corner of the airfield and a long way from the main camp buildings. Weekend race meetings became regular features of squadron life and families appeared with refreshments to cheer on their local heroes. The track was fiendishly difficult and some exciting duals were fought out. By great good fortune no bones were broken but it was not from lack of opportunity.

The Officers Mess at Laarbruch was new and rather plain, a typical NATO design, and we had to spend a lot of effort to transform it into a suitable location for our first Winter Ball. A very lively and enjoyable evening was our reward but late in the evening Marlies achieved immortal fame throughout the RAF. David Goodsir was one of our most reliable pilots and our exceptional drinker. He could be found every evening occupying his usual position at the end of the bar quietly slurping his ale. No one was sure of his intake but if he was asked if would like another pint and he said he would like a gin in his beer we knew he had downed about ten pints. He was very amiable and was the butt for many jokes. If this became intolerable he would remove his pipe from his mouth and utter some cutting remark such as "Drop dead, Ashley", replace his pipe and resume drinking. Late at night during the Ball he was obviously wrestling with a major problem but at last he removed his pipe and said the memorable words, "Marlies, would you like to dance?" A hush descended on the assembled multitude as David escorted Marlies to the dance floor and proceeded to dance the only Farmer's Polka ever seen in an RAF Mess. This never happened again and Marlies still cherishes the memory.

We were really beginning to settle in to Laarbruch when news was received that we and 79 were to move at the beginning of November to RAF Wunsdorf. Laarbruch was too far from the East German border and Wunsdorf was one of the airfields which were within spitting distance. The old routine was adopted of continuing to fly our tasks while trying to prepare for the move but this time I also had a wife to include in the plans. When moving day came I led the main convoy in my car with Marlies as passenger. She felt she was certainly one of the Squadron and our airman also enjoyed the novel experience. It was a long journey from the western to the eastern border of Germany and we were glad when we reached Wunsdorf. The Squadron equipment was soon unpacked and, as many times before, we were almost immediately operational again.

Officers Married Quarters for junior officers were always scarce and Marlies and I, with three other families from the Squadron, moved into a building in Wunsdorf town which had been converted into a hostel. We had our own bed and bathrooms but shared a lounge and dining room with our friends. Marlies and I knew that we would be leaving for Farnborough in early January so this was a very satisfactory arrangement.

Flying continued as usual but we had a new recreational facility to enjoy. RAF Wunsdorf used an ex-sailing club on the shores of Steinhuder Lake as an Officers Club. It was known as the Chequers Club and when an officer visited for the first time the small end of his tie was cut off and nailed to the wall. He was then a fully paid up member. Because 79 Squadron spent most of their time roaring around Germany at low level all their ties were nailed along the skirting boards. 541 Squadron ties in accordance with our motto, Alone Above All, were nailed into the highest part of the eves of the roof and a black velvet bow from Marlies' petticoat was included among them. I wonder if they are still there.

Christmas and New Year flashed by and on 4th January 1956 I flew the last sortie of my tour and it was spent converting Mike Somervell to the Prentice with a good measure of aerobatics thrown in. Within a few days Marlies and I were on the way to a freezing cold Farnborough. I was disappointed to leave the squadron and we would have loved another year on 541 Squadron.

At this time the RAF had a policy of allowing pilots on non-operational tours to return to their old squadrons to retain their operational status. In August 1956 during the summer break at ETPS I applied to return to 541 Squadron which was still at Wunsdorf. We stayed with Mike and Kay Somervell in their Married Quarter and it felt as if we had never been away. I managed to fly six operational tasks in my old friend VW376 "Charlie" and the detachment was all too short. Our daughter Jenni was born in May 1957 and I was seriously tempted to have "Made in Germany" tattooed on her backside.

CHAPTER 10
Empire Test Pilots School, RAE Farnborough

ARRIVING at Farnborough in January 1956 was like travelling on a pilgrimage to the RAF pilots' Mecca. Cody's tree, the Black Sheds and the old Officers' Mess still stood there and Laffens Plain disappeared into the winter haze. I was happy to absorb the atmosphere but Marlies was not impressed with the very cold damp air and general desolation. It was her first visit to England and the prospects were not good. No arrangements for our arrival had been made by the RAF but my old friend Tony Goorney, who was back at the Institute of Aviation Medicine, had booked us into the Ridgemont Hotel, just over the road from the Royal Aircraft Establishment (RAE) Officers Mess.

The reception area was empty when we sought shelter from the cold evening air but soon a large female dragon appeared and imperiously demanded, "Yes?" When we explained we had a booking and asked for our key we were told that they had no keys. We were shown a room with walls which closely framed a double bed and a few pieces of furniture. The centre of attention was the small single bar gas fire and huge meter which was designed to gobble up one shilling pieces. During the evening I collected as many shillings as possible and when we returned to the freezing room I began feeding the fire at about 20 minute intervals. I remembered to save a couple for the morning. Marlies was not impressed by England.

Newly married junior officers found themselves at the bottom of the waiting list for married quarters and the fact that Farnborough, which came under the Ministry of Supply, had very few service houses meant that we had to fend for ourselves. Our first task in England was to search or an affordable house within commuting distance of RAE. At last we found a small bungalow in Farnham and put our experience in the Ridgemont behind us. We quickly settled in and Marlies knocked it into a comfortable little nest. I had been advised by ETPS to brush up my calculus before starting the course but as my accelerated school education had only briefly touched calculus I had to give myself a quick do it yourself course which kept me out of mischief until No 15 Course assembled.

No 15 Course Empire Test Pilots School

ETPS was only 12 years old and flying had changed and continued to change every year. As a result the course content and method of teaching was continuously in flux. We all learned together. We had 32 members on the course but only 12 were RAF. 4 were Royal Navy, 3 Canadian Air Force and 1 Canadian Navy, 2 each from the Italian and Indian Air Forces plus another 2 from the United States Navy. The motley crew was completed by single members of the French, Belgium, Swedish and US Air Forces. The glue which held this group together was a love of flying and a rare amount of expertise was gathered together ready to begin a unique year.

We were fortunate to have a separate Test Pilots School Officers Mess in the form of a pleasant single story building immediately over the road from the Queens Hotel and in the 12 years since ETPS was founded both of these locations had become watering holes for the UK test flying community. The lecture hall was next to the Mess and the flying offices and hangar were a small walk past the Institute of Aviation Medicine (IAM) and down the hill towards Laffans Plain.

Empire Test Pilots School Mess

The first few weeks were devoted to the lecture hall where lectures on performance and stability were dominant but I had an interruption on 15th February when the Chief Test Flying Instructor called at our house in the evening and told me my mother was desperately ill in Louth hospital. He had arranged for a Piston Provost aircraft to be ready for me in the morning and as I had not seen one before he brought a copy of the Pilots Notes for me to read overnight. My first flight at Farnborough was typical of many subsequent flights with a new kind of aircraft in one hand and the instruction book in the other. On later flights I came to love the little Piston Provost but the task on 16th February was to get to RAF Manby with all due haste. At Manby I was quickly bundled off to Louth hospital to visit my mother. I was told she was in the very late stages of breast cancer and I spent as much time as possible with her before I had reluctantly to begin my journey back to Farnborough. She seemed much brighter when I left and I was told next day that she had rallied and after a few more days she returned home. Little did I realise that this was the last time I would see my Mother. When I returned to RAF Manby the airmen were not accustomed to Farnborough habits and they almost had fits when they noticed me trying to find various bits and pieces of the aircraft with the help of Pilots Notes and even more so when I started up and taxied out. By this time the book had been put away.

Back in the lecture hall the sessions were filled with lectures, discussions and blackboards filled with flute music about performance, stability, flutter, etc. These subjects played such a large and vital part of experimental flying before power operated controls became wide spread. The UK then had a score or more of aircraft manufacturers and nearly all were involved in some kind of experimental work. Our theoretical lectures were laced with talks by visiting test pilots and we were kept up to date with latest developments. Jimmy Laing was our Chief Ground Instructor and he was a very capable instructor with a wealth of pertinent information.

Towards the end of February we cavorted down the hill to our hangar to meet the collection of aircraft which had been prepared for our course. The remainder of February was devoted to familiarisation with the aircraft and we helped each other to fill in gaps in our experience. As I was fairly well up to date with the jet aircraft I elected to have a look at our helicopters. The RAF had only a few helicopters in 1956 and the Hiller, Dragonfly and Sycamore all had manual controls without auto-stabilisers. My first attempts at this completely unnatural method of flying were similar to a one armed paper hanger. Every movement of one control required compensating movements of all the other controls and I could not decide if I was flying the contraption or if it was flying me. Our Army helicopter pilot and the 2 RN pilots soon licked me into shape and I discovered that one of them knew almost every nudist camp in central southern England. The open spaces made good sites for practising engine off approaches.

Vampire F Mk 3

The Devon, Chipmunk and Varsity followed in quick succession and, for old times' sake, a work out in the Meteor Mk 8 kept my blood circulating. A Canberra sortie was wedged in between a Vampire and the Piston Provost.

Then the fun had to stop and we had to earn a living again. I very quickly discovered that much of test flying was rather tedious and repetitious in comparison with squadron flying. Air thermometer calibration, fuel consumption, partial climbs and accelerated levels were all straight forward but had to be measured at many different speeds or heights and care taken to obtain accurate results which were written down on our knee pads. On the ground the results had to be converted to the International Standard Atmosphere to ensure that results from different conditions could be compared with accuracy. This meant that for every hour flown at least 2 hours on the ground were devoted to pushing my slide rule back and forth like a fiddler. I had tasted operational flying and I wanted to go back. The only consolation was the range of different aircraft at our disposal. That was the part I liked. We had very little help from our tutors and they had a splendid time with their test pilot friends. Vast improvements in aircraft performance had been made since ETPS was formed and we were finding our own way through the jungle. It made a big contrast with Jimmy Laing and his instructors who made a great job in interpreting mathematical flute music into common sense

My old friend Tony Goorney was back again at IAM and was working on the early generation of protective helmets. An essential requirement for these prototypes was the ability to be worn for several hours without discomfort. I often took my results up to Tony's office, pulled on his latest instrument of torture and settled down to reduce my latest test results. All would go well for an hour or so and then pressure spots would be felt around my head which would slowly increase in intensity until I had to plead for it to be dragged off. Tony would then begin modifications and in due course the next session would be due. The time spent in reducing my results were put to good use. Tony was always short of time but several years later I was happily wearing the production version of his helmets.

One evening when I arrived home I told Marlies that I thought I had a fever so she promptly gave me some tablets and bundled me off to bed. Next morning I dragged myself to work feeling like death warmed up but when I paid a visit to the toilet I noticed that my urine was brick red. I then felt much worse. I went to see our Adjutant, old Whatty Whatmough, who had seen much overseas service before the war. He sucked his pencil and solemnly declared that I had jaundice. Transport was arranged to Aldershot Military Hospital and the sad tale was told to very high priced help. Of course a specimen was required and produced. I was left in the corridor and soon another specimen was requested. Heads began to appear out of the doors to survey the patient. Another specimen was asked for but I had to seek refreshments to keep the hospital in business. All the while I was beginning to feel near to death. At last they admitted defeat and asked me to return the next day. I made my way home and sadly told Marlies of my day's misery expecting some form of sympathy but she brightly replied, "Oh that, I forgot to tell you that the German tablet I gave you last night always does that!" After it had sunk in I immediately felt much better. Next morning I waltzed into work and after letting Aldershot Military Hospital off the hook the course was resumed as usual.

In the meantime our social life was coming to the simmer. Marlies laid on a party and introduced sundry Canadians, Australians, Americans, etc to the German Bowle which consisted of fruit such as diced pineapple which had been fermented in a bottle of Champagne and when ripe diluted with 1 or 2 bottles of white wine. The concoction was eagerly lapped up but many stalwart drinkers decided to eat copious amounts of the alcohol laden pineapple. They were happily carolling on their way home but the lecture room on the following morning was rather subdued.

In among the routine test exercises more new types of aircraft were steadily collected. In one week I went over to Instrument Flight of RAE to help a test flight in a hybrid Meteor which seemed to have been cobbled together from bits and pieces of several marks of Meteor. They had even managed to mount an FR 9 nose upside down. Then it was back to ETPS to make my first acquaintance with the Gannet T Mk 2, the Hunter Mk 4, the Seahawk Mk 1 and the Pembroke.

The Gannet was an extraordinary flying machine. The first problem was to climb into the cockpit. The built in steps were found round the other side of the fuselage. Two retractable steps led to a diamond of four footholds recessed into the fuselage side. If a pilot was heading for the second of three cockpits and began his climb with the wrong foot he would find that he could not knot his legs sufficiently to reach the cockpit. Back down on the ground again he then had to try to remember which foot he began with last time. When successfully tucked into his seat the next problem was to start the engines. The Gannet had two Mamba turbo prop engines joined by a gearbox which drove two contra-rotating propellers. The combination of engine, gear box and propellers required a lot of energy to rotate it up to idling speed for starting and large cartridges were provided to do the trick. However on colder days one cartridge did not provide enough bang to accelerate the engine to a self-sustaining speed and if fuel continued to be fed into the engine it would over heat and the turbine could be burnt out. The trick was to cut off the fuel, let the engine speed reduce a little and then fire a second cartridge to boost the engine up to the required speed. Experienced Gannet pilots were quite used to this but to newcomers it was quite a challenge. The counter rotating propellers gave a flickering effect but if in flight it was decided to fly on one engine for maximum range it was quite disconcerting to have a stationary propeller within a few feet from your nose.

Having challenged you to get it started it had another surprise in store for you during the landing phase. In order to reduce the speed sufficiently to land on an aircraft carrier the wing had to have extendable flaps on both leading and trailing edges. When the first tests were made deploying the flaps caused the aircraft nose to go down quite strongly. To counteract this rather alarming feature the manufacturer arranged for the tail plane to move nose down simultaneously with the wing flaps and thereby hold the nose up. All was well unless the pilot was too high or fast on the landing approach and had to throttle back below the minimum recommended setting. The propellers would form a giant disc which reduced the airflow over the tail plane and let the nose go down. Much height could be lost before the engines could be slowly wound up again. George Burdick, our US Navy pilot, was caught by this and only managed to avoid an untimely and inelegant arrival on the runway by an uncomfortably small height. Naval pilots who flew the Gannet regularly loved it but for an occasional pilot it was certainly full of interest.

At last my turn to fly the Hunter Mk 4 arrived. It was the RAF's leading fighter aircraft at the time and was well established in squadron service. It was lovely looking and the cockpit suited me well. At last manufacturers were beginning to put aircraft controls, knobs and switches where pilots could reach them and I was as happy as a dog with two tails as I got airborne into a clear Hampshire sky. The first requirement was to head to 40,000 ft out beyond the south coast by Chichester and make three supersonic dives. This was no great challenge but I had become a supersonic pilot at last. The remainder of the flight was a general evaluation and after about 40 minutes I felt I could live happily with the Hunter.

Hawker Hunter

A rather sedate session in a Percival Pembroke communications aircraft collecting data for the air thermometer calibration calmed me down again but my luck changed when I was allocated a Hawker Seahawk Mk 1 naval fighter. It was the same generation as the Meteor with non-swept wings and a sub-sonic performance. It looked absolutely right and it was a pilot's delight. The cockpit was excellent and I immediately felt at home. It seemed to be made for aerobatics and I was happy to take advantage of it. The only limitation was the manually controlled ailerons and at high speed they became very heavy and the rate of roll deteriorated. Later I was tasked to fly some high Mach number tests in the Seahawk Mk 4 which had power assisted ailerons and the problem was cured. In its performance range it was one of my favourite aircraft. The Royal Navy was lucky to have it.

Hawker Seahawk

Our program of lectures and flying was interspersed with visits to the main British aircraft and engine manufacturers. On a typical visit to the Fairey Aviation Company we all travelled by bus to the small grass airfield at White Waltham where we were greeted by the test flying staff. Gordon Slade, the Chief Test Pilot, gave us an overall view of their operations and then Ron Gellatley briefed us on his work with the Rotadyne, a twin rotor helicopter which was producing very promising results. It was typical of the times that after so much effort to develop it into a potentially successful project it was not continued because of lack of government funds. Peter Twiss then in his very modest way described his work with the Fairy Delta 2 in which he had recently raised the World Airspeed record to more than 1,000 mph. This project was one of the most successful in the history of aircraft development. Fairey Aviation, a relatively small manufacturer, was given the task of producing an aircraft to explore speeds well above Mach 1. Many companies were encountering all manner of problems with straight delta wings but Fairey Aviation built and flew an aircraft which, straight from the drawing board, provided excellent test data over many hundred flights. Normally such experimental aircraft of this kind had only limited life, some only a few flights, but the Fairey Delta 2 became a work horse. It required very sensitive handling but in Peter Twiss the company had a master hand. His handling of the attempt on the world airspeed record where he had to climb to 30,000 feet and make the first pair of runs and then land and immediately make another 2 runs all within 30 minutes was one of the best examples of superb flying on record. It was another tragedy that this airframe was not developed into an interceptor fighter but again funds were not made available. Some of the Fairey Delta's tests were made at a test centre in the south of France and perhaps it is significant that when the French developed their successful Mirage fighter it had the same configuration as the Fairey Delta.

We relished the opportunity to have detailed discussions with leading members of the British test flying community and our happiness received a boost when Gordon Slade announced that 4 light aircraft were ready for us to fly. We poured out of the briefing room to find 4 vintage light aircraft waiting with their engines running. Several pilots who had not flown the Tiger Moth made a bee line for it but Dave Kribs of the USN and I were the first pair to a small low wing monoplane known as the Tipsy. Dave confessed he had not flown a tail dragger before and suggested I should have the first stint. Like others of our party I climbed just clear of the circuit, threw it around a little to get the feel of it and then re-joined the circuit to see if my old Tiger Moth training was still working. Fortunately it was one of my better days and it sat down in a nice three point landing. Then Dave took over and qualified as a tail dragger pilot and could boast about it to his grandchildren ever after. The high spot of this entertainment was the sight of the Tiger Moth falling around all over the sky as our modern jet pilots attempted to slow roll it. The Tiggy was a great humbler.

Eventually we were dragged away and taken by bus to an excellent restaurant at the Monkey Island at Bray on the River Thames. A magnificent meal was laid on together with copious drinks. Our impression of the Fairey Aviation Company was improving hour by hour but when it was approaching the time for a nice afternoon snooze we were again loaded into our bus and taken to tour the factory where the Gannet was being produced. Maybe our concentration was not as high as in the morning and our walking pace was slowing but we had a first class insight into production problems in the mid-1950s. Back in the open air again our bus then headed for Kew Bridge where we found a river steamer waiting for us. It was loaded to the gunwales with food and alcohol and as soon as we were aboard it set sail on a journey to the Pool of London and return. I was drinking gin and tonic and Maurice Hedges, one of our naval pilots, was savouring brandy and ginger. As we passed under each bridge we saluted it with a new hand poured drink. On the return journey it took a long time before Hammersmith Bridge so we had an extra one to close the gap. When we arrived back at Kew Bridge the boat passed underneath and then turned about to return to the jetty. We didn't have time to refuel our glasses for the second passage but we had finished the course one up. When we disembarked someone noticed that it was still a few minutes before closing time and we were able to get one last drink in the pub by the bridge. We suffered no pain at all on the return journey to Farnborough where I was solemnly escorted back home. Marlies says she was wakened by loud cries of "Shush!" and that it took her an hour to get me to bed. Apparently I was sitting on the edge of the bed laughing and telling her jokes in German. Next day we counted the bridges. There were 22. It was 40 years before I repeated such a bender.

If the Inquisition had been still in fashion in 1956 the Institute of Aviation Medicine (IAM) would have been in great favour. It had one of the most comprehensively equipped torture chambers designed to put jet pilots to the question. Much had still to be discovered about the effects of flying at high speed and high altitude together with the associated temperature extremes and vibration. We had no G-suites to ward off the effects of increased pilot's weight in tight turns at high speed. In IAM's centrifuge we could be exposed to up to 8 G or more while the ghoulish doctors made their observations. On their vibration platform we could be shaken as if flying at low level in turbulence at 500 kts. In the decompression chamber we could be taken to high altitude and then have our oxygen switched off to demonstrate the effects of anoxia. While sitting at a cabin height of 25,000 ft an explosive decompression could be arranged which would reduce the cabin pressure to a height of 40,000 ft. In the climatic chambers one had the choice of torrential rain in jungle conditions, arid searing desert heat or strong arctic winds. Everyone could choose his own torture. A pilot's leg strength could be measured to check on his capability to handle the more powerful aircraft on one engine. This could make the difference between life and death in Meteors and Canberras. IAM could produce a fully calibrated pilot.

I always loved the opportunity to fly the Piston Provost. It was an ideal basic trainer with a very lively performance. It was a pity that it was pushed out of service by the requirement for all jet training. I was happy to be allocated it to fly a series of spinning tests. The programme contained a series of 12 turn fully developed spins to the right and left with various control positions held throughout the spin. As life is rather chaotic during the spin I had an early version of a magnetic wire tape recorder to record my comments. Some of the spins were wilder than others but I began to lose my enthusiasm when the cockpit slowly filled with more and more petrol fumes. After completing 12 spins I returned to base and headed for the operations room feeling very queasy. While I was sitting with a large mug of coffee and sucking in fresh air our Technical Officer made my day with the news that the tape recorder had jammed and the sortie would have to be repeated. I then discovered that the Piston Provost usually had the fuel fumes problem when spinning with full fuel tanks and the Flying Training Schools only flew spinning exercises on second sorties with half full tanks. I was learning the hard way. The second sortie and 2 more on the next day produced no problems and the experience did not spoil my affection for the Piston Provost.

Percival Piston Provost

Although the Hunter became a widely loved fighter it had a few problems in its early days and I became familiar with one of them when I was detailed to fly a series of lift boundary tests at 40,000 ft in a Hunter Mk 4. The object of the tests was to find the maximum turning performance at a series of increasing Mach numbers and then note the subsequent behaviour. The problem with the early Hunters was that when the point of the stall was reached in a turn at high speed the aircraft nose would pitch up and go deeper into the stall. I had to note the amount of G at which it reached the stall and then let it pitch up to find the maximum G attained. A squadron pilot avoided this situation by easing the control column forward as soon as the buffet from the stall was felt. I had to repeat the tests at increasing speeds and as the higher Mach numbers I had to climb above 40,000 ft and arrange things so that as I dived the required speed was reached as I pulled the maximum G when we arrived at 40,000 ft. This was intriguing but life became much livelier at the culmination of one pitch up when the engine went out. Everything became very quiet but when my heart starting beating again I had to get the engine restarted. During the remainder of the tests at the higher speeds with steeper dives and more violent pitch ups the engine quit 3 more times. For a pilot with only a few hours on the type it certainly increased the flow of adrenalin. I was relieved when I started a high speed descent back to Farnborough but the mood did not last. Suddenly the aileron controls lost their power and reverted to manual control. The ailerons were out of trim and it rolled quickly to the right until I could collect my senses and use enough strength to stop the roll and trim the ailerons. The aileron controls were very heavy in manual and my arrival back at Farnborough past the Town Hall and the Black Sheds was made with both hands on the stick and making occasion jabs at the throttle a bring me to the runway threshold in good order. As I turned off the runway I felt very relieved but when I got to the dispersal and climbed down the ladder I felt so weak that I had to hold on to the ladder to steady myself. As the adrenalin drained away I felt as weak as a kitten. The pitch up problem was cured in the Mk 6 by fitting a saw tooth wing leading edge.

We were fortunate that we could join in the social life of the RAE Mess and one evening we were involved with Tony Goorney in a motorised paper chase. Several crews in a motley selection of motor cars were given clues which led to a public house. After a drink the landlord could be persuaded to produce a clue towards the next pub and so on until most of the pubs in the area had been patronised. The clues were not too difficult but half way round the course we met up with Danny Clare's crew who were howling with laughter. They confessed that in an attempt to save time and effort while searching for a pub which obviously had a connection with The Iron Duke or Duke of Wellington they had decided to phone all the likely establishments in the area for information. Half way down the list they received a very stuffy reply and were then informed that it was the residence of the Duke of Wellington.

While searching for the pubs and sampling their ale we also had to collect a spider in a matchbox, some hair from the tail of a white horse and a signed photograph of Queen Victoria. We finished the course with the spider and the horse hair but Queen Victoria required more than average effort until Marlies remembered she had a suitable photo in a book. We quickly collected the book and someone signed it. However we had to settle for second place because Gp Capt Finlay had the genuine article which his parents had obtained from an Officers Mess after the death of the Queen.

After the high life with the fighter type aircraft I soon had to take my place at the navigator's table in a Canberra T Mk 4 to record data while two other students flew fuel consumption tests. It was rather like watching paint dry but at last we returned to base and I noted that the runway in use was from the Laffens Plain end. On the final approach I was packing my papers away when I heard one of the pilots say, in his best QFI voice, "I have control". This was most unusual so I ducked my head down to have a look out of the small window and was surprised to find myself looking up at a platoon of soldiers with an armoured car on a bank to the left of the approach path. A little judicious use of extra power and a tweak on the control column rectified the situation and saw us safely home. Even the duller trips had their moments.

Chipmunk T Mk 10

A change from the normal flying routine came when I flew our little Chipmunk and towed the Sedbergh glider over to Fairoaks, a small grass airfield nearby. I spent the day towing it up to 2,000 ft and releasing it so that the course members could familiarise themselves with a glider.

Then followed a quick low level run over the airfield to drop the towing cable and a smart circuit and landing. It was certainly a better day than air thermometer calibrations or reducing test results. The flight back to Farnborough towing the glider in the late afternoon reminded me of the contentment when riding a pair of cart horses home after a day's ploughing.

We were fortunate to have an Eon Olympia and a Slingsby Sky sailplane for our use and gliding sessions were often arranged at weekends. On 6th May my turn came round to fly the Olympia which had been a world record holder a few years earlier. I was towed up to 1,000 ft and then at 450 ft while manoeuvring to land was lucky to find a thermal. Then began the contest with nature to stay in the lift. I managed to tease my way up to 5,200 feet before losing it and landing back at base after a 1 hour and 15 minute flight. I was well pleased for a first flight. Later in the day I had another launch but found no lift and was back on the ground after only 15 minutes. Perhaps I was not God's gift to gliding after all.

The following weekend my place in the queue for the Sky came up. The Sky was a beautiful sailplane which was still breaking world records. Behind me in the queue was Bill Bedford, the Hawker's Chief Test Pilot, who was waiting to attempt yet another world record to a declared destination. Again I was lucky to find a thermal and managed to claw my way up to 6,200 ft and eventually landed after 5 hours and 20 minutes. In 8 days I had completed two of the three requirements for a Silver C Gliding Certificate.

July was a busy month with a range of new tests on nearly all the aircraft in our fleet but now our thoughts were turning to the summer break which was planned for August. While turning over various plans I discovered that the Air Ministry had introduced a scheme whereby pilots in non-operational postings could return to their old operational squadron to enable them to brush up their skills. I needed no second invitation and promptly applied to return to No 541 PR Squadron during my leave period. I was delighted when permission was granted and in early August Marlies and I departed for RAF Wunsdorf where the Squadron was still based. A very warm welcome was waiting for us and we were invited to share the quarter of our old friends Mike and Kay Somervell. It seemed as if we had come home again and mess life and evenings in the Chequers Club seemed to resume where we left off. My old aircraft, Charlie, was waiting on the flight line and within 7 days I used him to fly 5 operational sorties. The sun shone on us in all respects. Marlies, who had only been on the Squadron for a few months in 1955 before we were prematurely sent back to UK, was well looked after by the other wives and we could feel again the richness of squadron life. Although the chance to complete ETPS was too good to miss we realised how much we regretted missing the last year of my tour on the Squadron. Alas, my detachment came to an end all too quickly and we trudged our way back to Farnborough with mixed feelings

When we arrived back at Farnborough rumours were rife of spending cuts in the defence budget. Defence Reviews had not been invented at that time but it was a sign of things to come. Several aircraft projects were being cancelled and the Government was debating whether manned interceptor fighters still had a role to play in the new Surface to Air Missile age. It seemed certain that many of our smaller aircraft firms would either have to merge with bigger ones or go to the wall.

I had a very good day when Tony Goorney brought a Boulton Paul Balliol to Tangmere to ferry me back to Farnborough. The Balliol had been introduced as a high performance trainer aircraft but unfortunately, like the Piston Provost, it had to give way to jet trainers. It was a marvellous opportunity to fly behind the lovely Merlin engine which had played such a major part in the RAF's history.

When the course restarted high indicated airspeed tests in a Devon and rate of roll tests in a Seahawk were interspersed with my first flight in the Avro 707B. This was the earliest of three small delta wing research aircraft designed to gather data for the Vulcan bomber which was being developed. It was longitudinally unstable below 125 kts and above 250 kts but, like the curate's egg, the other parts were fine. We knew that it had crashed and killed an Avro test pilot during an early flight while making low speed tests. After the Avro test pilots had finished their tests it was transferred to the experimental establishment at Boscombe Down for further evaluation. During the tests it was involved in an accident while landing and severely injured the pilot. It was then moved to Farnborough for use by ETPS. The briefing for my first flight must have been a classic of brevity. I was given a single sheet of A4 paper which contained a summary of the aircraft limitations and its main systems. It included a brief note on the instability problem and noted the care required while landing. My tutor added that it had a Derwent engine, the same as the Meteor, and as I had flown Meteors I would be OK. When I had settled on the throne and closed the hood I found the view very limited. The forward windscreen was normal but the rest of the canopy was made from metal alloy and two small windows were set into the sides to give a little lateral vision. The controls had no power assistance but the flight produced no problems. The weather conditions were excellent and for 35 minutes I explored the full performance range. The unstable areas required extra concentration but it did not spoil the fun. Back at the airfield the approach to land was quite normal and it sat down on the runway nicely. I was happy to add one more type to my log book

Avro 707B

The Vickers Varsity prototype now appeared on the scene and I spent several flights flying lateral and directional stability tests. This big, comfortable and docile crew trainer made an interesting change from our more lively aircraft. In mid-September I had the opportunity to grab another flight in the Avro 707 and I spent the sortie exploring the slow speed flying and the buffet boundaries. It was a tiring sortie but full of interest. The approach and landing were again quite steady and straight forward. After more sorties in the Varsity, the Piston Provost and a Chipmunk the Avro 707 became available again. The weather was cloudy and I took the opportunity to fly on instruments in both the stable and unstable speed ranges. When I returned to the airfield I set up a normal approach but immediately after touch down the aircraft nose rose and the aircraft became airborne again. I pushed the nose down and put it back on the runway only for the nose to rise again but a little higher than before and start another larger hop. The airspeed was decreasing rapidly and more control movement was required to bring the aircraft down to the runway again. The nose came up again and off we went in an even bigger hop. I had to fight quite hard to keep the aircraft level but when I arrived back on the runway for the fourth time the port wheel came off and the undercarriage leg collapsed. The aircraft veered off the runway and ploughed its way across the grass of Laffens Plain. Everything seemed to be going very slowly and as we careered across the grass I cut off the fuel and switched off the electrical circuits. As the aircraft came to a stop I opened the canopy and was preparing to make a hasty exit when two sets of fingers appeared on the left edge of the cockpit followed by a friendly face and a rather concerned voice that inquired, "Are you all right, Sir?" From that moment on I was indeed all right. The crash wagon normally stationed by the runway controller's caravan had followed me down the runway and as I got slower it got faster and we arrived on the finishing spot together. I was reminded of an American test pilot who had a landing accident and when the crash crew arrived and inquired about what had happened he replied, "I don't know. I've only just arrived here myself!"

That was the last flight of the 707B and it was only in 2007 that a friend produced some detailed information on the aircraft and I discovered that the fuel tanks in the wings had no baffles fitted and when the aircraft was put into a nose up attitude the fuel could flow towards the rear of the tanks and make the aircraft more unstable. A feature of the 707's delta wing was that the aircraft could fly at much higher nose attitudes than previous aircraft. We live and learn.

The course continued until on 5th November and I made my contribution to the Suez War which was in full swing at the time. I was airborne with my tutor and other members of my syndicate in the Varsity making tests at forward and aft centre of gravity (C of G) positions. To change the position of the C of G small bags of lead shot were carried between two boxes which had been fitted in the fuselage. While we were examining the behaviour at the aft C of G we were contacted and asked to divert to Boscombe Down where they had an urgent task for us. We landed at Boscombe and were directed to a dispersal pan where several people were waiting for us. I was in the driving seat but as some of our crew went aft to open the door the aircraft began to rock back and forth and we realised we were in danger of the nose wheel lifting off the ground and the aircraft sitting on its rear end. After much scrambling around and calling for the people on the ground to keep clear some ballast was brought forward and sanity was restored.

In the first phase of the Suez War leaflets were dropped over Cairo but the bundles were not opening and scattering the leaflets over a large area. Cairo was being bombed by bumph and this was too belligerent in a modern war. Boscombe Down had leapt into action to produce a solution and we had been specially selected to test their modified leaflet bundles. A war load of leaflets was taken on board and we then flew to Imber Bombing Range and showered it with Arabic leaflets. I wonder if the local inhabitants realised that we were playing our part in the war. When we had ensured the successful outcome of the Suez operations we then resumed more mundane tasks.

Vickers Varsity Prototype

The course was slowly winding its way to the end. I flew several sorties in the prototype Varsity to prepare my Preview Handling Test and then we sat our ground examinations. During this time we were concerned about happenings in the UK aircraft industry. Several projects had been cancelled and the Air Ministry was working on proposals which were eventually published in the 1957 Defence White Paper. The most significant feature was the change in air defence policy from the use of interceptor fighters to reliance on Surface to Air Missiles. We had discovered that none of the students would be going to work in civilian aircraft companies and there would be a scramble for worthwhile test flying jobs.

I had already decided that if I could not have a top grade test flying job I would be much happier on an operational squadron again. The Cold War was still a major threat and there was plenty of work to be done. The only problem was trying to get a posting to a front line squadron. During this unsettling phase Marlies and I spent a weekend with an old PR friend who was flying at the Canberra PR OCU and we discussed the prevailing situation. Sometime later I discovered that my friend had discussed it with his boss who rose to the bait and promptly phoned the Air Secretary's branch to put in a bid for me. The personnel staff were delighted to have someone to help them with their problems and agreed to the suggestion. When the postings were announced at the end of the course I was posted to join the staff of No 237 PR OCU at RAF Wyton. I had been fortunate to have had the opportunity to complete the prestigious test pilots' course. I had increased my knowledge and experience considerably while having fun with a new range of aircraft. The course would stand me in good stead for the remainder of my flying career and I was frequently invited to try to sort out various sick aeroplanes. When the test flying future was becoming very gloomy I was able to return to PR but instead of the Meteor PR 10 which was coming to the end of its operational life I would be starting again on the Canberra PR aircraft which were coming into service.

We now had to plan for a move to Huntingdonshire but our life was about to change significantly. Marlies was now pregnant and the bed which had been reserved in the Aldershot Military Hospital would have to be given up and a new booking sought wherever it would be in the east of England. We were on the move again.

Empire Test Pilots School Crest

CHAPTER 11
No 237 Canberra PR OCU.
RAF Wyton

OUR arrival at RAF Wyton was typical of life in the RAF in the 1950s. First we had to find somewhere to live and the Cambridgeshire area was not a good place to begin. Cambridge was the only major town in the area but most of the accommodation was mopped up by the University and the remainder was competed for by 7 nearby RAF stations. A junior officer could only offer about £4 per week for rent so we were not very competitive. The RAF bases had a limited number of officers married quarters but places on the long waiting lists were allocated according to rank and family size. Junior officers could only dream. Eventually we found a small 2 bed roomed bungalow on the edge of the Fens about 3 miles east of RAF Oakington. Rampton was a small bleak village with a church, a chapel, a pub, post office, a disused school and a village pond. Our tiny bungalow was between the school and the pond and immediately over the road from the Rectory. Marlies, who was now 4 months pregnant, had to begin her usual task of turning it into a comfortable little home and I had to turn my attention to work at Wyton which was 15 miles away.

When I checked in at No 237 PR OCU I discovered that my first task would be to attend the Ground School at the Canberra bomber OCU at RAF Bassingbourn which was producing Canberra bomber crews as fast as possible. The Ground School was well organised and efficient. Most of the aircraft systems were identical with the PR version so I was able to obtain an excellent introduction to my new aircraft. Although I was itching to get back to flying again I enjoyed the opportunity to crawl all over the aircraft to find out what made it tick and the three weeks quickly passed. I got an endorsement in my flying log book that I was qualified to undertake Canberra PR3 and T4 servicing up to primary servicing level. This would be essential when operating away from base.

In the meantime we had not been able to find a hospital place for Marlies in early May when our baby was due. Apparently it was a vintage year and all places were fully booked. One weekend we were spending the day in Cambridge when we saw a beautiful litter of Golden Retriever puppies in a pet shop window. They were lovely and we would have loved to have bought one but there was no way we could afford to buy a pedigree Golden Retriever and we had to continue dreaming. Marlies' birthday was due in February and my thoughts kept returning to the puppies but all common sense confirmed that we could not afford one. Such is human nature that on her birthday I returned home via Cambridge and when I arrived home in the dark I had tucked into the front of my coat the puppy which we had found particularly attractive. I went to the back door and through the glass panel I could see Marlies in the kitchen. I tapped on the door and held the puppy at arm's length in the middle of the window. When Marlies turned all she could see was a small bundle of oatmeal coloured fluff. That was how Susie came to join our family and she proved to be an excellent investment.

Having got that settled I could now think of work again. Wyton was a big station with a long RAF history. It was the home of 3 Canberra PR squadrons and a Valiant reconnaissance squadron. In the southwest corner of the line of hangars 237 PR OCU was tucked away. It was very friendly outfit and I was made welcome by old friends and strangers alike. This phase was always facilitated by numerous mugs of crew room coffee. I met the CO, Sqn Ldr Dusty Miller, who I had previously encountered in the Canal Zone on No 13 Meteor PR Squadron at RAF Kabrit in 1954 but at Wyton I hardly saw him again. I was soon introduced to the Canberra PR Mk 3 which had quickly been developed from the very successful bomber version and it combined good performance and reliability with a rare simplicity. It was equipped for only one navigator instead of 2 in the bomber version and it quickly became one of my favourite aeroplanes. I had plenty of time to become familiar with it and also the Canberra T Mk 4 trainer version which had the same performance and handling characteristics but was somewhat spoiled by wedging 2 pilots into the cockpit side by side. A feature of the Canberra which I found unusual was the 6 fuel tank booster pump switches. Although the Canberra was a 100% British aircraft the switches were upside down from the normal convention. This could be a source of embarrassment to new Canberra pilots and I had to continually remind them that the switches were like knickers. When they were up they were on and when down they were off.

Before I could begin instructing I had to go through a time honoured RAF system of instructor standardisation. The training syllabus was divided into several different sections and each one was demonstrated to me by one of the experienced instructors and then I took my place in the right hand seat and taught it to an instructor. So it continued until I had worked my way through the whole syllabus. We also applied the same method to the ground lectures. While this was going on I managed to fly 3 sorties in a Chipmunk giving ATC cadets air experience. For good measure I also topped up my twin propeller and tail wheel expertise with an Anson flight.

While this was going on Marlies and I had to come to grips with Rampton village. It could have been disastrously boring but we found we had very rare neighbours. We lived across the main road from the church and the Rectory. The Rector was Donald Goodman and his wife was Nancy. A small simple village like Rampton which was divided between the church and chapel needed a good down to earth village parson but Donald was an academic. He was Professor of Aramaic at Cambridge University and was deeply involved in the deciphering of the Dead Sea scrolls which had been discovered soon after the war. After we came to know and like them Donald would come over to us with his latest letter from a fellow professor in Germany which was written in a mixture of some English, more German with copious sections of Aramaic and a smattering of hieroglyphics to add a little spice. Donald needed Marlies to help him with his German while I supplied coffee and a pinch of common sense. I remember learning much about the Nestorian heresy which seemed to be very topical at the time.

While Donald was so involved with his scholastic work he was completely out of touch with his village congregation and he could not come to grips with their church politics. Fortunately Nancy was absolute mistress of the situation. She was a handsome motherly figure who could understand the village completely and she had the marvellous ability to help the parishioners solve their problems without them realising that she was the master mind. It was fascinating to watch her operate. Donald got on with his academic work and preparing very uncontentious sermons. Occasionally he would come over the road looking completely exasperated and ask he could have a stiff drink. He was never refused.

Susie guarding a Canberra PR3

Between our bungalow and the school was a pair of semi-detached thatched cottages which clearly showed their age to be several hundred years. Soon after our arrival we were amused to see a man, a little older than us, in his dressing gown with a newspaper under his arm heading for the wooden thunder box at the bottom of his garden. With a cheerful wave he disappeared for a lengthy period. We soon came to know that our neighbour was Mike Bulleid, the son of the designer of the Battle of Britain class railway engines. In the middle of the war Mike had left his studies at Cambridge University and had joined the RAF and trained as a pilot. Towards the end of hostilities he was chasing the German army through NW Europe in his rocket projectile equipped Typhoon. After the war he had a spell in South Africa but soon decided to return home and resume his place at Cambridge but he changed his studies to architecture. While seeking a base for his studies he found the tumble down cottages next to us. The elderly tenant of the cottage next to us had recently died but the other end still had an even older couple in residence. Mike decided to buy the property with the intention of living in the empty house while renovating it. When we visited him we found that he was camping in the cottage with an absolute minimum of furniture. He had made some progress with the restoration and the quality of the work was remarkable. Even areas which would eventually be covered were of the same high standard. He had no bathroom so we offered him the use of our bathroom. Coal rationing was still in force and I was amused that when Mike appeared for a bath he was humping a suitable portion of coal in his old parachute bag. He was still a pilot at heart. Although Rampton appeared to be a dull and uninteresting village we had found charming and interesting neighbours. Marlies was getting steadily bigger but as she tried to work her way through the household chores little Susie would create havoc by stealing floor cloths and anything else which looked chewable.

I continued working my way through the Canberra training syllabus and when I thought I was ready for a check with a senior instructor to sign me up as a Canberra QFI I found myself on the flying program with a student crew. Like a loyal officer I did as ordered and began to earn my keep on the OCU. A week or two later on 17th April I discovered I was to have a check ride with Sqn Ldr Monty Burton. Monty was a well known pilot in the PR world who had been a previous CO of the PR OCU and had recently won the England to New Zealand air race in a Canberra PR3. I received no specific briefing for the sortie but when we got airborne I was asked to give him various parts of the syllabus but all the time we were wandering further and further north. Normally we planned an exercise so that by the end we were near to base and did not waste time on a return journey. When we had worked our way up to the Scottish border Monty asked me to make a practice diversion to Aberdeen Airport. I found this interesting as it was outside my normal bailiwick. When we landed at Aberdeen I was instructed to park on the west side of the airfield by a lonely hangar and wait with the engines running. Very soon a Rolls Royce car appeared and the chauffeur opened the door for an elegant elderly lady carrying a small parcel. Monty went over to greet her and after a very friendly chat, bid her farewell and returned to our aircraft with the parcel. I began to wonder what I was getting involved in. Soon after the huff and puff of getting airborne again was over Monty confided to me that he had recently been in the area for some shooting and had forgotten his binoculars. My QFI check was a recovery mission. Needless to say I passed the test and was duly signed up as a fully paid up member of the Canberra QFI's union.

Mike Bulleid was full of surprises so it was no surprise that he should own a 1925 Rolls Royce two seat drop head coupe which he garaged in one of our many sheds. When the weather improved Mike proposed that we should have day at Huntingdon Races. Marlies had never seen a provincial race day and looked forward to it but she was horrified at the thought of turning up at such an event in Mike's old car. The cabin was high and almost rectangular. Behind the cabin was a long boot and set into the boot lid was a hatch which when opened revealed a Dickie seat for 2 more people. This was an excellent place for Susie and me. After getting the beast started we bowled off to Huntingdon in Pickwick like fashion. The day was fine and when we arrived the car attracted a great deal of attention. It was mainly admiration but it did not ease Marlies' embarrassment. It confirmed her impression that English people were as mad as March Hares.

We still had not been able to find a hospital bed for Marlies' confinement and eventually we had to accept that the baby would be born at home. Fortunately we had in Cottenham, the next village, yet another marvellous character; a District Nurse with a bicycle who was well past her retirement age but was too busy to find time to retire. Almost every child in the area who had arrived in the last 40 years or so had been delivered by her and her experience was endless. I took some leave and on 5th May 1957 the Nurse rolled up her sleeves and I put on the kettles to boil. Marlies got on with her business for the day and after a short visit from our Doctor from Cottenham Jenni was born. I well remember doing what all new parents must do and checking that everything was in place and being delighted that although she looked rather wrinkled she promised to be marvellous. After a remarkably short time the Nurse hopped on to bicycle and set course for Cottenham and I was left holding the baby. I was holding the most complicated item I had ever had known and for the first time in my life I had not done a manufacturer's course or been given a comprehensive handbook or operating data manual. However looking after Mother and baby was not akin to rocket science and a liberal dose of common sense saw me through nappy washing and all the other delights of owning a new baby. Even Susie seemed to approve of the new addition to the family and from then on she was never far from Jenni. In no time at all mother and child were doing well, father was coping and Susie was busy.

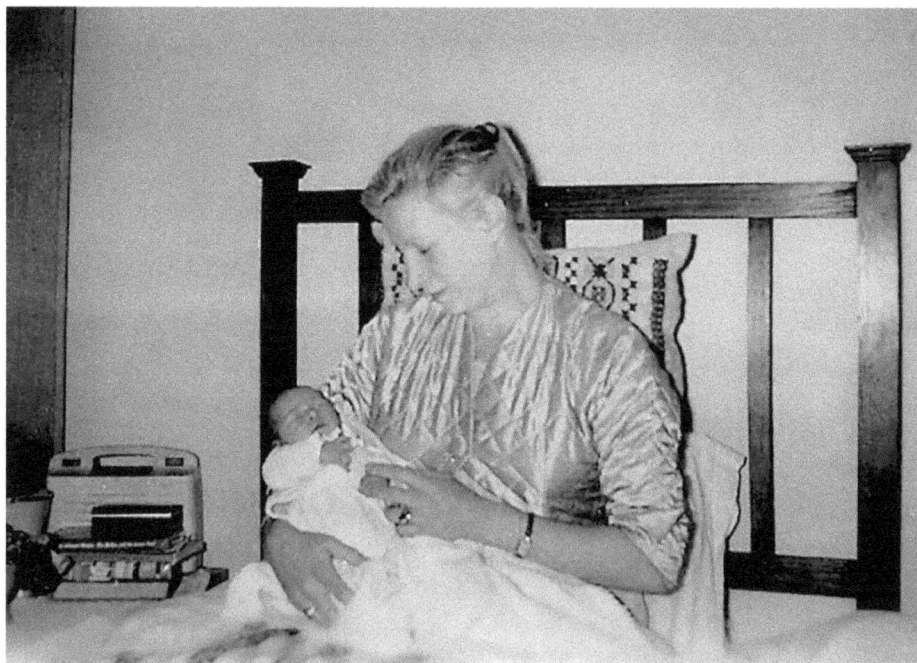

Mother and daughter both doing well

Eventually I had to get back to work again and the summer months were spent churning out students. A typical sortie would be about 2 hours and allowed much more scope for variety than we had with the Meteor. We often visited other airfields to practise using their landing aids or to give our students experience of diversions. Occasionally I could fit in some photography to keep myself up to date and at the end of July I planned my first long range cross country so that I could savour the delights of the PR3. However before I could fly it Sqn Ldr Bob Linford, or Joss as he was better known, joined our unit to make a Canberra familiarisation. Joss was a tall handsome man with boundless, almost boyish, enthusiasm for life. When he heard I was preparing a long cross country flight he immediately volunteered to come with us even though he would have to sit on the very uncomfortable folding canvas seat which filled all the very small space on the right of the pilot. The flight was planned to cover North Germany, the Swiss border and south western France and I was delighted to be back over my old stamping ground. The PR3 performed beautifully and Ron Paget was well on top of the navigation. The weather was bright and clear and the view of the Alps in sunshine was spectacular. Joss was like a little dog with two tails. I could not imagine a nicer way to spend a day.

Joss had been told that he was going out to Singapore to take over Nr 81 PR Squadron which was still equipped with the Meteor PR 10 but it was planned to re-equip with PR Canberras during his tour of duty. He was an old Spitfire PR pilot so he was very happy with his lot. When he discovered that I was a QFI and also a PR pilot on both types he said he would ask the Air Secretary to post me to join him when my tour came to an end. It sounded too good to be true.

In the middle of August I was detailed to fly Dusty Miller, our Sqn Cdr, to RAF Thorney Island and back. This was the only occasion when I flew with him and I never knew why he had to go to Thorney Island. He never did any instructing and was not often seen on the squadron.

Soon we began to hear rumours that our unit would be moved to RAF Bassingbourn to form a PR Squadron at No 231 OCU, the Canberra Bomber OCU, but that was a problem for the future. About this time Bomber Command began to experiences incidents during which the electrical elevator trim motor would suddenly decide to run away to the fully nose down position. This was potentially very dangerous and unless well handled could result in a crash. While the engineers were working on a solution to the problem it was also decided to fit an aluminium strip on to the trailing edge of the elevators and by trial and error file the strip either on the top or bottom until, with the tail trim fully nose down, the aircraft would come into trim at 450kts and be safely controllable. This involved several flights in every aircraft and much filing until the solution was reached. I seemed to be elected to do much of the testing and during the Autumn I sneaked plenty of extra flying until all our aircraft were modified. I still managed to fit in several Chipmunk flights to keep a good sense of proportion.

The summer in Rampton passed quite quickly. Jenni thrived and Marlies was never worried about turning her back on her because Susie was always in attendance. If Jenni was on the floor on a blanket Susie would be alongside and when Jenni was in her pram Susie would occasionally put her front feet on the edge and peer in to ascertain that all was well. On a typical weekend day Marlies and I would be in the garden. Susie would have charge of Jenni and Mike would be in the lounge reading our newspaper.

Bomber Command had introduced an exercise known as a Lone Ranger whereby bomber crews could fly a long navigation exercise and land at a base far from UK. To add a little spice the crews were allowed to stay over a weekend and return on Monday. The target airfields were selected by Bomber Command and offered out to their bases. Destinations such as Nairobi or Gütersloh were quickly booked but when RAF El Adem on the North African coast near to Tobruk came up I was able to bid successfully. I was paired with Flt Sgt Ron Paget as my navigator and we planned a 5 hour cross country to El Adem on 25th October and another back to Wyton on 28th October. Before we set course I arranged to have 2 sacks of fresh vegetables, 2 sets of daily newspapers and 2 crates of milk delivered to the squadron. With the vegetables neatly packed into the rear fuselage which made an excellent fridge and the two crates of milk and the newspapers sitting next to Ron in his compartment we set course on a very enjoyable weekend break. When we arrived at El Adem one sack of vegetables, a set of papers and a crate of milk went to the Officers Mess and the others went to the Sergeants Mess and Sick Quarters. Needless to say we were welcome guests in our Messes. We spent most of Saturday and Sunday in Tobruk or on the beach at the nearby club and relished a break from UK's October weather. El Adem was a very remote airfield and as usually happened the families homed on to the Messes on Saturday evening and enjoyed an impromptu party with an ad hoc 3 or 4 piece band. Apparently the make up of the band depended on who was passing through at the time. We returned on Monday to the grey autumn of Wyton having enjoyed 10 hours of navigation and an excellent weekend break.

Planning for our move to Bassingbourn proceeded quietly and as several of our officers were nearly at the end of their tours it was decided that I would take over as Flight Commander at Bassingbourn. We aimed to make the transfer without any break in the instructional flying. We would use Bassingbourn's Canberra T4s but we would take our PR3s and servicing personnel with us and it would be an almost new compact squadron. Marlies and I would be placed on RAF Bassingbourn's Married Quarter waiting list which we hoped would produce a bigger house for our growing family.

In the last fortnight at Wyton I had two unusual Canberra failures. It was normally a most reliable aircraft but within 10 days I had encountered a burst hydraulic pipe and then a burst flap jack. The incidents were no great problem to handle but I never saw either of the failures again. During the last few days at Wyton as each PR3 finished its last sortie it was parked at Bassingbourn and on 28th January 1958 I flew our last aircraft into Bassingbourn and we became the PR Squadron of No 231 OCU.

PR Squadron. No 231 OCU, RAF Bassingbourn

Our Sqn Cdr did not take up his job at Bassingbourn and I became not only Flight Commander but also acting Squadron Commander. Bassingbourn had been turning out Canberra bomber crew for about 8 years and had become a very competent and efficient unit. We fitted easily into the same hangar that had been the PR OCU when I completed my Meteor PR course in 1954 and I felt I was back home again.

While all the upheaval was going on Marlies took Jenni on a visit to her family in Germany and I moved into the Officers Mess with Susie. Within a few days of our arrival at Bassingbourn we had 2 student crews trying to complete their photography exercises but they were being held up by unsuitable weather. I sent them off to a likely looking area of good weather in north east England and as we had another navigator whose pilot was sick I decided I would be his pilot for the day and join them. While we were busily working near the Scottish border bad weather closed in over the whole of southern England and the only airfield left open for flying was RAF Kinloss near Elgin in the north east of Scotland. I rounded up my chicks and we all diverted into Kinloss and the students could mark that down as a landing away exercise.

Kinloss was a Master Diversion Airfield and was well used to having visitors calling in. We had no outer clothing except for our flying suites but the Mess members rallied around and I soon had trousers, jacket and roll neck pullover and the rest of our party looked as if they were heading for a day at the races. Our reception was very warm and by darkness I had hitched a lift in a Shackleton maritime reconnaissance aircraft heading for night low level bombing in Tain Bay. I was fascinated by so many people wandering round in such a large aircraft with everything happening in slow motion. When the serious business of bombing began I parked myself with my head in an astrodome from where I could see along the top of the fuselage and keep a check on all the proceedings. It was a lovely way to spend an evening.

RAF Bassingbourn airfield
The PR hangar is 2nd from right PR dispersal in NE corner

Next morning the weather was still excellent at Kinloss but still clamped all over England. The student crews still had plenty of film in their magazines so I sent them off to try to finish off their photography over eastern Scotland. My navigator still needed to complete one more cross country flight so we went on a long journey around the north of Scotland. England was still fogbound next day but we had a conducted tour along the Spey valley where several renowned single malt distilleries draw their unique water and I discovered single malt whisky.

My 2 student pilots also needed their introduction to night flying and normally the Canberra T4 was used. However, when needs must, I decided to take my life in my hands and to lead them through the night flying checks from the folding rumble seat in the PR3 and then sent them off to finish their night flying requirement.

Before I left the Mess at Bassingbourn I had received a note from Marlies in Germany where she mentioned she was running low on money and at Kinloss I was not well placed to send her any. Eventually I decided the only thing I could do was send her some cash even though it was illegal at the time. Then I found that the only suitable notes I could obtain were the beautiful old fashioned A5 sized £5 notes printed on thick crinkly white paper. To complicate the issue further they were Bank of Scotland notes which I was sure Marlies had never seen before. As I had no other options I sent them off as quickly as possible and when I discussed it with her after her return to England she told me she thought they were stage notes and it was only when she re-read my note that she became aware they were legal tender.

After the night flying the students had a day off but next morning England was slowly appearing out of the fog and we all climbed aboard and after a few very productive days we headed south. Bassingbourn was operating normally again and after a quick lunch we were able to fit in another sortie and we were back to business as usual. At about this time 2 of our students were detailed to fly a night high level cross country flight. All went well during the take off and initial climb but when the navigator called the pilot for the 30,000 ft checks of oxygen and electrics he received no answer even though the 20,000 ft checks had been normal. He called the pilot repeatedly and then he felt the nose of the aircraft go down. He threw off his harness and left his seat to check and as he reached the pilot's seat he found him slumped over the control column. He was convinced the pilot had lost his oxygen supply and had become unconscious. As a first measure he had to drag the pilot off the controls but as he reached out to do so the pilot reared up and struck at him quite hard. The navigator knew from his training that when people suffer from lack of oxygen they often become belligerent and his reaction was to try to knock out the pilot to prevent further damage. All this was above 30,000 ft on a black night!

Now we must turn to the pilot's view of the situation. When he did not get a call from the navigator at 30,000 ft he called him several times and then assumed that he had become anoxic through lack of oxygen. He decided to reduce height and return to base as quickly as possible but as he was leaning forward over the control column to reach the radio controls his navigator appeared alongside and tried to grapple with him. The pilot was now convinced the navigator was anoxic and behaving violently and he believed the only way to resolve the problem was to knock the navigator out. So now there was a violent fight between the only two occupants of an aircraft flying at over 30,000 on a black night and it was only when they realised that the other was very strong they decided to rethink the situation. After they had returned to their neutral corners they discover that the navigator, after making the 20,000 ft checks, had leaned forward and his radio lead from his helmet had snagged and become disconnected. Both were badly shaken by the experience and they decided to abort the sortie and return to base. I agreed with their decision when they arrived. This was a very good example of the daft things that can go on in aeroplanes and the incident was fully written up and published in Air Clues, the RAF flight safety magazine to warn other crews.

Soon after we moved to Bassingbourn a semi-detached house in the south of Cambridge became available and we were able to move in and life became much more enjoyable for Marlies. The house was owned by an elderly lady who lived next door; she had never been invited to the house by the previous occupants so was unaware of the dilapidated state of the house. We soon met and entertained her and found her to be a delightful person and when she saw how neglected the house had become she had much of the damage repaired. She became a delightful neighbour and we often enjoyed each other's company. Olga was the head of the ladies' department in the Robert Sayles store, the local version of John Lewis, and Marlies found this very attractive. Meanwhile Jenni was rapidly growing under the eagle eye of Susie and when she began to try to walk Susie would stand still while Jenni pulled herself upright by pulling on her fur. The six legged monster would then move gently around the arena.

Susie with PR Sqn ground crew

Bassingbourn was a very efficient station and the PR squadron had settled in without missing a beat. I had a pleasant office overlooking the airfield and I could keep a watchful eye on my PR3s. One morning I had a shock when I saw one sitting on its tail bumper and looking like a little dog begging for goodies. An airman had been told to defuel the aircraft prior to servicing. Unfortunately he began by emptying the forward tank and the centre of gravity moved aft until it was behind the main wheels. As the aircraft began to teeter backwards the fuel in the 2 rear tanks sloshed backwards and up went the applecart. Fortunately no damage was done and the situation was soon restored.

The efficiency of the Flying Wing was mainly the result of excellent leadership by the Chief Instructor, Wg Cdr H G (Bert) Slade. He was one of the most competent officers that I served under in the RAF. He had a distinguished flying background and he ran the OCU with a great amount of that rarest of qualities, sound common sense. I was having a very hectic time while doing my share of instructing and also running the flight and the squadron and I often worked a little later in my office in the evening to clear my paperwork. Invariably I would hear the steady tread of Bert plodding along the pathway and he would come in to my office and perch on the edge of my desk. While chatting to me about the day's work I knew he was quietly checking the students' progress board. After a short while he would be on his way but I knew that if I needed help he was there. One evening he asked me if I had ever thought of applying for Staff College. I was aghast and said, "Good lord, I'm a flying man not a pen pusher". Bert spent a little while inquiring if I didn't want to have a say in how our aircraft were procured and used and also be involved in planning operations or would I rather leave all that to pen pushers who had forgotten how aircraft were flown. I often chewed over this conversation and of course 4 years later I was at Staff College. I was very fortunate to serve under several officers who were of enormous value to the RAF and Bert Slade was one of the best.

The squadron was running well and life was very pleasant but one morning my Flight Sergeant came into my office and ruined my day by telling me corrosion had been found in the battery bay of a PR3. The battery bay was just underneath the entrance door and corrosion caused by battery acid very quickly erodes the aluminium structure and weakens the airframe. I asked the Flt Sgt to have the remainder of our PR3s checked to see if was an isolated case and he quickly returned to say that another one was also affected. This was serious and Bomber Command would have to be told and all PR3s would probably be grounded until they had all been thoroughly checked and rectified if necessary. While I was sucking my pencil and pondering the wording of the bombshell one of our student crews came into the office to say they had heard the news and they had a confession to make. They were both known to enjoy their ale and when they began to fly the long high level cross country flights they ran into a problem. After several hours at high altitude they both needed, in modern language, a comfort break but in a pressure cabin the only provision for relief was something similar to a hospital bottle but in soft waterproof canvas. A pilot clad in thick clothing and strapped into his parachute harness and secured on his ejector seat with another harness would have to be a contortionist to achieve any relief and the navigator who could leave his seat to go down to the nose position was very little better. Eventually the navigator hit upon a solution. He came round from his compartment and stood next to the pilot and then had a pee on the floor next to the exit door. With the very low cabin temperature it immediately froze. He then moved forward and turned to face aft and held the flying controls while the pilot dismounted from his seat and followed suit. Normal business was then resumed but instead of making a cruise descent from about a hundred miles from base they stayed at altitude until near to base and then pushed the aircraft down as quickly as possible and landed without delay. As the aircraft rolled down the runway the navigator would open the door and kick out the ice before it melted. Unfortunately the operation was not as neat and efficient as they thought and the corrosion in the battery bay which was underneath the scene of the crime was not caused by battery acid. As soon as we knew the cause of the problem it was a straight forward task to get rid of the corrosion and everyone except the guilty crew breathed easily again.

Meanwhile, back at home, living in Cambridge was very enjoyable. It was a lovely city with all the amenities we could wish for and Susie was bringing up Jenni like the best of Nannies. When Jenni began to stand and try to walk Susie was always available to be used as a climbing frame. Jenni would pull herself upright clutching Susie's fur and then Susie would gently lead her through her earliest steps. When Jenni could walk I had a welcome when I returned home in the evening. Our front gate had a bottom ledge and holes along the top and as I turned the corner into Lichfield Road I usually saw two blonde heads peering through the holes and waiting for me. Susie's clock was very accurate.

The Cold War was still very tense and Bomber Command was on high alert. Accurate weather information was essential and every morning an experienced crew would fly a special flight in any weather conditions to glean actual weather reports. When Bassingbourn's turn came round I took my place in the queue. The flights took off early in the morning and either flew at high level a westerly route out to the southern Irish Sea and then north until level with the northern tip of Scotland or an easterly route to the southern North Sea and again north to the Orkneys before returning to RAF Waddington for a let down and roller landing before returning to base. One of my flights in the autumn was memorable for me. The early morning weather was a cold thick fog with visibility only a few yards. I had practised many instrument take offs but never flown one in such conditions. My aircraft was towed out to the take off point and carefully aligned with the runway. From the cockpit I could see only the powerful sodium lights at the side of the runway next to me and I could see one of the white dashes which formed the centre line ahead of me. I had 2 staff navigators but they could not help me at this stage. The Senior Air Traffic Controller drove slowly down the runway and back again to check that it was clear. I began the take off paying great attention to keeping straight and the dotted line appeared a only few yards ahead of me and quickly disappeared under the nose. After what seemed like a long time take off speed was reached and we lifted off and immediately I ensured we were in a positive climb as we flew in a dark grey gold fish bowl. We soon broke out of cloud and as far as we could see was nothing but a carpet of flat cloud. We flew the westerly route through a good selection of clouds with no problems but with no sight of land and only a few gaps over the Irish Sea. When we began out let down to RAF Waddington we soon entered cloud which slowly became thicker and darker. Waddington was a Master Diversion Airfield and had very good navigation and landing aids. I had often been into the airfield in quite bad weather but even with a forecast of visibility of 400 yards when the aircraft was at a height of 200 or 300 feet the high intensity runway lights appeared out of the murk and the runway quickly followed. Very strict rules were used to control instrument approaches and on every approach the height was calculated below which it was forbidden to descend unless the runway or a full set of approach lights was visible. On our approach the minimum approach height was 200 feet and as I was coming down to it I could see nothing but thick fog. I climbed away and when we flew along the runway not one light was seen. This was the only time I had failed to make any contact and as we had plenty of fuel I made 2 more approaches and still saw nothing. This was very unusual because normally on a second or third approach the conditions such as wind are different. Having convinced ourselves that Waddington was closed we climbed away and were diverted to RAF Acklington near Middlesborough which was the only open airfield in England. The weather conditions there were good and when I started my landing I began to feel that I had rounded out too high. I was thinking about easing down a little when I realised that the wheels were rumbling along the runway. I thought that must be my best ever landing when I realised that neither of my navigators had made a comment. This was rare for the breed.

All we could do at Acklington was to wait for England to appear out of the fog and the forecasts indicated that it would clear by teatime. Eventually we got on our way and when we appeared at Bassingbourn all trace of the fog had disappeared. Normally we landed towards the west but the wind which had dispersed the fog was blowing from the east and we had to land on the other end. I trundled round my home circuit without a care in the world but as I was about to land I hit a small step on the end of the runway and arrived with a clatter. Immediately a chorus of abuse came up from both navigators and I dreamed of being a single seat pilot again.

Young pilots straight from training were now coming to us and we usually gave them an experienced navigator to form a promising crew. One of the experienced navigators who had been crewed with a seasoned pilot was Doug Tew, a burly and rather weather beaten navigator who was an enthusiastic rugby player. During a station game Doug twisted his knee and suffered severe pain when he walked but he still continued to fly. For their first flight I walked out with Dave Watson, the pilot, to supervise the pre-flight external checks of the aircraft and when we completed our circuit of the aircraft we were standing by the entrance door together with two ground crew when one of them noticed the approach of Doug. He was hobbling along with his thinning hair blown all over the place with his navigator's bag in one hand and a walking stick in the other. On airman looked at the other and said, "Bloody hell. I've seen everything now!"

Amid all the routine of the instructional sorties an opportunity came out of the blue which gave me terrific enjoyment. Bassingbourn was host to a summer camp for ATC cadet flying and we had a contingent of Chipmunk trainers weaving in and out among our Canberras. Among the Chipmunk pilots was Flt Lt Ken Wilson who, as P1 K N Wilson, had been my first instructor on Tiger Moths at RAF Heany in 1950. Ken had been a superb instructor and had set Bob Barndon and myself on very enjoyable flying careers. The opportunity was too good to miss and we arranged a repeat of my first RAF flight. Ken was captain and went into the front seat, as in the Tiger Moth, and we flew all the exercises that he had taught me 8 years before. Stalling, spinning, aerobatics and a few circuits brought back a sackful of happy memories. All I missed was Ken's head sinking down in the front cockpit until he was almost out of sight and apple cores being tossed over the side. Ken had gone on to be a Britannia captain and had continued to give the RAF excellent value. We also drank a few beers.

Our nominal Squadron Commander had still not taken up his post at Bassingbourn and we eventually heard he was being replaced. In August 1958 Sqn Ldr Dick Arscott, our new CO, arrived and was welcomed by the Squadron. Dick was an experienced Canberra pilot and had recently commanded a bomber squadron at Upavon. He was quiet and intelligent and soon had the Squadron in his very sure grip. We could all settle down to a normal squadron life. His wife Jan was equally charming and the Squadron could look forward to a happy period. Dick was new to PR and as part of his introduction to the black art he arranged to visit some of our customers and he chose the Canberra PR squadrons in Germany. On 17th November I flew with him to RAF Wildenrath to visit No 17 PR Sqn. While Dick was on his liaison visit I took the opportunity to fly with a crew in a Canberra PR7 on a low level cross country exercise through the rolling hills of southern Germany. I was quite alarmed when I discovered that the flight would be in haze with visibility down to 1,000 metres at times. The Canberra was fitted with a Doppler navigation aid, Green Satin, which I had not used before and I was astonished by the competence they displayed in navigating through the rolling terrain and fulfilling all their tasks. The weather closed in behind us and we were diverted to RAF Laarbruch. I had led the first flight into Laarbruch on 28 Oct 1954 and was happy to renew my acquaintance. When Dick finished his visit to Wildenrath he flew our PR3 and my kit from Wildenrath to visit the PR squadrons at Laarbruch and we flew back to Bassingbourn via RAF Marham on 21 Nov.

The party season was quickly on us and Christmas came all too quickly. Life had settled down to a very pleasant routine and after a very busy year we were very well established in all aspects of Bassingbourn life. It made a great difference to us to have Dick and Jan Arscott living on the station and Marlies and I saw more of the station's social life than before. 1958 had been a good year.

Life in Cambridge was very enjoyable and our Squadron was churning out well trained students to equip the steadily increasing number of Canberra squadrons. Occasionally staff officers flying desks in the Air Ministry were able to break their shackles and escape to a flying unit and enjoy some welcome flying practice. Gp Capt Bird-Wilson chose to drive up from London in the evening, fly a night sortie and be back at his desk next morning. He had a distinguished war record and I had great pleasure in flying with him as a safety pilot. He did not have time to revise all the Canberra drills and emergency procedures so I sat quietly alongside him and acted as human Pilots Notes. We discussed what he wanted to do and then I watched a very competent pilot perform his party pieces. A practice diversion and a few GCAs at RAF Cottesmore added to a very enjoyable evening before he had to set course back to London. I was delighted to find that when I was posted to Central Flying

School Examining Wing in 1965 he would be my Commandant. I knew CFS was in good hands.

Our crews had to be competent in night flying and while they were away on long night cross country flights around east and southern Europe we had to make available an experienced PR3 pilot in case they ran into any problems. When my turn came round I tried to arrange that I was on duty the same night as our Senior Air Traffic controller, Sqn Ldr Dinty Moore. At the beginning of the war Dinty had been on a Whitley night bomber squadron as a Flt Sgt QFI which in those days was a post of considerable authority. One of his junior pilots who he ruled with a rod of iron was Plt Off Clementi. While Dinty rose to be a Sqn Ldr SATCO his fledgling did even better and had become not only a Group Captain but also our Station Commander. He often visited the control tower while Dinty was on duty and I noted that they still had a great mutual respect for each other. I used my time to encourage Dinty to recall tales of pre-war flying and I relished his accounts of flying open cockpit biplane bombers and being alerted by his rear gunner that one of the engines was short of water and boiling. The gunner had made this discovery by feeling spots of hot water on the back of his neck as he stood in his open rear turret. This fairly common occurrence was rectified by locating a suitable grass field near a farm house, making an emergency landing and requesting a bucket or two of water. While the engine was cooling down the supply of water was usually accompanied by cups of tea.

I received a letter from Joss Linford in Singapore to tell me that he had spoken to the Air Secretary about a posting for me to 81 Sqn and been told that it would not be possible. My hopes of another PR tour in the Far East went up in smoke. Soon afterwards I received another letter from my old friend, Jim Campbell, to tell me that he was being posted to Bassingbourn to take over my post later in the year. The end of my time at the PR OCU was approaching. I managed to squeeze in a very enjoyable Lone Ranger sortie with a weekend stay at my old German base at Gütersloh before we began our preparations for the annual AOC's inspection. Our AOC was the very popular AVM Gus Walker and we wanted to put on a good show for him. Our Squadron's contribution would be to take an aerial photo of him as he arrived on the Control Tower balcony and deliver prints to him before he left it. During practice I found that I could land and slow the aircraft in time to turn off at the runway intersection and arrive very quickly in front of the tower where our photographers were waiting to smartly remove the magazine and transfer it to a motor cyclist for delivery to our photo section. On the great day, 23rd June, Murphy's Law of meteorology arranged that the wind was blowing gently from the east and I would be faced with a down wind landing and I might have to roll to the end of the runway before returning much later than planned to the control tower. As my time to perform approached I positioned myself to the east of the runway and waited as I was informed where the AOC was. As he approached the steps to the control tower I worked up a good head of steam and as he reached the centre of the balcony we swept past and photographed his arrival. Throttles were closed as I hauled the PR3 round in a steep climbing turn to reduce speed as quickly as possible and then position myself for an approach to land at the lowest safe speed. As we crossed the runway threshold I decided to have a go at turning off at the runway intersection. The PR3 did not have anti locking systems on the brakes and friends who were watching said the only unusual feature of the landing was the two plumes of black rubber spraying behind the tyres. We taxied smartly round to our spot before the tower and the magazine was quickly on its way. We then briskly exited stage right and trundled along the taxi way until we had to stop before crossing the runway to our parking area. As we stopped we heard a mighty bang and a wing lurched down as the right tyre burst. While I contemplated my next trick I noticed that a tractor was already on its way to us towing a trailer with jacks, spare wheel and all equipment to save my day. Our Flt Sgt had taken the precaution of planning for such an event and as soon as he saw the tyre burst he blew the bugle for the advance. The crew arrived and very smartly jacked up the wing, changed the wheel and gave me the clearance to carry on taxying. Before I moved forward I was able to see the photographs being delivered to the AOC on the balcony. I felt very proud of our Flt Sgt and his team who had dug me out of my hole so competently. Later I heard that the AOC thought it was all part of the exercise and was impressed by the team's efficiency.

Jim Campbell had arrived much to my delight and had started his QFI standardisation and I was fully aware that my days at Bassingbourn were limited and I was worried that I might be heading for a ground posting. On a particularly glum day my posting notice arrived and, lo and behold, I was posted to No 81 PR Squadron at RAF Tengah, Singapore. Such were the machinations of the Air Secretary's branch. I could hardly wait to tell Marlies. Although the flying continued as usual my thoughts were focused on the forthcoming moves. Our biggest worry was about the future of our faithful Susie. We considered taking her with us but it was soon shown to be impractical. The problem was solved when we learned that Jim Campbell would take over our house in Cambridge. Jim asked what we proposed to do about Susie and then asked if would consider leaving her with his family. He had a young son and daughter and they all loved her. We soon realised that this would be an excellent solution for all concerned and we were happy to agree.

From now on most of our attention was devoted to Singapore but I looked back with affection to my days at Bassingbourn. It was a very efficient station and we had fitted in well. After Dick Arscott and Jan arrived we had a happy unit with very competent ground crew. When Wg Cdr Slade signed my logbook for the last time I had an Above Average assessment as a flying instructor and an Exceptional rating in PR. He added, "A very sound, competent and reliable instructor who has achieved excellent results throughout his tour". With these remarks from Bert Slade I felt well satisfied with my tour at the PR OCUs. I was steadily learning my trade.

My final flight at Bassingbourn was a night standardisation flight with Jim Campbell before he took over from me and I wished him as happy a tour as mine.

CHAPTER 12
Non Solum Nobis.
No 81 PR Squadron

A T the end of June 1959 the Ashley family bid farewell to Cambridge and headed towards Singapore. Our first step was to get ourselves with nearly all our possessions by rail to Southampton. After much huffing and puffing through London we steamed into Southampton harbour station and there awaiting for us was The Empire Fowey, one of the fleet of old passenger liners which plied the Southampton to Hong Kong route depositing and collecting service families around the Empire. The Empire Fowey had been the ex-German pre-war liner Bremen which had been requisitioned at the end of the war and was still doing yeoman service.

We were soon settled into our three berth outside cabin on the starboard side which although comfortable enough was not POSH (Port Out, Starboard Home) and we therefore had the sun on our portholes. The air conditioning worked well so we had no problems. Jenni was installed in the lower bunk while I assumed my rightful place at the top. Marlies had the delights of the single bunk. A net was fitted around Jenni's bunk to prevent her falling out during high seas.

Young children were not allowed to eat in the dining room during adult meal times so we had to take her to her meals. Officers were expected to wear mess kit for dinner except on the first night at sea. With Jenni installed in her cage and the faithful Ali, a Pakistani steward, to watch over her we went to assess the dining facilities. We were allocated to the ship's doctor's table and shared it with Major Harry Orr, RAVC and his wife Pat who were to join us in Singapore. Our sixth member was Major Polly Hoyle, a QARANC nursing sister who was on her way to Hong Kong. The ship's doctor was Donald Miller who was making his first voyage in that role. He was very naïve and as Harry was an experienced veterinary surgeon and Polly equally experienced in medical matters we had Donald seriously out gunned. Within 24 hours Harry had convinced him that he needed to take plenty of salt when living in the tropics and as there was always a good supply of salt tablets on   the table Donald was soon like a baby's rattle. The food was excellent which was very welcome after UK austerity. I discovered later that the ship had 28 beautifully varied menus, one for each day to Hong Kong. For the return journey they began again at the beginning.

Before we went to our lunch and dinner we had to take Jenni to the children's nursery which was a big play pen attended by a very nice and competent nanny. Jenni was only a little over two years old and she had never been separated from us before. When we left her in the nursery she sat in the middle of the floor and howled her head off. We were very worried about this so we spoke to the Nanny and she told us not to worry: it usually happened. Next day after leaving her we returned after only a few minutes to peep round the corner and she was playing very happily with a pile of toys around her. When we had to leave her in our cabin Ali looked after her and he would give her a paperback book which she loved to reduce to confetti. He collected a steady supply of the books from around the ship and as he did not mind cleaning up afterwards everyone was happy.

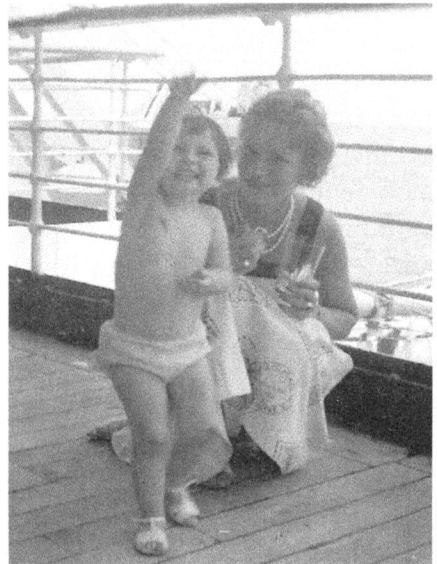

Marlies and Jenni on the Troopship Empire Fowey

Often after dinner we would all descend on Donald's sitting room and if he was away on duty Harry would phone the galley and order toasted sandwiches for all of us. Of course we left some for Donald. The ship's crew soon realised that Donald was a very soft touch and within only a few days an unusually high proportion were sick and off duty. This situation could not last and after a visit to the bridge where the Captain read his palm Donald became much better acquainted with the realities of life.

The weather in the Bay of Biscay was kind to us and by the time we arrived at Gibraltar I was heartily fed up with gin and tonic. Gin was about a quarter of the price of tonic so the temptation was great. In Gibraltar Marlies and Jenni had a good look at an outpost of the Empire and met the Barbary apes. On the voyage to Malta I tried brandy and ginger but by the time we arrived I couldn't face that either. On to the Suez Canal and all the distractions of Port Said which was bursting with activity all around the ship. Soon we were in the southbound convoy heading through the Canal but halfway through we had to wait in a side canal while the north bound convoy passed us with much hooting and waving. While we were waiting a cocktail party was laid on to greet the new passengers who had joined us at Port Said. While were enjoying ourselves the ship began to resume its journey south. Waiters were busy circulating with trays of drinks when suddenly the ship hit the side of the Canal and stopped dead. Trays and passengers flew in all directions and a waiter announced, "Hell, this always happens!" Everyone squeezed outside to watch the proceedings and very quickly the crew had a dinghy in the water to attach a rope to a bollard on the bank. A little bit of winching and the ship was again pointing straight along the Canal. As we moved slowly ahead it turned slightly to the right, then a little more to the left and then even more to the right and hit the bank again. The recovery action was repeated and we managed to get away successfully on the second attempt. The problem was caused by the rudder which was operated by single speed electric motors and if the ship was not exactly in the correct direction the rudder could not act quickly enough at the ship's low speed to keep it going straight. At higher speeds all was well. Just before we left the Canal at Suez we sailed along the eastern boundary of RAF Kabrit airfield and I was able to show Marlies and Jenni where I operated from when on detachment with a 541 PR Sqn aircraft from RAF Gütersloh in Germany.

By the time we entered the Red Sea the temperature was beginning to show us what the tropics would be like and I told Harry my problem with choice of drinks. He said the only drink in the tropics was whisky but unfortunately I could not swallow the stuff. Harry explained that initially I should drown the whisky in lots of water. This was an excellent solution and the rest of the journey was without problems. In a very short time the whisky was not being drowned. This and subsequent visits to RAF Kinloss introduced me to the joys of single malt whisky and I have never looked back.

After a day in Aden we set course for Ceylon and the usual cocktail party was organised to greet those joining from Aden. The party was in full swing as the ship sailed out of the shelter of the East African coast and Socotra Island and into the rolling waves of the Indian Ocean. The ship began to roll and the waiters were busily climbing up and down the deck in time with the rolling. We were happily swaying in rhythm and watching the drinks in our glasses also swaying when a roll to starboard did not stop at the usual place but continued until a waiter lost his balance and skidded towards the lower side of the bar with his tray of glasses preceding him. Almost at the same time a passenger decided to do the same closely followed by many more. The party broke up very quickly. Marlies is not a good sailor and took to our cabin to weather the storm. Next morning there were only half a dozen passengers at breakfast and there was plenty of the best food for everyone.

We were not allowed to go ashore at Ceylon because of a threatening political situation and we had to view the beautiful green island from offshore. Then we were off on our last leg to Singapore. The voyage had been very enjoyable with excellent companions and Jenni was now an experienced school girl who would go off to her "school" with enthusiasm while we dined. However we felt we had been at sea long enough and we were ready to tackle everyday life in Singapore. At last we wove our way through the islands surrounding Singapore and we were in Keppel Harbour. We were fascinated to see what would be our new home and the outlook seemed good.

In a very short time we were visited on board by our splendid new Squadron Commander, Sqn Ldr Bob "Joss" Linford and all the squadron aircrew who were available. What a superb way to be welcomed! We had a small party in our cabin until the luggage had been removed and the crew was threatening to throw us ashore. The assembled multitude then drove us through Singapore to our temporary accommodation in the Yoks Garden Hotel close by Newton Circus. Several of the newly arrived aircrew were still living there while awaiting allocation of hired accommodation. After a short period which was useful to enable us to adjust to the Singapore life style we moved to a hiring which was a comfortable bungalow at Raffles Park, near to the Singapore race course. It was 10 miles from Tengah and only 4 miles from the city centre. This turned out to be an optimum arrangement for us. Marlies began the task of turning the house into a comfortable home and, having found a house we decided we needed a dog to fill the gap left by Susie. We visited the local dogs' home expecting to find a lovely young replacement. However we were drawn to a terribly broken spirited, mal-nourished dog with skin sores. We took a gamble and when we took her home she began to recover very quickly and very soon grew into a lovely 90% Alsatian that became Jenni's constant companion, Trixie.

On the boat Jenni had become very fond of the nursery or school as she referred to it and when we moved into our house she demanded to go to school again at the grand old age of 2¼ years old. We found an excellent nursery school run by Catholic nuns and she happily began what became a multi-cultural education which is still going on.

David Tay's pretty little girl

Soon after we settled in Marlies made contact with the fashion world and was soon instructing at the Singapore Model Academy. Roland Chan, Singapore's leading fashion designer, soon picked her to model many of his best creations and he allowed her to buy many of them at cost price. What could be better? David Tay of Westlake Studios was recognized as the leading fashion photographer and while photographing Marlies he came across Jenni who was rapidly growing into a pretty little girl. He asked us if he could use her as a model and we agreed. In return he supplied us with his best prints of her and when we left Singapore he still used a picture of Jenni with her teddy bear as a centre piece in his display window.

Marlies strutting her stuff

When I joined No 81 PR Squadron I had been flying continuously for 8 years and had just finished a posting as Flight Commander on the PR Squadron at the Canberra OCU at Bassingbourn. Now the gods in their wisdom had sent me back to my old love, the Meteor PR 10, and I could not have been happier. No 81 Squadron was the RAF's last single seat PR Squadron and this was the only chance I would have to fly my favourite role again. I had been on No 541 PR Sqn flying the PR 10 based in Germany from 1954 to 1956 but had been short toured after only 18 months and sent home to the ETPS Course in 1956. Now was the chance to carry on where I left off.

Flying with 81 Squadron was very different from the Cold War confrontation in Germany and the Squadron's main task was flying Firedog operations over the Malayan jungle against the communist terrorists led by Chin Peng. The tasks were set by the Army and usually consisted of rectangular areas of jungle which required 3 photo runs side by side from 30,000 feet to give a small area coverage. The flying had to be precise otherwise gaps were left in the coverage but the really tricky part was finding the switch on points in large areas of virgin jungle. We had no downward vision from the Meteor so the switch on point, when found, was approached in a steep turn and the aircraft rolled out exactly over the switch on point, on exactly the required heading and with wings level exactly at 30,000 feet. At least that was the intention.

A major problem with low level sorties from Tengah was the high cockpit temperatures. When the aircraft were standing on the tarmac any parts of the fuselage which were exposed to the sun became hot enough to burn a bare hand. Locally made sun shades were used but they had to be frequently moved to protect the cockpits. Taxying out to the take off point was no great problem with the hood open but as soon as the hood was closed for take-off the cockpit became a green house and the temperature began to rise. The aircraft had no cooling air and the cockpit temperature control when selected to Cold merely allowed warm ambient air to enter the cockpit. We normally flew low level sorties clad in flying suits over socks and pants but our Mae West life jackets and parachute and seat harnesses prevented any air circulating. I don't know what temperature was reached after one and a half hours flying but when we returned to dispersal we and our flying kit were wet through. Our airmen were well aware of the problem and as they climbed the side to put in the ejector seat safety pins the first thing that came over the cockpit side was an ice cold bottle of drink from the flight line cooler. It normally disappeared in one quaff. The overall effect was to leave us very tired.

No one complained about lack of flying but among the operational flying tasks we also had to fit in a comprehensive training program. I had been appointed Squadron Training Officer and in my office I had a large board on which were recorded each pilot's number of monthly training exercises such as let downs, single engine let downs, single engine landings, flapless landings, instrument flying, night flying, etc. We had a Meteor T7 mainly for me that I used for dual checks and instrument flying. This was in addition to my operational flying so I had little to complain about.

Meteor PR Mk 10 of No 81 PR Squadron

Operating the Meteor PR10 at maximum weight from the old runway at Tengah was dangerous. The runway was 2,000 yards long and when taking off in the middle of the day the high outside air temperature reduced the thrust from the engines. With 795 gallons of fuel and three cameras with full magazines the aircraft was very heavy. The acceleration down the runway was slow and the nose wheel was still on the ground at 95 Kts or more with the little wheel spinning around at speeds for which it had not been designed. Eventually the aircraft was hauled into the air at about 130 kts just before the end of the runway. It crossed the overshoot area very low and still accelerating slowly. At the south end of the runway we had rocky ground quite unsuitable for a forced landing and at the north end mangrove swamps which were equally uninviting. At full weight it was not possible to climb away on one engine until a speed of about 165 kts had been reached. If an engine failed before this speed the aircraft was bound to crash land. Our ejector seats had a minimum ejection height of 200ft at a minimum speed of 200 kts. Breathing was resumed when both these criteria were met.

Meteor T Mk 7 off Pulau Tinggi

We had an occasion when a Meteor PR10 on take-off burst a main wheel tyre just before lift-off. The wing dropped and the wing tank hit the ground. A hole was filed in the bottom of the tank and 100 gallons of fuel flowed onto the runway and caught fire. The take-off was abandoned and the aircraft stopped in one piece. The blazing fuel had been left behind and did not reach the aircraft. We eventually discovered that we had been supplied with tyres which had been re-treaded three times. It did not happen again.

Malay island with light house

One Saturday morning in October 1959 I was detailed to fly a low level task in the southern part of Thailand and because of the long range I would have to fly at high level to the Thai border, descend to do my task and then refuel at Butterworth, the RAAF airfield just south of the Thai border. I filed a Flight Plan with Air Traffic Control and set off on my task. All went well until after I had finished the task and came from behind Gong Kedah, a big hill just north of Butterworth, and called Butterworth for permission to join their circuit. I was disconcerted when they asked me who I was. I told them I had filed a flight plan to land there and they informed me the airfield was closed because a trench had been dug across the runway. I checked my remaining fuel and I had only 80 gallons per engine. The nearest diversion airfield was Ipoh which had a short runway but was about 80 miles south of me. I did not have enough fuel to fly at low level. If I tried to fly at high level I would run out of fuel on the climb so I chose the good old English compromise. I climbed as quickly as possible to 25,000 feet and then flew on one engine. Slowly the valley in which Ipoh lay came into view but it was covered in low cloud. The airfield had no approach or landing aids and it was therefore no place to be. I had no alternative but to continue on towards Kuala Lumpur as long as my fuel lasted. After an agonisingly long time the area of the airfield came into sight but the valley was full of haze and the sun prevented me from seeing the runway. I continued at height until eventually I could see the runway and with the throttles closed I began my descent. Kuala Lumpur had been told about my problem and all was cleared for me but by this time I had no idea how much fuel I had remaining. I spiralled down keeping well above a normal approach height. Unfortunately the approaches to the old Kuala Lumpur airfield were tricky. At the end I intended to use a huge jam factory that was situated near the runway threshold but just off to the left side. At the far end of the runway was a railway embankment which would certainly stop me if I ran off the end of the runway. I began to breathe again when I safely arrived on the beginning of the runway. As I turned off the other end of the runway my port engine stopped but as I only had one more left turn to make I could continue taxying. When I reached the dispersal area and started the left turn the starboard engine came out on strike in sympathy with the port engine and also stopped. While the aircraft was being prepared for the flight back to Tengah the ground crew brought up an old wartime 900 gallon fuel bowser and my aircraft gobbled up all the contents.

Malay fishing village taken during a low level sortie

On 16th December 1959 81 Squadron flew its 10,000[th] Firedog operation. Fg Off George Paul, who had flown very many of them, was given the honour of flying the task. I flew our Meteor T7 with Cpl Court, one of our ground photographers, and we took a series of photos as George departed from Tengah en route for the great occasion.

In November one of our Meteor PR10s was found to have developed some dangerous behaviour and I was asked to investigate it. When a Meteor lost one engine at high thrust and low speed it would rapidly roll towards the dead engine but WB165 rolled much faster to the left than to the right. The rate of roll was sufficient to be very dangerous. Problems of lateral and directional stability can be tricky to diagnose in older aircraft and during November and December I flew ten air tests until the fault was cleared. Several adjustments made minor improvements but the main problem was asymmetric friction in the rudder control circuit; a seemingly minor defect but a potential killer. The controls were refurbished and WB165 became a normal, well behaved PR10 again

At this time No 60 Squadron was at Tengah equipped with Meteor NF14 night fighters and I was asked to have a look at one of their aircraft WH805 which was throwing tantrums. Before flying the new type I had a good look at the Pilots Notes and the flying was no problem. I found the NF14 a nice old lady and its handling was rather like driving a London bus. Later I discovered that the 60 Squadron navigators were not keen to fly with me again. They complained I flew it far too slowly on the approach. This surprised me as I was spot on the speeds recommended in the Pilots Notes. I often wondered about the approach speeds used by their own pilots.

Fg Off George Paul outbound on No 81 Sqn's 10,000th Firebird operation

For a little light entertainment we also had a Pembroke CPR Mk1 for any survey tasks which required the use of vertical cameras. It was flown only by a handful of pilots but it provided a pleasant change from undiluted jet flying. In May 1960 I was detailed to fly the Pembroke to Kuching in Sarawak and on to Labuan Island and return. I soon discovered my passengers were to be five RAF padres. As they were boarding the aircraft one of our nice, polite airmen asked the last padre "Going up on a visit, Sir?" When we flew from Tengah for tasks in the Borneo area we had a problem with the sun rising in front of us. We usually took off early so that we could be in the operational area by first photo light. Later in the day cumulus clouds would build up quickly and cover our targets. In the clear visibility over the South China Sea the sun was very strong and streamed into cockpit directly into our eyes. It could be very tiring and, after an hour or so, disorientating. The Pembroke had a simple form of autopilot with very limited authority and it frequently disengaged itself. On this flight I was glad for its assistance because half way to Kuching I suddenly woke up! I think I had only dozed off for a moment or two but when I checked around John Stanton, our navigator, and all five padres were also dozing or sleeping. It was the only time I have been in an aircraft with all seven occupants sleeping.

Our Squadron Commander, Sqn Ldr R J "Joss" Linford, was an old PR hand who had served his PR apprenticeship on PR Spitfires, a job which I would have loved. He was an excellent boss but he ruined my day when he told us we would be visited by CFS Examining Wing in October 1959 and that he had put in my name for an A1 Qualified Flying Instructor (QFI) recategorisation test. I protested that recats were only taken on established training units in UK where the QFIs were kept up to date with all the latest developments in training. This cut no ice with the Boss so I had to get on with my preparations in my spare time. At that time an experienced Mosquito and Canberra PR pilot was posted to the Squadron to await the arrival of our promised PR Canberras. Master Pilot Tommy Tomlin was keen to convert to the Meteor and it gave me the opportunity to give him a complete old fashioned Meteor conversion course before the Trappers arrived. Although Tommy was our oldest pilot he became a very enthusiastic Meteor pilot. If the T7 became available and I asked if anyone wished to come for some aerobatics Tommy would be right there. He also had a taste for formation flying and if we had had two more like him we might have formed the RAF's first PR squadron formation aerobatic team.

Singapore waterfront taken from No 81 Sqn's Percival Pembroke CPR Mk 1

When the Trappers team arrived the leader, Sqn Ldr Reg Jordan, came to 81 Sqn to discuss the test program and at first would not agree to conduct an A1 recat on an operational squadron within a 100 miles of the equator. However the Boss was adamant and persuaded Reg Jordan to go ahead with the test. Jim Rutter was allocated to the task. I knew that Jim was a very thorough examiner and he lived up to his reputation. For two days we slogged it out with two flights and long sessions on the ground in a temperature of 38 C with over 90% humidity which was not ideal for good aircraft performance or concentrated thinking. Although 81 Sqn was a Meteor squadron we also had at Tengah 45 Squadron RAF and 75 Squadron RNZAF with Canberra bombers so to add some spice to the test I gave my specialist lecture on "Handling the Canberra at Extreme Centre of Gravity Positions". At the end of the second day Jim announced that I had passed and we both collapsed. Later that evening we went to the Raffles Club with the Trappers and while the rest were having a high old time Jim and I sat watching the ripples on the swimming pool. We were absolutely drained. One of our pilots' antics resulted in a three months ban from the club but we did not even notice it. Thanks to the Boss's insistence I had got myself an unexpected A1 QFI category which carried an exceptional assessment and as far as I know this is the only time it has been gained on an operational squadron overseas and far removed from a flying training unit.

Suddenly I had a re-occurrence of the iritis of my left eye which I had encountered while on No 541 PR Squadron. Again I was packed off for a holiday in the RAF Hospital Changi. I had a very enjoyable rest in ideal surroundings while the apothecaries made more allergy tests. Nothing was identified, the iritis went away and I have never had a repeat attack.

During this time I remembered the wise words of Wg Cdr Bert Slade at Bassingbourn and began to think about applying for a Staff College course. A pre-condition for the course was a pass in the Staff College qualifying examination, known as the Q. This was based on a broad knowledge of current affairs and had to be prepared for in one's own time. The local pundits said that no one passed the Q in the tropics but an excellent Gp Capt from the Education Branch volunteered to run a course for candidates in the hope it might produce more applicants. I immediately booked a place and found it to be a fascinating break from my continuous flying tasks. I learned a great deal and enjoyed the experience. In due course Dickie Littlejohn, also from 81 Squadron, and I duly sailed through the exam and became eligible for Staff College.

On 1st August 1960 No 81 Sqn was invited by the Malay government to participate in a large fly past of aircraft over Kuala Lumpur to mark a national celebration day. PR squadrons do not normally practice formation flying but relations with Malaya were very good and we were keen to take part. We managed to fit in some practice and produced a nine ship Meteor formation. Only one full scale rehearsal was planned and then the great occasion was upon us. The fly past was led by the slowest aircraft and followed by successively faster flights. Our place in the fly past was behind a flight of Beverley transport aircraft and we were followed by an RN squadron of Seahawk fighters from a visiting aircraft carrier. The timing of the previous flights was not good and as we approached Kuala Lumpur we could see ahead the Beverleys looming larger and larger and we reduced our speed and weaved from side to side to attempt to stay behind. Of course this passed the problem on to the Seahawks behind us and as we approached the saluting base the Seahawks drifted slowly under us and won the race by a short head. Perhaps this is now recorded as another great naval victory.

Soon afterwards news circulated that we were about to re-equip with Canberra PR7s. The usual method of changing aircraft types on a squadron was for new crews to be trained at the OCU in UK and then fly out the new aircraft. When Joss Linford went through the Canberra OCU at Bassingbourn on his way to become OC 81 PR Sqn he said he would ask for me to be posted to the squadron. Soon afterward he told me that the Air Secretary had said it would not be possible. After two more months I received my posting to the squadron! When I arrived on the squadron Brian Olive, a PR navigator and Staff Navigator, was already there and was the Pembroke navigator. He had been with me at Bassingbourn and we were well qualified to convert the aircrew to the Canberras. Joss convinced HQ FEAF that the conversion was possible and we were all set to go.

In January 1960 a Canberra T2 trainer was delivered and after flying the first Canberra sortie on 81 Sqn we put Peter Eden, the Flight Commander, into the left seat and the conversion began. When Peter was ready to convert to the operational aircraft a PR7 was delivered and a qualified navigator, Eric Gladwin, also appeared. He also had been a Staff Navigator at Bassingbourn with me and also was able to help with the conversion. Next Dickie Littlejohn, the Deputy Flight Commander, went into the sausage machine and as he was churned out another PR7 and navigator arrived. So it went on for most of 1960 until Steve Armstrong, who was to become my navigator, arrived and the conversion had been completed at a bargain price.

I had flown with many navigators but I had never been crewed up with my own and I was dreading that I would finish up with the last available third rate navigator. It was a mighty relief to find that Steve was an experienced and vastly competent PR navigator. He was tall and slim, unlike myself, and he appeared to be rather quiet. However I soon discovered he had a dry sense of humour and his temperament suited me well. We became a very good crew.

During the conversion period I managed to get my share of Meteor operations so I had few complaints. We continued to operate both Meteors and Canberras until 7th July 1960 when Dickie Littlejohn and I delivered the RAF's last 2 Meteor PR10s to the MU at RAF Seletar to be written off. I made sure I was last one down! I taxied into the MU expecting to be marshalled to a place of honour but instead a scruffy airman waved me off the taxiway and immediately stopped me and asked me to shut down. I could not believe the RAF's last Meteor PR10 was being left so shabbily parked. Before I climbed out I took the crowbar provided to break the canopy in emergency. Fifty five years later I still have it!

I did not realise it at the time but I had just become the last single seat PR pilot in the RAF. Sidney Cotton had acquired his first Spitfire in about 1940 and by great single minded drive had bullied or cajoled the RAF into forming small units and then expanding them into bigger units. RAF commanders were desperate for up to date information from inside Europe and Sidney Cotton's results were so impressive that in a short time the first PRUs were established. The Spitfires were eventually joined by PR Mosquitoes but they had navigators. Both continued to the end of the war. After the war money was so scarce that both types had to continue in service until jet aircraft could be introduced to replace them. The Meteor PR 10 took over the Spitfire roll but by the late 1950s they were replaced in Europe and the Middle East by Canberra PR 3. No 81 PR Squadron was the last remaining Meteor PR unit but my flight with the last aircraft to RAF Seletar had brought the era of single seat PR to an end. The whole period of the single seat PR operations had only lasted a bare 20 years and I felt very proud to have closed the last chapter of the great contribution made by the unsung heroes of the PRUs. It had been my ideal role and I was happy that I had been the last of the cold and lonely pilots.

Last 2 Meteor PR10s fly over No 81 Sqn flight line
en route to Seletar before last Meteor PR10 flight in RAF service

Most of my earlier flying had been as a single seat pilot but when I was crewed up with Steve I was very conscious of the fact that if anything untoward happened to Steve I could safely fly the aircraft back to an appropriate airfield but Steve would be stranded if anything happened to me. Every time we had the opportunity to fly the Canberra T Mk 4 alone Steve would fly in the right hand pilot's seat and fly as much as possible. Eventually I was happy that he would be able to land the aircraft in emergency. I am glad he didn't become a pilot because he was an excellent navigator for me. During one of Steve's dual sorties we were bounced by a Javelin of No 60 Sqn. Although the Canberra T Mk 4 had heavy controls it was very manoeuvrable if brute strength was applied. The Javelin pilot was soon surprised to have a Canberra sitting on his tail. I often wonder if he told his fellow pilots.

When No 45 Sqn arrived at Tengah with their Canberra B2s they did not have all their aircraft and they brought with them an old Bomber Command spare aircraft. When their last aircraft arrived the great topic of conversation in 45 Sqn was about who would fly the old aircraft home? It was in poor shape and restricted to a range of 1,200 miles. HQ FEAF, in their great wisdom settled the problem. They decided that Steve and I would fly WH922 to UK and bring back our last Canberra PR7. I had the task of visiting 45 Sqn to announce the glad tidings and then escape without major injury. Steve and I spent 8 days in February 1961 nursing WH922 along the pretty way back to Wroughton. We developed a routine at the en-route airfields whereby Steve did all the hard work. He trudged around ATC, Met, Customs and all the other departments who always got into the act while I looked after the aircraft. I ensured they refuelled us with the correct fuel and oil and refitted the covers properly. I reloaded starter cartridges and made a thorough check of the aircraft.

We had a night stop at Delhi and after collecting nine office stamps on one piece of paper we were allowed to travel to our hotel in the city centre. Our taxi was an ancient Morris Minor and we were somewhat surprised when the driver and his mate had to push start it. Halfway into the city they had an intense discussion in Hindi which finished when they asked us if we could pay them then so that they could buy some petrol. We wondered how they knew that they needed to refuel because there were no instruments on the dash board, only empty spaces.

Next morning we had to collect another nine clearance stamps on our piece of paper and then we were on our way to Karachi, Masirah and Aden. After being one of the first aircraft to land on the new runway at Karachi airport which had opened that morning we were soon on our way again.

All went well until we arrived in the circuit at the old airfield on Masirah Island. The airfield had compacted coral runways and the edges were marked with dashes of old engine oil. Unfortunately a brisk wind had covered all the marks with sand. I had with me a large map of the airfield from the old Pilots Handbook and noted that the runway we were looking for started near the control tower. We made a low approach to where we suspected the runway might be and then applied full power and flew down the line of the runway as low as possible to try to blow some sand away. After a very quick circuit we approached again and, lo and behold, in front of us were sufficient marks for us to land on the runway.

No 81 Sqn aircraft in 1960

As we came to halt on the Khormaksar parking strip in Aden the door was opened and the head of an old friend, appeared. It was Mickie Murden who had been our Engineering Officer at Bassingbourn and he brightly inquired, "Have you got your mess kit with you? It's our Winter Ball tonight". We didn't have our mess kit so, like Cinderella, we couldn't go to the ball but instead we found ourselves in a 1 star transit hotel in Aden known as The Rock. Our first floor room had no air conditioning but a single ceiling fan. It was hot and sticky so we opened the window and discovered just below us a makeshift pen holding a herd of about 50 very pungent goats. We had the choice of closing the window and risk becoming steamed puddings or sharing our room with the goats. When we went to the dining room we found a Transport Command Comet crew sharing the hotel with us. Having travelled to Khormaksar in luxury they were provided with air conditioned rooms while we, having flown three stages through Karachi and Masirah unassisted, felt definitely steerage class. If we had taken some loaded camera magazines with us the magazines would have been entitled to air conditioning and Steve and I could have shared their room with them.

Our new PR7 was not fully serviceable at Wroughton and we had to spend 10 days living in wooden hutted accommodation at RAF Clyffe Pypard during a particularly cold part of the winter. Singapore seemed to be far away. My original Tiger Moth instructor, Ken Wilson, was now a Flt Lt and a Britannia captain at RAF Lyneham and he came up to Clyffe Pypard for a very happy re-union. At last we got away but for some technical reason we not allowed to use the Gan route and we had to return via the Indian route. This time the British Embassy had booked us into the Ashoka Hotel which at that time was the best in New Delhi. This was a very welcome time-out during the journey and I have rarely seen such a well organised luxury hotel and unobtrusive excellent service. However such good things do not last and we were soon in our flying suits again and on the way to Calcutta.

On the tarmac at Karachi Airport with Shell mechanic

We arrived back at Tengah after a 24 day absence to a welcoming committee of the Station Commander, OC Flying Wing, my wife Marlies and daughter Jenni.

Return to RAF Tengah from UK
Jenni, Marlies, BA, Steve, Gp Capt JES Morton

At this time groups of the Squadron's airmen organised trips away from the island. They went by lorry to the east coast of Malaya near Mersing and then by local boat to a deserted island such as Pulau Tingii. They took with them all their rations, including water, and personal kit and spent about a week doing their own version of a survival exercise. Every day one of our pilots would include in their planned sorties a visit to the island in either a Meteor or Canberra to check if there were any emergency messages in their signal square. They never had any problems but we loved visiting them.

Visiting airmen at Pulau Tinggi in Meteor T Mk 7

And in a Canberra PR Mk 7

Continuous operations over the jungle inevitably resulted in aircraft crashing into it and during my time on No 81 Sqn I was involved in three intensive searches for missing aircraft. The first two, in June and November 1960, were for Austers which had been operating into the jungle forts. Full effort was mounted for these searches and I flew six sorties. When a small Auster crashed into the trees it would easily slip through the tree tops and disappear under the jungle canopy and was extremely difficult to locate from the air. After much effort one Auster was located but as far as I know the other was not found.

The third search was for a RNZAF Canberra from No 75 Sqn. It had been tasked to fly a high level navigation sortie over Malaya by night. It was a moonless night and cumulonimbus clouds were scattered over Malaya. In Northern Europe such clouds often rise to over 30,000 feet but in the tropics they can be much bigger and stronger and rise up to 50,000 feet. An aircraft cruising at around 30,000 feet on a dark night can enter one of these monsters accidentally and not realise it until he hits severe turbulence. The Canberra had suddenly entered a particularly violent area of the cloud and after fighting to control the aircraft the pilot was overpowered and the aircraft entered a spin. The pilot ordered his navigator to eject and after hearing a bang he also ejected and the aircraft crashed into the jungle. Another maximum effort was mounted and we photographed large areas of jungle around the estimated site of the crash. The Canberra made a larger mark in the jungle canopy and the crashed aircraft was located. A major ground search was organised and the aircraft was reached. The pilot who had landed nearby was also rescued. Unfortunately the body of the navigator was found in the wreckage.

Perhaps it was appropriate that about this time Steve and I were sent on the FEAF jungle survival course which lasted two weeks. The first week was spent in a camp at Changi where we were given lectures and practical exercises to prepare us for a week in the jungle. Steve remembers eating a very tasty fish wrapped in banana leaves which had been cooked in a pit on the beach at Changi. Then we were taken by lorry to the east coast of Malaya where we spent a day and night on the edge of the jungle by the sea. We had been allowed to bring a dead chicken with us and we were shown a very effective way to cook it. At breakfast time we made our fires in a shallow hole in the sand on the beach. We cleaned the chicken, added some salt to taste and then put it in the bottom part of our mess tins, closed the top half over it and then put it on top of the embers of our fire, covered it over with sand and left it while we did an exercise in the jungle. When we returned several hours later the chicken was beautifully cooked but perhaps it tasted so good because we were hungry.

To begin the serious part of the course we were taken in parties of six by road to an area of primary jungle, shown our position on our maps and told to make our way through the jungle to a rendezvous point at another road several miles away. They said they would be waiting for us in five days' time. Within five minutes we had learned one basic fact about jungle travel. In the first few metres we came across a fallen tree obstructing our route and we had the choice of burrowing under it or climbing over. Either way we finished up wet through. The Malayan jungle is wet! It is wet under foot and every branch of a tree has enough water clinging to it to make a shower bath. We were wet and we stayed wet for the next five days. Steve still remembers that it rained every night we were in the jungle. In our packs we had a spare set of jungle fatigue suits and it became essential to try to keep the spare suit dry.

The jungle was so dense that we had to hack a clearance for almost every step with a machete. One of the party went first wielding the machete, behind him at a safe distance came a man with a compass whose task it was to keep the machete man heading in the right direction. Behind him came No 3 whose task was to make steady strides and count them. He would log every 10 steps with a notch on a stick which he carried. The remainder of the party kept a general look out while regaining their strength. At regular intervals of perhaps 20 to 50 steps, depending on the density of the trees and creepers, the leading man would go to the rear of the party and all other members moved up one place. Sometimes, in old virgin jungle, the going became easier but the next problem was deep valleys which had to be crossed. If we were to make our rendezvous point we had to stay on track. A journey of one mile in a day was good going.

Before night set in we had to decide where to bivouac for the night. We needed to find a site near water and this was generally no problem. Shelters had to be built and food prepared. Each member of the party had a 24 ration pack to last us for the whole journey. Any extra food we had to find in the jungle. When shelters and food were taken care of we then stripped off our soaking wet, dirty clothes and went to the river to wash, downstream from the place from which we drew our drinking water. While washing we inspected each other to locate our day's supply of leeches. Even the non-smokers carried cigarettes and matches to remove the leeches. The hot tip of a cigarette made them withdraw their heads from their feeding bowls (us) and they could then be removed. When cleaned up we returned to our shelters, being careful not to pick up more leeches, and donned our dry suits before getting in to our shelters. In the morning the first thing after washing was to put on the wet, dirty suit for the day's march and pack the drier suit away. It was a great temptation to wear the dry suit and one or two members did just that. The result was two wet, dirty suits and no dry suit to sleep in. They discovered why we had been briefed to keep one as dry as possible. How we came to hate the horrible wet, muddy suits!

We were always on the lookout for food and on one occasion Steve and I killed a green mamba snake and we found that the tail which was like a cucumber was similar when cooked to a light meat such as chicken. A good tip was to leave the greasy paper from a butter pack out all night and let it trap a layer of ants. We had been told they were a good source of protein and who is going to argue when you are hungry. Each day was similar but some were easier when the jungle thinned out but others were exhausting when we came into patches of secondary jungle which had been cleared by natives and had then grown again. We had planned our route to arrive at the road south of our meeting point so that when we hit the road we knew we had to turn north and all would be well. We were all very relieved when the lorry arrived.

WHAT ? NO CHOCOLATE FLAVOUR ?

The Jungle Survival Course as seen by Robin Brown

We had learned that we could live and travel in the jungle. Water was in abundance and enough food could be obtained to survive. The major problem was getting safely on to the floor of the jungle. Our most likely method of arrival would be by parachute but most of the trees were up to 200 ft high. The parachute canopy would invariably be caught by the trees and we would be left dangling way above the ground, too high to risk releasing the harness and falling to the ground. We all had our own solutions to this problem and I always had a 200 ft length of parachute cord placed handily in my flying suit and I had a method of threading it through my parachute harness before cutting my parachute lines and abseiling down complete with dinghy and emergency pack.

The lorry took our party back to Changi but the best was still to come. We were taken in the evening to a point about two miles west of Changi jail and told we had to make our way eastwards to the road which ran north to south just east of Changi jail. It was a night escape and evasion exercise and the police and RAF Regiment were guarding the route and waiting to capture and interrogate us. I travelled with Steve and to minimize the risk of capture we walked about 100 metres apart so that if the first one was caught the other might be able to escape. We changed the lead frequently to even out the risk of being captured. All bridges and junctions were guarded and we worked our way across country. To cross one water drain we had to wade across up to our necks in the water and up to our knees in mud. All was going well until we were nearly home and dry. Steve was leading and we were sneaking along the side of a road approaching a well-lit cross road which we saw was guarded by local soldiers. Steve was treading very carefully while deciding what to do when suddenly a patrol of RAF Regiment thugs leapt out of cover on my left and grabbed me. I let out a yell to warn Steve and he immediately set off at full gallop and charged straight through the check point on the cross roads and he was away before they reacted. In spite of my predicament I was amused by the sight of Steve in full flight. It was the only time I saw him moving so quickly.

I was taken to an old gun position on the coast by Changi airfield where I was stripped naked, blindfolded and frog marched in to a room for interrogation. Although they were pretty rough and put a metal bucket upside down over my head and beat it with a metal bar at irregular intervals it was no great problem to avoid disclosing any information. For being uncooperative I was taken to an old ammunition locker built into the side of a gun position, wedged inside and the metal door closed on me. The concrete had been heated up by the sun during the day and acted like a night storage heater. I was in a slow cooker and to make things more interesting my tormentors would sneak along occasionally and beat on the metal door with the same old iron bar. When I was almost cooked I was dragged out of the locker, a bag was put over my head and I was made to stand about 4 feet away from a wall and lean against the wall resting on my finger tips. After a while the pain in my hands built up and my whole hands seemed to be on fire. If any attempt was made to rest the palms of the hands against the wall retribution immediately followed with a hefty thwack on my backside with what seemed to be a wooden lathe. When they tired of this amusement I was shoved back in my cooker but they took me out when dawn was appearing and threw me into a concrete block house which had an opening in the roof. Several other prisoners were already inside and we were still naked. To prevent us sitting or lying down the enemy would frequently throw a bucket of water and gravel into the chamber through the top hatch. Have you ever tried sitting on gravel with a bare backside? We were not allowed to attempt to escape unless we outnumbered the captors by three to one. We reckoned that when they brought new prisoners there were three of them. When we had eight prisoners in the room we waited for the next to arrive and when the door was unlocked we forced it open, barged the guards aside and fled. We saw a camp gate nearby and six of us galloped through, crossed the road and sat on the side of a ditch. Three others had been held by the guards. By this time it was daylight and the occupants of several cars passing along the road were surprised to see six naked but obviously happy men sitting on the roadside. An umpire came along and declared that our escape was invalid because there were two guards on the roof and we had not over powered them. However by this time the exercise had ended and we could not have cared less. During the exercise I had let my beard grow and my final memory of the course was at home when Jenni was sitting on my lap playing with my beard.

Operating the Canberra PR7 at maximum weight from the new Tengah runway had a similar problem to the Meteor PR10. Although now the runway length was adequate we still had a dead man's gap after take-off. If an engine failed between take off and about 150 kts the aircraft could not be controlled without throttling back and thus being committed to a crash landing in the very rough overshoot areas. At 150 kts control could be maintained with difficulty but it would not climb away. Not until about 190 Kts could a climb be established. Our ejection seats were similar to the Meteor PR10 and could not be used below 200 ft and 200 kts. We proposed to HQ FEAF that unless maximum range was essential we should be allowed to operate with empty or removed wing tanks. The proposal was rejected. By great good fortune we never had an engine failure in Dead Man's Corner.

In the Canberras we had another similar problem to the Meteors with high cockpit temperatures. They were fitted with cooling units which drew air in from the leading edge of the wing but with the fixed canopy the temperature began to rise immediately the cockpit door was closed and the cooling unit had to work hard. At slow speed while taxying there was very little airflow into the intakes and they would begin to overheat. When the aircraft was airborne the problem disappeared but we could not afford any delays before take-off. A rule was eventually introduced to compel crews to abort their sorties if they could not take off within 20 minutes from the cockpit door being closed.

During 1961 the squadron had very interesting tasks in Hong Kong and Steve and I were chosen to fly one in October. As I was not familiar with the approach patterns at Hong Kong's old Kai Tak runway I had to fly there before our planned visit in a Hasting from Changi. After the passengers were disembarked the Hastings' captain and I flew all the approaches by night in an otherwise empty aircraft. One of my lasting memories was the approach to the south east runway which ran out into the harbour. The let-down was to Cheong Chow island, west of Hong Kong Island, then at low level through the harbour over Stonecutters Island and directly towards a huge red and white chequer board painted on a rock face high above Kowloon city. When the chequer board was close in front of your nose at a height of about 500 feet you turned hard right and there was the runway straight ahead. All that was then required was to land without running into the harbour. When Steve and I returned to Hong Kong in our Canberra we had the task of peering over the border into China. Before we flew from Kai Tak we were given very enjoyable conducted tours by an Army Captain along the border in an Auster AOP Mk 9. When Steve's turn came I was amused to witness an Army Auster being navigated by one of the RAF's best navigators. At least the pilot could be sure of his position once in his flying career. When all conditions with the weather, the aircraft and Tai Mo Shan's surveillance radar were all favourable we climbed out of Kai Tak and returned overhead at altitude and then tip toed very quietly over the border. If any air activity was detected in our area we were recalled and we high tailed it back to the airfield. Several attempts were sometimes needed to complete the task.

We had a survey task to fly over Hong Kong but instead of the normal 30,000ft we flew it at 50,000 ft and we managed to capture most of Hong Kong on one frame of the film. I wonder what the Chinese thought about a Canberra floating around at 50,000 ft on their doorstep. After that the return to Tengah was all downhill.

HQ FEAF ran a Sea Survival Course which all operational crews were supposed to attend and so it was inevitable that Steve and I soon found ourselves at the Sea Survival School at Changi. We spent several days attending lectures and demonstrations before being thrown to the sharks. During this phase they also took the opportunity to brush up our parachute training. After falling all over the training hangar floor forwards, backwards and sideways after been suspended and swung around in a parachute harness we were invited to climb up to the very top of the hangar and, after being attached to a cable which ran outside to the ground about 50 metres away, cast ourselves into space, fall about 3 metres and then career off downhill until we arrived on the ground in a crumpled heap.

NO. 81 (PR) SQUADRON
BACK L-R.
M/N TAYLOR.W.J.C.- F/L P.R.BARTLETT- F/L J.H.M.BEVER- F/O R.B.OLIVE.- F/O F.W.POOLE.- F/L S.W.ARMSTRONG- F/L J.R.STANTON- F/L T.B.CHILTON.
(ADJ.)

No 81 Squadron aircrew 1961

This was a horror for me as I have always had a fear of standing unsecured on even moderately high surfaces. I had no problems when flying and when I was in the BBC and Royal Navy I took great delight in climbing and working on high masts. In the first few days of our course we had to carry out dinghy drills in the swimming pool and part of the training was to put on our parachute harnesses and dinghy packs, climb up to the high diving board and jump into the pool. This was always the worst part of any RAF training throughout by career. Steve was a very reliable comrade and I let him go ahead while I followed well behind. I hoped he would keep steadily moving when we reached the top and he never let me down. When I arrived on the diving board Steve was on his way down. From that moment I went on to autopilot and nothing on earth was going to stop me walking along the board and off the end. If they had drained all the water out of the pool I would still have gone!

When we came to do the practice parachute descent I adopted the same procedure. Off went Steve and I trailed behind. At the top of the hangar was a small platform high above the ground on which an RAF parachute instructor checked that we were securely attached to the cable before we jumped into space. Steve had disappeared as I came on to the platform and I hoped I could get it over quickly. My harness was checked and the PJI gave the order to jump. As I jumped his bizarre sense of humor took over and he called, "As you were", meaning, "Come back". In the brief time before my parachute harness jerked me upright I died a thousand deaths. With friends like that who needs enemies? I often wondered if Steve noticed that I was slow in following him on these occasions.

Return from Hong Kong

The culmination of the course was a day at sea. Early in the morning we were taken on a launch way out to sea. As Steve and I flew with single seat dinghies we were thrown into the sea individually. We were dragged for a while to simulate landing in a high wind and being dragged by the parachute. After stabilising ourselves in the water we were cast off and the launch disappeared on its way to the horizon. We then retrieved our dinghy pack, found the inflation bottle, inflated the dinghy, hauled ourselves aboard and then pulled the protective covers over ourselves to shade us from the sun. Then began one of the most boring days of my life. The most exciting part was setting up the water distillation kit and waiting for it to produce water. I have heard people talk about watching paint dry but that is far more exciting. I also dug out a simple fishing kit and trailed it hopefully in the sea. If I had caught a fish I think the excitement would have given me a heart attack. After I had contemplated my navel for about 8 hours the launch returned and returned us back to Changi and we had all survived.

While we were operating the Meteor PR10s they were in very short supply but as they were very serviceable we were able to maintain Squadron strength until they were withdrawn. On the other hand the RAF had plenty of surplus Meteor T7s. If we had a seriously unserviceable T7 it was more economical to draw a spare from the Maintenance Unit than to spend time and money repairing the sick one. During my time on 81 Sqn we had several T7s but in November 1959 I took some leave and when I returned to duty I had the shock of my life. Standing on the strip was Meteor T7 WH226, one of my oldest and favourite friends. I first flew WH226 on 16th May 1952 while I was instructing at 207 AFS at Full Sutton. It had a grand total of 1hour and 10 minutes and was one of the straightest Meteors that I flew. It became my favourite and I used it during the next 18 months as often as possible and particularly for any aerobatic displays. In 1959 it was much dirtier and creaked and groaned a bit but it still flew beautifully. When flying aerobatics with the manual controls the pilot had excellent feedback from the control surfaces and one could feel what was happening to the aircraft through the control column as if it was talking to you. In return I used to talk back to it. I had many interesting conversations with WH226.

Naturally I was delighted to resume my love affair and dual checks etc became almost enjoyable. In April 1961 the Singapore Government opened Payah Lebar International Airport in the middle of Singapore

Island. They decided to have a grand opening ceremony lasting ten days. They assembled aircraft from the RAF, Royal Navy, RAAF, RNZAF, Royal Australian Navy and the Royal Marines for the occasion. I represented the RAF in WH226 on the first day and relished the idea that we were repeating our first show after 8 years. I repeated the display as the last item on the final day. An ex-RAF reporter for the South China Morning Post wrote an over the top account of the display in the paper and I had the Mickie taken out of me for some time. PR pilots were not expected to perform such unseemly antics!

And what an air display it was! Crack flyers from the Royal Navy, the Royal Australian Navy, the Royal Air Force, the Royal Australian Air Force, and the Royal Marines thrilled the crowds for hours on end. For sheer virtuosity in the split-second art of controlling an aircraft at near-sonic speeds, a solo flyer of the R.A.F. must surely take the prize.

Variations

He staged his display with all the artistry of a great musician. Beginning with the standard routine of loops and rolls, he then proceeded to execute variations of the highest elegance on these basic themes in a performance that I have never seen surpassed and I served in the R.A.F. for 13 years, so I am not easily moved to wide-eyed wonder by an aerobatic display!

Extract from South China Morning Post

HQ FEAF decided to lay on an Exercise Pluto for the benefit of the local media during which they would be shown aircraft landing, camera magazines being removed, aircrew debriefing, processing of the film, interpretation from the wet film, printing and eventually to view the finished films. A huge tent was erected on the edge of the flight dispersal and we were supposed to make a smart line for the tent to give our debriefing reports. Robin Brown, a recently arrived pilot, was also an excellent cartoonist with a sharp eye for anything unusual and he was around at the time and produced a drawing to mark the occasion. It was a very apt commentary on the events. On 24th October we had a party in the squadron's crew room and Robin produced the invitations. As usual they were collector's items.

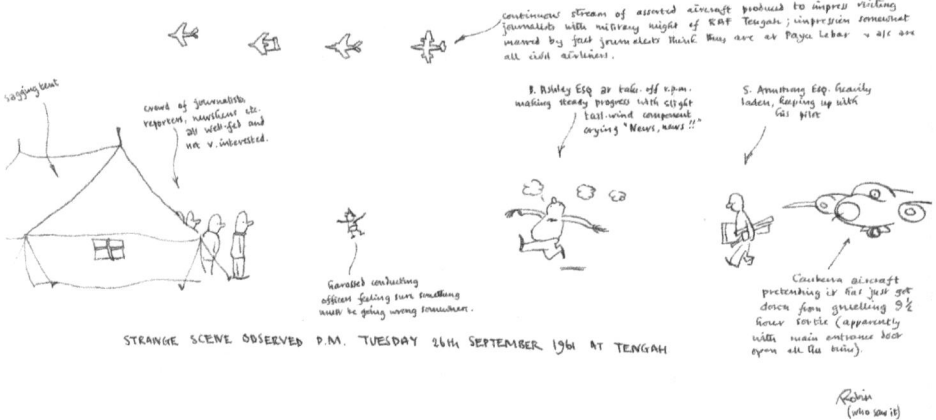

Exercise Pluto as seen by Robin Brown

When I left the Squadron Steve stayed behind and was crewed up with Robin. They flew a low level sortie in Borneo in the early days of the Borneo Confrontation and Robin, in poor weather, managed to leave 3 or 4 feet of the aircraft's starboard wing tip on a radio mast. The starboard aileron was damaged and much fuel was lost. Steve was in the nose at the time and had a close up view of the incident. The Canberra was a tough old bird and Robin did a good job in landing it safely at Labuan Island.

In the early days of P.R......

After the dawn patrol, crews would come back for wine and cheese in the local Estaminet —

No: 81 Squadron

invites Flt. Lt. & Mrs. B. A. Ashley to partake in the old P.R. custom on Tuesday 24th October 1961 at 8 p.m. in 81 Sqn. Crew room. Dress: living suits & gosport tubes, or informal.

R.S.V.P. The Adjutant No. 81 Squadron

Party invitation by Robin Brown

Survey tasks made a pleasant change from the normal operational sorties and in November 1961 Steve and I were fortunate to fly part of a high level photographic mapping task for the Thai government. The RAF had been requested by the Royal Thai Survey Department, a part of the Thai Army, to cover all of Thailand and a few gaps remained to be filled in. We flew from Tengah and spent a pleasant morning trundling east and west over southern Thailand until our fuel state demanded a refuelling stop at Bangkok. The old runway at Dom Muang Airport had a small hump about a third of the way down the prevailing runway and if a pilot was not alert it could lift the weight off the main wheels sufficiently for the brakes to lock the wheels and burst a tyre. We were met by our liaison officer, Lt Somnoek of the Royal Thai Survey Department. He was their only pilot and he flew an old Dakota aircraft which had a camera mounted on the floor of the cabin with an appropriate hole cut in the underside of the fuselage. It was rarely serviceable. He met us with a large, impressive American car and took great delight in driving us past the resident Sabre F86D squadron to show that he had good friends. When we were leaving the airport to go to Bangkok the car broke down and had to be replaced by a tatty service vehicle. At least he had had his moment of glory. The evening in Bangkok was an excellent example of Thai hospitality away from the sleazier tourist areas. Somnoek guided us around Bangkok and his favourite shops and insisted we were his friends and not tourists. Good bargains were easily obtained. In the evening we were taken with his wife and a small group of his friends and relations to a restaurant with floor show and we enjoyed one of the most enjoyable evenings. Next day we flew another survey sortie before returning to Tengah but before take-off we were each presented with an engraved silver cigarette case from the Royal Thai Survey Department to commemorate our visit. We were very sad to hear some time later that Somnoek had been killed while flying his Dakota. He had been hit by a RTAF Sabre F86D in the circuit at Dom Muang Airport and both aircraft were destroyed.

During our tour we had many civilian friends in Singapore city and we were invited to help out a pair of close friends. Rex had an important business visitor who had a reputation for being extremely difficult to entertain. He asked us if we would join them to try and liven up the occasion. The pre-dinner drinks period was very hard going and every conversation ground to a halt. Eventually dinner was ready for serving and as we wandered through into the dining room their Malay amah came through the kitchen door carrying a tray of soup. She was an attractive little girl and was wearing the traditional sarong and white lace blouse. The family's little white dog had been banished to the back rooms for the evening but as the amah opened the kitchen door it seized its chance and raced into the dining room. It did a couple of high speed laps around the room skidding around the corners of the slippery floor and as it passed the amah on the second lap it seized the bottom of her sarong. It gave it a shaking as if it were savaging a rat and off came the sarong. The evening never looked back.

Towards the end of the year when the end of my tour was looming on the horizon I received a letter from Jim Campbell who was soon to finish his tour at Bassingbourn. He was delighted to tell me that he had been posted to replace me on No 81 Sqn. He asked if we would like to take Susie back again which gave us much food for thought. Jim told us that his parents had fallen in love with Susie and, if we could not take her back, they would be very glad to have her at their home in the Kent countryside. I had been told that I would probably go to Staff College but it was not known whether it would be Andover or Bracknell and as the starting dates were 5 months apart the crystal ball was very muddy. After much emotional deliberation we told Jim to let her go to his parents where we knew she would have a secure and happy future. She stayed with the Campbells until she died when she was 14 years old.

The domestic arrangements at the end of my tour were quite chaotic. Even though the RAF could not decide what to do with me they decided that Marlies and Jenni would have to return to UK in November. We had no home in England so Marlies chose to go to Germany to her family until my future was resolved. I was not happy as I watched them depart on a Britannia aircraft for Stanstead. Robin Brown took over my house and Trixie and I moved into the Officers Mess.

In November 1961 I was sent for by AOC 224 Group, AVM Ramsay-Rae, who was very concerned by the results of a recent CFS Examining Wing visit. A Flight Commander on the Target Facilities Flight at Seletar equipped with Meteor TT Mk 22s and a Meteor T7 had performed so badly that the examiner had recommended that he be withdrawn from all flying. The AOC showed me the report and asked my opinion. I thought the recommendation was very severe as it was based on one 40 minute duration flight. The pilot had a DFC from WW2 and was coming to the end of his flying career. His last posting would be to ATC duties. I suggested that I should fly with the pilot to make my own assessment. Trusty old WH226 was saddled up again and we flew a couple of sorties with the condemned man. The Trapper was right; he was awful. After the flight I talked at some length with the pilot and discovered that he had never had any training on the Meteor or any twin jet. He had been a Flight Commander on a Vampire squadron in Germany. They used a Meteor T7 for instrument flying training and dual checks. He had flown virtually as an observer while the other pilot had made the checks and flown the various procedures. At the end of his tour in Germany his flying record showed that he had flown quite a few hours on Meteors and Air Ministry had assumed he was a qualified Meteor pilot and posted him to Seletar. The AOC was reluctant to see an otherwise meritorious career ended so ignominiously and I suggested that I should give him enough Meteor instruction to see him safely to the end of his tour and the end of his flying career. The AOC agreed and WH226 and I finished in FEAF where we started in 1952; giving Exercises 1, 2, 3 and 4 from the Meteor training syllabus. During the instruction I noticed that every time he went near a Meteor he became full of stress. Before we climbed aboard he had a quick nervous pee on the edge of the strip and as soon as he was away from the parking strip he smoked continuously. He had obviously been living in fear of flying during his tour and I admired him for not throwing in his hand. It was very satisfying to see him gaining confidence as the instruction proceeded and by the end of his short course he was at ease with himself. I had never before seen a pilot frightened of flying and I tried to imagine what it had been like for him returning to duty every morning. It took more guts than for pilots who loved flying. On 21st November 1961 I flew my last session with him and it was also my last flight on 81 Sqn. It also ended my love affair with WH226 which soldiered on with No 81 Sqn.

Steve also stayed on and became the longest serving navigator on the Squadron. He was the best navigator I ever flew with. For me Staff College and a desk loomed ahead but first I had to find Marlies and Jenni.

Steve as seen by Robin Brown

CHAPTER 13
No 15 Course. RAF Staff College, Bracknell.

MARLIES and Jenni had been flown home from Singapore in November 1961 and as the RAF had no idea about my future they decided to stay with friends in Germany. At very late notice the Air Ministry was able to find a place for me on No 15 Course at the RAF Staff College Bracknell and so my immediate future was settled. My departure from Singapore and arrival at Bracknell was chaotic. Because of my late addition to the course we did not have a Married Quarter available to move into. The quarter which had been allocated was occupied by Peter Latham who had 5 children, a dog and a 6 months pregnant wife. Under these abnormal circumstances he had been given permission to stay in the quarter until the situation normalised.

I arrived in UK in mid December and decided to join Marlies and Jenni in Germany where we spent an unexpected Christmas and New Year. I returned to Bracknell just after New Year and moved into the Mess until our quarter was available. On 3rd January I was having breakfast with Charlie Slade who had just finished 14 Course and while savouring our coffee Charlie said, "Oh, congratulations!" I asked for the reason and he told me he thought my name was in the New Year's promotion list. Immediately after breakfast I went looking for the list and, sure enough, I was to begin the course as a brand new Squadron Leader. I could hardly wait to send the news post haste to Marlies and Jenni.

The College was accommodated in the lovely old Ramslade House with its beautiful flower laden grounds. A lecture hall, an assembly area known as the Flag Room and administrative offices had been added to cope with 96 students and staff but our syndicate rooms were prefabricated huts behind the offices.

Soon our course assembled and we were divided into syndicates of six for the first of the usual three terms of the academic year. All the students were of post graduate status and we were all specialists in our own branches with only a glancing knowledge of the remainder of the RAF. We were all cleared for NATO Secret information so that was the course classification. A typical syndicate had three RAF officers, an Army, Navy or Civil Service officer, an old Commonwealth and a NATO representative. An indication of the diversity of the students was the different backgrounds of me and our civil servant, John Dole. For 13 years I had been happy flying aeroplanes around the world at the lowest levels of the Air Force while John had served on the top floor of the Air Ministry building and had arrived at Bracknell after a tour as Private Secretary to the Vice Chief of the Air Staff. I had rarely been in contact with anyone above station level but John had been in close contact with decision making at the very top of the Air Force. We could and did learn much from each other.

We were fortunate to be allocated to the syndicate of Wg Cdr Peter Vicary, an experienced Administrative Officer, who had the task of beating our written and spoken English into acceptable shape. This was the foundation stone on which Staff College training was based and was essential if we, in our later jobs, were to produce orders and briefings which would not lead to unnecessary casualties. The mnemonic ABC for accuracy, brevity and clarity will stay with me for the rest of my life. I had brought with me from Singapore an Olivetti portable typewriter and I burnt much midnight oil pounding at it with two to 4 fingers to produce my best possible work. During the first three months we all had to choose a subject for a ten minute talk which would be given to the whole course and Directing Staff (DS) on the stage of the lecture hall and which would be followed by questions and criticisms by the whole assembly. I chose as my subject Tunku Abdul Rahman, the charismatic Prime Minister of Malaya and while I was preparing for the big event I watched, every morning, one of my colleagues being put to the Inquisition. The comments were ruthless and if the victim had any failings in his lecture technique they were mercilessly exposed. Of course the whole process was designed to put the students under stress and it certainly succeeded. I discussed various options with my DS and he pointed out that nearly all students mounted the steps to the left of the stage, walked across to a lectern on the right side, arranged their notes and then gave their magnum opus from the shelter of the parapet. He posed the question; why not stand in mid stage where the audience had a clear target to snipe at? I would have been quite happy to take refuge behind the lectern but Staff College was looking for future leaders so I decided to risk a heart attack. On the day I walked to the middle of the stage and then turned to face the enemy. I knew of the exposure felt on a steep rock face but it is no comparison with facing 120 critical faces all focused on you. I had my notes in my jacket pocket but I had rehearsed thoroughly and did not need to dig them out. At the end I received my allocation of adverse comments but was pleased to note that no one had noticed that my left knee had been shaking uncontrollably. I had been saved by a good pair of Gieves Bros trousers!

A major subject during the course was problem solving and before any major operation a formal document known as an appreciation was prepared by the Commander to produce his plan of action. The appreciation set out the aim of the operation simply and clearly, reviewed the forces available to both sides and all relevant factors before setting out the enemy's possible courses of action. This led to the Commanders courses of action and eventually the choice of the best course and finally the plan. This was our next task and we were provided with all the information available to the German High Command in 1940 and asked to produce an appreciation named See Adler for them to fight the Battle of Britain. It was an individual exercise and after a detailed briefing we were allowed two weeks outside of lectures to produce our final plan. During the debriefings we found that almost every plan would have won the battle for the Germans. The amazing fact was that the Germans never produced such a plan and failed to win. Exercise See Adler had been used at the Staff College and updated annually for about 15 years but we were the last course to use it. The whole procedure was changed to a more informal service paper which used similar methods but was much more streamlined. In retrospect I found that learning the full technique never let me down. Later I learned that another important acronym for planners was KISS, keep it simple, stupid.

At last our married quarter became available and Marlies and Jenni returned from Germany and we began settling in. Marlies began her usual role of making a comfortable home. The large houses were not equipped with central heating or insulation and keeping them warm was a major problem. We decided to buy an enclosed anthracite stove and I devised a method of installing and removing it. It was used from autumn to spring every year until after I retired from the RAF and always kept us warm. Jenni was approaching her fifth birthday and we were lucky that the Staff College had its own junior school and she was able to settle in with an excellent teacher. It was here that she received the foundation of the 3 Rs which always stood her in good stead. On most sunny days she could be found outside exploring Ramslade Road on her new acquisition, a bicycle with outrigger wheels.

The Ramslade Road Patrol

We were all slogging away at our exercises but we soon had welcome respite, the first of many visits. The course assembled early and embarked on three of Mr Smith's Luxury Coaches which then set course for RAF Scampton. When we were in the Midlands and beginning to wriggle with sore backsides the coaches pulled into a carefully selected lay by with urgently needed toilets. We were surprised to find that our mess staff was already fully deployed and a late breakfast was prepared for us on neatly laid out tables. It was not only a welcome break but also a lesson for us in detailed planning.

We were very familiar with living under the threat of a surprise attack from the east but it brought home to us the constant danger of a nuclear war when we visited four Vulcan bombers armed with nuclear weapons sitting on the end of the runway ready for immediate take off. We could expect a maximum of four minutes warning of an attack and the immediate task of the Vulcans was to scramble and be clear of the base within two minutes and be prepared to launch a counter strike.

The Staff College course was serious work but it was not designed to train monks and plenty of social life was woven into our activities. It was not long before we discovered that Mike Dawes, our senior RN student, was an accomplished beer brewer. Les Reading, our Australian bachelor who lived in the Mess, could not believe it was legal and he soon undertook a deep study of the art. Each quarter was furnished with a 7 gallon wash boiler but most occupants had their own washing machines and the boilers were not used. Les very soon had 3 of them in his room and was producing a continuous supply of Readings Best Bitter and never had a surplus.

A new civilian doctor, Mac, was appointed to tend for our needs and Marlies and I became friends with him and his wife. Soon after his arrival the Summer Ball hove into view and we planned to take them with us. We lived next to a Canadian student, Ruff Johnson, and as he was holding a small party prior to the ball he invited us to bring Mac and his wife .When we arrived the party was already well under way and on arrival we were given a glass of drink which raised the hair on the back of my neck. It would have been a very effective paint stripper. Mac was soon surrounded by new faces which were keen to meet him. While he was surrounded and chatting enthusiastically the hostess, Pat, was circulating with a jug of the paint stripper (later revealed as Drambuie and gin) and topping up any available glasses. Mac was too naive to realise the peril and thoroughly enjoyed himself. Eventually we found our table in the mess and within a few minutes Mac disappeared to the cloakroom but when he had not returned after a while I decided to go to find him. In the cloakroom all the compartment doors were closed but I noticed a pair of shoes with toes facing downwards under one of them. Fortunately it was not locked and I was able to squeeze in to restore order. Mac had passed out but I was able to sit him down while I went to give a situation report to our wives. Elfrieda decided to bring their car round to the main entrance while I prepared Mac for his great retreat. Fortunately the cloakroom was very close to the main door and I was able to use a very firm grip on his arm to propel him to his car without anyone noticing his departure. Within a very short time Elfrieda was back in the Mess declaring she was not going to miss a good party.

Next morning Mac was not very well but Elfrieda heaped on him more misery when she told him he had behaved disgracefully and he would have to visit his new friends to apologise for the awful things he was alleged to have done. It was only after a few visits that Mac realised that no one had noticed his absence from the Ball and Elfrieda was extracting the last bit of fun from the incident.

We ground our way remorselessly through the course and at last a major event of the course advanced upon us; the European Tour. Our usual three coaches were packed with our luggage and several crates of provisions and the expedition set course for Dover. During the ferry crossing of the channel John Dole confessed to me that this was the first time he had been out of England. He could hardly wait to see Paris but in this he was not the only one. Our evening began with a meal followed by a visit to the Follies Bergere. A stroll along the Champes Elysse and leisurely coffee was rounded off by French onion soup in Les Halles. John finished up by walking home in his stockinged feet.

Next morning detailed briefings had been arranged at NATO's HQ at Fontainebleau, just south west of Paris, where we were giving the latest review of the Cold War and I was left in no doubt that if the Soviet Union made a attack in Europe the result would be a catastrophic nuclear war within 3 or 4 days. We were prepared for such an attack but this was a very sobering thought.

We resumed our tour through Western Europe via HQ 2nd Allied Tactical Air Force, a US Air Force base, an RAF base and the British Sector of Berlin where we inspected the Wall and visited the Soviet Sector. Although this was depressing we managed to maintain high spirits during the off duty periods.

On return to Bracknell we settled at our work benches to continue grinding our way through the course but we soon had a welcome diversion with a well organised visit to the Epsom race course for the running of the Derby. We travelled in an open topped double deck bus which when parked close to the railings made an excellent grand stand. We had easy access to the fairground just over the course and the bookies were readily available. For the Derby we found an excellent position on the rails near to the finish and as the field swept towards us I was impressed by the speed at which the horses were travelling and the thunder of hooves. The grim determination on the jockey's faces reminded us that this was serious business for them. The lunch provided by the mess staff was excellent and a great day was enjoyed by us all.

A little later the exercise was repeated at Ascot for the Gold Cup. The bus was positioned inside the course opposite to the royal box and the royal coach procession passed close in front of us. The ladies enjoyed the day particularly but the men suffered no pain. We were given a demonstration of how to organise a social event with meticulous detail to the planning.

More welcome breaks to the pressure of the course came with a visit to Salisbury Plain for a presentation on the capabilities of the Royal Artillery and the tank regiments. In a spectacular demonstration of main battle tank fire power a single tank fired on target tanks at varying distances from 1,000 to 3000 yards and scored 9 hits in 60 seconds. We had been demonstrated the old saying that the British Army could beat any army in the world provided they fought on Salisbury Plain. The RAF would not accept second place so a little later we departed to RAF Wattisham for a demonstration of our air defence capability. After the presentations and lunch the course gathered on the veranda of the control tower to witness a scramble of Lightning fighters. After they had punched holes through the cloud the Lightning display pilot, Bugs Bendall, gave one of his exceptional performances which ended with a high speed run before the audience. He had many friends among our course and obviously wished to give us something to remember and as he appeared from our left we realised by the vapour forming over the wings that he was very close to the speed of sound. He came a little closer than usual to the control tower and flashed past with a mighty bang. A couple of seconds later another loud bang occurred and we were suddenly up to our ankles in broken glass as all the glass in the tower was shattered. We later learned that the prefabricated hut used by the Met Office had been moved on its concrete base. It was certainly a performance to remember.

Apart from Jenni the only other small children in Ramslade Road were the 3 boys of Ruff and Pat Johnson from next door. They were around Jenni's age and a trio of crew cut, boisterous American kids. Jenni, of course wished to play with them but they made her play a high price. All of the boring roles in their games fell to Jenni. I gathered from odd remarks and observation that she had a hard time with them. But Jenni was not to be outdone. A favourite game was to play cowboys and Indians from holes in the lovely rhododendron bushes over the road. Jenni inevitably had to be the squaw and she decided that to be proper red Indians they should wear war paint. Jenni knew where I kept my model making paints and as expected by the boys she acquired a colourful collection. She then supervised an impressive display of red, yellow blue and green patterns all over their faces and into their hair. The first we heard of this when an irate Pat appeared at our door demanding that we should come to her kitchen to witness an atrocity. Sitting on the draining board was the youngest boy yelling his head off as a result of Pat's efforts to scrub cellulose paint off his face and out of his hair. His brothers had obviously sampled similar treatment. We tried to persuade Pat that the outrage had obviously been a joint effort and not by Jenni alone. The boys were older than Jenni and they should have been looking after her. We did not notice any paint on Jenni because squaws don't wear war paint and we did not have to do any scrubbing!

A unique feature of the course was the series of lectures by high ranking politicians, Generals and Air Marshals, trade union leaders and captains of industry who gave 45 minute presentations on their part in running the country. It was rare that they could speak to such a diverse audience in absolute confidence and we were given a true insight into their responsibilities and problems. After a coffee break in the flag room where they were able to mix and chat with the students and staff they returned to the stage and faced unlimited questions from the audience. An Air Marshal later told me that it was the most harrowing experience he had been through. With about 100 sharp brains arraigned against him he could hide nothing. These lectures were a rare opportunity given to very few people and they were greatly appreciated by us.

We were very fortunate to have one of the best of the Staff College Commandants, AVM David Lee. He was an excellent example of an English gentleman with a sharp mind and a nimble pen. Our colonial students loved him and he was destined for the highest ranks. His ability to sum up an embarrassing lecture was a superb example of tact.

A feature of the course was several syndicate exercises in which operations were planned against fictitious countries in the Middle and Far East and large scale administrative exercises such as setting up air transport routes to the Far East. Joint service exercises with the Army and Royal Navy were being introduced and management studies were replacing what had been known in the past as leadership.

Eventually our thoughts began to turn to the future and the question of our next posting. Most pilots like me had been flying continuously until our arrival at Bracknell and we could only expect to be given our first ground tours and the choice could bring either happiness or misery. In late November I was ordered to visit HQ Technical Training Command for an interview with the Air Officer Commanding in Chief who was seeking a new Personal Staff Officer. This was all uncharted waters for me but I soon discovered that HQ TTC was located in the small village of Brampton near Huntingdon and was responsible for not only all technical but also administrative training for the RAF and was the largest Command. I sought out my first DS, Peter Vicary, who was a mine of information on the RAF and how it worked and he told me that the job depended on the master and the slave as it was a personal appointment and the two worked together as one. He said that very few people knew the AOC in C, Air Marshal Sir Alfred Earle, but those that had worked for him worshipped him. He could give me no more information because my future would depend only on the AOC in C and me.

It was with some trepidation that I set course for Brampton to ascertain what my future would be. When I arrived at Brampton Grange, the HQ building, I was redirected to the C in C's residence, Water Meadows, on the road between Huntingdon and Brampton because the C in C was in bed with an attack of flu. The sergeant steward was waiting for me and he apologised for the absence of Lady Earle who had an official appointment. He asked for my taste in coffee and then showed me up to the C in C who was propped up in bed. A chair and a small table were arranged by the bed and I was cordially greeted and invited to sit down and have coffee. I can only describe what followed as a cosy chat. AVM Lee was an old friend of the C in C and he had obviously supplied a detailed brief on my background and in a very short time I came under the influence of a very remarkable man. He was a short and burly man but only chunky enough to justify his widely used nickname of Tubby. His nose had been broken in a flying accident and he chain smoked. In spite of these apparent disadvantages I was aware of a great charisma and I discovered later that he had a formidable memory and one of the sharpest minds in the RAF. He asked me if I would like the job and soon it seemed to be assumed that I would be his next PSO. On my journey back to Bracknell I had much to churn over in my mind and I could only look forward to working with this extraordinary man. I only hoped I could live up to his standards.

The course was rapidly winding up and much effort was being devoted to the annual stage revue known as Clueless which was an opportunity for the students to poke fun at the events of the year and when DS wondered which of them would be the butt of students' wicked humour. The Winter Ball raced upon us and after the dinner Clueless was unveiled. Postings were being announced piecemeal and I was glad that I had not been included in those going to be members of planning teams in dingy offices around the RAF.

I was amazed to be phoned by the Station Commander at RAF Brampton and he welcomed me to the station. He told me that a married quarter had been allocated to us but it was being redecorated and refurbished before we arrived. He asked Marlies to contact the Barrack Warden and to her surprise she was asked to choose the colours for carpets, curtains and walls. It began to dawn on me that this was no ordinary Squadron Leader's job.

Such a tremendous year could only end in a mother and father of all Christmas parties as we celebrated finishing the course and at the same time bid farewell to close friends who were departing for the outposts of the Empire. I mentioned to a USAF friend who was returning to the States that it would be nice to be moving back near to his home and he replied, "Hell, no. I live in Florida and I'm posted to Alaska. I'm nearer to home now!" I remembered Bert Slade asking me at Bassingbourn in 1958 if I had ever considered applying for Staff College and I told him, "Who, me?" Now I had 'psc' after my name in the Air Force List.

CHAPTER 14
Life on the Top Floor

A S the dust settled after the death throes of our Staff College course we found ourselves on a bright morning in January 1963 heading along the Great North Road to Brampton. After the chaos of our arrival at Bracknell we were happy to be travelling as a family again. Jenni was with us and in May she would be 5 years old and ready to start full time school. We drove directly to our new quarter in Brampton Park where the Barrack Warden was waiting to show us with pride the splendid state of decoration that he had supervised. The weather was bright and clear but turning very cold and it was the beginning of a period which was to become the coldest on record for the area that was well known as one of the coldest spots in England. Fortunately Pickfords' pantechnicon promptly arrived and I was able to begin installing our heating stove and as the house warmed up Marlies set about her usual conjuring act which transformed an empty house into a very nice home and Jenni began exploring her new territory on her bicycle. In front of the house were the playing fields and behind them we could see the Officers Mess which was housed in an old manor house which had been converted into an individual but comfortable mess.

The Officers' Mess, RAF Brampton Park

On Monday morning I presented myself at The Grange, an old Georgian house in the middle of the village High Street that had been adapted to house the Command HQ. The senior staff officers were all shoe horned into the house and the overflow was housed in a motley collection of Seco huts in the large yard behind the main house. Among all this muddle I had to find my work bench and was delighted to discover that my office was in pole position at the top of the stairs and over the front door with a very convenient small veranda overlooking the High Street.

Next to me were the ADC's office and then our clerks. Across the landing at the top of the stairs was the C in C's office so we had a close little enclave. To my right were the offices of our two Air Vice Marshals, the Senior Air Staff Officer and the Air Officer Administration with their staffs.

My hand-over from my predecessor David Tew was very brief and the main task was to take over custody of the office safe with its classified documents and my aiguillettes and sword. The very personal relationship between the C in C and his PSO dictated that our method of working would be sorted out between us. I was fortunate to have the help of a very efficient Aide de Camp, Flt Lt Terry Morgan, who had been with the C in C for more than a year. Terry and I had to work closely together to ensure we were singing the same song. His task was to look after the ceremonial and domestic side of life and was in close touch with Lady Earle. My task was to act as business manager.

I soon discovered that the C in C was a Devonshire grammar school boy who had joined the RAF in about 1921 as an apprentice at RAF Halton. His outstanding ability won him a cadetship at RAF Cranwell and he graduated as a pilot in 1924. He served in UK and then in Mesopotamia before returning to the UK to serve during WW2 at every level of command. He joined Churchill's staff and attended the Cairo and Yalta conferences. After the war he advanced steadily and when Lord Mountbatten became the first Chief of Defence Staff he chose Sir Tubby as his Vice Chief. This was an excellent team. He was known throughout the RAF as Sir Tubby and he signed his personal letters "Tubby".

Every morning Terry and I would synchronise our diaries and discuss our day's plans while waiting for our Master to arrive. At precisely two minutes to nine the C in C's car would appear round the corner of the road and Terry would trot down the stairs to welcome him. After Terry had discussed the day's ceremonial and domestic events it would be my turn to enter the lion's den for my morning prayers. I would detail the day's tasks which were awaiting him and show the preliminary work I had prepared and the C in C would give me his plans. I would also give him any news which I thought he ought to know. I was his eyes and ears around the Command and my reports often began with "You're not supposed to know this but....".

Sir Tubby

I had no work of my own. Everything which came through my office was Sir Tubby's work. I opened all the mail except the letters which were obviously personal and I listened to all his phone calls, kept quiet and took notes. As every new task came in I would assess it and then make a round of the officers who could provide me with advice and information. I would then prepare a brief for Sir Tubby with my proposals and usually a draft paper or letter to answer the task. I soon discovered that he had the sharpest mind I had ever encountered. He had the ability to seek out the root of a problem and apply his formidable intellect and memory to produce his solution. I learned much from him as he revised my efforts. I produced my work in standard English and he built in his own style and phrases. As time went by I was able to draft my work to anticipate his style and eventually I could produce for him an answer for a straight forward task in final form which he usually signed. We were becoming a team with Sir Tubby supplying the brain power and me doing the leg work.

Jenni was looking forward to being enrolled into the village school but we soon discovered the problem of children who move from school to school. At 5 years old it is difficult to settle into an established group and she suffered from being the newcomer particularly when they learned that she spoke fluent German. She had been to a convent school in Singapore and junior school in Bracknell and she had a different background from the local children. Perhaps this was her first lesson in coping with all kinds of people. However she was a bright little girl and she coped well.

I soon found out that Sir Tubby had his VIP aircraft and crew based at RAF Wyton, only 20 minutes or so from the HQ. It was a Devon and I had come to like it when I flew airspeed calibration trials on it at Farnborough. It was not long before I visited the Communications Flight to meet the VIP pilot and navigator and in due course I began a thorough training course to get myself fully qualified on type with an instrument rating.

Sir Tubby made a series of visits around his stations and the next one came along very soon. This is when I met Sgt McCoy, our VIP driver, who was not only a first class driver who always got us to our destinations safely and on time in all manner of circumstances and difficult weather but also one of a breed of General Factotums who could fix or acquire things which were too difficult through normal service channels. I had a key to Water Meadows and for a long road journey I might arrive at the house around 0430 or 0500 hrs and have breakfast with Sir Tubby before we set course. When we arrived at the station being visited the Station Commander would normally be waiting at the top of the steps of his HQ to receive his visitor and a corporal policeman would be waiting to open the car door with a smart salute. However at RAF Yatesbury the Station Commander was Group Captain Tom Lloyd Davies who had also started his RAF career as a Halton apprentice but one course ahead of Sir Tubby. When we arrived at Yatesbury he would be standing ready to open the car door with a big salute and a remark such as, "Good morning Sir. It's nice to see the junior entry getting on so well!"

The long car journeys were a good opportunity to chat with Sir Tubby and I loved to encourage him to talk about his experiences particularly during his time with 55 Sqn in Mesopotamia in the 1930s. He was a Flt Cdr flying Westland Wapitis when Britain was experimenting with policing the overseas territories by air. He told me that on one occasion he was leading a flight of 3 Wapitis when they ran into an unexpected sand storm. After exhausting all normal methods of escape they had to resort to an emergency landing. In a safe area the formation would close up and the leader would set up an approach with normal approach engine power and speed. The aircraft would be descending at a few hundred feet per minute and the formation would be maintained until they hit the ground when the throttles would be closed and a formation landing was terminated. Usually the desert was flat and hard and all they had to do was wait until the sand storm cleared and the exercise could be continued. Unfortunately for Sir Tubby on this occasion a successful landing was made but by mischance he found in front of his aircraft the only large rock in the area and the end result was a broken nose from banging his face on the cockpit edge.

3 Wapitis in the desert

An early task for me was to prepare a draft speech for Sir Tubby to the RAF Staff College at Bracknell. This gave me the opportunity to visit nearly all the staff to collect information which was not only needed for his speech but also for my better understanding of the Command. I was surprised to discover that Sir Tubby had 105,000 people under his control. The magnitude of his task is best illustrated when one considers that the size of the whole RAF in 2014 is about 37,000. Sir Tubby took my draft and breathed on it to transform it into his own style. He was an excellent lecturer and he always seemed to be delivering his message off the cuff. I was taken by surprise one morning when I went into his office and found him standing behind a lectern in the corner rehearsing. He told me later that giving his lecture to 144 post graduate experts was one of the most harrowing tasks he knew. After a coffee break he would sit on the stage and field unexpected questions for an hour and a half. Even 144 idiots could still find any cracks in the system. I sat up at the back of the lecture hall with the tutors and he would often call to me to provide the answer to a detailed question. If I did not know I ensured that the questioner was sent the answer as soon as we returned to Brampton.

Sir Tubby after flying into RAF Cosford
being met by AVM Cosworth

The hard work was often rewarded by very pleasant visits. In his command Sir Tubby had the Depot of the RAF Central Band at RAF Uxbridge and he had to attend music festivals where the band played next to such recognised world class musicians as Black Dyke Mills Band and the Brighouse and Rastrick Band. I was pleased to discover that the RAF Central Band was held in very high esteem by the experts. One of our trumpeters delighted in playing the Post Horn Gallop on an army rifle with a mouth piece fitted in the muzzle. The RAF Police Depot at RAF Debden mounted the RAF Police Dog Championships and I loved the whole day.

RAF Cosford was the venue for the RAF Boxing Championships and the Wakefield Trophy. The ADC never had the chance to go with the C in C to these events. We never missed the RAF Athletics Championships and as the Ten Tors Marches over Dartmoor were competed for by several RAF Apprentice teams they were compulsory viewing for us. The School of Physical Training produced a gymnastics display team which participated in major national events and we were very proud of them. RAF Uxbridge was also the home of the RAF Regiment's guard of honour which represented the RAF at major occasions such as royal weddings, state funerals, coronations etc. They also maintained a ceremonial drill squad which produced a quick fire display of rifle drill without any words of command. All these displays were world class performances and I never thought of them as work.

Most of our stations could be reached by air and we normally flew in the Devon. At any opportunity Sir Tubby loved to fly the aircraft himself and our pilot moved over to the right hand seat. Sir Tubby never had time to go flying for fun but he loved the chance to keep his hand in.

Water Meadows was the scene of many official parties and Marlies and I would be asked to act as assistant hosts. Several of the parties we held in our house were also attended by Sir Tubby and Lady Earle. We decided we would give a party for the junior members of the HQ staff and they agreed to come along too. The younger members normally had no opportunities to meet the C in C informally and the evening was a great success. In the middle of the party I found Sir Tubby sitting on the landing, half way up the stairs, surrounded by a throng of youngsters. He had a good time. After one particularly good party we were in the kitchen trying to restore order from the wreckage at about 2 o'clock in the morning and Sir Tubby and Lady Earle were helping with the washing up.

Life continued at a hectic pace on the top floor and frequently Sir Tubby would emerge from his office and clatter off down the stairs clutching a file. One of a PSO's golden rules was "Never lose your Master" and I would have to rush across the landing so that I could see where he was going into the back yard to tackle a junior officer. Imagine the surprise of the unsuspecting man when he heard a clatter of footsteps in the corridor and his door burst open to be confronted by the C in C demanding "What's all this nonsense about the establishment of doctors at Halton Hospital, Benny?" After the encounter the officer felt 10 feet tall and would recount the incident to his friends with pride. That was Sir Tubby's style.

Sir Tubby and Lady Earle

I was working under pressure but I always had to ensure that no mistakes occurred. On one occasion I fouled up Sir Tubby's itinerary for the next week and when I discovered the problem I had to confess immediately that I had landed him in the mire. His reaction was to ask, "What is the problem and what can we do about it?" When we examined the program he told me that he was not happy about one of the appointments and would be glad to rearrange it. As I was leaving the office he told me "Remember, Brian, the man who never made a mistake never made anything." On another occasion he decided that something must be done immediately and when I said I would do it right away he gave me another of his sage adages "Brian, when you have a kennel full of dogs, don't bark yourself".

The exceptionally cold winter had slowly immerged into a splendid summer and Marlies and Jenni spent more time than usual sunbathing on the lawn behind our house. Just round the corner lived the Command Accountant, Gp Capt Dundas and his wife. He had an avuncular, friendly personality and his wife was plump and matronly. In Jenni's wanderings she had met Mrs Dundas and they became great friends. The Dundas' had no children of their own and Jenni filled the gap. If we could not see

Jenni around the area we had no worries because we knew she would be with Mrs Dundas helping with the day's chores. Jenni still remembers her.

The summer and winter balls were quite splendid events at the HQ. They were preceded by a reception for the VIP guests at Water Meadows and Marlies and I were invited to assist with the hosting. To provide extra space for a dance floor two large marquees were erected on the lawn behind the dining room. They were connected by an opening that was topped by a large beam to take the weight of the canvas. During the 1963 ball a large thunderstorm threw down a huge volume of water while the dancing was in full swing. The canvas of the roof on either side of the opening collected the water and very soon it looked like the fat lady's bottom on a Blackpool post card. Eventually the beam gave way and a torrent of water flooded the area. It added a spice of adventure to the ball.

Sir Tubby at the Ball

Marlies in all her glory

Big changes were being made in the Ministry of Defence and a single Chief of Defence Staff (CDS) to sit above the single services Chiefs was to be appointed and Admiral of the Fleet Lord Louis Mountbatten was to be the first incumbent. Very soon afterwards we had to make arrangements for the great man to come to Brampton to visit Sir Tubby. He flew in by helicopter and we had him for the whole day. When he had been CDS as the senior of the Chiefs of Staff he had chosen Sir Tubby as his

Deputy Chief and it had been an inspired decision. Like many brilliant leaders Lord Louis could be rather erratic and he needed a steady hand standing behind him to occasionally tug his jacket to suggest a more practical solution. The steady hand was Sir Tubby and Lord Louis knew and appreciated that. He had come to Brampton to ask Sir Tubby to get back in harness again. We all realised it would not be long before Sir Tubby was on his way.

Now began an anxious time. Terry knew that a new C in C normally chose a new ADC or brought one with him and he began to wonder about his new posting. I hoped he would be promoted because he deserved it. The old PSO normally stayed in post for about 3 months to see the new C in C into his chair without a hiatus. I could expect a move fairly soon.

Sir Tubby with Admiral Mountbatten

All too soon we attended the farewell guest night for the great man and it was a full house. Also being dined out was our very popular female US exchange officer Captain Norma Brown, who was very well chosen by the USAF to represent her country. In her farewell speech she told a futuristic tale about Sir Tubby when he took up his post in Whitehall. On his first day he was sitting at his desk in a room next to CDS but next day he had moved along the corridor to be among the Chiefs of Staff. On the 3rd day he was down on the next floor among the hewers of wood and drawers of water. On the 4th day he had his desk in the toilet. When he was asked what was going on he replied, "This seems to be the only place where people know what they are doing".

On the day of Sir Tubby's departure Terry went down to Water Meadows to supervise the arrangements and when they were about to depart he called me and I hurried down to the house. When all was ready the staff was lined up outside the door and Sir Tubby and Lady Earle said a fond farewell to all of them. Lady Earle came to say goodbye to me and then Terry saw her into the car. When Sir Tubby had said farewell to Terry he came round the back of the car to where I was waiting to see him into his seat and as he came past he gripped me hard just above my left elbow and got into the car without saying a word. I felt the same. The super boss then drove off at the end of his tour. I kept in regular contact with him for the rest of his life and will never forget him.

The new AOC in C arrived almost immediately and was Air Marshal Sir Donald Evans who had been a war time pioneer of airborne night fighting and had a great reputation for detailed planning. He was quiet and had a delicious sense of humour. He was very similar to Wilfred Hyde White, a very popular film actor at the time, and I warmed to him from the beginning. His wife was small and dark with a very attractive personality and I immediately felt a firm rapport with her. To my relief it seemed as if my next few months would be enjoyable. Sir Donald chose John Dixon to be his ADC and Terry was promoted and went on his way. The HQ machine continued to grind away without pause.

Sir Donald's style of working was completely different from Sir Tubby's but I liked working with him. He directed affairs quietly from his office and used the staff to action his plans. When he was in MOD he lived in The Boltons without a garage and his car had to stand in the street. It was often nudged by other cars and was rather more battered than a normal C in C's car. The fact that it was a Mini Cooper S, the hottest little car on the market in the mid 60s, made it all the more interesting. Soon it became apparent that I would be driving Lady Evans quite often and my name was added to the rather expensive car insurance policy.

When the Royal Tournament came around Sir Donald was invited to be one of the reviewing officers and he decided to make it a memorable event. Along with several other personal friends he invited me, Marlies and Jenni, now a little charmer of nearly 8 years, to accompany him to Earls Court. While we were settling in to the Royal Box I took my usual place with Marlies and Jenni just behind Sir Donald but Lady Evans came round and took Jenni by the hand and led her to sit between herself and Sir Donald. She sat where the Queen had been sitting the night before and had the best seat in the house. As each display finished the team leader saluted Sir Donald and then came up to the Royal Box for a chat. At the end of the splendid tournament an excellent buffet meal had been arranged in the ante-room behind the Box and a happy party was soon in full swing. The previous performance had been before The Queen and Prince Philip and the occasion was commemorated by their signatures in the visitors' book which was laid open in a central position. During the merriment Marlies suddenly noticed that Jenni, who by now could write well, was about to add her name to those of the Queen and Prince Philip. Disaster was narrowly averted and Jenni was saved from the Tower of London.

When Sir Donald was told that Sgt McCoy, his driver, played football for RAF Brampton he decided he must go to watch him play. He and Lady Evans wrapped themselves warmly in sheepskin coats and hats and drove in his Mini to the station playing fields which were sited between the Officers Mess and the senior officers married quarters. He found an excellent parking position just by the pitch's half way line and was settling down ready for the match to begin when a Corporal RAF Policeman appeared next to the car window and said, "You see that house over there. That is the Station Commander's house and if he sees your car here he will have your guts for garters". Sir Donald apologised and said he would move immediately. This story quickly circulated round the station and Sir Donald recited it frequently.

While the routine work was being churned out in the HQ I became involved in much more important matters at home and I was required to perform a duty which nearly all fathers have done. The out riggers had been removed from Jenni's bicycle and the large area of well mown grass with small trees became my next battle ground. A period of slowly accelerating trotting with a slowly reducing grip of a wobbly bicycle seat soon began to produce results. The speed increased and the wobbles reduced until at last Jenni was away on her first solo ride. All that remained was to reduce the encounters with the small trees. Mission accomplished.

Sir Donald with USAF Colonel

When I had time alone with Sir Donald I encouraged him to talk about his experiences in the 1930s and he recounted to me the time when he was serving on 45 Sqn in Egypt and flying Fairey IIIFs. All squadrons in the 1930 were keen to set records and 45 Sqn decided to fly the first squadron flight from Cairo to Cape Town. After lots of huff and puff the squadron set course and all went well until they were passing over the Rift Valley in Kenya. Sir Donald then encountered the worst event that can happen to a pilot; his engine began to fail. He hastily searched around for a suitable area where he could possibly force land his aircraft. To his surprise he saw a small area of quite reasonable grass and was able to plan his descent into the tiny area. He made an excellent engine off approach into his chosen landing area but his day was ruined when he touched down and found that his field was in fact a shallow lake and his arrival finished with his aircraft sitting in a few feet of water. The episode had been witnessed by his squadron and photos were taken, one of which I found in 45 Squadron's photo albums in Singapore 30 years later.

Although he did not know about the photos he knew that a rescue party would soon be on the way. His flight to Cape would have to wait a while.

While I had my nose to the grindstone Marlies decided to take Jenni and drive to Germany for a holiday with family and friends. The best route was via Harwich and the overnight ferry to the Hook of Holland but Marlies was not a good sailor. When the ferry put to sea she had to seek refuge in her cabin and did not see much more of the crossing. Jenni however is a good sailor and had an enjoyable time making friends. Next morning they were soon ashore in Holland but fog was slowly thickening. The exit from the Hook of Holland to the autobahn was very difficult to follow at that time and Marlies was soon groping for directions. She found herself behind a well driven car that was apparently going towards the autobahn so she decided to follow him. All went well until he turned into his home driveway and stopped. Fortunately the gentleman was very helpful and he was able to direct Marlies to the autobahn which was not too far away. After they returned home we received a postcard from Radio Hilversum, the Dutch national radio, saying that Jenni's part in a radio program recorded on the ferry would soon be broadcast and it gave us the details of the schedule. Unfortunately we were not able to listen to it and we will never know what our little broadcasting star got up to while Marlies was fighting her way to Holland.

Young James Evans was at school near Cheltenham and when Sir Donald had a visit in the Gloucester area he would fly down to Staverton Airport with the ADC in the Devon and I would drive Lady Evans in their Mini across country to arrive at about the same time. I could fly back in the Devon and they had the use of their car to visit James. Lady Evans enjoyed brisk driving and was a calm passenger. The drive through the back roads of central England in such a lively car was invigorating and she was a delightful companion. I hoped they would visit James more often.

A great amount of RAF business was carried out between the PSOs of all of the other Commands and Air Force Board members. It was a tightly knit band that worked closely together and we soon got to know each other well. Wg Cdr Tim Lloyd, the PSO to the CAS, had the marvellous idea of arranging a PSO's party in the crypt of the Banqueting Hall in Whitehall. This was the building from which King Charles 1st made his last public appearance and is full of ancient history. Parking slots were reserved for us and we were able to drive into central Whitehall with very little trouble. The buffet meal was excellent and we were able to meet the wives of our friends. The PSO from Bomber Command soon afterwards married the ADC at Fighter command. They formed a formidable team and he became a C in C in due course. Several other PSOs also became Cs in C in time and Tim Lloyd became a very popular Chief of Air Staff. The CAS, Marshal of the Royal Air Force Sir Sam Elworthy, also came to join us and we all had a great time. The efficiency of high level work throughout the RAF was improved with the wave of a wand.

As time passed I began to wonder when I would be replaced but Sir Donald never mentioned the subject so, to demonstrate my loyalty, I did not either and as work continued I assumed I would probably stay with Sir Donald and I had no objections. In between gaps in my work I was continuing to steal flying at any opportunity. I took my chances to fly Canberras at Bassingbourn, Varsities at Oakington, Chipmunks at Henlow and Wyton, Jet Provosts at Cranwell, Hunters and Meteors at Chivenor and a Gnat at Little Rissington with my old friend, Dave Goodsir. I managed to steal about 120 hours of interesting flying to maintain my proficiency on both jets and piston engine aircraft. Of course the Devon was my regular nourishment.

In June 1964 a Command Garden Party had been arranged at No 22 Group HQ at Market Drayton and Sir Donald was determined to take Marlies in his VIP party. The plan was for us to fly in the Devon to RAF Ternhill which was near to HQ 22 Gp but a snag arose when we discovered that the party was one person too many for the Devon. Sir Donald soon solved the problem by deciding that his personal pilot would stay behind and I would fly the Devon. I had no objections and it gave Marlies the rare opportunity to fly with me in an RAF aircraft. Normally wives were not allowed to fly with their husbands unless it was on a scheduled flight in Transport Command.

The weather was good when the full aircraft took off from Wyton but as we progressed along the airway over the Midlands a huge thunder storm build up on our route and soon I found myself in a very vigorous storm and the aircraft was bounced around like a cork in water. It was not possible to maintain our allotted height but I had to concentrate on keeping the aircraft on an even keel. Any other aircraft on the airway would also be going up and down with us. The rough ride did not last long and soon we were back in the sun light and I was able to demonstrate that I could fly just as well in good weather. The flight is highlighted in my log book

De Haviland Devon

Marlies was usually keen to undertake any work which would keep her busy and she soon found part time employment as a supply teacher, filling in gaps at junior schools in the area. She often recounted hilarious incidents which occurred during the day. Funny episodes are not only contained in jokes; they also happen in real life. A favourite topic in the classroom at the time was for children to relate what had happened out of school recently and many parents never knew what was revealed in the classroom. Little Larry is alive and well and living out there.

By the beginning of 1965 the long awaited replacement for the Canberra aircraft, the TSR2, was nearing completion and as our command would be involved in introducing it into the RAF we began a series of visits to the Weybridge works at Brooklands airfield where the first 5 aircraft were being assembled. I had a personal interest in the TSR2 because it would be entering the RAF just at the right time for my next posting and I was particularly well qualified to be one of the first pilots. I was an A1 instructor on both Meteors and Canberras but I also had exceptional ratings as an operational pilot in the reconnaissance role. Sir Donald knew that I would be the obvious choice to run the first TSR2 training unit and the timing would be right. I took every opportunity to get into the cockpit and keep up to date with progress. I liked what I saw and was sure it would be a winner. It looked like my aircraft

TSR2 BAE picture

Sir Donald had a history of severe stomach illnesses and the RAF had protected his career as much as possible because they knew his value to the service. In 1965 it became clear that the problem was returning and he was visiting the hospital more frequently. Eventually it was decided that he would need a longer period of inpatient treatment. We had 2 Air Vice Marshals in the command that could stand in for Sir Donald but the more obvious choice was very ambitious and loved the pomp and grandeur of his position. The other was a much sounder officer who would keep the main work of the Command on track. Sir Donald gave instructions that all work entering his office would come to me and I would allocate it out in accordance with his wishes. This would be a very delicate task for me and would require very much tact. Lady Evans had lost her first husband, Sqn Ldr Philip Hunter, during the Battle of Britain and she knew Sir Donald's problem well. It was a very worrying time for her and I gave her all the support I could. I found that the allocating of work was usually straight forward because I knew Sir Donald's wishes quite well but if I had any doubts I often discussed the problem with Lady Evans and as usual she was very perceptive and gave me very sage advice.

While I was working in my office I received a very worrying call from Jenni. She had been out walking with her mother when Marlies suddenly became ill. Jenni managed to get her back home and then phoned me. Marlies had sustained the first attack of heart irregularity and after good care by the medical staff she was sent to the RAF hospital at RAF Ely where she was well looked after.

During this time our SASO, AVM Ben Ball, was invited to take a passing out parade of pilots at RAF Feltwell. He was delighted to do so and after a very pleasant day he decided to call into Ely Hospital to visit Marlies and give her the lovely bunch of flowers that had been given to his wife, Pam. In due course the big car bowled into the hospital and drove straight across to the ladies' ward. Ben had forgotten that Commanders don't usually visit one of their stations without warning. I was with Marlies when the visitors, with the flowers, arrived at her bedside. We were pleased to see our next door neighbours and coffee was soon arranged. While the jollification was going on I could see a phalanx of high priced help advancing across the grass from the main buildings and in no time at all we were joined by the CO and Matron with their retinue. Eventually Ben and Pam had to get on their way back to Brampton and the dust settled. The great benefit that followed the visit was the splendid treatment given to Marlies. The hospital staff thought she was Ben and Pam's daughter and as they did not ask us we did not deny it.

Soon a rather frail Sir Donald was released from hospital and resumed his duties. The storm had been weathered. Soon I heard from my PSO's grapevine that Sir Donald would be the next Air Secretary and thus responsible for all personnel matters and postings. This would be useful for me when my next posting came under review and as time went by it became accepted that I would be going to the first TSR2 unit. My obvious posting would be to command the TSR2 OCU and I had already decided I would fight to get Steve as my navigation leader. The visits to Weybridge became more important.

Soon we had to make plans to receive a visit from Lord Winterbourne, the Conservative government's Minister of Defence. He wished to discuss with Sir Donald probable changes in the RAF that would happen during Sir Donald's next appointment. We had a very enjoyable day but it was overshadowed by the fact that a general election was due soon and the Labour party, who were likely to win, were making great play on the huge savings in defence spending they would make. They were quoting savings of £750 million and anyone with reliable defence spending figures could forecast that the only place where such savings could be made were to cancel a new aircraft carrier for the Royal Navy and the TSR2 for the RAF. As sure as night follows day the Labour Party won the election and the new Harold Wilson government cancelled both projects. My dreams of TSR2 were dashed. This was a tragedy because the aircraft was already flying with very good results and it was all set to be a world beater with great export sales potential. To ensure that the TSR2 was not resurrected the government ordered all jigs and other manufacturing infrastructure to be destroyed and all unfinished aircraft to be used as targets on air to ground firing ranges. As far as I know no RAF pilot ever hit one and most of them are now in museums. What a pity! I was now in limbo. What would my future be?

Sir Donald with Lord Winterbourne

Confirmation came that Sir Donald would be the next Air Secretary and I was coming towards the end of my full tour. I did not monitor conversations between the C in C and the Air Secretary but eventually Sir Donald told me that the only post he could find which matched my qualifications was OC Advanced Standards Squadron at the Central Flying School at RAF Little Rissington. Ever since I had left my flying instructor's post at RAF Full Sutton in 1954 I had tried to avoid a return to the flying training world because experience showed that once caught in the training machine it was very difficult to escape. I had never heard of the new post and it felt as if the roof had fallen in. Fortunately the future was to be better than I expected.

So we began packing and saying goodbye to old friends and Jenni was preparing for a new school. In particular I felt sad to leave the Evans family because the nature of my job led to very close ties and I had come to be very fond of them. Marlies as usual was hardest hit because she had to give up the home she had lovingly built up and take to the road and begin all over again. I often described our lifestyle as middle class gypsies and our caravan was on the roll again.

Back to my aeroplanes again

CHAPTER 15
CFS Examining Wing — The Trappers

I N the middle of 1965 I had been earmarked for the TSR2 but no one told that to Harold Wilson's government and they cancelled the program. Full of disappointment I was posted to Central Flying School as OC Advanced Standards at Little Rissington. I had been away from Little Rissington for 13 years and my response to the news was "What on earth is that?" I was told that it was something like the old Examining Wing and that I would have a magnificent fleet of obsolescent aeroplanes consisting of a Meteor T7, a Vampire T11 and a Mosquito. I soon discovered that it was the most interesting part of the old Examining Wing and my bailiwick would include the RAF's Advanced Flying Schools, Operational Conversion Units, front line squadrons and foreign air forces when invited. I would have the use of aircraft from the relevant units when I needed them. I was cheered up immensely and we moved quite happily to our Cotswold hill top. Marlies set about building us a snug little nest and garden and Jenni who was now 8 could look forward to a few years in a good school. She had suffered from being dragged around from school to school and was due for some stability at last. We now come to the parts of the story she can remember.

Examining Wing had originated in about 1927 and had begun a series of visits to home and overseas RAF stations. Over the years their reputation had spread around the world and eventually their program not only included all of the RAF but also, by request, many leading overseas air forces. I was very proud to join this team. When I arrived the Wing was housed in a fairly small building of their own which was conveniently situated behind the hangars and the Advanced Squadron had half of it. I inherited a team of first rate examiners who were divided into Fast Jet and a Multi Engine flights. The existing boss was still in post and the program for the year was running smoothly. They did not need any interference from me until I was up to speed and I could start to prepare myself for what was probably the best pilot's job in the RAF.

Normally pilots who had been pushing desks for over 3½ years were sent on lengthy refresher courses before returning to flying duties but it had not been suggested to me. Instead of wasting my time trying to get more action rather than noise out of a Jet Provost I could arrange my own rehabilitation. My first task was to get myself qualified as an A1 QFI on the Gnat, the Meteor and the Varsity as a beginning. I still had current instrument ratings on the Canberra and the Devon so I decided to begin with the Varsity. I had flown the prototype at Farnborough and was keen to meet my tubby friend again. My multi engine examiners were involved in their series of visits and I took the opportunity to become familiar with the Waterfront, as the instructor training squadrons were known. I was made very welcome on the Varsity squadron and soon got stuck into a streamlined program to qualify me as an A1 Varsity instructor. In any gaps I was able to renew my love affair with the Meteor and we were soon on very friendly terms.

Next I could turn my attention to the prettiest little aeroplane that the RAF ever owned, the Folland Gnat. I had watched it since it was introduced into service and I was itching to fly it. The CFS Gnat squadron was based at RAF Fairford which had recently been the base for the USAF's giant B36 bombers. The airfield had a 3,000 yard runway and ample accommodation so the Gnat squadron had lots of elbow room. I decided to fly my first sorties with the squadron instructors and as usual was made very welcome. The Red Arrows shared the accommodation and of course Gnat student QFIs were in full flow. I soon discovered that the Gnat was more complicated than most contemporary fighter aircraft and I had to spend a couple of weeks attending the ground school with the other students. The Gnat had emergency systems for almost any failure and if a pilot was to be master of it the systems must be thoroughly understood. I was very familiar with Martin Baker ejection seats but Folland had produced a smaller and lighter one for the Gnat so that also had to be digested. Before I could get to grips with the aerial skateboard I had to be fitted with my first sound proof helmet and anti-G trousers. The helmet was too late because I later discovered that my hearing had already been damaged by Harvards and other noise generators.

A Gnat over the Welsh mountains

My first encounter with a Gnat was with a scarlet Red Arrows aircraft and I was surprised to find that I could look over the top of the cockpit with space to spare. A box of two wooden steps was provided to enter the cockpit but I discovered later that if no steps were available it was easy to hoist a leg over the side and haul oneself into the cockpit. I know of no other fast jet where this is possible. I slid down into the seat and was again surprised that I had so much elbow room. When we began to taxy I noticed how near my head was to the tarmac and that the very narrow undercarriage allowed the aircraft to roll from side to side rather like my old Springer Spaniel when it had drunk some beer. I felt very happy with my new toy and I soon relished the sparkling performance. Its small size increased the impression of high speed and as soon as we were in clear airspace I was able to confirm that it was a very spritely little aircraft with excellent maneuverability. However the fun soon had to stop and we had to get down to business of mastering all the emergency systems. It is still one of my favourite aircraft and the Red Arrows were very fortunate to be able to use it for their brilliant displays. It was an excellent aircraft for experienced pilots but too complicated for students. Too much time had to be spent on teaching the emergency systems instead of advanced flying.

Look out! Here comes a Gnat

I flew three sorties with the Waterfront instructors before I enjoyed my first solo trip but then one of my examiners became available and I was able to sample their abilities. Alan East had been on Gnats from the very early days and was rapidly becoming the recognized expert on the type. We had to get down to the serious business of making me into a Gnat QFI but I enjoyed flying with him. I found much of his approach to Gnat flying very similar to mine. He always wanted to know more and to fly better. He was a very down to earth character with an excellent instructional technique. I was well satisfied with my first encounter with one of my team. If they were all as good as Al I would be very happy.

After Al had set a firm foundation I spent all of December flying four sorties per day with other members of the staff, Red Arrows members, students on the current course and occasional flights with Al to keep me on the straight and narrow path. I was introduced to high level aerobatics which Al loved. I was competent at aerobatics in the rich air at lower levels but when trying to perform in the rarified air at high level I fell around all over the sky but Al soon sorted me out. I can't remember a more enjoyable period.

In January I took the opportunity to bring myself up to speed in the back seat of the Meteor and took the first of my 4 Command Instrument Rating Examiners (CIRE) tests. I was able to fly a couple of sorties with my RN examiner, Lt Keith Rawlinson from the Fast Jet flight. Keith was mainly involved with Hunter and Meteor examining and was a very sound pilot with a quirky sense of humour. By now I was looking ahead and planning for my first Examining Wing visit to RAF Oakington with their Varsitys. To prepare myself I flew with one of my Multi Engine Flight examiners, Vic Stanton. In eleven sorties he licked me into shape and I got to know Vic very well. He proved to be solid gold. He had escaped from Poland and had eventually joined the RAF. He was an excellent pilot and had settled down into the transport role and then instructing. He was a mature character who spoke and wrote excellent English better than the average Englishman. I enjoyed his companionship on many visits and he became a valued leader of the Multi engine trappers. He was my oldest trapper and he lived in his own house at Charlton Kings with his charming wife, Sheila, and his two typically bouncy teenage daughters. I thought it was an ideal family. We discussed the problem of choosing a new name in a strange land and Vic assured me it was no problem. His Christian name was the Polish equivalent of Victor so that was only a cosmetic change. His brother had married an English girl and he had taken her name. Vic thought it would be a good idea to have the same name as his brother. I could only agree.

Vickers Varsity My tubby friend

RAF Oakington was the main training unit for students heading in to the multi engine piston force and was a well-established unit. I arrived for a two week visit with Vic and another examiner and found many friends. The Chief Instructor (CI) was Wg Cdr Stan Wandzilak who had been my deputy Chief Instructor at Full Sutton and we arranged to fly together during the night flying phase. The days passed quickly with checks made on QFIs, students and supervisory staff. I already knew that the CI was a very experienced instructor but was very happy to find that his Varsity flying was quite exceptional. On the last day of the visit we gave a presentation to all available staff to summarise our proposed report. I insisted to my team that we would never put anything in our reports which had not been discussed with the unit. Any praise due must be given and any weaknesses must be highlighted but advice must be given on corrective action. Occasionally the fault was not caused by the unit but by external sources and we would have to take up the issue for the unit. On return to base the report had to be written and then circulated so that all relevant units could benefit from the visit. At all times our intention was to improve the RAF and not destroy it.

On a typical weekend I would arrive back at Rissington on Friday evening and go into my office to dump my draft report for the week's visit and pick up the contents of my in-tray and the Pilots Notes and Operating Data Manual for next week's aircraft. A lot of time was spent sitting on the edge of my bed doing emergency drills and flying let downs and circuits. My bed became the flight simulator for about 30 different types of aircraft.

Such a high workload also had its brighter times. In 1967 Vic Stanton and I were involved in the introduction of the Dominie into the RAF. It was a very attractive version of a civilian executive jet to be used as a navigator and rear crew trainer and we relished the opportunity to explore it. To enable us to keep our hands in we were allocated 6 hours per month of Stradishall's and Strubby's flying allotment. We accumulated our hours and before going to examine Stradishall we would have a concentrated flying session at Strubby and vice versa. The Dominie at that time was probably better equipped than any other squadron aircraft and we delighted in getting up to speed on the systems and we probed into every one of its secrets. During subsequent examining our biggest problem was encouraging the pilots to use the new whistles and bells. We thought the ability to fly an auto pilot coupled ILS approach better than sliced bread but most pilots preferred to fly manual ILSs. During this time we had to introduce an Instrument Rating Test for the Dominie and when it was ready we had to prove it. As the boss I claimed the right to have first attempt in the left seat with Vic's eagle eyes glinting from the right. I managed to struggle through the test and Vic gave me the nod. We then changed seats so that Vic could demonstrate his usual prowess. Unfortunately during the latter stages of an approach he slipped out of the limits and I failed him. Bosses can be vicious! In mitigation I knew that if I had tried to pass Vic he would not have accepted it. As a consolation prize we went flying in our Meteor and I put Vic in the front seat and took the opportunity to practice my back seat flying. We flew much better aerobatics than in the Domini or Varsity.

BAC Dominie

To bring me down to earth I travelled with the Coastal Command CFS Agents during their annual check of the St Mawgan Shackleton Maritime Patrol squadrons and polished up my taxying and flying of these enormous aircraft. During an Atlantic patrol with anti-submarine exercises I was fascinated by a crew of 14 wandering around the spacious interior. I witnessed the competition during every sortie to produce coffee in the shortest time after the wheels were selected up. Of course anti-submarine operations went on continuously but the next major event was tea time. The next wife on the duty roster had been tasked with providing a better tea time meal than the previous one. At every hour a call of, "Signalers amidships", would produce a line of aircrew waiting to be re-allocated the various tasks such as manning the radar or radio stations, and, most importantly, taking station as the new duty cook. Four powerful engines, each with 2 counter rotating propellers, were aligned just behind the pilot's head and they formed the nastiest noise generators I have ever encountered. We only wore light canvas helmets with no sound proofing and after our fourteen hour sortie I arrived back on the tarmac like a drunken sailor.

Avro Schackleton

As a welcome break I was able to arrange a flight in one of my favourites, the Chipmunk, to my old stamping ground at South Cerney and return to keep in practice with a tail dragger. It was rather like a delicious sorbet between main courses.

A pleasant contrast was provided by a Command Instrument Rating Examiner (CIRE) from Boscombe Down who was due for a renewal of his rating in a Hawker Siddeley Andover transport aircraft. He brought his aircraft to Rissington where we agreed a suitable Instrument Rating Test and then I demanded Shylock's pound of flesh. In order to validate the test I decided to fly the test before rating the CIRE. I used this procedure several times later and found no pain.

Hawker Siddeley Andover

The remainder of May was filled with a mixed bag of Gnat night flying, testing, a couple of Final Handling Tests, back seat night flying in the Gnat and Meteor and again an A1 QFI check for me in the back of my Meteor. I had a feeling I might have been there before. At the beginning of June I managed to sneak away on my own to spend a week checking No 85 fighter squadron at RAF Binbrook. My clients were at the Target Facilities Flight which was mainly equipped with Canberras and Meteors. In the program I managed to squeeze a Canberra check with Tommy Tomlin, my old sparring partner from 81 Sqn in Singapore. Even trapping has its pleasurable side.

My Meteor Mk 7 and Vampire T11 which became the Vintage Pair

In a small gap I was able to fly with Keith Rawlinson in our Vampire T11 trainer. I had enjoyed the little Vampire F5 fighter in the 1950s and expected the Vampire T11 trainer to be as good but was very disappointed. Two ejector seats were wedged side by side in the cockpit but the seats were too uncomfortable for me. It was heavier than the Kiddy car and its performance lacked any sparkle. I do not like side by side instructing and the T11 became my least popular aircraft. In future I avoided flying it as much as possible.

Marlies had slowly been settling in to life on a flying station for the first time. The wives of our examiners that lived on the base were very friendly and they soon had an exclusive social life operating. Stow on the Wold and Bourton on the Water were our two very attractive neighbouring villages with CFS friendly hostelries. Bourton was the home of Patrick the Pelican, the mascot of CFS who lived with Len Hill at his Birdland. Perhaps most important of all, Mr Coleman ran the best fish and chip shop I have known. Marlies discovered that our nearest large town, Cheltenham, was an excellent town for her weekly shopping. Jenni was getting some continuity in her schooling and she met for the first time the man who became her great love, David Goodsir, our good friend from Laarbruch days who had recently arrived at Rissington to be Unit Test Pilot. Our house had nicely settled down and Marlies had planted several hundred bulbs so that we would have a good show of flowers in the spring when the fickle finger of fate struck again. We had been watching a row of new style married quarters being built in Bristol Road which was only a hundred yards or so up the road from us and we were impressed by their desolate appearance in comparison with the old style of quarters. We had heard they would have no fireplaces or central heating but in the modern era of 1966 they would have overnight electric storage heaters. Our day was really made when I was told that they would be occupied by senior officers and we would have to move in. Who was going to tell Marlies?

As we had very little furniture but quite a few personal possessions we decided we could move our bits and pieces up the road by ourselves. This was possibly the worst decision I ever made. We must have made hundreds of journeys up Avro Road to our new living machine. I resolved that next time it would be Pickfords whatever the cost. When we had assembled all our goods and chattels we then had to face a bare plot of land which was supposed to be a garden. It nearly broke Marlies' heart. It normally takes a whole year to find the optimum settings for a night storage heater system but we had no-one with any experience to help us. The result was huge electricity bills. No wonder they decided the houses would be occupied by senior officers. Alan East and Thelma took over our old quarter and one bleak morning in springtime Marlies had a lovely surprise when Thelma stood at our door with an armful of daffodils, etc. She thought that Marlies would appreciate some of the flowers she had planted. Suddenly it was a sunny day.

Visits to overseas air forces were usually high spots of a Trapper's year but I was surprised when we discovered that our 1966 hunting ground would be Iraq. The RAF had left Iraq in 1955 and relationships had been strained over the intervening years but now we had received an invitation and even the Foreign Office had no idea what kind of reception we would receive. We would have to dip our elbows in the water. While a suitable team of Hunter, Jet Provost and helicopter examiners was being assembled I encountered a typical Trapper's problem. The team would travel in one of our Varsities and I would be the only Varsity qualified pilot on board. Since my arrival at CFS my Varsity instrument let downs had become works of art and my single engine landings were like poetry in motion but I had never taken one outside England. The navigation aid for the Varsity in Europe was the Decca navigator which used a local chart and I had never flown off the edge of one chart and had to change it for another.

CFS Varsity (Adrian Balch)

While we were waiting for diplomatic clearances through the Middle East and into Iraq I found time for a splendid solution to the problem. During the depth of the Cold War Berlin was still isolated and could only be approached by air via three corridors and the Eastern Block continually harassed our air traffic. If the corridors were not regularly utilized they threatened to close them. A gallop along a corridor and back would give me the opportunity to gain experience and also help the Western cause. I hastily arranged a journey and I took a Varsity to RAF Oakington to pick up Sqn Ldr Hugh Field, the OC Standards flight, and Sqn Ldr Chris Christie who was suffering from a staff posting at Group HQ. Hugh had been at CFS with me and later on the same test pilots course. I had met Chris during my Meteor instructing days and we thought the combined level of experience would see us through our ordeal. We set course via RAF Wildenrath to begin our corridor passage and then bowled merrily along to the delightful airfield at RAF Gatow. It is possible that a dear old Varsity has rarely been flown with such tender loving care. Although the exercise was taken seriously and we extracted all possible experience the whole journey was great fun. In Berlin Marlies and I had a favourite Aunt Elschen who had lived in central Berlin all through the war and was immensely proud of her city. She ran an important advertising agency for TV, radio and national press and this brought her into contact with all forms of social life in Berlin. She was great fun to visit and this time I was able to visit the Deutsche Oper to see Marriage of Figaro with Dietrich Fischer-Dieskau which was rated as one of the best performances. Next morning we trundled back along the route direct to Oakington and after bidding farewell to Hugh and Chris I presented myself back to Rissington as a fully-fledged Varsity international operator. Problem solved!

While I was away learning my trade Transport Command HQ had decided our route for us and obtained single day diplomatic clearances for the flights. We would be able to canter along the route as far as RAF Nicosia but then we would have to cross Jordan, Syria and arrive in Iraq on the precise dates. Before we set course we had to decide on the load for the aircraft. I would have with me two Hunter examiners and three for the Jet Provost. We had our CFS helicopter agent from the Wessex force and we always took a sergeant servicing engineer to try to keep our Varsity on the rails. We pilots thought it was a huge joke that Transport Command insisted we must have a navigator even though we only had one at CFS. I think none of the squadrons wanted him and he was sent to us to supervise the planning and map sections. To complete our load we took some spare parts such as an exhaust manifold and a radio compass which experience told us might be required. That was the easy part. We now knew our forecast weight but our first leg would be to Istres, a French test centre near to Marseilles, and after we had calculated the amount of fuel required for the flight we then knew how much we would be over the Varsity's maximum all up weight. We did not tell HQ Transport Command.

We expected to be away for two weeks so we had to make all our domestic arrangements including trying to ensure there was always a Duty Dad in our HQ to look after any domestic emergencies. Marlies prepared to watch over our wives and Jenni could be their Gofer. At last on 18th June 1966 we climbed aboard our Varsity and you may have noticed that I was the only pilot qualified on type. A one eyed pilot was about to lead the blind. We had no auto pilot so our bird would have to be flown manually all the way to Habbaniya and back but I solved that problem by installing myself in the right hand pilot's seat and detailing the other pilots in turn to do the hard work from the left seat. After making the external checks and girding up our loins I started the engines, did the cockpit checks and operated the radio. I then asked one of the Jet Provost examiners to demonstrate his versatility and taxy out to the runway. I kept a beady eye on him during his first take off and we were on our way to Istres.

The weather forecast for Istres was reasonable but the usual thunder storms were forecast over the Central Massif and because of the limitations made for us by our diplomatic clearances I decided to press on. We were cruising around the 10,000 feet level and as we crossed the French coast we entered solid cloud. It steadily became much darker and we ran into severe turbulence with heavy rain. In such conditions it is not possible to hold a steady altitude but every effort must be made to maintain the aircraft in a level attitude and let it ride out the storm. The noise in the Varsity was unbelievable. Huge hailstones and heavy rain were noisier than the 1812 Overture. Frequent lightning and St Elmos's fire on the wings were quite spectacular and water was finding its way into the aircraft. My student pilot needed a little help but it must have been a great experience for him and he is no doubt still telling his grandchildren about it. The other crew members in the back had a severe beating and some were airsick for the only time in their flying careers. We hung on and eventually we appeared into much more benevolent weather and then enjoyed the ride to Istres.

The Officers Mess was well known for its excellent food and plentiful supply of wine on the table but unfortunately we were continuing on our way and only the passengers could really enjoy the brief lunch. When the aircraft was replenished we remounted our chariot and repeated the exercise with another Jet Provost examiner as my auto pilot. We had a pleasant flight to Malta and Chick Hemsley made his first Varsity landing at RAF Luqa where we made an overnight stay. Next day our Wessex examiner, Harvey Thompson, who had not flown a fixed wing aircraft for several years took his seat alongside me and impersonated a Varsity pilot. I think he enjoyed the occasion and he managed to make a tidy arrival at RAF El Adam as if helicopters had never been invented. We made it a joint service exercise by inviting Keith Williamson RN to do the chores on route to RAF Nicosia and he did his duty as Nelson expected and his landing at Nicosia raised no rude comments from the back. We stayed overnight in the RAF Officers Mess. We planned to fly next day over Jordan, Syria and into Iraq along a zig zag route and we would have to be careful with our navigation. We pilots were all experienced pilot navigators and all the way along the route we had been mentally checking our navigator's directions and we had frequent differences of opinion. The pilots usually won. I had saved Syd Taylor, my senior fast jet examiner, for this last leg and as I expected he rose to the occasion with his usual unflappable reliability and delivered us on to the runway at Habbaniya like an experienced Varsity pilot. The team had looked after me and ensured my safe arrival in Iraq.

The British forces had left Iraq 10 years previously and since that time relationships between the two countries had varied from cold to icy. We could only wait to see what our reception would be like. We had a very high priced reception line waiting for us and the greetings were warm. The tension quickly faded. After the reception we were whisked off to a large house on the base in well-kept grounds which during RAF times had been a senior officer's quarter. We were told it was Jiblee House but we soon discovered it had originally been christened Jubilee House. The house had been chosen and spruced up and volunteers had been called for from bearers with experience of serving British officers. The large number of volunteers who could not be given jobs was very disappointed. We were looked after impeccably and most of the bearers recalled the Good

Old Days with pride and fondness. We were also invited to be members of one of the five officers' messes which once served RAF Habbaniya.

While we were quickly unpacking we were told we would be taken into Baghdad to attend a reception for us at the Ministry of Defence. A bus duly appeared and we caught our breath during the long journey to the Capital. The reception was being held in a large Officers Mess with a very well-tended garden and a large gathering was spread around the lawns. The party was lively and friendly but by about 10 o'clock we remembered that we had not eaten since breakfast; our stomachs were rumbling and we realised that no mention had been made of a meal. We were mightily relieved when we were invited to step around a corner to discover tables laden with food. I was being escorted by an Air Force colonel and I was taken aback by a wall made up of the backs of junior officers who were attacking the buffet. The main items of the meals were roasted whole sheep and I was fascinated to watch them being torn apart with the bare hands of the diners. The crowd ahead of me was about 3 deep and I could not get near the table. I saw a red dish and I asked my host what is was. He reached over the obstacles, grabbed a handful and dumped it on my empty plate and told me it was red rice. He reached out again and tore off a hunk of lamb and deposited it alongside my red rice. So the meal continued. When the carcasses of the sheep were well stripped it became obvious that the enthusiastic diners were retreating from the tables and their places were being taken by the bandsmen who had fallen out for their attack on the buffet. We withdrew and after a while the bandsmen went back to their task and they were again replaced by the waiters. We could not help contrasting it with a recent lunch at Little Rissington with our Commandant in Chief, HM the Queen Mother.

The evening had been a great success because we had made many useful contacts and learned much background information. Next morning we had to buckle down to work and as our examiners departed for their client squadrons I had to deal with a special request from the Iraqi Air Force. They wished to establish an Instrument Rating System for their pilots based on the RAF system. Major Mohammed Adwan had been proposed as the officer to build up the system and I spent the morning briefing him on our system and requirements. I would supervise a test with him but first we had to devise a suitable Instrument Rating Test. His specialist aircraft was the Bristol Freighter which had been very popular as a cross channel ferry in UK just after the war. We soon agreed on a flight profile for the test but we had to verify it. I thought my solution to this problem was impeccable: I would fly the first test and then Major Adwan could demonstrate his prowess. When all was ready we entered the capacious cargo bay, climbed a vertical ladder and installed ourselves in the cockpit high above the aircraft nose. I sat in the first pilot's seat and while Major Adwan started the engines and performed the checks I familiarized myself with the controls and instruments. We taxied out to the runway and then I donned the visor which prevented me from seeing outside the cockpit. The instruments were similar to those used by the RAF in the 1950s and I was familiar with the lovely Bristol Hercules engines. I was determined not to let the RAF down and struggled through the test. After a mug of coffee we climbed the ladder again and I was able to enjoy my first views of the huge Habbaniya air base and Euphrates valley. Major Adwan had been well chosen to launch the scheme. He was the only competent pilot I encountered during our visit and his mature outlook gave me confidence that he would supervise the scheme very soundly. He flew the test with much more ease than my attempt and I had no qualms about certifying him as competent to launch the project. I had been dreading that he might fail and thereby create a diplomatic incident and precipitate the Iraqi War by 25 years.

Bristol Freighter

My afternoon was a vast contrast to the morning. Colonel Hussain Aurain, the colonel in charge of training in IAF HQ, insisted that he must be checked by our team and his chosen aircraft was the Antonov AN2. I was happy to indulge his request because I believed that he wished to acquire the prestige of being trapped by CFS but he would be quite happy to allow me to fly the aircraft. When we arrived on the tarmac I found the nearest approximation to an aerial tractor that I have ever encountered. It had been produced in Russia just after the end of the war and was intended to be the simplest, cheapest, utility aircraft for use for agricultural and other general purpose tasks. As such it was a great success. It was claimed to be the largest single engine biplane in the world and many people laughed at it. It had no frills and every system was the simplest available. The greatest feature was that it was self-contained and required no extra equipment to operate from remote areas. It was a successful workhorse and over 5,000 were built and used for every imaginable task. We took our place in the enormous greenhouse of a cockpit and the colonel started the huge engine with its internal battery. It cranked over and spluttered before settling down to run steadily. I was invited to taxy to the runway and, as I expected, nothing could have been easier. The take-off run began with a huge bellow from the lusty engine and we were airborne within about 200 yards. The aircraft was empty and when safely airborne it could be hauled around without a care. I was told that if a pilot ran into trouble in bad weather all he had to do was set a moderate power setting and then pull the stick back. The aircraft would not stall but mush down with the wings level until it hit the ground in the landing attitude. All that remained was to walk away. I was allowed to play around with this unique toy and for the first time in my life I flew an aircraft into wind at minimum speed and allowed it to drift backwards over the ground. Unfortunately I could not think of a use for this capability. I gained the impression that the Colonel operated it like a lorry and he was greatly amused by my antics. Some of the instruments were labeled in Russian script but it did not seem to matter because they were not important. I can't imagine that it would be possible to make a dangerous landing in this remarkable machine. Any reasonable approach speed seemed to suffice and it could be comfortably operated from a cricket ground. We walked away from it with the colonel proud that he had been trapped by CFS Examining Wing and I tried not to look too smug.

Antonov AN2

In June the midday temperature was very hot and the air became sufficiently turbulent to cause fatigue damage to jet fighters. When the RAF operated from RAF Habbaniya the flying day would begin at 6 o'clock and a full program of training would finish by midday. The program board in the Operations Room would be prepared every morning and 20 to 30 sorties would be planned. Syd and Keith joined the IAF fighter squadron which was based at Habbaniya and equipped with Hunters and found that it was being operated like a young gentleman's flying club. The pilots would wander into the squadron at about 8 o'clock and one of them would give a rather superfluous weather briefing which was exactly similar to the one given the day before. They would then sit outside next to the buildings' walls where they could shelter in about three feet of shadow and order breakfast. When the important things of life had been safeguarded they would at last decide who would fly and what they would do. After one or two sorties the turbulence would be too uncomfortable and they would quit for the day. Syd and Keith needed great tact to convince them that if our team was to finish our task a more active flying rate would be needed. When they began flying they soon discovered that the pilots were quite competent at routine flying but they had obviously not been required to practice any emergency procedures which might be somewhat unpleasant. High levels of proficiency can only be maintained by practicing the nasty bits. While Syd and Keith were stirring up the pilots our navigator was sent to check the Operations Room and found that he had entered a time warp. The operations board still showed the last day of flying by the RAF before No 6 Sqn left Iraq ten years previously.

In the next four days I flew six checks with the transport force. The first four were in the DH Dove and as it was the civilian version of the Devon which I flew regularly a few years before I was happy to renew our acquaintance. The remaining two were flown in the DH Heron which was a larger version with four engines. It was like a big brother and I liked it also. The transport pilots were similar to the Hunter ones: competent at routine flying but completely out of practice with their emergency procedures. On every sortie when I gave a practice emergency the flight eventually headed towards a fatal accident. One pilot was given an instrument let down into Baghdad Airport and forgot to reset his altimeter before approaching the airfield. When I took control and asked him to remove his blind flying visor the aircraft was in the middle of tall chimneys in what might have been a brick factory and it was below their tops. If I had taken control before we entered the danger zone he would have told me that he was just going to reset the altimeter. I asked a Dove pilot making a single engine approach to go round again from just above his decision height and he applied climbing power and kept the aircraft straight but he then failed to retract the undercarriage and flaps. The aircraft would not climb or accelerate on one engine and I was dragged around the Habbaniya cantonment at the same height and at a speed not much above the stall until he eventually arrived back on the approach. I had to demonstrate to him the correct procedure and he was amazed that a circuit could be made at normal speeds and at 1,000 feet.

The final meeting with the staff required a great deal of tact. We had to maintain our integrity and bring all the shortcomings to their attention and we left them detailed briefings on how to correct them. Care was needed to avoid offending their pride and dignity

We were invited to a farewell reception at MOD in Baghdad on the evening before we were due to leave Iraq and our bus duly arrived and we set course but we were stopped at the main gate and asked to return to our quarters. Something was afoot but they did not know any details. Back at our house I contacted the Station Commander and he told me the situation was unclear but apparently a group of Iraqi Air Force officers had mounted an attempted coup d'état from Mosul. Very soon we were surprised to see a continuous patrol of a pair of rocket armed Hunters over Habbaniya. Our Varsity was the only aircraft on the tarmac and we were worried that they might use it for target practice. The Station Commander was then arrested by some of his junior officers. We returned to our house, destroyed any compromising documents and packed our kit and stood by to make a hasty departure. We went to the Officers Mess which we had been using in the hope we would be able to gain some information. Most of the officers that we knew were sitting around in the anteroom acting quite normally except that the subject of a coup was never mentioned. Any experienced officer makes no comments until he knows for certain which side is winning.

Next morning the Station Commander was free again. He thought the coup was collapsing and advised us to get airborne as quickly as possible with radio silence and head for the nearest RAF base at Akrotiri. Our navigator was with the British Air Attaché in Baghdad but they promised to send him on by civilian airlines when the coast was clear. We made all speed to the Varsity and I did the outside checks while all the team piled on board. Chic Hemsley, a Jet Provost pilot, went in the left seat and Keith Rawlinson RN took station on the navigator's table. I started one engine and Chic started taxying out. The second engine came on line while taxying and I managed to complete all the essential checks before we turned on the runway and started the take-off. By the time we reached our cruising height of 1,000 we were all ship shape and Bristol fashion. We were airborne within 30 minutes from Jubilee House. We cantered along to Akrotiri much better than when we had to continuously check our navigator and we were able to keep in phase with our diplomatic clearances. However, when we returned to the tender loving care of the RAF we then had to sit and wait for our navigator to arrive. I took great pleasure in sending a Trans Delay signal, which included as the reason for the delay "Waiting for navigator to catch up with the aircraft".

After a couple of weeks in Iraq, Akrotiri in July was an ideal place to kick our heels while waiting for our redundant navigator to arrive. He caught up with us after four days which was not too bad for him and we made haste to get ourselves home. We quickly passed through El Adem and Keith took us on to RAF Luqa where we stayed our last night before our return to UK. Next morning Syd had the unique experience of landing us on the Nice Airport runway which runs parallel to the beach. This airport is rarely used by RAF transport aircraft but unfortunately we could not stay to enjoy it. Keith soon got us on the road again and brought us safely home to Little Rissington. The team had taken me to Iraq and back and I had not flown the aircraft once.

Normally when aircraft arrive from overseas flights they have to clear through a customs airfield but for a long period of time it was usual for the Customs Inspector to come up from Gloucester and clear us on our base. He knew that we were not dedicated smugglers but he usually charged us all a nominal sum of about £4 for presents which we brought for our families. We had a small respite with our families who had as usual looked after themselves well but not necessarily happily in our absence before returning to the grindstone. The remainder of July rapidly passed with Dominie flying with Vic at Stradishall, Varsity and Valetta examining with Vic at Gaydon, a two day trip to Wildenrath in a Canberra and to round off the month I checked out Syd as a Meteor QFI.

Gradually a routine was established for the couple of years in the best pilot's job in the RAF. I tried to do some flying during every test because I believed that pilots would accept criticism or praise better it they knew you could cut the mustard. Every flight had to be one's best performance and there were no relaxed flights. A check flight with an A1 QFI such as Mike Vickers, who was then the doyen of Gnat QFIs, was a major challenge and might include a practice fire in the air at high level followed by all the emergency procedures and a practice forced landing through scattered cloud into Mona airfield. My adrenalin was maintained on high flow.

The domestic side of our lives also had its better moments. Keith had a notorious reputation for rarely taking his wife, Pat, out for a meal. One day he and I were due to spend a day trapping at Exeter and about 6 of our well behaved wives planned a coffee party at Pat's house. Before he left Keith told Pat that he had left a gallon of sherry for them and if they finished it he would take her out for dinner. Keith and I disappeared off to Exeter but Syd Taylor was in the office for the day. At lunchtime he found his house empty but before he returned to work he left a note for Kay to say that her lunch was in the oven. When he returned home in the evening the note remained on the table. He wandered round to Keith's house and found it in darkness. He entered through the back door and eventually found Pat and Kay comatose side by side on the bed. When

I returned to Rissington with Keith my house was also in darkness and Marlies was blissfully fast asleep on the bed. Our loyal group of wives had supported Pat and demolished the sherry. Marlies had even driven Pat's batwoman home before being overcome with stress and overwork. Their efforts were rewarded with a night out for Pat.

We were very fortunate to have as our near neighbours Syd and Kay Taylor. We soon realised that they were a very special family. Their eldest daughter Sue was away at Tubingen University. Johnny, Tim and Debbie were at our local school with our Jenni and little Alison, who was waiting to join them, was a frequent visitor to our house. Domestic chores were well organised and everyone had their part to play. Syd was active with the Scouts and Kay was a leading light in the Guides. Outside the house was a sailing dinghy and a frequently used caravan. Somewhere in between an Old English shepherd dog managed to keep everyone in check. Granny came to stay and at one time Jenni stayed for the weekend with them. They always had time for one more task or person.

After a Ball in the Mess at about 2 o'clock we walked home together and then Marlies and I discovered we had left our keys inside the house. Jenni was asleep upstairs but no amount of stone throwing or calling could rouse her. Syd fetched his tools and we set about a determined effort to break into the house. In retrospect I was amused to note the number of other people returning from the Ball who cheerfully wished us good night while we were attacking our house.

Hawker Hunter

At about this time a Hunter training Squadron was introduced into Nr 4 FTS at Valley to supplement the Gnat training. The Hunter was a well-loved fighter and we were pleased that this decision would bring our squadron more Hunter flying.

When we first arrived at CFS the Commandant was the same Air Cdre Bird-Wilson (Birdie) that I had flown with at Bassingbourn when he would escape from his MOD office to steal some Canberra night flying. He had a distinguished war record as a fighter pilot and it was pleasant to have a good friend in court. He was an excellent Commandant but I was equally delighted to learn that he would be succeeded by Air Cdre Frank Dodd. Frank Dodd was renowned among the PR force as an exceptional operational pilot. Together with his navigator they demonstrated their ability to persuade a Mosquito to fly greater distances than all other crews and played a leading part in major operations such as the finding and sinking of the battleship Bismark. As a dyed in the wool PR pilot I knew his background but he also had gained a wealth of experience in the bomber and instructional world. He became an excellent Commandant. He sucked his pipe and said little but I soon discovered that he was aware of everything that was happening at CFS.

Early one afternoon the phone rang and he said, "Brian it's a lovely afternoon. Can we go Meteor flying?" After I regained my breath it took me very little time to ensure that the Commandant's wish was my command. We met at the aircraft and he went into the front seat and I took my usual place. He was not an experienced Meteor pilot but he needed very little guidance to see us on our way. He took us up to medium altitude in a clear area and then flew various general handling maneuvers to get his hand back in and then produced a very competent set of aerobatics. Very little was said and we were both enjoying the workout. When he paused to draw breath he said, "Now show me your aerobatics". As I usually kept my display sequence up to date I was pleased to brush it off again. He then resumed his afternoon out and returned to the airfield, flew a few circuits and taxied back to our dispersal. Very little was said but he thanked me before returning to his grindstone. I can't remember a more pleasant or satisfying afternoon but when I thought about it later I realised that it was his very tactful way of checking my aerobatics. I was the Meteor display pilot and in a couple of days' time we were expecting another visit from our Commandant in Chief, The Queen Mother. We always mounted an air display for her and the Commandant was responsible for ensuring the safety of such events. He had not seen any of my displays but now he had fulfilled his responsibilities in the nicest possible way.

CFS Meteor 7 (Photo - Keith Watson)

He also held responsibility for the Red Arrows formation aerobatic team but as he was not an up to date Gnat pilot he knew he was not able to directly supervise them. I was in frequent contact with them as we operated alongside them at RAF Kemble and often shared aircraft when I was in a Gnat flying phase. Ray Hanna, their leader, was an old friend of mine from our RAF Gütersloh days and their next leader, Dennis Hazel, was my next door neighbour so it was easy for me to keep a discrete eye on them. They were a very professional team and I saw no problems with their operations but it gave me the opportunity to fly with them. Sometimes I flew in the back seat with Ray, Dennis or a new member of the team. I also had the opportunity to take another Gnat and fly behind as a chase aircraft to watch the overall formation manoeuvres. It was a golden opportunity to mix with such an elite team.

It was most appropriate that Queen Mum should be Commandant in Chief of the RAF's premier flying unit and I doubt if the Royal Family ever had more loyal subjects than at CFS. She was always a welcome visitor and she managed to escape as often as possible to visit for a day usually with as many of her family as could find an excuse to join the fun. Princes Philip and Charles had been trained as pilots at CFS and usually flew in for the occasion. After the reception and a walk around the station to talk to people engaged in their daily tasks we always gave a lunch in the Officers Mess before mounting the usual flying display. CFS normally had an interesting collection of aircraft to entertain her but my old Meteor was the daddy of the lot. She normally met all the display pilots but I think as the vintage pilot she felt I had a little in common with her. A memorable occasion for me was in September 1967 when Vic Stanton and I began the display by leading the tradition mixed aircraft formation in a brand new Dominie and closing it by cajoling my old Meteor to strut its stuff.

Trappers, together with other esoteric visitors such as Courts Martial members and auditors on working visits to RAF stations were not allowed to live in the Officers Messes for fear we may be nobbled by the residents. Instead we had to find our own accommodation in the local area. The RAF was always mean with allowances and we had to provide lodgings from what was known as a Rate 1 allowance which at that time was just over £3 per day! Over the years the teams had discovered a wide range of small hotels and pubs which provided an amazing range of rooms. It was not unknown for the landlord's family to give up their own bedrooms for the trappers but in return we would run the pub for an evening while the family had an evening on the town. The only person I knew that made any money on the Rate 1 was Al East. During one of our visits to Chivenor Al booked into a camping site near Croyde Bay. He had a magnificent 1930 vintage Alvis Silver Eagle car and he had been on a camping holiday with his family. He managed to arrange to install his family on the site and then join us for our trapping session. Every morning he appeared out of his tent in full uniform and disappeared over the horizon in his vintage car: thus proving that not only the English but also the Welsh are mad. The accommodation policy was misguided because we normally spent our evenings in the mess bar with our clients. This gave us much information and also allowed us to assess the morale of the unit.

Al shared his office with another major player in our team. Gerry Honey was one of the happiest men I knew and I looked upon him as our court jester. He was an accomplished pilot and soon became a solid examiner and with his wife, Valerie, he fitted very well into our team. He went on to become a leading and valuable member of the Harrier force.

The exciting range of flying continued apace and I managed to fit in some night flying in Hastings transports followed by some Lightning supersonic flights with our agents at RAF Coltishall. This earned me my coveted 1,000 mph club tie which was fairly rare at that time. Our next major overseas trip was to Singapore where I was delighted to revisit my old stamping ground after 6 years absence. No 81 PR Squadron was still in their ranch house and I took every opportunity to bring myself up to date with their operations.

BAC Lightning

I had a great contrast between flying the Javelin night fighter with our agents and getting my hands on the Pioneer short take-off and landing utility aircraft. After recently hurling a Lightning at the runway at 165 knots the task of approaching into a 200 yard landing strip cut into 100 feet high rubber trees in the Malayan jungle at 28 knots increased the flow of adrenalin noticeably. The small strips were usually built on a gradient and, as there was very little wind below the trees, landings were invariably made up the hill and take offs downhill. The approach was made to just clear the trees at the exact speed and as soon as the aircraft was on the ground heavy braking was required. As soon as the situation was under control the aircraft had to be taxied to the very uphill edge of the strip and turned round with the tail as near to the trees as possible. For take-off the engine was run up to full power before releasing the brakes and charging downhill with the intention of hauling the monster off the ground and clearing the trees again. We also flew into small strips on the offshore islands and I found this form of flying more demanding but satisfying than operating the fast jets.

Scottish Aviation Twin Pioneer

When I last met Sir Donald Evans he told me that when he took over as Air Secretary he proposed to make a tour of all operational stations to get a better feel for personnel problems and Tengah had just been told that he would visit them soon.

No 45 was now at Tengah flying Canberras and I visited them to remind them that Sir Donald was an old 45 Hand. The CO dug out the old photo albums from the 1930s and, lo and behold, we found a photo of the Fairey IIIF sitting in the bog. I suggested to the CO that during the visit the itinerary should be arranged to include a visit by Sir Donald to his old squadron for a coffee break and that next to the visitors book the old photo album should be place with the photo on the open page.

I later checked how the ambush went and was told that the forced landing was way back in his mind but after glancing at the photo alarm bells began to ring and he looked more closely until the penny dropped. He roared with laughter and congratulated 45 Sqn on their research and after a little thought asked, "Was Brian Ashley here?"

During the visit I had to check a target facilities flight which operated the heavy Meteor TT21s out of RAF Changi. During my tests I noticed that the pilots were having problems with single engine overshoots and I doubted if they had been practicing them. I took an aircraft on my own to examine the problem and, to my horror, found that in the worst case the aircraft had very marginal power to complete the manoeuvre. The high ambient temperature reduced the thrust from the engines and the extra drag from the target towing winch placed the aircraft in a potentially dangerous situation. I had to arrange with RAF Changi that if a Meteor TT21 lost a starboard engine during a flight the occurrence must be treated as a major emergency and special procedures followed.

Gloster Javelin

Another task which I enjoyed was visiting the Royal Navy Standardisation Flight at Yeovilton to sample their particular aircraft which included a wartime Swordfish biplane torpedo bomber. We had to ensure that the RN and RAF kept in step with our testing and recategorisations but as this was Keith Rawlinson's home ground we were always welcome.

The time had come when I must decide what to do about Al East. He had become the major Gnat expert and was giving excellent support to the training units and the Red Arrows. I had no doubts that he had easily attained A1 QFI status on type and, because of my daily contact with him, I would have been quite justified it I had decided to award him the category. However I decided that the integrity of Examining Wing must be protected and it must be demonstrated that there were no easy pickings. I therefore arranged that Al would have to sing for his supper by taking the full test. For me these were two of the best days I can remember. We went head to head in the lecture room and during a couple of flights and I learnt a lot. During the first flight I gave him a simulated emergency and he had to make a landing at RAF Valley, the base of the Gnat training unit but as I expected he sailed through with flying colours. He had his well-earned A1 category.

This pilot's paradise could not go on forever. I could see the end of my tour approaching but I was nearly exhausted. When I thought back to the small boy in 1935 who wanted to be an RAF pilot or the young man before the gates of RAF Heany who was worried about being able to make the grade I realised I had just about reached the top of the pile. With my exceptional ratings in all my main roles and pilot navigation, my test pilots course, my A1 QFI category, my Command Instrument Rating Examiners ratings in all 4 categories of aircraft together with the wide range of aircraft that I had been operating I reckoned I had a Grand Slam hand. I was glad that I had been given this first rate posting.

Among all the flying we had maintained a wide range of the usual station activities with summer and Christmas balls etc. and the Squadron had maintained a close social life. All the members of the squadron are still some of our best friends and Marlies and I were lucky to have met them. I am certain we gave the RAF excellent service during our time at CFS and Jenni, who had also been part of the team, had managed to gain 3 years of continuous education for the first time.

I was reluctant to give up my job and I continued flying a wide range of tests until my last day. When I left the Squadron was divided into two.

'Our teaching is everlasting'

In June 2012 the Central Flying School celebrated its 100th anniversary of its formation at RAF Upavon

CFS Centenary Medallion No 12

My CFS Pelican

The Vintage Pair

CHAPTER 16
Return to Staff College

Ternhill

AFTER the high pressure atmosphere of the trappers the world suddenly went flat and I realised that Air Ministry had no idea what to do with me. Until then I had been in practically no contact with the Personnel Branch and I was soon to discover that personnel management in the RAF was third rate. After the Trappers I was expecting a ground tour but I imagined it would be associated with aeroplanes. I was surprised when eventually I was told I was posted to the Officers Advance Training School at RAF Ternhill as a tutor. I was rather disappointed.

In early February 1968 I trundled about 100 miles north in my little Austin A35 known as Fitzroy to find RAF Ternhill. After inspecting a map I was expecting bleak scenery in the Potteries area but I was pleased to find that the airfield was in the middle of very pleasant countryside. It was surrounded by Chester, Shrewsbury, Stoke and Wolverhampton. The officers mess was the familiar 1936 pattern and as usual very comfortable. The Officers Advanced Training School (OATS) shared the station with the CFS Helicopter Wing so I had plenty of old friends nearby. I was made very welcome by the staff of the OATS course and I began to feel that the social life at Ternhill would be enjoyable but I soon discovered that no married quarter would be available for some time. I would have to commute between Rissington and Ternhill and Marlies and Jenni would have to stay at Rissington until a quarter became available. At least Marlies would still be among her friends and Jenni could stay in the school she knew.

The OATS 3 month course was very well established and had been developed into a very efficient training course for Flt Lts and Sqn Ldrs who were likely to progress through Staff College to the higher ranks. I was given a 6 member syndicate and soon settled down to sharing the course with them. Almost any group of people is full of interest and it was only when Bob Miles, an up and coming navigator, gave his 10 minute short talk we discovered he was a fully qualified London taxi driver. We were fascinated by his description of his efforts to learn "The Knowledge" by cycling around all the minor roads and side streets of Central London.

The CFS Helicopter Wing trained new helicopter QFIs and I decided that now was an ideal time to become one in any spare time I could find. My helicopter flying had been restricted to my time at the Test Pilot's School and was flown on early types which had no auto-stabilisation and the task was similar to a one armed paper hanger. The Helicopter Wing had small Sioux helicopters and when I began my part time course I discovered that life for helicopter pilots had become much easier and their chariots much pleasanter to drive.

Life could have been enjoyable except for the separation from one's family and the dreary commuting to Rissington on Friday evening and back to Ternhill on Monday morning. Time dragged by and after 3 months I was told that I had been allocated a quarter. Our joy was abated by the fact that while I was working at Ternhill Marlies would have to pack up our possessions and arrange the move. This was the first time she had faced the problem but like most RAF wives she buckled down to the task and on a Friday in May she arrived with Jenni and Pickfords' van at our new quarter. I was proud of her and the sun started to shine on us again. The quarter was quite nice but the garden, as usual, would need a lot of work but we were glad to be together again. My group director, David George, and his wife, Molly, made Marlies very welcome and we soon found out that the Station Commander, Gp Capt H G Davies, was a forward looking officer who was introducing weekend activities in the officers' mess for our families such as a curry lunch followed by a film show. Up until this time families had very limited access to the mess.

Sioux Helicopter

We spent our first weekend meeting new friends and getting the feeling that we would have a pleasant social life but the fickle finger of fate was not finished with me yet and on Tuesday I had to go home and tell Marlies that I was being posted again almost immediately. My new posting would be to the RAF Staff College at Andover and I would be promoted to Wing Commander. Andover was about 50 miles south of Rissington and I would have to commute about 150 miles and pass Rissington on my journey. Why could not the Air Ministry have left me at CFS for 3 months where there was plenty of work to keep me usefully employed? Marlies would not have had another lonely time and Jenni would have avoided a short time in her new school at Market Drayton. She settled in to the local Brownie pack and soon shared the pleasures of a Brownie camp in the area. It looked like chaos but the inmates were enjoying it.

Jenni, centre with friends at Brownie camp

She was a bright, enthusiastic little Brownie. I was beginning to worry about Jenni's education. She was coming up to 11 years old and continuity was very important at this age. I was also aware of the problems of a young girl changing schools so often. She had to be tough to weather the storm.

At a time when industry was waking up to the importance of good personnel management the RAF was dragging its heels and sticking to old draconian rules which insisted on rigid posting rules. With a little imagination the date of a posting of an officer could have been delayed or advanced to avoid the type of inefficiency with which I was now faced. Feeling that I already knew the answer I enquired when a quarter would be available at Andover I was not surprised or happy to be told that we would have to wait for a few months. I thus began the drudge of 3 months of unnecessary commuting to a job which I would otherwise have been delighted to begin.

Andover

The RAF Staff College at Andover had been founded in 1921 and was the first of its kind in the world. Each course normally had 42 students. Half were from UK and the remainder came from almost every part of the world. It soon established a reputation for excellence and many air force commanders around the world were Andover graduates. Unfortunately some were in gaol because their political grouping fell into disfavour. After the war the RAF expanded staff training and a new and larger college was formed. In 1968 it was at Bracknell and trained students from the old Commonwealth and NATO with a high security clearance. The old staff college was so well established and valuable that it was retained to train students from our friendly nations around the world. The small single story rose covered building alongside the road passing Andover airfield was an ideal location.

I was immediately appointed to be a tutor and was allocated a syndicate of 6 students ready to begin the second academic term. We had our own syndicate room but the tutors shared a large room for general work. This was an admirable arrangement because I found it useful to share views while marking papers or organising new college work. We combined our work happily and Alan Hume became a lifelong friend.

A typical syndicate had three UK, one NATO student and one each from an old Commonwealth country and a country where English was not spoken as a usual language. As they were all graduates from a wide range of colleges the amount of expertise brought to bear on the subjects under discussion was formidable. I soon settled down to extend my own education,

I was surprised to find that Dickie Littlejohn was a member of the course. He was a Cranwell graduate and I had followed him to 541 Sqn and 5 years later to 81 Sqn. He had married the AOC's daughter and was generally regarded as a high flier. Nine years later I thought I had overtaken him.

Nothing was more important at this time than getting Marlies and Jenni to Andover. After a very tedious period of commuting we were at last allocated a quarter in summer 1968 and Marlies had to repeat the process of packing up our effects and getting them to Andover. Service wives had much asked of them but it was amazing how they accepted the life and got on with it. Before they arrived I had discovered that because of more defence economies the Andover Staff College was to close at the end of 1969 and all students would be absorbed into Bracknell. I was nominated as one of 3 tutors to move to Bracknell to ease the overseas students into the sausage machine. I would therefore have only eighteen months at Andover and a year at Bracknell. Poor Jenni! I could only see more disruption of her education at the most important time. We were aware that eventually Jenni would have to go to boarding school to guarantee her a satisfactory education but how many parents want to see their young daughters leave home when they wish to enjoy their company and guide them through the mine field of adult life. At last we found a school with a good reputation only a short distance from us in Andover town. Rookwood was a private girls' school which catered for both day girls and boarders and we decided that Jenni could join as a day girl for the one and a half years we would be at Andover and then become a boarder in a school she knew well. At last we could contemplate a normal life.

The social life slowly increased in tempo as the end of the course loomed over the horizon and Marlies was able to join in the fray. Many of the overseas students were not accompanied by their wives and they were regular visitors to our house. A typical example was Keisuke Masakari from Japan. A daughter had been borne to Keisuke and his wife, Keiko, just before he left for England on his own and he faced the prospect of not seeing his baby girl for her first year. He was very lonely and he was always welcome in our house. Ten years later when I was visiting Japan frequently I always saw Keisuke and Keiko. Keisuke had become a Lt Gen and was able to direct me to the best contacts in the Air Force HQ. Often when I contacted one of his recommendations I was told "Ah, you are General Masakari's guru". Every year we have exchanged Christmas messages and he always addresses me as "Dear Sir".

The college made many friends for Britain in influential places around the world and as the course came to an end the warmth of these friendships was consolidated. More and more parties were organised in the mess and around the married quarters and after a year together we were heading for a special Christmas. The staff college had worked its magic.

Germans, South Africans, a Philipino and an odd Englishman

In preparation for the 1969 course letters had been sent to our client countries to warn them that the College would be amalgamated with Bracknell in 1970 and that 1969 course would have the distinction of being the last from the world's first Air Force staff college. We wished to ensure that after such an illustrious 47 years the final year would be one to end like a celebration and not fizzle out like a damp squib.

The tutors' room was working flat out to finish marking final papers and agree the assessments which would be so important to the graduating students. I was told before I went to Bracknell that it was better not to go to staff college than go and do badly. We were also aware that many overseas students would soon have to re-adjust from the freedom of speech which they had gradually acquired to a much more prudent manner of speech and their wives would have to hide exotic dresses under a shroud. They would never forget their brief freedom.

Major Jack Duffy of the US Air Force was very short but he made good use of it and I took great delight watching Jack at any of our dances. Bente Rasmussen from Denmark was a lovely statuesque girl who was over 6 feet tall and Jack's party piece was to invite Bente to dance and then lay his head on her bosom. I have rarely seen such bliss.

May the staff college course never end!

It was a time of great expectation as the students waited for their postings. Would their year's hard work have brought them the reward they hoped for? All too suddenly the course came to an end and they were gone. The pressure was removed from the staff and the married quarters' area became quiet. We could relax and spend a comfortable festive season with our permanent friends. The reduction in tempo was all too obvious. We could recharge our batteries and wonder what 1969 would bring us.

In early January we girded up our loins and the new course arrived. The reception party was a sea of unknown faces and I was given a list of 6 names of the lucky lads who would form my first term syndicate. When we assembled in my syndicate room I introduced myself and explained that from now on we were a team and what happened in our room was up to us. What they would learn depended on what we put in to the process. I had in front of me:

Lt Col Yohannes Woldemariam (Johnnie), a pilot from the Ethiopian Air Force

Sqn Ldr Don Bandula Senat Weeratne (Bandu), an administrative officer from the Sri Lankan Air Force,

Major Lutz Mundhenk, a pilot from the German Air Force,

Sqn Ldr Brian Batt, an RAF pilot.

Sqn Ldr Jack Broughton, an RAF navigator

Sqn Ldr Geoff Gwynn, an RAF engineer.

I asked them to spend about 10 minutes introducing themselves to the syndicate giving their careers and any specialities which might be useful in our studies. We were going to live in each other's pockets so all detail would help. Their overviews were followed by a question period during which we discovered what expertise we had to throw in to our pot of knowledge.

It was quickly apparent that Johnnie was an outstanding personality and he was the obvious choice for the senior student and course leader. He came from a modest family in the west of Ethiopia and soon after he joined the Air Force his outstanding ability won the attention and trust of the Emperor. He steadily rose to become the top pilot in the air force and had recently commanded the Strike Wing which was equipped with Northrop F5 fighter bombers and had been operating against Somali insurgents on their southern border. He was the only member of the syndicate with recent operational experience. He had also spent some time with West African air forces helping with their training and development and I soon discovered the great respect which he commanded in the area. He was a fine athlete and if he had not joined the air force he might have been an international footballer.

As we buckled down to work and became deeply involved in our studies it became obvious that racism did not exist at Staff College. All of us knew the colour of our skins and we all had the confidence to know we could compete with our peers. Free discussion on all topics of international news could be discussed with well balanced inputs. Thank goodness Political Correctness had not been invented in 1969. As we worked together we came to know and respect each other and a close knit team emerged.

The overseas students who were living in the mess without their wives were obviously lonely and our house had an ever open door. Johnnie, Bandu and Lutz were regular visitors. Marlies persuaded Bandu to ask his wife for his favourite recipe and she soon received one for a curry and a second for a splendid rice dish to accompany it. She set off on a round of stores as far afield as Winchester to find all the ingredients or the nearest available substitutes. When the heap was assembled arrangements were made for Bandu to come to the house on a Sunday to cook the feast. When I collected Bandu from the mess Nazir Khan from Pakistan decided to come along to help him.

Marlies hovered in the background to supply an ever increasing number of pots and pans. Bandu methodically worked his way through his wife's instructions with a little pinch of this here and a teaspoonful of that there but when he was not looking Nazir would throw in a handful of something else. The pots slowly filled up and just before midday I went to the mess to collect any hungry students. When everyone was refreshed we sat down for lunch with 12 different nationalities around the heavily laden table. Only Germany was represented by two members because Marlies was aiding and abetting Lutz. The Sri Lankan gods were working well and the meal was enjoyed by all. My bar slowly diminished as the afternoon passed away. By early evening the students slowly decided to walk back to the mess and Marlies and I were left with a kitchen that looked as if a tsunami had passed through it. Every pot and pan had been used. We rolled up our sleeves and set about the great salvage operation. By mid evening we could at last sit and contemplate our lounge walls.

We came to know and respect each other
Geoff, BA, Johnnie, Brian
Bandu, Jack, Mike Lintell

We were not only under siege by day but also by night. After a late dinner party Marlies and I were clearing up the kitchen at half past two in the morning when the doorbell rang. When I opened the door I was confronted with Lutz's face and two pairs of white teeth in the darkness. He marched in followed by Johnnie and Bandu. They had been returning from a dinner party when they saw our lights still burning so they decided to visit. Johnnie and Bandu settled on the carpet in the lounge while Lutz made a detour via the kitchen to find my Scotch bottle. It was still dark when they left but my Scotch bottle never recovered from the onslaught.

I found it amazing that we were able to fit in serious course work into our very active social life but the course surged ahead. While I was working Marlies and Jenni took our friends to visit Longleat House and Park for a little cultural activity. Sport was an important part of the course and all the usual games were well represented but not football. Marlies had a good supply of tennis partners. The college played annual games against the other service staff colleges but the 1969 course decided that they had enough talent to produce a useful football team and a challenge was issued which was accepted. Training began and shortly before the match a final workout was planned. Players could be found to field two full teams for the rehearsal except for one player. As they cast around to find a stop gap player the finger was pointed at Bandu but he protested that he had promised to play golf with Rudi Abad Santos. Pressure was brought to bear and he was harangued about the honour of the course etc but he still resisted. Eventually Johnnie was brought in to persuade him. Johnnie delivered a long oration to bring Bandu into line and finished with the immortal words, "Come on Bandu, be a white man and get your boots on!" Bandu played in goal.

In the summer Johnnie's sister came to UK for a short time and brought with her Johnnie's youngest son Soni and of course they came to Andover. Johnnie was immensely proud of Soni and took him to meet all his friends. Soni was quite small for his 8 or 9 years but was an absolute charmer. His round smiling face captivated all of us as he gravely shook hands on introduction. Most of our wives would gladly have stolen Soni.

The tutors did not receive any entertainment allowance to help defray our expenses but it was not possible to run a good syndicate without including the students in a full English lifestyle and we soon noticed we were having to dig into our meagre savings. However we did not regret this because we believed that the results were well worthwhile. Not only did we enjoy the students' company but we also considered it to be a sound investment in friendship for Britain from around the world.

Deep discussion on modern trends with Leslie Waterfield

In summer we had the great good fortune to take the students to witness the Trooping of the Colour before the Queen on Horse Guards Parade. The weather was good and the Queen was magnificent as she reviewed the parade on horseback. I was proud for the course to see Britain at its very best. No one does these occasions better and the students were most impressed.

Farewell, Johnnie

All too quickly the course entered its final phase. The town of Andover had always been excellent hosts to the Staff College and to mark the end of a very enjoyable era the Rotary Club invited the staff and students to a dinner in the town. Warm compliments were paid on both sides and Johnnie, as the senior student, was invited to respond on behalf of all students who had enjoyed Andover's friendship over the years. He could not have been a better choice and his dignified but warm hearted speech was well received by the Rotarians. I particularly remembered an allegorical story about the time when the Mayor of Andover was invited to visit Ethiopia. He was guided around the country by a very ambitious government minister who took every opportunity to address gatherings of local people. His spirited harangues were invariably followed by the crowd leaping to their feet and calling "Hosanga!" The Mayor was most impressed and towards the end of the visit he was invited to inspect one of Ethiopia's greatest exhibits, the deposed Emperor's herd of magnificent bulls. Before the visitors entered the enclosure to inspect the marvellous animals the mayor was asked to change his shoes for a pair of rubber boots and the curator explained that even Imperial bulls will always be bulls and one had to be careful to avoid the hosanga.

Inevitably the course ground its way to the end. Posting were received and sad farewells were made. A remarkable year ended in many parties among packing boxes. The students dispersed and the staff closed a memorable staff college. The tutors were also posted except for Bob Wilson, Gerry Watson and I who were destined to integrate the next crop of overseas students into the enlarged course at Bracknell. Marlies and I packed our goods and chattels ready to move back to Bracknell and Jenni prepared to rejoin Rookwood in the New Year as a boarder. She was familiar with the routine after spending eighteen months as a day girl and the change would not be too horrific. Even so Marlies and I did not relish the loss of Jenni when she was developing so well.

Goodbye Andover

All the Directing Staff were presented with silver replicas of the Egyptian Hawk of Horus to commemorate their tour of duty and Bob Wilson, Gerry Watson and I prepared to welcome the next course at Bracknell

Postscript

Johnnie returned to Ethiopia and as expected became the Chief of Air Staff in 1972. Soon afterwards a coup d'état was mounted and the Emperor was deposed. All his senior service officers were executed except for Johnnie who, because of the great respect for him, was sent out of harm's way to Washington as the Defence Attaché. After two years he was ordered home but declined and retired from the Air Force. He joined the Northrop aircraft company as their African consultant and was made a Director in 1974. We stayed in close contact with him until he died in the USA.

Bandu returned to the Sri Lankan Air Force and progressed steadily until he became the head of the Administration Branch. During a time of political turmoil I followed his progress via the RAF Air Attaché in Colombo. His health declined and he died while still quite young.

Lutz returned to the Luftwaffe in Germany to a senior administrative post in NW Munich. He was fortunate to meet through his work a civilian lady doctor psychiatrist who was working with the Luftwaffe and a sound relationship quickly developed and in a short time they married. When I made solo visits to Munich during the Tornado project I was happy to stay with them in a SW suburb of Munich. Lutz and Katherina visited us in England and, when they retired, we visited their lovely house and garden in the Krefeld Gardens area and met their busy little dog that rejoiced in the name of Zwiebel (Onion). We are still in regular contact with them.

My Andover Hawk

Bracknell

Our anthracite stove was dismantled and in January 1970 the Ashley caravan took the road to Bracknell. We were happy to return because we had fond memories of one of the RAF's most attractive units. A good quarter was waiting for us in the Crescent but the stove had to be installed to get some warmth in the house before we could begin the settling in process. The ground was covered in a few inches of snow but we were happy with the environment. We had quite a few mature trees with squirrels in our garden and a bank rising up about 3 feet to a high wooden fence at the back. It was only when a slow thaw began clearing the snow we discovered that the attractive bank was in fact a long heap of fallen leaves carefully raked up for us by the previous occupants and it took many days for a continuously burning incinerator to dispose of them.

In our absence the old syndicate huts had been demolished and a fine new instructional building erected on the site. As there would be four groups the building had four floors and each one had a staff common room, a Group Director's office, six tutor's offices and across the corridor six syndicate rooms. As I would be in D Group my office was on the top floor and I was D2. The main lecture hall was just below us and I found it to be an ideal teaching environment.

In the New Year Jenni set off for a new period in her life as a boarder at Rookwood School and we waited for our new big course to arrive. When we had sorted out all the shining expectant faces I was pleased to find that I had Alan Parkes in my first term syndicate. Alan and his new wife, Mavis, had joined us on 541 Sqn just before we left and we had lived for a very happy period in a hostel together. Mavis was an ex-WRNS and we could share our ex-RN reminiscences. They lived above us and I still remember a large thump from above as we were dressing for dinner. Mavis had slipped in the wet bathroom and landed on her bottom and hit the base of her spine. She had a marked limp and severe pain for several days but, like gout, most people thought it was amusing. Alan was a bright young lad who would probably be a RAF high flyer and his arrival on the Staff College course showed that he was still running well. We met them very regularly about 10 years later when Alan was Station Commander at RAF Akrotiri and we are still in contact.

I had an excellent Group Director, Roy Crompton, who ran his group very well and we settled down to a very happy routine. Roy and his wife lived near to us in the Crescent and they were very kind to Marlies and she soon resumed her old relationship with Bracknell. The term quickly passed and when the second term began I was given the most enjoyable syndicate I could have wished for. The senior member, and also for the course, was Wg Cdr Joe Hardstaff, the son of the well known English cricketer. The big, tall Joe was a Canberra pilot and captain of the RAF cricket team. Sqn Ldr Jim Sawyer was an RAF fighter pilot, Sqn Ldr Geoff Hawk was an RAF Engineer and Sqn Ldr Colin Milner was an RAF Education Officer. Our NATO representative was Major Jim Baker, a huge USAF pilot from Texas who had recently returned from strike operations in Vietnam and our rest of the world student was Major Ali Farivah a very small but charming engineer from the Iranian Air Force. They were a lively bunch and our syndicate sessions were full of interesting argument. I soon came to realise that their activities ranged outside the syndicate room and several pranks and high jinks around the college resulted in the finger being pointed at my syndicate D2. Ali followed the gang and the big boys looked after him very protectively.

Colin Milner should have been a politician. He had an Arts degree in History so he was a wordmonger by trade. He could make a long impressive sounding speech but say nothing. While marking one of his major papers I was puzzled by a sentence which lasted for 6 lines of print but was rather vague. I went over it several times before I discovered the sentence had no verb. Occasionally I would introduce a topic for discussion which I expected would be contentious but was disappointed when during the first round of opinions it looked as if everyone was agreeing and we had a damp squib. Then Colin Milner would talk a load of rubbish at length and Joe would immediately put him right whereupon the two Jims would savage Joe. We immediately had a debate on our hands and Colin our catalyst would sit down.

Our Commandant, AVM Nigel Maynard, came to the end of his rather undistinguished tour and a final Ladies' Guest Night was arranged to speed him on his way. I was annoyed to hear that the dinner was to be for the staff only and the students would not attend. I believed that the Staff College was centred on the students and they should have been there. After the meal we were continuing the party in the bar when a mess steward came to me and told me that I was urgently needed outside.

I excused myself and followed the steward. He led me to a small store room behind the bar and there was my syndicate sitting on the floor and enjoying their own party. I joined them and after a few minutes asked the steward to retrace his action and summon Marlies from the bar. She joined us and the party proceeded but soon Marlies suggested that we should all adjourn to our house. As we wended our way across the grounds in the moonlight she was discussing making a breakfast when she realised she had no bacon in the house. Jim Baker thought that Beverley, his wife, had some which might solve the problem. The only complication was that big Jim was dominated by his tiny wife and he would have to sneak into his house and steal the bacon without waking Beverley. He was a resourceful lad and accomplished his mission and the party with bacon went ahead. The momentum was retained and my bar stock was steadily diminishing when Maurice Harvey, who had joined us, decided to do his party piece and make Crepe Suzettes. His pancakes were average but his sauce depended on the contents of his host's cocktail cabinet. Mine was well primed and Maurice was declared to be a hero but my cabinet had taken a pounding.

One of the squirrels in our garden began to wait for Marlies when she appeared in the kitchen and they soon became good friends. When Marlies appeared he would hop up on to be window ledge and Marlies would feed him bits of peanut butter sandwiches. He often sat on the stay bar of the open window and when he had munched enough he would take the pieces and bury them in one of his winter caches at the base of a nearby tree.

One morning I was in the lounge when all hell was let loose in the kitchen. Our squirrel had fallen into the kitchen and when I arrived on the scene Marlies and the squirrel were chasing each other round the kitchen table. The squirrel was slightly in the lead. The chase continued until I could squeeze through a gap and open the outside door. The squirrel fled the scene but Marlies stayed behind. The squirrel was again waiting next morning.

We were introducing a period of management training into the syllabus and invited the heads of the UK's biggest companies to partake. The invitation was gladly accepted and we had a period of morning lectures from the leaders of such organisations as the BBC, BOAC, a large electronics firm, Tesco and a leader from the Trades Union Council followed after a coffee break by a 90 minute questioning from the students. Most of them stayed to take part in our syndicate discussions and I was often told that it was like a breath of fresh air for them to hear new ideas for their problems. I found it interesting to discuss with the Director General of the BBC the comparison between the BBC of 1944 with that of 1970.

We were also concentrating much more on joint service exercises and spent more time at the Army Staff College at Camberley. We were surprised to note how little respect and politeness the Army officers paid to their female counterparts. In one major exercise set on a group of islands in the South Pacific I had my own people plus Naval and Army students including Major Margaret Harle of the Women's' Royal Army Corp. Margaret wore spectacles, screwed her hair up in a bun and wore low heels shoes. She was also comfortably plump and we could see why the Army treated her and the other WRAC officers as second class citizens. However she was a bright and friendly person and she fitted in well with our team and we became quite fond of her. When the solutions to the planned operation were submitted two diametrically opposed plans were chosen to be presented to the whole course and one of them was ours. We chose to give the presentation on stage before a background of a south sea island and one of the students remembered that his wife had a grass skirt and many tropical beads. Margaret was outnumbered and she was reluctantly given the role of a senior local inhabitant who could provide essential local knowledge to the planners. When she unravelled her bun she had long hair which hung over her shoulders and with a large flower in her hair, the grass skirt, colourful bra, no spectacles and a tasteful amount of sun tan lotion she was unrecognisable as Major Harle. The presentation went well but the Army members could not think where we had found the dolly bird and how we had smuggled her into a restricted site. It came as a shock when they realised what was hidden in their midst. The RAF could be trusted to find it.

The new Commandant was AVM Michael Beetham and although he rose to become Chief of Defence Staff we were rather disappointed by him. I had a brilliant Commandant during my course, AVM David Lee, and the comparison was not good. The tutors were responsible for choosing and briefing visiting lecturers and we had to submit to the Commandant notes for a welcoming address and also a closing thank you speech. David Lee could quickly change our suggestions when required for what were very tactful comments after a sometimes unexpected talk. AVM Beetham rigidly ploughed through our notes even if the lecturer had not followed his brief and the tutor who produced the notes would be embarrassed.

My Bracknell Hawk

As the end of the course approached I was given the task of overseeing the students as they prepared for the end of course pantomime, Clueless, which was their opportunity to hurl good natured abuse at the Directing Staff. During an early rehearsal two students in uniform appeared from one side of the stage. At the same time another in full AVM's uniform with medals and a clipboard under his arm appeared from the other side. As they crossed the students saluted and said, "Good morning, Sir". The AVM looked at his clip board and replied, "Good morning". Before they disappeared into the wings one student said to the other, "I wonder who wrote that for him?" I mused that students could be very perceptive but it had to come out of the panto. Cruelty was not included in our syllabus. The course rolled to an end and the final Guest Night was followed by Clueless without any disasters. Gerry Watson, Bob Wilson and I were given second silver statuettes of the Staff College Hawk of Horus thus making us the only RAF officers to hold two Hawks. The two together with my CFS Pelican make a unique collection of which I am very proud.

331

The Unique Three

CHAPTER 17
Aphrodite's Isle

I N late October 1971 I was told by the Air Secretary that he had a job for me in Cyprus and he asked me how quickly I could get there. It was a Friday so I told him I would have to discuss it with Marlies but would let him know on Monday. I hurried off home and we spent the weekend in deep discussions and consultations with friends. Life in general had become quite serious and we were ready for a new adventure. On Monday morning I phoned the Air Secretary and told him we would go by car and we had started planning already.

For about a year we had been driving the top model of the new Ford Capri range with a 2 litre V6 engine, automatic gearbox and the top GT specification. It was such a pleasure to drive that we welcomed the chance to drive it across Europe.

A major reason for taking this unusual decision was the fact that housing was easy to find in Cyprus and we could avoid Marlies waiting for a quarter to become available. We decided to pack 6 boxes to be sent by sea and apart from the cases we would take with us the rest of our possessions would go into store. I then began a wealth of detailed planning and I found all the route information I needed from the AA. A small travel agency in Bury St Edmunds put together a wonderful package of ferry bookings at Harwich and Piraeus, petrol vouchers, a ferry booking from Piraeus to Limassol and hotels in Athens and Limassol. All bookings were paid and I was amazed at the very small bill. I did the most comprehensive route planning that I have ever done and in early November we set course. We planned to cross the North Sea on the overnight ferry from Harwich to the Hook of Holland and drive through Holland, Germany, Austria, Yugoslavia and through Greece to Athens. Delays would always be possible so I built in a weekend in Athens before sailing from Piraeus to Limassol.

We had made the overnight crossing of the North Sea several times before and we were soon on our way in Holland. The route from the

Hook of Holland to the east bound motor way was very tedious until we reached it near Delft. Then we settled down to very enjoyable driving. Our itinerary was mainly determined by re-fuelling stops. I drove to a service station near to Cologne where we topped up with fuel and food. Marlies then took over and drove down the Rhine valley in good weather. I had planned to stay overnight near Munich but when we approached the city it began to rain and as darkness fell the glare from all the lights on the wet roads was quite unpleasant so we refuelled and I took over and we continued driving. We were listening carefully to the weather forecasts because next day we had planned to drive over the top of the Alps via the Tauern Pass into Yugoslavia. The reports began to forecast snow over the Alps and road conditions were deteriorating. We emerged from the rain and eventually decided to stop for a lovely clear night in Salzburg. We had time for a good Austrian meal and a stroll before sleeping well.

Next morning the weather forecast was not good so I decided not to try to drive over the top of the Alps but divert to travel through the Tauern tunnel. Good fortune was with us and before long we were bowling down the southern side of the Alps on our way to the Zagreb area. We had the choice of following the coast road through Dalmatia which would have been very attractive but with endless corners so I decided to take the quicker inland route through Belgrade and Skopje. The road to Belgrade was the most boring I have ever driven. It was almost dead straight for nearly 250 miles and all the villages were set back about a mile from the road. The surface was poor and undulating. Our attention was maintained by the sight of huge lorries bearing down on us in the centre of the road. The only overnight stop was a service station with hotel where we had a very basic standard of service. We had been warned to take all removable attractive articles such as hub caps and windscreen wiper blades into the hotel with us and we were able to continue next morning with a complete car.

The approach to Belgrade was on a new motorway but as we were passing the city the road stopped at a barrier with a notice that directed us into the city. The diversion was well signposted until we came to a sign that pointed us in a direction almost opposite to the one which my pilot navigator's instinct told was correct. The signs then disappeared and I eventually reappeared back on our original new motorway. When I reached the barrier again I followed the diversion signs until I reached the one I doubted. I turned the opposite way to that indicated and we found the way out to Skopje.

Refuelling stops which accepted fuel coupons were becoming few and far between but our AA route plan was accurate and we stopped in a very remote area as the hills began. Marlies disappeared to find a toilet and almost immediately I heard a cry for help. She had found a small shed with a door only half the size of the frame and a large hole in the ground and two concrete foot prints on which to stand. She was wearing leather slacks which complicated the issue so I stood guard while she practised some problem solving. We wound our way through Skopje and then the road became quite spectacular. The road though the deep valleys was usually halfway up the mountain side and Marlies will never forget the nearness of the cliff face on her side and the sheer drop so close to the car on mine. As always we survived and we trundled down to the Greek border in Salonika. Darkness was settling in and we decided to look for a night stop. When we had the sea on our left we came across a small motel which looked as if it would fill the bill. The room we were provided was adequate and we quickly found the restaurant. It was long and narrow but a group of waiters was gathered in a bunch at the far end. They made no effort to come to us to take our order so eventually I went to see why they were avoiding us. The reason immediately became obvious; they were watching a television set showing a black and white episode of Coronation Street in Greek. I couldn't detect if it had a Lancashire accent.

This was our first encounter with Greek people but we found them to be friendly and helpful. The fact that we had no common language was no problem and we were soon sampling a typical Greek meal.

Next morning we had ample time so we could cruise along the east coast and admire the scenery. I quickly realised that through my knowledge of maths and physics I could read the Greek signposts. I planned to stop for lunch at the site of the Battle of Thermopylae where a small Spartan army made a heroic stance against an overwhelming Persian army until they were betrayed by a peasant who revealed a hidden track and they were overrun. In 480 AD the pass was only a few hundred metres wide and a restaurant had now been built in the narrowest part of the defile which would be an ideal place for lunch. When we entered the restaurant we saw a sight which would become very familiar in the next few years. A huge bare room was filled with small tables and chairs and about half of them were occupied by local people. They immediately showed keen interest in us but the numerous greetings of "Kali mere" reassured us that all was very friendly. Again the lack of a common language was solved when we were taken by the elbow and lead into the kitchen to see a good selection of local dishes on display in large metal pans suspended over hot water. We had no problem in selecting a very enjoyable lunch. As we left we were bid farewell by most of the other diners. We had a very favourable impression of the ordinary Greek people.

We cruised steadily southwards and in mid-afternoon arrived in Athens. We had stayed on schedule and could look forward to a weekend in the city before leaving Piraeus on Monday afternoon. In 1971 Athens had a terrible reputation for smog and the whole city was normally obscured but we were lucky because the sky was blue and visibility good. The whole city was bathed in sunshine.

We had bookings in the Queen Amalia Hotel near to the Parliament building and it was an excellent base for our explorations. During the weekend we covered nearly all of the many ancient and modern sites. The political situation was quiet so we saw Athens at its best.

Our passage by ferry to Limassol was booked so all we had to do was drift along on Monday afternoon to Piraeus and drive on to the ferry boat. For the first time we found ourselves immersed in a large group of Greek people and we came into close contact when we were seated for our first meal with four other passengers. Most of them knew a few words of England and a very helpful large plump elderly lady was quite fluent. They made every effort to help us and we began learning basic Greek language and customs. They seemed to enjoy it as much as we did. The very pleasant two day journey on a calm sea was a suitable introduction for Marlies' first sight of Cyprus.

Early on Wednesday morning, 18th November 1971, we were cruising along the south coast of the island and before us we could see aircraft operating from RAF Akrotiri. We had a clear view of the centre of the island including the Troodos mountains and as we rounded Cape Gata we saw before us the Bay of Limassol and the old town nestling on the shore. The harbour was only a small fishing port with 2 small jetties so our boat had to drop anchor in the bay about a kilometre offshore. Very soon a small lighter appeared alongside a hole in the side of the ship and two wooden planks were manoeuvred into position to form a bridge for our car from the ship on to the lighter. My confidence was not boosted by the knowledge that Cyprus had very few cars with automatic gearboxes.

I asked if I could drive the car on to the lighter but was immediately informed that it was not allowed so I had to bite my finger nails while the car was precariously shunted onto the lighter. We were onshore in time to see a repetition of the procedure at the dockside. When the car was safely ashore I could resume breathing.

When all the disembarking processes were complete we drove leisurely along the coast road to the Pavemar Hotel; one of the fairly modern hotels in Limassol. It was small but we were given an adequate room and at last we were safely ensconced in Cyprus.

After we had taken a coffee break I decided I would have to check in at RAF Episkopi to let them know we had arrived in Cyprus. I took a very pleasant 20 mile drive westwards along the south coast to find Headquarters Near East Air Force. I located the Gp Capt with whom I was going to work who told me he had been wondering where I was. No married quarter had been allocated to us so we would have to find our own house and furniture in Limassol. He was in a very magnanimous mood and told me that to help with our search I need not appear for work until Friday. I could have the whole of Thursday off! RAF personnel management was maintaining its reputation.

Limassol was a faded, sun bleached town of about 75,000 inhabitants. Although it seemed sleepy it had a lively industry of wineries, distilleries and a wide range of light industries such as leather and silver ware and pottery. Small tavernas and restaurants abounded and a busy old market was in the old town. A unique feature was the presence of a large number of British servicemen and their families. The overflow from the two large bases at Akrotiri and Episkopi occupied about 3,000 houses with 14,000 people and brought an income of about £20 million per annum into the town.

Houses were continuously being built with the hope of renting them to the British and into this market we had to plunge to find a house as quickly as possible. The RAF had centred their housing activities at Unicorn House on Makarios Avenue which formed a ring road around the town. We quickly found one of many house agents, Sammy Andros, and he began to drag us around numerous inadequate houses which seemed to be getting worse and worse. He often referred to a house which was out of town with a bad road connecting it to Limassol. As we became more depressed we asked him to show us the house but he was reluctant until we twisted his arm.

St Andrews Street

The Old Post Office

The Yellow House

He headed out of town along the coast road to the west towards Akrotiri and as he had forecast the tarmac road gave way to a rutted track and steadily the ruts became deeper. After five miles we arrived in Zakaki village, a small settlement centred on a crossroads, surrounded by small fields tended by market gardeners. We stopped before a new bungalow that was raised up on its foundations by about three feet. It was surrounded by a quite large bare garden and a neat metal fence. Immediately we knew that this was the house we were looking for. When we entered the house we liked what we saw but after a few moments our spirits dropped when we were confronted by a fierce looking lady dressed all in black who stood in front of us and gave us a close inspection. She was about my age and was very plump. She said something to Sammy in Greek and then left us. When she returned she held a plate of green and purple fruit about the size of small apples. We had no idea what they were but the lady split one open and offered it to us to eat. This was our first encounter with a fresh plump fig and we never lost our love for them.

The fierce lady was Vasiliki who was to become a major feature in our lives. She was a simple village woman but was one of the nicest people I have ever met and had not one evil thought in her mind. She became our close friend until she died far too early in 1998. She disappeared while we looked at the house but when she returned with a lovely smile on her face we knew we had found our new home.

The bare garden after a few flowers had had been planted

The house had been built as a dowry house for her daughter, Androulla, who had recently been married but her husband, Michael, was working in Famagusta and the house was vacant. Vasiliki and her husband, George, heard that houses were required by the British and had offered it for hire. Several people had come to look at the house but Vasiliki had turned them all down. We had obviously been given her seal of approval and we became the first British residents of the small village of Zakaki. The house was unfurnished so all we had to do during the rest of the day was find a kit of parts to make up a home. Sammy told us, "No problem", and took us to a huge warehouse where the workers had obviously seen this problem before. In very little time we had crossed off the items on our shopping list. As a grand finale to our first full day in Cyprus Sammy took us to a material shop where Marlies bought some excellent Cypriot curtain material and the rest of the day was ours. All this was accomplished without any assistance from the RAF personnel branch who had no interest whatsoever where we slept for the night.

I had to check at Episkopi next day but Vasiliki visited Marlies before she set to work to make our curtains by hand. While she was busy a large burly villager appeared at our door with a smile and a large bunch of shiny red radishes in his hand. Marlies thought he might be trying to sell them and offered by sign language to pay but immediately more vigorous hand waving refused the offer and the radishes were put into her hands. We later discovered that this friendly visitor was Vasiliki's elder brother, Andreas, who sold his vegetables in the Limassol market. While Marlies was sitting in the middle of our sitting room sewing the curtains she noticed a group of four men walking down the middle of the road carrying what appeared to be a small table. When they turned into our entrance she saw it was a treadle sewing machine which they brought into the house and set it down before her. Days later after she had mastered the art of using a treadle machine and the curtains were finished and in position the men returned and took the machine away again. We never discovered where it came from but this was another introduction to the generosity of our village neighbours. While Marlies worked several old ladies dressed in black wandered into the house individually, patted Marlies on the cheek, strolled through the house and disappeared after muttering friendly greetings to her in Greek.

And after a few more flowers

It was obvious that Vasiliki and George were very fond of each other and were never apart for very long. Vasiliki was the same age as I and George was a couple of years older. The Cypriot villagers set great importance on being a Good Man and George was one of the best. He tended a large field behind our house where he raised a wide range of high quality vegetables which he took to the Limassol market early every morning. We would often see George picking figs from his trees about 5 o'clock in the morning before he went to the market. He would return about 9 o'clock and he and Vasiliki would pick more before he returned to the market. That is what they meant by fresh figs in Cyprus.

Their little house was next to ours and was an old wattle and daub single story building consisting of a line of four rooms with a kitchen and bathroom behind. It was set back from the road behind two rows of tall eucalyptus trees which Vasiliki had planted when she was young. A pleasant open space stretched along the front of the house. The room nearest to our house was used as a simple grocery shop which supplied many of our daily necessities. We quickly discovered that the local baker delivered fresh warm bread three times a day and put the loaves into a large wooden cupboard. The new loaves were hidden behind the older loaves but we noted the delivery times and Marlies became very adept at fishing lovely crisp village bread out of the pile.

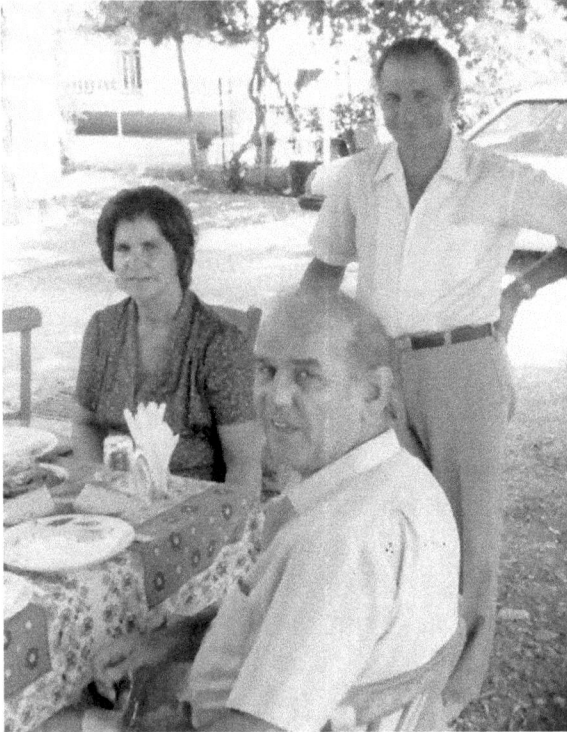

Vasiliki and George

Evyenious, the youngest son was about 15 years old and he lived at home. He had not yet discovered girls and spent most of his spare time practising football against the front wall of his house. His older brother Herodotus (Rodi) was aged about 20 years and was an officer in the Army but was attending a course at the Greek School of Artillery in Crete. We had to wait to meet him but the rest of George and Vasiliki's family seemed to shoot out of the ground at regular intervals and we began to realise that we were becoming part of the family.

Vasiliki's older sister, Aleki, lived in the next house along the road with her husband, Kostakis, who was the manager of the Smedley's tinned fruit factory which was the village's biggest industry. The last building before the corner was a taverna which was owned by Kostakis but run by his brother, Andreas Vashis (The Fat One).

Our road was set back from the sea by about 1 kilometre and George's younger sister Cleoniki lived in a small house in the middle of the fields with her husband Bambos and three children. Bambos worked in the HQ NEAF as the driver for the Director of the Ministry of Public Buildings and Works, known as Works and Bricks, and spoke almost fluent English. Their daughter, Soulla, who was aged about 15, was a bright, confident girl who also spoke good English. Marlies and I buckled down to learning Greek and as we learned our new friends discovered that they already knew a lot of English words from television, etc and together we made good progress. Cypriot is a dialect of Greek and has many differences. Marlies preferred to learn colloquial Cypriot because she was in continuous contact with the villagers while I turned towards Athenian Greek because it suited my purposes better. Marlies became very adept at gossiping with her neighbours.

In our early days Soulla was very helpful and when she was talking to Marlies she offered to take her into Limassol on our village bus. She arrived at our door on the arranged morning and Marlies asked her in and offered a soft drink. After a little while Marlies asked what time the bus came and Soulla replied, "Oh, it's waiting outside!" After dragging around the world in the RAF we had now found ourselves in a new world.

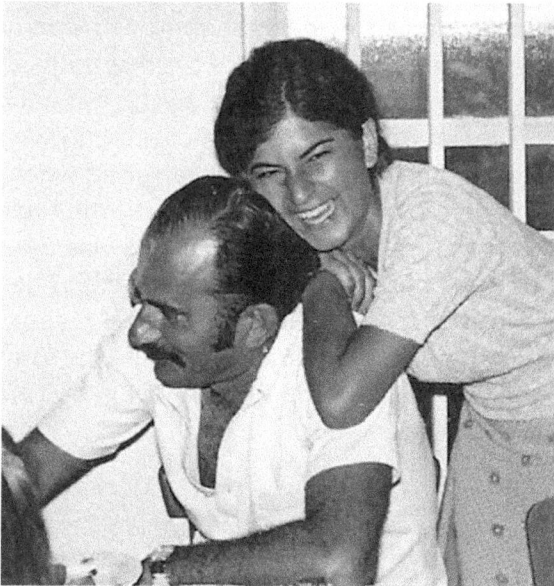

Bambos and Soulla

On Sundays and special days George would set up and light his charcoal grill on their forecourt and set about preparing large chunks of lamb which he slid onto long spits which were then set to rotate over the hot charcoal to produce Cyprus's favourite dish, souvla. We would wander round in mid-morning and join him while the ladies prepared salads and put potatoes in the oven to roast. We were introduced to ouzo, an aniseed flavoured drink which is known by many other names around the world. A generous helping of ouzo with plenty of water and accompanied by long strips of cucumber seemed to be the ideal preparation for a barbecue. The excellent Keo lager type beer was a good alternative. Just before the souvla was ready George would take his knife and cut off hot bubbling parts to taste the flavour. Of course he invited us to join in this evaluation and we both thought these samples were the best part of the dish. When the souvla was ready we would then relax while the remainder of the meal was completed. Tables were set out under the trees and all members of the family who were available sat down for a happy family meal. Who cared if the souvla was only warm by then?

When Christmas was bearing down on us Jenni flew to join us. She was well established in Rookwood School by then and this was a welcome break into the warmer weather. She was very quickly swept up in to our new family and she found that Soulla was a close soul mate. We decided to give a traditional English Christmas dinner to our neighbours and Marlies pulled out all the stops to produce a turkey with all the trimmings, Christmas pudding and all the rest. Rodi was still not back from Crete so we had George, Vasiliki, Androulla and Michael who were visiting from Famagusta and Evyenious. They were very surprised when the turkey was brought direct from the oven and was carved on the table while still hot and even more so when the Christmas pudding was doused in Cognac, lit and brought to the table covered in flames. We had been worried that they might not like the food but we were soon reassured. The whole turkey disappeared and the only person to dislike the Christmas pudding was Evyenious, the young boy. I thought he would be certain to enjoy it. A good time was had by all.

Androulla and Michael visiting Evyenious joins us

Every morning a long stream of cars passed by our house on the way to RAF Akrotiri and a similar number were making their way to RAF Episkopi on a road which ran north of us. I had to join the queue of cars to Episkopi and after suffering the delays caused by the large number of vehicles I decided to buy a motor cycle for my daily commuting. It considerably reduced my travelling time and was the only form of air conditioned transport available at the time. Marlies was free to use our Capri and she began to use Limassol for her shopping but she was surprised to receive a traffic police ticket for speeding on the sea front road. She had been caught speeding at 38 mph in a 30 zone. We would have to wait to see how vicious the punishment was for such villainy.

In the evening we were introduced to the village coffee shop. We only had to walk about 100 metres along our road to Kostakis' kafenion and meet his brother Andreas Vachis who was the host. A good cross section of the village men regularly wandered through and we began to meet more and more of our neighbours. Ladies did not normally use the kafenion so Marlies was a great novelty. The Cypriots are great talkers but very little new happened in the village and they quickly ran out of news and they had to repeat old stories. Our arrival was a major event and they were curious to know all about us and we were involved in lively sessions around the bar. When news of Marlies' speeding ticket became known it was repeated with gusto but each time it was recounted the speed increased until it passed the 70 mph mark. We did not know at the time that one of Vasiliki's older brothers was a sergeant in the police HQ but we learned of the Cypriot habit of mislaying speeding tickets of good friends. Marlies is still waiting for her summons.

A few friends would gather around the bar and share a bottle of local brandy which had a soft taste but proved to be just as strong as French cognac. Marlies soon began to add a little water to it. The rest of us drank it neat. About 10 mm would be poured into a long tumbler but if too much was poured in accidentally a little would be poured out until the accepted level was found. Obviously too little was considered to be mean and it was quickly adjusted. The bottle stood on the bar and it and frequent renewals were common property. The nearest free hand topped up the glasses when necessary. As we drank small dishes of sliced cucumber or carrots would appear on the bar and as we continued drinking more titbits would follow. If another friend came in for a short visit he would be given a drink and bite and would then leave without paying. At the back of the room a juke box loaded with Greek folk dance music was available and as the evening warmed up spontaneous dancing would begin and before long several of our companions would be demonstrating their prowess. Needless to say Marlies and I were readily joining in and being offered advice by our zealous instructors.

Andreas Vachis, our host

As the evening wore on more people would join the fun and the bar counter was quickly laden with empty bottles and plates. When at last someone asked Andreas how much we owed he would waddle along to us, take out of his pocket a scrap of paper, lick his pencil, count the bottles and plates and then say something like, "Seven Pounds". The remaining six or seven revellers would share the cost and disappear to their homes; all sober.

A German lady who owned a hotel with her husband came to stay with us and we warned her that the Cyprus brandy tasted mild but was still potent. She shrugged off this warning and assured us that with her experience it would be no problem. When we took her to our taverna she was the centre of interest and did not notice that her cognac glass was always topped up to the 10mm mark. As we walked the small distance home she began to plait her legs and she suddenly veered off to the right side of road as if her right leg had suddenly become shorter. Opposite our garden gate she turned violently left and I was just able to open the gate before she shot through. She negotiated the steps with difficulty but then continued the journey into the house on her hands and knees. I had to look the other way as Marlies helped her to bed after unlacing her corsets and finding her abandoned wig.

Kostakis shows the way with Juke box in background

347

The political situation in Cyprus is always volatile and at that time the main issue was the conflict between followers of the President Makarios who was supporting an independent Cyprus and the EOKA party lead by the Greek General Grivas who were struggling for a union with Greece. The division of loyalties often divided families but Kostakis' coffee shop was neutral ground and we mixed with both groups and as time went by we were regarded as neutrals in the argument.

Unfortunately Kostakis had to give up his coffee shop but a stranger from outside Zakaki took it over and soon we all assembled to rate his service. The meze was not as good as Andreas' and in general we were disappointed but when the new landlord presented his bill our friends were outraged. The price was about double that of Andreas'. The indignant assembly retired to our house and a Council of War was convened. The unanimous verdict was that we would not go there again and Dinos revealed that in protest he had taken a knife and fork from the tavern.

For a few weeks we arranged to go with the usual congregation to various tavernas in Limassol but a new taverna was being built next to our house and Andreas decided to take it over as landlord. We would only have to walk about 20 metres back to our house so we thought it advantageous to transfer our custom to him again. Life in the village could return to tranquil normality and we still have an extra fork in our kitchen drawer. The Grivas faction used another kafenion in the village but we were still friends with its clientele.

In summer we sat on the coffee shop terrace under the grape vine to enjoy the cooler evening sunshine. When more grapes were required Dinos climbed up the corner post and solved the problem. This provoked much macho discussion until Marlies shinned up the vine and collected more grapes. In Cyprus ladies had not climbed up grape vines before and she was regarded as super woman. On another occasion two villagers appeared on their big, heavy bicycles with panniers which they used to take their vegetables to the market every morning. Claims were made that only Cypriot men could ride such hefty machines but Marlies and I decided to defend Britain and confuse the locals by taking the bikes and riding after each other in circles around the crossroads.

Early in 1972 a quarter became available for us at Paramali where all the senior staff lived but we had become so entrenched in Zakaki that I turned it down and said we would stay in the village. The reaction at

Episkopi was amazing. The waiting list for houses was as long as your arm and many people were desperate to get out of Limassol and on to the bases. I came under very strong pressure to move and eventually I was told my marriage allowance would be stopped. This made me more adamant not to move and eventually the pressure dropped and a keen volunteer happily moved into the house.

We became more involved with family and village life and went on picnics on the hills, etc. Bambos took us to visit his parents in Kolossi and Marlies for the first time in her life found herself in a goat pen. She was delighted to discover how soft haired and playful the lovely young kids were until she noticed that a friendly little one had been nibbling the hem of her silk dress.

Cypriot girls were closely chaperoned and Soulla was delighted when Bambos and Cleoniki allowed her to go into Limassol with Jenni and they took the opportunity to go as often as possible. Jenni later told us that Soulla had a steady boyfriend, Byron, and he just happened to be in Limassol at the same time.

Much later we were invited to visit Bambos during the evening for a meal and to meet some friends. We were surprised to discover that it was much more formal than we expected and we had been invited to support Bambos in his negotiations with Byron's parents to decide if Byron and Soulla could become engaged. Soulla was sitting anxiously with us and the talks continued well into the evening. Bambos was initially not in favour of Soulla being engaged to a baker's son but by gentle persuasion he was converted and just before midnight his two small sons were dispatched to the coffee shop to fetch Byron who was then told that the engagement had been agreed.

Next day a party was arranged at lunchtime for about 200 guests and all their friends rallied around to produce tables and chairs, chickens, vegetables and all that was needed to produce a feast for their friends and neighbours. Marlies and I could not imagine this happening in England or Germany at such short notice.

Cyprus had an abundance of olive trees and every rural family owned some of them. Towards the end of a long dry summer we were invited to join Bambos' family in their annual olive picking. We were warned to wear old clothes because it was a dirty process. When the family was assembled in their orchard plastic sheeting was spread under a tree and then it was violently assaulted by vigorous shaking, beating with long poles and small boys shinning up the branches. We helped in recovering the fallen olives from the ground and we learned the hard way why we had been warned to wear old clothes. Dust had collected on the trees during the dry summer and it now came showering down on top of us. The particles were very fine and found their way into every crevasse in our clothes and into our hair. At the end of the day we all looked like light brown ghosts and after a picnic we made our way home to seek the bathroom. After much scrubbing, the shower pan was full of muddy water. Some olives were chosen for the kitchen but the bulk of them went to the local olive press to provide the annual supply of olive oil.

I had to share my time between living in the village and going to work. I was one of a of a three man team which CAS had set up to carry out a management review of the Near East Air Force which at that time stretched from Gibraltar to Hong Kong. Our bailiwick was quite large! I had to disappear quite often to the far flung parts of the Empire but my travels were compensated for by an enjoyable mess life. In addition to the RAF Officers Mess we also had an officers' club which provided an excellent curry buffet on Sundays and produced various forms of entertainment. Our old friend Alan Hume had arrived at RAF Akrotiri as the Gp Capt Administration. We had been close colleagues when we shared the same room as tutors at the Andover staff college and we were happy to resume the friendship. Alan and Liz had a very comfortable house in the best area of Akrotiri and we able to share mess life and village life. Alan also had a beach hut on the bathing beach at Akrotiri which was well used. Jenni and Alan were great friends and she has very pleasant memories of Akrotiri.

On Alan's beach

We also travelled around the island together and we often on a winters' day drove up the mountain to the Forest Park Hotel at Platres to enjoy a Sunday lunch in the sunshine before descending back into the clouds. A cruise along the coast road to Paphos for a fish meze on the harbour wall made a pleasant diversion.

On the harbour wall

RAF Akrotiri was the base for three Vulcan Squadrons and No 5 Squadron which was equipped with Lightning fighters and a Canberra. Fortunately the Sqn Cdr was Martin Bee who had been a student at Bracknell while I was a tutor and this gave me the opportunity to slip away and fly as often as possible. Even flying a Canberra as a target for practice interceptions was not boring for me.

The RAF used any spare capacity on the transport aircraft plying their trade between UK and Cyprus to bring children at boarding school in England home for their holidays. We were fortunate in finding seats for Jenni and she never missed a visit. On one occasion the aircraft was full and Jenni was allocated the nursing mothers' seat for take off and landing but spent the flight on the flight deck on the spare seat with the crew. Our old friend Vic Stanton was a VC10 captain at Brize Norton and I suspect he was behind this plan. While they were en route Jenni was asked if she was related to Brian Ashley, who had been the Boss of the Trappers.

When Jenni pleaded guilty to this heinous offence the crew decided it was a good opportunity to dump her overboard. However they relented!

Jenni soon made contact with a number of other A level students and undergraduates in Episkopi who were also on holiday on the island and when they hired a bus and made frequent visits to Limassol for a night out she was never forgotten. Their evening usually began with a visit to a Turkish kebab house where they enjoyed a meze and free kokinelli (local red wine). After hiding away a liberal quantity of the kokinelli they then went on to a disco for the remainder of the evening. Girls were admitted free into the discos and it was not unknown for the smaller boys to borrow girls' capes to sneak in free. This ploy also had the advantage of hiding more kokinelli. Jenni was just over 14 years old and the youngest of the group and I used to spoil her fun by insisting on picking her up at midnight. Cinderella lost her slipper but the prince never rode into Zakaki.

A bright and shining Jenni

The other Jenni

She was also slowly mixed in with other Cypriot girls by Soulla and she gained a good insight into the lives of both worlds. George's eldest sister who lived in the fields near to Bambos had three sons and then six daughters. She shepherded a small flock of goats during the day and life was very hard for her. The boys all did well and the girls were growing up to be a very nice bevy of beauties. In the 1970s every village family was required to provide a dowry house for their daughters and the three boys were determined to live up to the custom and build 6 houses for their sisters. This was a daunting task and I think it would not even be considered today.

When weather became warmer the wedding season began. In the villages weddings were major events and even the poorest families gave their daughters a magnificent start to married life. Very few of the old five day events still took place and had been replaced by a three day ritual.

On the Sunday the bride would be prepared by her family and many bridesmaids while the groom was being dressed by his numerous best men before they paraded separately along the village street to the church where the whole village was gathered.

Towards the end of the ceremony small crowns were placed on their heads and long tapes unrolled. All the best men signed the groom's tape and the bridesmaids signed the bride's. Each of the signatories later made a contribution which covered the cost of the service. The whole party then paraded back to the new dowry house and the celebrations began. On the first day the main guests were from the groom's village, on the second day the bride's village friends and families made up the crowd which could be over a thousand strong. On the third day the extended family provided chickens and all joined in to prepare a family finale. A full meal was served on the first two days and local musicians churned out a steady stream of traditional music. The mattress was danced through the house and a small baby rolled on it as a fertility rite. The mothers danced together followed by the fathers. Next came the best men and then the bridesmaids. While the bride and groom were dancing close friends pinned bank notes on the bride's dress until it was well covered. Usually several hundred pounds were contributed. During the summer we received invitations nearly every weekend and often we did not recognise the name of the couple and were tempted to excuse ourselves until we learned that the bride was a relation of Vasiliki and the scene changed. Once more Marlies visited our silversmith for yet another present.

Jenni, during her summer holiday, was swept up into the whole affair and was involved with preparing the food and was seen up to her elbows in a large wooden trough making spaghetti. When she was invited to be a bridesmaid she had to learn to dance the kalimatianios, the bridesmaid's dance. Her education was being rounded out.

Limassol was the liveliest town in Cyprus and every evening the many restaurants and tavernas were happy places to be. Most of them had three or four piece bands usually with a bouzouki and all of Limassol danced. The Miramare Hotel was the most modern hotel while several bigger hotels were still being built and we went regularly on Friday nights for dinner. The four piece band was very good and the members became our lifelong friends. Kostakis played the guitar but was learning to play the bouzouki. He was rather hesitant about showing his prowess but late in the evening when many diners had left we encouraged him and he rapidly became very good. The main attraction of the evening was the Appolon folklore dancing group which staged a display of Cypriot and Greek traditional dances. They had recently represented Cyprus in Mexico during the Olympic Games and often performed abroad. They were the pioneering group in Cyprus and we became fascinated by the lively Greek dances but the Cypriot dances were rather solemn and boring.

Apollon dancers in full flow

The power house behind the group was Marios Sophroniou who was a secondary school teacher who had studied in Greece. During his studies he had researched Greek regional dances and had become an expert on the subject. Marios was the driving force but he was ably assisted by another gymnastics teacher and dance enthusiast, Andreas Lanitis To see Marios and Andreas dancing an energetic dance such as Samikos was quite spectacular.

Kostakis and bouzouki

They collected together a very likable group of boys and girls who worked hard in response to Marios' leadership. Girls were rather limited by strict chaperone rules but the group was considered to be a very respectable organisation and they were allowed a much appreciated freedom to work with the group and we enlarged our circle of friends. We often attended their weekly rehearsals and when Marios saw our serious interest he volunteered to visit our house to give us individual tuition. After the group performed at the Miramare they would change their dress, have a meal and then return to the ballroom to enjoy themselves and after we became proficient we often joined the group in the main dances. This opened up a new relaxation for us and at Easter time we were invited to join the local Army Depot in their celebrations.

At Polymidhia Army Camp

and Jenni too

The Miramare was very ably run by Tony Skyrianides who often joined us on Friday evenings. We came to know him very well and we began to drive up the mountain to the coolness of the Forest Park Hotel for their very good Cypriot buffet on Sundays. The hotel was owned by Tony's family who were the leading hoteliers in Cyprus

Forest Park Hotel

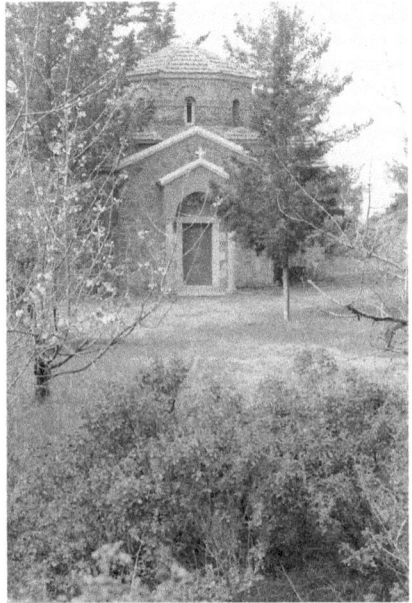

Forest Park Church

We came to know the whole family very well and their daft Great Dane puppy Oscar. Hercules, the elder brother wore a hairpiece with gay abandon and every time we met him we looked forward to seeing if he was wearing it forward, backwards or sideways. Eventually he threw it away but he was always the same nice man.

Hercules, Oscar, Marlies and Tony

Easter was the most important holiday time in Cyprus and we often spent the weekend at Forest Park and enjoyed the festival with the family. We went with them to the midnight service and witnessed the light spreading from behind the altar throughout the darkened church as worshippers lit their candles from the new flame. Outside the children played as Judas was burned on a bonfire and firecrackers exploded around the church. We then carried our lighted candles back to the hotel where a traditional Easter breakfast including margaritas soup and coloured eggs awaited us.

The time at the hotel gave a good opportunity for walking in the woods around the hotel. The scenery was spectacular and it was obvious why the hotel had been so popular with Egyptian visitors in the 1930s before air conditioning had become available.

Marlies in the woods

Around Easter time in Zakaki the annual football match between the married men and the bachelors was staged. George was planning to play but at the last moment he was sabotaged when Vasiliki and Androulla burned his shorts. The rules were rather vague and the timekeeping was questionable. I never discovered the results of the game.

Bambos and Evyenious waiting for the talent scouts to appear

Towards the end of the year the roads around Limassol were busy with heavily laden lorries bringing grapes from the hill villages to the Limassol wineries. The weight of the grapes crushed the lower layers and grape juice dripped on to the road. Cyprus is the only country where I have seen roadside notices saying, "Road slippery from grape juice." After the first rain of the winter arrived the journey home from Episkopi was very interesting. After the long dry summer the roads had absorbed motor oil, grape juice and other debris and the newly arrived rain brought it all to the surface. On the winding road downhill past the ruins of Curium Theatre the ditches were peppered with sundry cars and motor bikes that had slid off the road. The drivers never learned.

During July 1972 I was working in my office when I began to notice sharp burning pains in the centre of my chest and my friends persuaded me to visit the unit doctor. I described my symptoms and his reaction surprised me when he had me dumped on a stretcher and called up an ambulance to deliver me with great urgency to the large RAF Akrotiri hospital. Apparently I had described the classic symptoms of an imminent heart attack and the Cardiology Unit was at full alert when I arrived. After much prodding and poking at me they were able to announce with confidence that my heart was purring like a Rolls Royce and the search for my chest pain must begin again. Fortunately I was put in the care of a very experienced consultant who after a few preliminary onslaughts filled me up with barium solution and strapped me on a vertical turntable and turned me upside down while watching an X-ray picture of my middle body. In no time at all he was able to declare that I had a hiatus hernia that allowed gastric juices to creep from my stomach up into my oesophagus and thus create the pain. He believed the damage had been caused by too much negative G during the inverted flying parts of my aerobatic displays. The manoeuvres were forbidden but in the early 1950s we were expected to include them in our show and they were accepted by our authorising officers.

I was in no danger and could carry on normally but I had to take care to avoid any violent upside down antics such as diving into swimming pools. Two weeks later a warrant officer was supervising the burning of confidential waste at RAF Episkopi when he noticed similar pains in his chest. He reported to the doctor and was diagnosed as having severe indigestion and given medicine to ease the pain. Soon afterwards he collapsed and died from a heart attack.

Fate must have decided that the good life was too rich to continue so in summer 1973 the fickle finger poked me again. After I returned from work on a Saturday I began to develop severe pains in my stomach rather similar to the belly ache I had as a small boy after scrumping too many apples. By evening they were so painful I visited the RAF medical centre in Limassol where a nurse was on duty. She gave me the standard kaolin jollop and advised me to return to see the doctor if I wasn't better by Monday. The pain increased over the weekend and I was on the doorstep at opening time. The Senior Medical Officer was away but a young locum tenens gravely informed me that a nasty bacterium was going around the Limassol area and prescribed some antibiotic tablets. They had no effect and by Wednesday I was in so much pain that I asked Marlies to drive me down to the clinic where the Squadron Leader doctor was back on duty. As soon as he looked at me he laid me on a stretcher and called for an ambulance to take me to Akrotiri hospital. Marlies said our car was outside and volunteered to drive me while the doctor phoned ahead. She made good speed and the medical staff was waiting to perform a medical inspection but when they saw me they poured a couple of litres of saline solution into me and wheeled me into the operating theatre for a surgical inspection. The surgeon opened up a long incision from my waist to my pelvis expecting to find a cancer of the colon but he immediately found a much more desperate situation. I had suffered a burst appendix four days previously and my whole stomach cavity was inflamed from a raging peritonitis. The burst appendix was removed and my stomach cavity cleaned up and then they put me together again. All I had to do was fight the fierce poisoning in my system. For the next week in intensive care I grew steadily weaker and lived in a fantasy land. When Marlies and other visitors came I could hear massed bands playing outside the ward and I could talk to people they could not see. Then suddenly I began to improve and for a further week I slowly regained some of my strength. We were later told that if I had been one hour later in arriving at the hospital I may not have recovered

Marlies had an appointment for an operation on her left wrist to ease the nerve sheaths which were giving her pain and she drove down with Jenni who was with us on holiday and parked the car. She came to visit me and then went to the Ladies Ward. I was then discharged and with Jenni collected the car and drove very tentatively to Alan and Ann Hume's house which was nearby. I was as weak as a very old man but after we spent the day in the sun I slowly gained strength and then we drove carefully home. We collected Marlies and her new wrist a few days later and life returned to normal.

Our new way of life was set against the background of Cypriot murky politics. Cyprus is in the centre of the Middle Eastern bazaar and every form of devious activity is widely practised. The veneer of civilisation is very thin. Personal vendettas were avenged and a bomb under a car could be blamed on some political cause. Many Cypriots believed that Greece was the mother country and demanded enosis or union with Greece. From our experience we knew that Greek Cypriots (GC) and Turkish Cypriots (TC) could live and work together. In our village the TC worked happily in the factories or on the farms while the more adventurous ones drove buses or taxis. They made good policemen but the most successful ones owned the kebab houses. The GC preferred to keep their hands clean and filled managerial and secretarial posts and they all sought well protected pensionable jobs in the Civil Service. The ubiquitous coffee shops were frequented by both sides and we never saw any tension between them. The TC rarely stayed late.

Since Cyprus became independent in 1960 the majority GC government had not played fair with the TC population and most infrastructure funds were spent on GC projects and hardly any on the TC side. By 1963 the

TC members of the government refused to co-operate. Politicians were constantly seeking power and were the cause of most unrest. Several well-known figures formed private armies and murderously raided villages. The majority of such raids were GC against TC but the TC were sometimes provoked to retaliate. As tension increased the TC authorities ordered many of their people to withdraw from mixed villages and relocate to TC ones.

The clamour for union with Greece increased and General Grivas arrived from Greece to command the pro-enosis EOKA forces which were carrying out guerrilla warfare against the government police of the President Archbishop Makarios. The police formed a para-military Tactical Reserve and by 1974 regular raids were being made to seek out EOKA bandits who retaliated by killing many innocent civilians with random bombs. This was an ideal scenario to settle private vendettas and the opportunity was not missed.

Early one morning in June 1974 Marlies and I were returning home from a summer ball at RAF Episkopi and while driving through the Phassouri plantation we closed up behind a battered old Land Rover that was travelling quite slowly. I flashed up my headlights to indicate I was going to pass and we saw two people crouched in the back and one of them appeared to be holding a rifle. Old Land Rovers were popular vehicles with EOKA as they could be driven cross country when necessary so I held back. When all seemed to be clear I overtook the Land Rover and continued on our way. As we came into Zakaki village we saw a tight convoy of four police Land Rovers slowly coming towards us and in the moonlight we could see that each vehicle had four police standing and facing outward while holding sub-machine guns at the ready position. They were obviously on high alert so I drove to the side of the road and stopped. The convoy slowly passed us and they could see my mess dress and Marlies' ball gown. No doubt some of the police recognised our car. When the police had passed I drove the small distance to our house and parked the car in our car port at the rear. As Marlies got out of the car we heard loud shouts of "Stamata" (stop) followed almost immediately with several bursts of machine gun fire. We could hear bullets coming into the side of our house near to Marlies who had crouched down for protection. Confused noises were coming from the road in front of our house so I carefully shepherded Marlies into the house through the back door and then went to investigate. Police were milling around the road and the suspicious Land Rover had driven over to the other side of the road and had crashed into our opposite house.

As the story unfolded I learned that the Land Rover had not stopped but had continued driving past the convoy. The police had looked down into the rear seats and seen what we had already seen. They assumed that a passenger was holding a rifle and in their high state of tension had simultaneously called for the car to stop and also opened fire. The bullets hit the car and the driver was killed. The car then veered across the road until it crashed into our neighbour's house.

It was all a tragic unnecessary accident. The occupants of the Land Rover were two water sports instructors from the Amathus Hotel who had been to a folk music festival at RAF Akrotiri accompanied by two young girls who were staying at the hotel. They were happily returning to the hotel and the suspicious "gun" was the neck of a guitar. The gun fire killed the driver and badly injured the other boy and one of the girls. If the driver had shown more care and the police had not been too hasty the incident need not have happened. As Marlies and I were the only two independent observers we were involved in the subsequent high level inquiry.

In July 1974 Jenni came out to join us as usual and I decided to take three weeks local leave so that we could explore the island. On Monday morning, 15th July we went to the Miramare beach club for a lazy day. I had offered to repair the sewing machine of the manager's wife so while Marlies, Jenni and Zozo went to the beach I went to Zozo's flat to look at the machine. While I was working the room was suddenly filled with loud martial music. The radio had been switched on but the program had been closed down and abruptly replaced by the music. An announcement in Greek quickly followed which I understood to say that President Makarios was dead and citizens were told to rally around the newly formed Government. I decided that the sewing machine was of secondary importance so I went down to find Marlies and Jenni and quietly told them that we were caught in a coup d'etat and we should be alert to take any necessary action. Soon other people on the beach heard on their radios that the Army, led by Greek officers, had attacked the presidential palace in Nicosia and killed and replaced Archbishop Makarios. Later we discovered on a loyalist radio station that Makarios had survived and been flown out to Paphos by helicopter. A curfew was imposed so all we could do was sit and await developments. Soon we were joined by Andreas

Mavromatis, the son of the owner, who was a Makarios supporter and we discussed possible outcomes. Soon gunfire was heard from the local police station which was only a couple of hundred metres away across a river bed. While more random gunfire was heard from the Limassol area Pavlina, Andreas' sister and Grivas follower, brought into the hotel a family who were well known for sheltering Grivas in their basement for a long time. They were accompanied by a group of nasty looking body guards armed with sub-machine guns and the group settled at the other end of the veranda from us. Sporadic gunfire was still being heard around us and if the police forces had known that the Grivas party was in the Miramare bloodshed would have resulted.

Because of the curfew we could not leave the hotel so we tried to make the days as normal as possible while carefully trying to find any snippets of information about how the coup was developing. The desperate parliament was trying to find a president but all the leading contenders were turning the position down. The Grivas party was still at the other end of the veranda and we could not avoid encountering thuggish body guards lounging around and sub-machine guns lying on the steps of the hotel. In the evening Jenni and I sat on the jetty and watched towards Limassol from where a steady noise of gunfire was heard. We tried to identify the various noises as heavy machine guns, pistols, rifles, grenades etc and we wondered how many people were being killed in all the chaos.

We were provided with a free room to stay overnight and we only paid for our food and refreshments. The hotel operated as normally as possible but many of the local guests were verging on hysteria and we tried to calm them down.

On Wednesday morning we were told that a cease fire in Limassol had been arranged and the curfew was being lifted for two hours to allow people to shop or, in our case, to return home. Our journey would be about 15 miles from the east of Limassol, through the centre of the town with several bottle necks and out to the west side. We set course as soon as possible but we were not surprised when gun fire could be heard as we passed through the city centre. We saw many bullet marks in the walls of buildings as we passed. Fortune was on our side and we were relieved to park our car behind our house.

When we reached our back door we found that the lock had been shot out and the glass around the door handle smashed in. The house looked neat and tidy with no trace of the broken glass but as we walked through the house to the front door Marlies noticed a few spots of blood on the floor. We went round immediately to George and Vasiliki's little house and we were aghast at what we saw. Their living room was wrecked by gunfire.

We learned that on the previous day Makarios supporters from Paphos had set course for Limassol to help their compatriots and they chose to approach the town via the road through our village. The Grivas rebels heard that they were coming and set up an ambush outside our house and George's. No one in Cyprus can keep a secret and the Paphos fighters soon heard about the ambush and stopped short of the village. They came round the sides of the houses and attacked the Grivas party who shot their way into our house and George's. As they entered George's house they saw a wardrobe which might hide gunmen so they sprayed it with machine gun bullets. George and his family were lying on the floor while the gunmen prepared to fight it out. A fierce battle was then waged until all the Grivas party had been killed in both our houses. George's house sustained more damage and although they were badly frightened they were not injured.

As soon as the family had recovered from the considerable shock they went round to our house to check the damage and then cleaned up all the debris and blood they could find. They had looked after our house first before they turned their attention to their own much more seriously damaged house. George and Vasiliki did not possess many clothes but what they had was in the solitary wardrobe and the machine gun fire had ripped them to pieces. Marlies later collected a small pile of bullet cartridge cases from around our house which we still have.

I was still on leave and we tried to settled down to normal life but our village friends were afraid and excited. We had to spend much time trying to calm them down and reassure them that all would be well. All the men of military age had either gone to join the Grivas fighters or to help the Police to put down the coup. One of our neighbours brought her young baby and pleaded with me to take it into the British bases for safety and I had to explain to her that there was no danger and when her husband returned he would expect to find her safely in their house. Our village friends were confused and could not understand what was going on. We tried to give them some stability and in the evening I would sit on our veranda with the light on reading a book where I could be seen along the village street. I discovered later that many friends checked regularly to see if we were still there.

The politicians were still trying to find a President and eventually Nicos Sampson who led a private army in attacks on TC villages was nominated and a TV news bulletin in which he addressed the nation was very chilling. The sight of him flanked by bodyguards with sub-machine guns was not re-assuring for the future. Traffic passing our house usually had arms reaching out through the windows brandishing machine guns and bursts of fire were often heard as the owners shot at Coca Cola cans for fun. None of our friends understood what was going on and the whole atmosphere was highly charged.

When I was at Staff College in 1962 we had studied a Turkish government document in which they declared that if the Cypriot government chose union with Greece they would have to intervene to protect the Turkish Cypriot population. It showed a line from Morphou through Nicosia to Famagusta that they called the Attila Line which delineated the area they would occupy. The coup was aimed at such a union and Turkey fulfilled its long stated policy. On Friday 19th July Turkish forces invaded the Kyrenia area by sea and air and the Cypriot army had to turn to resist the invasion.

The Commander NEAF ordered all military families living in Limassol to take refuge in either Episkopi or Akrotiri. We did not want to leave our friends but military police soon appeared to enforce the order. We were asked to take clothing for a couple of days and all available food with us. The husbands who had gone to work on Monday morning had not been able to return home and many families were without cars. We were reluctant to leave our friends but we had no option. After we left some of our friends slept out in the fields for a few nights. Marlies took Jenni and two wives of 9 Squadron from Akrotiri who lived nearby in our car and I rode my motor bike alongside as we joined a huge queue of vehicle heading west. As we wended our way through Ypsonas and Kollossi villages the streets were lined with villainous looking spectators many of whom carried guns but we were rather re-assured when we heard calls of "Hello Mrs Marlies" or "Hello Mr Brian". It was impossible to tell the goodies from the baddies. As the convoy approached a long straight road, the M1, military police were controlling the flow because gunfire was being exchanged across the road near Episkopi village. When we received our green light we hurtled off down the road but we could still hear gun fire around us and we resumed breathing when we reached the safety of the western end of the road. When we reached RAF Episkopi we were ushered to a parade ground where harassed workers were struggling to restore some order. We were sent to an officers married quarter which eventually contained 35 people. We handed in our food and were allocated a bed. Others slept on settees or on the floor. Our passengers were moved on to RAF Akrotiri by bus to be re-united with their husbands.

I put on my uniform and went to report to the Station Commander and tell him I was available. He was delighted to gain another helping hand and asked me to take over the Sovereign Club which was normally an NCO's club but was now being brought into action to co-ordinate the welfare of the families brought in from Limassol. The staff I had available was Legal, Education and any other officers without essential station duties. Undergraduates and A level students on holiday were my most potent weapon and we began a round the clock effort to fight off the chaos which was near the surface.

Many of the young wives and children had been on their own in Limassol for 5 days with only radio as their outside contact and they were frightened and nervous. The accommodation at Episkopi was over flowing and soon petty squabbles were common. A system of street wardens was introduced where mature wives such as Marlies tried to settle minor problems but could call for help when needed. In the Sovereign Club my best assets were pairs of boy and girl senior students who I could send out to relocate families or resolve other problems. They would not return until they had taken babies to the doctor, found extra beds and rations etc. and the task had been completed. A junior officer was often defeated by red tape. Jenni was swept up into this effort but I did not see her in my teams. Every evening I had a meeting with the station's warrant officers who were an excellent source of experience and information. We assessed if we were still in control of the situation and often decided it was a marginal issue. They had the all the experience and only needed someone to authorise their action. I readily provided the authority if it was essential to save the day. Later in the evening the new Station Commander, Gp Capt Parfitt, would come round to review the situation with me. He had been pitched into this situation at short notice and had other problems such as a Turkish refugee camp in Happy Valley, civilians in St John's school and all the evacuees from the married quarters at

Berengaria in Limassol. He rose to the occasion splendidly but he needed all the help he could get.

All the senior officers reported to their offices inside a secure compound every day and played no part in the domestic emergency except for the Army logistics staff and the AOC in C, Air Marshal Sir John Aitken, who was a calm tower of strength. The C in C arranged a British convoy to transport British personnel from Nicosia into the safety of the Bases in the south.

Bambos, Jenni Cleoniki, Marlies and Vasiliki

Life in Episkopi was made more unpleasant by the heat and humidity. Late July was the hottest period of the year and water was scarce. We had no fresh vegetables and we were fed from compo ration packs. One day I was at our temporary quarter with Marlies and Jenni when Bambos arrived with Vasiliki and Cleoniki bearing a bunch of flowers from Marlies' garden and a bottle of our favourite cognac. They had gathered a collection of fresh vegetables and Vasiliki had been into our house and packed for Marlies a case of clothes and a coat. She even included a spare handbag. Bambos had used his pass to bring them into the base and a happy reunion took place.

Bambos, Jenni and Cleoniki

The struggle continued day after day and the coup seemed to be collapsing as the Turkish forces easily occupied half of the area inside the Attila Line. To relieve the congestion in the bases a decision was made that all families whose head was within three months of the end of their tour would be sent back to UK. We protested that we were happy to stay and return to our village but even though many young families were desperate to go home our request was turned down with the reason that senior officers must set an example for their juniors.

This decision gave us major problems. We had no home in England and it would be difficult to arrange money for Marlies and Jenni's departure. Our old friend Vic Stanton was a VC10 captain at Brize Norton where Marlies and Jenni would arrive so I phoned him to ask if he and Sheila could look after them until other arrangements could be made. Of course he agreed. I managed to obtain a limited amount of cash to help Marlies' journey into the unknown. In the early hours of the morning of our 19th wedding anniversary on 31st July I had to say goodbye to Marlies and Jenni not knowing where and when we would meet again.

While Marlies was flying home past Rome a radio message was received in the VC10 for her. Vic had been caught up in the evacuation and was passing her on his way to Akrotiri. However he had arranged for Ken Newman, one of my navigators from Bassingbourn, who was then at Brize Norton to meet Marlies and Jenni when they arrived. Although I was now out of contact with my family I eventually learned that Marlies had been offered married quarter as far removed as Scotland but as I had no idea where my next posting would be she turned them down and decided to go to Germany to her family and friends until I could re-join them.

The Turkish invasion in the north of the island had diverted attention away from the coup and it slowly fizzled out and soon after Marlies and Jenni were thrown out of Cyprus I was allowed to return to our very lonely house. Normally when coming to the end of a tour the contents of the house are slowly reduced until only essentials are left but we had left the home we had occupied for nearly three years and no thinning out had been made. I managed to obtain some wooden boxes and in my off duty hours I began the task of packing our belongings and disposing of the rest. Marlies had become very good at bottling prunes in Armagnac and other exotic treats and we had several bottles in store. When I came to pack them I found that several had been started and as I sat on the kitchen floor filling boxes I decided to finish off the opened ones. The packing slowed down but as I rode back to the Officers Mess on my motor bike I was happier than on my earlier journey. I booked a place on a ship or aircraft to return our car back to UK and hoped that it would find a place in the queue.

After two weeks the fighting in the north was resumed and the Turkish forces moved up to the Attila Line which is still in existence in 2016 and is now known as the Green Line. Although the Cypriots blame the Turks for the invasion they brought it on themselves with no help from anyone else.

Every morning the C in C held a meeting with his senior staff to assess the latest news from Limassol but they discovered that a vital source of information was missing. In cities such as Delhi or Singapore the senior service officers had lived in the city in the middle of the community and the services were involved in all activities and all the important people knew each other. In Cyprus all senior officers on arrival occupied houses on the bases and they never lived in the Cypriot community. In the midst of all the news coming in were Cypriot names which were not known to the HQ staff. I was the only senior officer that had lived in Limassol for two and a half years and when the C in C realised this he often called me to his office to give him a Who's Who of Limassol

Marlies had suffered a great deal of stress during the time in Episkopi and had been involved in difficult tasks as a Street Warden. When I had returned to England I was delighted when I received a letter for her which contained an official Letter of Commendation from the Station Commander to thank her for her work.

In October I was told that my next posting would be to the Ministry of Defence (MOD) in London as the RAF Project Officer for the Multi Role Combat Aircraft (MRCA) and I would be a member of a three man team with German and Italian colleagues. No more information was given but it could wait till later while I was more interested in the fate of Marlies and Jenni. Earlier in the year while we were enjoying our life in Zakaki Marlies had said it was too good to last and suddenly in July her prophesy had come true. We had been brought down to earth and I was only waiting until we were together again and we could get back on our feet. In November my three years in Cyprus expired and at last I was flown back to England leaving behind our car and boxes of possessions. I wondered if we would ever see them again

Post Script

Marlies and I returned to Cyprus in 1975 to ascertain how our friends had fared. The economy had been hit hard but our villagers were managing reasonably well. While we were on the island we bought a flat on the sea front in the east part of Limassol and have had a foot hold on the island ever since. Our family continued to grow but unfortunately Vasiliki died on 5th January 1998. George had lost his lifelong companion and although he has never recovered from his loss he is still a lively 89 year old. He no longer cultivates his vegetables but he goes to the market most days to have a coffee and chat with his old friends. We are still in contact with the family and every year on the nearest Sunday to 5th January we go with the family to a memorial service for Vasiliki. On my 85th birthday we gave a party in our local village taverna for the family. Herodotus (Rodi), George's eldest son, was back from a very successful career in Athens as Chief Engineer for a very large construction company and was now in charge of all onshore buildings in the new Limassol Marina. He made a speech which summarised the life of Marlies and me in Zakaki and we were very grateful to him.

85th birthday party with Rodi speaking

Marlies with George 2013

Yiota, Elena and me 2013

Jenni and me at 85th birthday party

ROYAL AIR FORCE
EPISKOPI
BFPO 53

20th November 1974

Mrs B.A. Ashley,
c/o Wg Cdr Ashley,
RAF Uxbridge,
Middlesex
UB10 0RZ

Dear Mrs Ashley,

Throughout the recent emergency situation I was constantly impressed by the way in which many of the ladies of the Station rallied round and unbidden applied their energies to the areas of our greatest need. I resolved then that I would write to as many as I could expressing our gratitude.

I am sorry that it has taken so long to get round to this but assure you that the sentiments are no less sincere for that. Indeed if anything, the passing of time has lent perspective to what at the time was a confused scene and has served to convince me more deeply that without your efforts and those of like minded willing spirits we could not have managed as we did.

Please accept my warmest thanks and admiration for your excellent work under the most difficult and trying circumstances, as a Street Warden and for helping Brian to do an excellent job also with the refugees, British and Turk.

Yours sincerely,

Ken Parfit

Marlies' Commendation from the Station Commander

CHAPTER 18
Tornado. The MRCA Project

I N November 1974 I had been given my new posting as the MRCA Project Officer for the RAF. I was happy with the posting because it would be a major task which would shape the future of the RAF's front line for at least 40 years. The Personnel Branch at the Air Ministry having posted me exactly on my tour expiry date had decided it had finished its responsibilities to me and I now had to contend with their absolute failure to exercise any form of personal management for the domestic side of my life. I was flown home from Cyprus but Marlies and Jenni were in Germany where the RAF had no interest in them whatsoever. Although the post was a key post in the RAF I had not been allocated a married quarter and after much haggling I was offered a temporary house at RAF Medmenham near Henley. The only reason why it was available was because it was one of a group of about 10 obsolete quarters that had been withdrawn from use until they had been renovated and heating systems installed and they were standing empty.

The only ray of sunshine came when I was told that our well-loved car had arrived in England and I could pick it up. Muttering muddied oaths about RAF personnel management I went over to Germany and spent Christmas with Marlies and Jenni but soon afterwards I brought them back to England. Jenni returned to boarding school and Marlies and I tried to make a home out of a cold, empty house with only a minimum of essential furniture. To make matters worse we then encountered a period of very cold weather. I'll pass over this miserable period until we were allocated a quarter at RAF Northwood at a time when Northwood was undergoing an overhaul to make it a major NATO headquarters. The officers' mess was closed and there was no social life so Marlies would be all alone while I began to think about the MRCA.

When General Rall, the Inspector General of the Luftwaffe, was visiting ACM Humphries, the RAF CAS, he asked what was being done about the MRCA because it was due to enter service in 4 or 5 years' time. I now know that the answer should have been, "Nothing". A decision was made to set up a team of three officers; one each from the German Air Force (GAF), one from Italy (IAF) and one from the RAF to plan the introduction into service. This was the post which came to me so I was in fact a Joint Project Officer. All the administrative work had already been done and I found that I had been allocated an office in Lacon House in Theobalds Road. As this was my first MOD posting I had to become accustomed to strolling down Kingsway in civilian clothes on my way to my work bench. I shared an office among the Flying Training staff and would use their secretarial facilities. The Flying Training department was as good as any for me because they would be involved with the MRCA from the beginning.

When I first sat at my desk with a mug of coffee I asked myself, "What on earth is the MRCA?" I quickly learned that it was the Multi Role Combat Aircraft but was known by the cynics as Must Replace the Canberra Again. After the debacles of Anglo French Variable Geometry Aircraft, the TSR2 and the F111 it was essential that we made this project work. The Canberra was still doing yeoman service after more than 20 years and would have to do so until our new bird joined it.

My next question was who else in MOD was working on the introduction of the aircraft into the RAF? The Operations Staff were all beavering away with their Vulcans, Victors, Harriers, Jaguars, Buccaneers, etc but there was no MRCA desk. A check on the Engineering and Supply staffs revealed that the coast was clear and we had a clean sheet of paper. I decided to visit British Aerospace (BAE) at Warton to see if they could fill in a few gaps in my knowledge. They were making the British parts of the MRCA and would take the lead in the flight test program. The visit was very useful and they gave me an oversight of the aircraft and its equipment. I also saw bits of the still incomplete aircraft. The Warton team, particularly the training staff became an invaluable help to me throughout the project. One of the most useful snippets of information they gave me was a simple diagram of what the beast would look like.

This is it! The MRCA

The first prototype had recently been flown by Paul Millet of BAE at Manching in Bavaria and the first indications were that it would be a splendid aircraft.

Paul Millet lines up for the first flight

I should have reported to the Vice Chief of Air Staff but the post had been deleted and the duties taken over by the Air Member for Personnel (AMP). I was fortunate because the incumbent of the post was Air Chief Marshal Sir Neil Cameron who I had met at Staff College and considered by me to be the sharpest brain on the Air Council. He was an excellent choice to be overseeing the MRCA project.

I knew that my German and Italian team members had already set up their offices in Bonn and Rome so I invited them over to London. They gladly accepted and we had our first looks at each other.

Lt Col Klaus Rimmek was an F4 Phantom pilot and he had his office among the flying training staff in Bonn and as the Deputy Inspector General was a logistics officer he worked for General Limberg, the Inspector General. Klaus was over 6 feet tall and had a very amiable personality. I soon discovered he was a very capable officer but his experience was limited to the ground attack role and he had no previous staff or instructional experience.

Our first home

Lt Col Federico Zamparelli was an F104 and G91 ground attack pilot and he also had his office among the flying training staff in Rome and reported to the Vice Chief of the IAF. He was another very pleasant character but he was short as Klaus was tall and he also had only ground attack experience from F104s and Fiat G91s but no staff or instructional training. I was the piggy in the middle. Their London embassies had booked them hotel accommodation and they easily found their way to Lacon House by underground railway. We spent three days eyeing each other up and sharing our knowledge and views. At lunch time we wandered round to a nearby pub and had the MOD standard lunch: a pie and a pint. We found we had very similar ideas for the project and we knew we could work together well. We agreed the general path we would follow and after a month's work we would meet again in Bonn.

Before I could devote all my attention to the MRCA we decided to buy our own house. While I was being pushed around the RAF we could not decide where to live or how to find the money for a deposit. Now that my disenchantment with the MOD's lack of interest in our domestic welfare was increasing the need for our own house was paramount. I could also see that my full time flying days would soon be coming to an end and that was the last push required and we began our search for a house. We were very fortunate and found an ideal property at Grove End, near to Hemel Hempstead. A group of 12 friends in the building trade had decided to form an association and build their own houses. As they had members from all branches they had the capability and as the houses were to be their homes the quality of the work would be their best. They built 6 semi-detached houses in a cul de sac and occupied them. After a settling down period one of the partners who lived in an end house had to move and it was put on the market. We found the property and when we inspected it we were very pleased because it seemed to be ideal for us. We moved in as soon as possible, installed our stove, and after 20 years of married life we had our own home and Jenni her very own room.

The layout of the rooms had been carefully planned and Marlies had a large kitchen, Jenny had a large bedroom and we all had a large bathroom. What more could we ask for? I bought an MG 1600 to drive down to Apsley station for a 30 minute train journey to Euston Station and a walk down Kingsway to my office. Marlies very quickly found a job as a Scientific Officer at The Radiochemical Centre near Amersham which was pioneering the production of radioactive isotopes. She loved the job and very soon we exchanged our old car for a lovely little Triumph Spitfire IV which she used to scoot to work. Jenni was at boarding school and could only savour our new life during school breaks.

The prettiest car ever built – our Spitfire IV

Now that I was soundly based I could begin to identify the MRCA tasks which we must solve in the next few years and the list grew longer and longer. It was an enormous jigsaw puzzle with very many pieces. It was the most expensive and complicated program for any of our three nations and it was more complicated by the need to consider the tri-national aspects.

Before we could make any meaningful plans we had to produce a Concept of Operations document which would describe the aircraft's capabilities, the weapons it was likely to use and how it would be used. We spent much time consulting our Air Force staffs and I again had very useful discussions with BAE. We cobbled a document together and it became the datum point for our plans. I worked within the Air Ministry at Air Commodore or Director level and they consolidated their staff's views. Klaus and Federico did likewise.

It soon became obvious that I was the only one with staff training or experience of working with the administrative departments. The language used for the project was English and we did not need to discuss who would draft our papers. Word processors were not in use in 1974 and all my work was created in pencil, double spaced on lined foolscap paper. It was then typed on a manual typewriter and even the best of typists made several mistakes in a complex document. The draft had to be corrected and re-typed. Word processors are a marvellous innovation.

Soon the time came to meet at Bonn. I had only a modest daily allowance for such visits and Klaus found for me a very suitable small bed and breakfast hotel in the centre of Bonn just off the market place and near to the Beethoven house. The hotel was run by the Gross family and they made me very welcome. I had breakfast with them before taking a taxi up the hill to Defence HQ at Hardhoehe. Klaus had arranged security clearance for me and I easily found his office. We began our day before 0800 hrs and his staff had a bigger than average coffee pot fully prepared and large mugs in the start position. As we worked, argued and laughed an NCO's arm regularly appeared over my shoulder to keep us refuelled. At mid-day we took a half hour break to stroll down to an all ranks dining room to take an enjoyable meal. Usually the Inspector General would be dining there but few people shared his table. In the evening we had a meal in a Bonn restaurant or Klaus took us to his house near Hangalar, just east of the river where his wife, Barbara, prepared a meal for us and we filled the evening with comfortable chat and sudden ideas. I found Barbara very different from Klaus as she was rather stiff and cold and probably more ambitious than Klaus. We made good progress because we all had the same aim. It would have been a disaster if our team had been 6 or 9 instead of just 3 and we would never had made such progress.

I decided to celebrate our good week's work by buying a bottle of Courvoisier cognac at the Bonn airport duty free shop. When I arrived at Heathrow I was standing outside the terminal waiting for the bus to take me to Watford railway station where my car was parked and I put my plastic bag with the cognac on to the pavement. Unfortunately I was too heavy handed and I heard the tinkle of breaking glass. My heart sank but I looked inside the bag and saw that the bottle had neatly broken into three large parts. I carefully picked them out of the bag and as I put them in the nearby waste bin I noticed that no liquid was dripping from the bag. I carefully nursed the bag home and tried unsuccessfully to convince Marlies that the Bonn duty free shop was selling draught cognac. After passing the cognac through a coffee filter and topping up my empty cognac bottle we were in fine fettle again.

On a lovely summer's day in July we loaded ourselves into the open topped Spitfire and galloped along the M1 motorway to Silverstone to see the British Formula 1 Grand Prix. Everything went smoothly and we had excellent seats to watch an exciting day's racing. As we sauntered home we were well satisfied with life. For some time I had been experimenting with making my own white wine. I now began buying German grape juice and I bought much better filters. The wine improved and I bought my own bottle labels. Suddenly we had 12 bottles just starting, 12 more in mid-stream and another 12 waiting for us to dispose of them. The sun began to shine on us. An old German friend who knew his wine could not identify if it came from the Rhine valley or the Mosel

Back at my bench I began to look at one of the many problems we had to solve. The RAF had assumed that they had plenty of pilots to man the future MRCA squadrons but when I decided to check the facts I soon discovered that we had plenty but they were all the wrong types. Most were senior pilots in the V bomber squadrons and many others from transport and maritime units. Many were coming towards the end of their flying careers and were certainly not the kind of young tigers we needed to man the MRCA squadrons in a few years' time. After working on the problem in detail I dropped the bombshell in Whitehall but after sucking their teeth the staff had to extend the production run of advanced jet trainers to produce sufficient numbers of pilots.

We had sufficient navigators because the ones from the Canberras, Buccaneers and Phantoms were in mid-career and were quite suitable but we had a different problem. They were all experienced and able navigators when working at their desk in a conventional aircraft with paper charts, rulers, compasses and navigation slide rules but the MRCA was a different animal. Having seen various bits of the aircraft I knew we had a problem so I visited BAE again to find more detail. The navigator would have no desk and chart board but would be faced with a series of TV displays to show the navigation plot and a moving map with a radar display superimposed on top.

Although I was not able to see all the equipment I was able to collect enough information to define the problem which would devour much of my time.

In the meanwhile Klaus and Federico were also working on their national problems. Both nations had only a few navigators for transport aircraft and none for combat aircraft. They would have to train some in the next few years. Italy did not have English language training and would have to introduce a program. We all had plenty of work until we met in Rome.

A navigator's cockpit in a production Tornado

When Klaus and I met in Rome we stayed in the same hotel and found ourselves in a different world. The splendid Air Ministry building, like most of the Rome's finest buildings, was built during the 1930s in Mussolini's time near the centre of the city. We shared a taxi to go to our first meeting but about a kilometre from the Air Ministry building our taxi came to halt in a traffic jam forming at a blocked traffic roundabout near to our target. Eventually we paid off the driver and walked the remainder of the distance. This became our usual practice. When we arrived we had to wait for Federico because he lived about 20 miles away on the coast near to the Rome airport and travelled to work in a service bus. While we waited we enjoyed the view of the traffic locking itself up at the nearby roundabout. There were no traffic lights or police to control the crossing and every time a small gap appeared it was immediately filled in. We never did discovered how it eventually unlocked itself.

Eventually Federico's bus arrived and he spent a few minutes discussing the day's office work with his deputy before we could turn to the important business of coffee. In London and Bonn we had a constant supply on tap in our offices but when Federico asked us if we would like coffee we walked to a small kiosk on the corner of the corridor and were presented with the smallest coffee I have ever seen without the usual glass of water. After more time wasting we settled down to work. We made good progress until 1200 o'clock when all work ceased and the officers left the building and wandered over to smaller single storey building next door. Klaus and I were amazed to find ourselves in the best restaurant in Rome. The room was beautifully furnished and the tables laid with silver and flowers. Several wives and children were already present and waiting for their men. The waiters must have been selected from the best hotels in Rome and we were presented with excellent menus. The wine was also first class. I wished Marlies could have been there. While Klaus and I were champing at the bit to get on with our work most of the officers seemed to be reluctant to return to their offices until 2 o'clock. We settled down to another session of work but we had to cease before 4 o'clock because Federico had to catch his bus back to his home. This was the pattern for our future visits to Rome. Fortunately Italy had only a 15% share of the MRCA project and had little to offer for our planning. However we had to ensure that they were consulted and agreed to our plans. When we asked Federico if the cost of the Italian parts of our plans were being built into their defence budgets he reminded us that in the 30 years since the war they had been ruled by 31 governments and as they could not be certain who would be in control in a few years' time they had to get on with their planning and assume the new regimes would pick up the bills.

Klaus and I made as much progress as we could in the evenings and we got as much as possible out of a very disappointing visit and we returned home to our national work before our next meeting. The construction of the Tornado, as the MRCA had been christened, was being overseen for the 3 nations by a management agency known as NAMMA that had its HQ in Munich and it was time we attended one of their meetings to co-ordinate our plans. I shared my office in Lacon House with Wg Cdr Mac Furze who had been placed second in the England to New Zealand Air Race in a Canberra PR3 and was now responsible for the RAF's advanced flying training and who would be one of the first RAF Tornado users. We had much in common and became firm friends and we arranged to travel to Munich together. During the next 3 years I came to know the city well and I thought it was lovely. When I travelled there with Mac we stayed in a small hotel together and in our spare time we explored the delights including haxen, spare ribs and good Bavarian beer. We soon had our favourite cafes in Schwabing. When I was on my own I was able to stay with Lutz and Katherina Mundhenk and catch up with his life since Andover Staff College. They had a house in the south east quarter of the city that was easy to commute to and I very much enjoyed their company. This was the better side of the project.

On one of my trips to Munich I met the training manager of BAE in the duty free shop at Heathrow; he was going to the same meeting. I had the usual bottle of Scotch in my basket for Klaus but he had two. When I settled into my seat on the aircraft I saw he was seated across the aisle from me. He immediately asked a stewardess for two glasses, opened a bottle of scotch, poured 2 large measures and gave me one. I liked to go through my notes for the meeting during the flight but it was a challenge I could not resist. I got on with my reading but during the hour it took to reach Munich the bottle slowly emptied without any further assistance from me. I thought I was the one who liked my scotch!

When I returned to London I had to devote some of my time to the problem of producing a navigation trainer for the Tornado. We did not have time to go through the whole procurement procedure so I had to draw up a specification and then take some short cuts. Redifon and Singer Link were both producing flight simulators for the RAF Tornado and they would have much in common with my idea of a navigation trainer so I discussed my ideas with them. I was able to identify about 8 units of the aircraft equipment which would have to be taken from the production line to form the core of the navigation trainer and then I wrote a description of what was required.

My more difficult task was to persuade the 3 Air Forces that no service crews could operate the Tornado until the navigators had been trained in it. At this time Air Marshal Neil Cameron called for a progress report on our work so I had the task of writing it and clearing it with Klaus and

Federico. The plans for the navigation trainer were of course prominent in the report. A little later AMP called for me to report to him so I scampered down to Whitehall to his office. He had studied our report and made a few very useful points. He then told me to keep on going as we were and let him know if we had any problems he could solve for us. This was a powerful endorsement that we could use in the future. I was relieved to know that we were in step with him and I was not surprised when very soon he became Chief of Air Staff and then Chief of Defence Staff, a Marshal of the RAF and a Baron.

The pattern for our visits was soon established but we soon came across a small problem. Germany was the richest of the three nations but Klaus had a very tight budget. Just before a meeting in Munich he called me to say that he had run out of travel money and could not attend the meeting. He asked if I could represent both Germany and UK. I was fortunate because I had almost free access to the Luftwaffe HQ, much to the envy of our Air Attaché. I galloped across to Bonn and was briefed by the Staff before I continued my merry way to Munich.

ACM Sir Neil Cameron

Klaus, Federico and I had no major differences of opinion but plenty of arguments about details. We often blackmailed our Air Forces without qualms to force the project ahead. If the RAF was dragging its heels I would tell them that Germany and Italy were insisting on the issue. Meanwhile Klaus and Federico were telling their Air Forces how stubborn the RAF was being.

In the meantime Jenni steadily changed from a school girl to a young lady. She had achieved good O level grades at Rookwood but we then discovered that they could not teach her German and mathematics for A level exams. We were able to find her a place at The East Anglian School for Girls at Bury St Edmunds, a public school run by the Methodist Church. Soon after she began her advanced studies the school was merged with a well-known public school for boys at Culford. Her education continued to follow an interesting path but she still managed to be given good A level results. We then had to go through the normal procedures for choosing a university and waiting to see if she would be given a place. All her friends were in the same boat. While she was at home with us and occasionally working with Marlies at The Radiochemical Centre she decided to visit London for the day. When she returned home she announced that she was not going to university but had found a job in the city. Trade with China was at that time was regarded as a black art and very few British firms had good contacts and were doing business. Jenni had found a company which was well established in China and almost had a monopoly. She had taken a job with them and started her connection with the City of London. During our lunch breaks Mac and I would often stroll down to Hatton Gardens to buy some apples and Jenni would often join us. She also formed a lifelong friendship with Mac. During our visits to the market Jenni told me about a money shop which sold at bargain prices heavy Deutsch Mark coins which were too heavy to export back to Germany. Before any future visits to Germany I picked up a large bag of 5 DM pieces that helped out my expenses in Bonn or Munich.

The team had slowly been forming a picture of how the first Tornado training unit would look and after searching many options it became obvious that it would have to be based in England. I then began my search for a suitable airfield and I paid several visits to the Air Ministry Organisation Staff to look into their crystal ball to guess which locations might be available in a few years' time. The picture was always murky.

In the future when German and Italian aircrew began flying in England a number of interpreters would be useful when dealing with emergencies. I applied to take the German Colloquial Interpreters Test and during my morning train journeys I began to revise and improve my German. I could not continue the work on the return journey because I, along with other regular members of our compartment, usually fell asleep. Fortunately we soon knew our companion's destinations and we were able to wake the sleepers in time. Later I sat my exam and gained my certificate.

When Klaus and Federico came to London I would take my car to the office and take them home after work where Marlies prepared one of her excellent meals for us. Afterwards we sat around, chatted and peered into our crystal ball. New ideas invariably bubbled to the surface. Late in the evening I took them down to the station for an easy journey back to London.

Me, Klaus and Federico at Grove End

Our house was proving to be an excellent home and the layout suited us very well. One night a very noisy storm blew up and the wind was howling round the house. When we heard the sound of breaking tiles on our veranda we knew we had lost some from our roof. I went into the loft and checked that no water was coming in. Next day we discovered the advantage of living with friends who had built our houses. I had some spare tiles and ridge tiles stored in our garage and other people had other replacements. In a very short period of time we had a friend on our roof with some tiles and a bucket of cement and our house was repaired. The wind had blown down the wall between our garden and our neighbour's but he was a builder and very soon the wall was back upright. The exercise called for a few beers.

The contract for 3 prototype Tornados had been extended to 8 but the work was very complicated and we soon realised that delays would be encountered. The major players in each country were anxious to get their hands on the aircraft as soon as possible and we began to plan the order in which each new aircraft would go to the test centres, maintenance units and the training units. The number of flying hours would be pathetically small and the task of rationing them to all the eager pilots was a headache. Klaus, Federico and I ensured that our slots were well protected. Our task of keeping all the balls in the air was similar to a one armed paper hanger.

We now had a very clear idea of what we wanted and our work settled down to a mass of detailed planning to devise flying syllabi, number of crews to be trained, flying hours required and number of aircraft for the first training unit. ACM Cameron often remarked that I would be the ideal man to be the first station Commander at Cottesmore and I saw no reason to argue with the Air Member for Personnel.

As we delved deeper into the Tornado problems the RAF slowly woke up and separate Tornado departments were being formed. A Tornado Operations team was formed and of course they faced a similar problem to me when I first looked at the blank piece of paper. They came over to visit me and I brought them up to date with our progress. I gave them a copy of the Concept of Operations documents which we had devised for our use and as far I know it became their foundation stone.

The routine of detailed planning was enlivened by a gathering at the Luftwaffe flight test centre at Manching. All the test pilots were gathered together for detailed briefings before their flights in the Tornado and Klaus, Federico and I were included in the list. The group was a unique collection of pilots from the manufacturers, test centres and user formations such as Strike Command. We had many old friends among the group and as our hotel had a bowling alley and a well-stocked bar the ambience was ideal. All of us picked up new pieces of information which helped us in our tasks.

The concept of a tri-national conversion unit was now set in concrete but we still had to solve the problem of how to provide weapons training. Germany thought they might be able to use Jever but the plans fell through. It would not be fair for UK to host both parts of the training so we looked towards Italy. A major NATO weapons training establishment was already operating at Decimomannu in Sardinia and we decided to investigate the possibility of expanding it to take on Tornado training. By this time more departments in all three air forces were taking an interest in the Tornado and quite big teams were assembled to visit Decimomannu. At last Italy would be required to make an input into our plans.

When we arrived in Sardinia Klaus and I thought we had wandered into Alice in Wonderland. It was apparent that considerable expansion would be required to the base but whereas Klaus and I tried to ensure that all our plans were carefully costed and built into the budget forecasts the Italians were not able to made even rough estimates. The whole team was accommodated in a hotel in Cagliari but it soon became a Tower of Babel and Klaus and I decided to move into the officers' mess on the base. We could deliberate in peace and enjoy the company of the German Richthoven Phantom wing who were making their annual visit. We soon found that they told many scurrilous stories about people from East Friesland which were similar to the ones being told by RAF pilots about their navigators. I took great delight in bringing their stock of jokes up to date and they discovered that they could tell them about their rear seat crew men, combat observers. A typical example was about a pilot and navigator who were in a supermarket when the electricity failed. When they joined up later the pilot complained that he had been stuck in a lift for nearly an hour but the navigator moaned that he had been stranded in the middle of an escalator for the same time.

One of the problems we investigated was messing for the airmen and NCOs. Federico assured us that we would have no problems with the airman's mess as they had just built a new one. When we inspected it we found a huge barn-like building with long lines of tables with forms arranged on either side. By the entrance doors were huge bins of apple sized chunks of bread and dried fish. As the airmen came in they took handfuls of each and that was their lunch. Roberto explained that one of the prime features was that the whole room was tiled up to shoulder height and when lunch was finished it could be cleaned by using a hosepipe. Klaus and I looked at each other.

The difference in life between the officers and airmen in the Italian Air Force was enormous. We saw airmen in uniform kicking their heels around the railway station in the evenings eating the hardest bread rolls I have ever encountered. When we had a break during our planning Roberto arranged for one of their transport aircraft to pick up his family and car from the nearby airfield and take them to Trieste and return two weeks later to bring them back.

While the specialist teams were doing their own thing we were slowly bringing all the loose strands together and the way ahead was becoming clear. We still had major arguments mainly caused by the Italians inability to formulate firm plans and make financial estimates. One evening the British and German teams held a meeting to discuss the issue and a German Colonel burst out in exasperation, "If we have another war, you can have them".

Intensive planning in progress in Sardinia

During the visit our hosts often said that at the end of the visit we would have a dinner at a restaurant in the west of the island which was well known for producing their own special fire water. Unfortunately it was illegal so we had to refrain from talking about it in public. On the great evening we hired buses and the whole team travelled west. The meal was a very good selection of Sardinian dishes and eventually the moment came for the revelation of the magic liqueur and, after checking the police were not likely to descend on us, the elixir of life was produced. It was colourless schnapps which turned out to be exactly similar to Cypriot zivania. Distilleries were closely controlled in Cyprus 40 years ago and any private distilling was illegal but this small detail did not deter the wine producers in the hills from re-distilling the grape skins from the original pressing to produce their own universal cure. It could be used as a liniment for aching joints, cleaning windows, paint stripping or even drinking. The Sardinians had re-invented the wheel but who were we to spoil their fun?

The Tornado project was now well established and the RAF departments were involved in their particular parts of it. We were now drawing together the strands and I began to give serious thought to my future. I had been happily flying and had achieved nearly everything that was available in the RAF. ACM Cameron talked freely about me being the Station Commander at Cottesmore but by now I could see that the production of the Tornados was so slow that no flying training would begin until early 1981. I would have an airfield in chaos while it was being converted to a Tornado base but without any aircraft. If I could steal any flying I would be robbing precious flying hours from young pilots who needed them more than I. I had flown my fair share and the prospects did not appeal to me.

I knew my early training and experience as an electronics engineer would be a valuable asset in the modern world and with the contacts I had made in recent years I knew there would be jobs for me in the aviation industry. It was therefore with a heavy heart that I decided to leave the RAF and I chose 5th May 1977 as the final day, Jenni's birthday. My decision was influenced by the fact that people under the age of 50 were still considered as a good employment investment but people over 50 were over the hill. My 50th birthday would be in January 1978.

I had a farewell round of visits and instead of a grand Dining Out Night in a big RAF mess the Flying Training Staff gave me a very pleasant lunch in a London pub. During the lunch the Director produced a signal from the German Air Force HQ to speed me on my way. I was delighted to receive it because I had been very happy memories of working with them.

TO

MINISTRY OF DEFENCE
UNITED KINGDOM
AIR, DFT/RAF
LACON HOUSE

LONDON

SUBJECT: TORNADO JOINT TRAINING

THIS AIR STAFF HAS BEEN INFORMED OF WING COMMANDER BRIAN ASHLEY
RAF RETIRING FROM ACTIVE SERVICE AT THE END OF THIS WEEK.
WING COMMANDER ASHLEY HAS WORKED WITH THE LUFTWAFFE ON MATTERS
PERTAINING TO TORNADO JOINT TRAINING FROM THE VERY BEGINNING.
HE WILL BE REMEMBERED AS AN OUTSTANDING INDIVIDUAL, A FINE OFFICER
AND A GOOD FRIEND.

I SHOULD NOT MISS TO EXPRESS MY SINCERE APPRECIATION OF THE WORK
WING COMMANDER ASHLEY HAS DONE NOT ONLY FOR TORNADO JOINT TRAINING
BUT ALSO FOR ANGLO-GERMAN RELATIONS.

WITH GRATITUDE I THING OF THE SPIRIT OF GOOD CO-OPERATION AND TRUE
AIRMANSHIP SHOWN BY WING COMMANDER ASHLEY.

ON BEHALF OF THE MEMBERS OF THE AIR STAFF KNOWN TO WING COMMANDER
ASHLEY AND MYSELF I EXTEND BEST WISHES AND "HALS UND BEINBRUCH"
FOR THE YEARS TO COME.

BY ORDER

KARL H. GOLDBERG
OBERST I.G.

Postanschrift: Postfach 13 26
5300 Bonn 1

Telefon
Vermittlung
(0 22 21) 12-1

Telex
0 886 575
0 886 576

Paketanschrift: Paketausgabe
5300 Bonn 7

Wg Cdr Mac Furze and I had shared an office and became close friends. We sat facing each other smoking our pipes and producing clouds of smoke which poured out into the corridor as visitors came coughing into our office. We both wore the ribbons of the Air Force Cross and I assumed that Mac had been rewarded for his part in the London – New Zealand air race. I stayed in contact with him after we both left the RAF and it was much later that I read an article in a well-known aviation magazine which described a series of operations when the RAF borrowed RB45 reconnaissance aircraft from the USAF and made some penetrations deep into Russia during the depths of the Cold War. Mac was named as one of the pilots. As it was top secret at the time Mac had never discussed it with me and he never knew that I had been up to similar tricks. He married a New Zealand girl who he met in Christchurch. They were a well matched couple but unfortunately she died while quite young. Mac later came closer to a charming old family friend and they shared their lives until Mac also died unexpectedly. We are still in contact with Gillian.

Klaus Rimmek also became a very close friend and he made rapid progress in the Luftwaffe. He was a Brigadier General as the Base Commander of the first NATO Airborne Early Warning Wing at Nörvenich and subsequently a Lieutenant General in command of the Luftwaffe's 3rd Air Force. After he retired he took a senior post as consultant with CAE Electronics of Canada. Then I lost contact with him with no response by letter, phone, Christmas card or Email. While I was on holiday in Germany in 2002 I bought a CD containing the German telephone directory. To test it I typed in "Klaus Rimmek" and immediately an address in Aachen appeared. I quickly phoned the number and asked, "Are you General Rimmek?" The answer was, "Yes"

After he left the Luftwaffe his marriage fell apart and he and Barbara were divorced. Klaus was over generous and Barbara kept the house while he lost his address and his phone number. I was based in Hong Kong at the time and contact was broken.

We were very glad to be back in contact and within a couple of weeks Klaus came to visit us with his new, younger and much friendlier wife. We had a superb re-union before we had to return to Cyprus. In 2003 we returned to Germany and were promptly invited to visit them in Aachen. We had a fine time with them as we had a guided tour of a lovely old town. Within a couple of weeks of returning to Cyprus we were devastated to be told that Klaus had suddenly died. We were very fortunate that we had had some time together again before the tragic event.

Klaus and Marlies

Klaus and I happy again

Federico continued in the IAF and was promoted to Colonel and moved to a HQ in Vicenza. Slowly we lost contact with him and Annemarie but he is always well remembered.

Post Script to Chapter 18

As I write this in early 2015 RAF Tornados are deployed only 20 miles away from me at RAF Akrotiri and are operating against ISIS forces in Iraq. I am a member of the Officers Mess and glad to have the opportunity to visit the base and have lunch with them. The aircrews are an impressive collection of professionals who are in good heart and talk to me very freely about my bird. I met Wg Cdr Mark Frewin, OC of the AEW that had been formed to control the operations, and he quickly realised that I had a great interest in my bird and he gave me every opportunity to meet the crews. On 26th November 2014 I was delighted to be invited to visit No 2 AC Squadron at their base. I had only dealt with the basic aircraft and to be confronted with the latest operational version was a revelation.

The Tornado meets its Grandad for the first time

After 37 years I was given all the answers to my questions and shown things which I did not know existed. I watched two crews preparing for a strike against the IS in Iraq and saw them take off. The Tornado had been in service for over 40 years and had proven itself in the Iraq war when it had been the only aircraft capable of making the most dangerous low level tasks against the Iraqi airfields. It obviously shows its age but by resorting to cannibalisation from other aircraft the RAF has kept it flying and it is regarded by the aircrews as a well-liked, reliable and potent aircraft. What more could I ask for?

All the aircrew were on unaccompanied tours and they had spouses and children alone in England and the squadron was operating every day or night over the Christmas period. On Christmas Eve I collected members of the Wing who were available and brought them to our flat to give them a typical German Christmas meal. After a very happy gathering I returned them to Akrotiri to continue their war. We were pleased to have with us a female navigator who was not only charming but obviously very competent.

A pair of No 2 Sqn Tornados taxi out for a strike against IS forces in Iraq

CHAPTER 19
The Revelation

THE book is nearly finished and I don't know how much more I will be able to churn out. Time is running out. Happy memories from long ago still keep bubbling up and I will continue to set down as much as I can. I am writing this concluding chapter now so that it is in place if I unexpectedly fall off my perch.

The book only deals with my life until I retired from the RAF. Jenni knows the story from then on and I won't have time to write volume two about what came afterwards. It is therefore centred on flying from 1949 until the present day but this was a golden age and I believe it represents the best of flying. I am very happy to be an active member of the Officers' Mess a RAF Akrotiri where I can mingle with aircrew lucky enough to still be flying and share their experiences. I tend to keep quiet about my time because it is their era and I can see how happy they are with modern day flying but I can't help thinking how flying has changed in the last 65 years. It is, after all, about 60% of the history of flying since the Wright brothers.

The real thing

I was very fortunate to begin my flying on wood and canvas biplanes and then quickly move on to aluminium monoplanes and early jet fighters. The Tiger Moth and Harvard were recognised as the best trainers of their era. They explored all the nasty tricks of flying and if one did not obey the rules they taught you they would kill you: and they did. It is worth noting that the Sopworth Camel, with 1.294 kills to its credit, was not only the top scoring fighter of WW1 but also killed more of its pilots than any other. If a pilot understood swinging the nose while taxying, swing on take-off, ground looping, high speed stalling, spinning out of bad turns, dropping a wing on landing, pilot induced oscillations and three point landings he was well prepared to face any new aircraft. Even starting large piston engines in winter was a challenge. The knowledge of how to pick the most suitable stone before clouting a magneto on the obvious scratch marks was valuable when encouraging a reluctant engine to start. When test flying we spent hours trying to sort out stability problems, unbalanced controls, flutter and the various effects of approaching the sound barrier.

Every cockpit was different and the first problem on entering a new aircraft was to find all the controls and switches. Cockpit ergonomics was not invented and even the renowned Spitfires and Hurricanes had the throttle by the pilot's left hand as usual but the huge undercarriage retraction lever was on the right cabin wall and everyone at their training units was familiar with watching the usual wobble after take-off when the student pilot had to transfer his left hand from the throttle to the stick while he moved his right hand from the stick to the undercarriage lever.

A pilot confronted by a new type of aircraft for the first time had four problems:

1. Can I find all the bits and pieces?
2. Can I get the engine started?
3. Can I get it airborne?
4. Finally, can I get it down again?

Aeroplanes in the 1940s were like ladies. Some were attractive and some were ugly but they were all fascinating in their own ways.

The Vintage Pair

Designers struggled to improve their creations but the biggest change came when powered flying controls began to appear. No longer could a pilot feel his aircraft talking to him through the controls as they trembled and twitched when approaching the stall, tightened up as the speed increased, began to snatch as the sound barrier was encountered or went crazy in a well-developed spin. When aircraft began to be controlled by a pilot making his demands through the autopilot aircraft lost their individuality and took on the mantle of pretty Hollywood film stars that looked good but were plastic images of the real thing.

Modern aircrew have to concentrate on a mass of ever more complicated black boxes, spend too much time entering information into their computers and interpreting the mass of information which is thrown back at them. They do not have the spare capacity to worry about flying cantankerous aircraft. Designers have been compelled to make aircraft as easy to fly as possible and in response to my four problems from the 1940s the answers have become:

1. Make all cockpits as similar as possible.
2. Press a button and the engine starts.
3. Point the aircraft down the runway, open the throttle and it takes off.
4. Point the aircraft at the runway, reduce the throttle and it lands.

QED.

My slice of aviation history has fully lived up to the expectations of the small seven year old boy who was determined to be an RAF pilot but was always anxious about being able to clear the next hurdle. By the time I had finished my tour on Examining Wing I had collected exceptional ratings as an instructor, a photographic reconnaissance pilot, a pilot navigator and an Examiner. I was a Command Instrument Rating Examiner on all four groups of aircraft and I was a test pilot. In the process of gaining this experience I had been fortunately enough to have flown a larger range of aircraft than most people can dream of. I was content with my lot and had never been worried about promotion or reward.

The icing was put on my cake when I was told I had been awarded the Air Force Cross. I was surprised but delighted because I had little regard for orders and decorations but considered the only medal worth having in peacetime was the Air Force Cross. I have never seen the citation for the award nor do I know the date.

The investiture would be at Buckingham Palace and I would be able to take Marlies and Jenni with me. Later we learned that HM The Queen would be presenting the medals. Thus Marlies would be rewarded for being dragged around the Commonwealth with me without complaint and Jenni would have the chance to see the Queen in her home. Ladies' fashion at the time was dominated by the film Dr Zhivago and Marlies, who had become a very capable dress maker, created two very topical outfits; one in black and a red one for Jenni. I decided to wear Queen's wings for the occasion.

We arrived at the Palace in good time and were able to admire, among many other items, the superb collections of paintings as we passed through the house on the way to the reception area. Marlies and Jenni were then ushered to very good seats in the ballroom where an RAF orchestra was playing pleasant music. I joined the line of equally proud recipients and when the Queen walked through from her private quarters I was reminded that she is a very small lady and when she took her place on the receiving stage she was still at eye level with the waiting men.

On the Mall

I noticed that although the Queen congratulated all the recipients she had a small chat with only a few. I hoped that I might be lucky because I had always been her loyal supporter and admirer. When at last my name was announced and I stood before her, hoping that my imperfect hearing would not let me down, a small glitch occurred and we both laughed. The Queen then asked a question which got an unexpected answer but it prompted another question which also received another unexpected answer. She was intrigued and pursued the problem. I enjoyed my small chat with my Queen.

Post Script

Written after Brian Ashley's death

Brian died suddenly & unexpectedly at the age of 87 on the night of 31st July 2015 after spending the day of his & Marlies's 60th Wedding Anniversary hosting their annual golf tournament & celebrating with their friends in the evening.

Brian's ashes were buried with full military honours at St Pauls Church at RAF Akrotiri directly under the flight path & his favourite poem 'High Flight' was read by Flt Lt Debs Borrie the same female navigator he mentioned at the end of Chapter 18 – he would have been so proud.

This book is for Jenni

who has waited a long time

Lightning Source UK Ltd.
Milton Keynes UK
UKHW011208030820
367620UK00003B/1016

9 781912 145126